In *Rampant Women*, Linda J. Lumsden offers an in-depth look at the intersection between the woman suffrage movement and the constitutional right to assemble peaceably. Beginning in 1908, women activists took to the streets in a variety of public gatherings and protests in a bold attempt to win the right to vote. Lumsden shows how outdoor pageants, conventions, petition drives, soapbox speaking at open-air meetings, the use of symbolic expression, and picketing—all manifestations of the right of assembly—played an instrumental role in the woman suffrage movement. Without these innovative forms of protest, Lumsden argues, women might not be voting today in the United States.

Tracing the strengths and weaknesses of American women's struggle for freedom of expression prior to the twentieth century, Lumsden shows how the suffragists' new tactics forged solidarity among women and legitimized the movement. When they spoke, marched, and picketed, suffragists not only challenged legal restrictions regarding public assemblies, they defied traditional ideas about how women should behave. Lumsden also examines the legal and social origins of the right to assembly and contends that women's exercise of their First Amendment rights helped prod the legal establishment to ensure protection for gatherings by other political dissidents as well.

The right of assembly provided the foundation for every step of the fifty-year struggle for woman suffrage. As Lumsden

Rampant Women

ESISTANCE

TYRANY

OBEDIENCE

TO GOD

Linda J. Lumsden

RAMPANT WOMEN

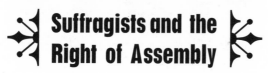

Suffragists and the Right of Assembly

The University of Tennessee Press / Knoxville

Library of Congress Cataloging-in-Publication Data
Lumsden, Linda J., 1953–
Rampant women: suffragists and the right of assembly /
Linda J. Lumsden.—1st ed.
p. cm.
Includes bibliographical references and index.
ISBN 0-87049-986-6 (cloth: alk. paper)
1. Women—Suffrage—United States—History.
2. Assembly, Right of—United States—History.
3. Feminism—United States—History.
I. Title.
JK1896.L86   1997
324.6'23'0973—dc21   97-4627

To my family:
Mom, Dad, Laurie,
and Jessalee and Samuel

Congress shall make no law respecting an establishment of religion, or prohibiting the free exercise thereof; or abridging the freedom of speech, or of the press; or the right of the people peaceably to assemble, and to petition the Government for a redress of grievances.

—U.S. Constitution, First Amendment

The right of citizens of the United States to vote shall not be denied or abridged by the United States or by any State on account of sex.

—U.S. Constitution, Nineteenth Amendment

The assemblage of rampant women which convened at the Tabernacle yesterday was an interesting phase in the comic history of the nineteenth century.

—*New York Herald*, 7 September 1853, on the 1853 Woman's Rights Convention

CONTENTS

ILLUSTRATIONS

ACKNOWLEDGMENTS

This book had its genesis as I listened to a lecture about female abolitionists during an American women's history class taught by Jacquelyn Hall at The University of North Carolina at Chapel Hill. It dawned on me that few if any books discuss the relationship between women and freedom of expression. I began scribbling notes about a history of American women and free speech. These notes grew over several years into my doctoral dissertation on suffragists' use of the right to assemble peaceably. The dissertation evolved into this book.

Many people offered professional expertise and emotional and financial support along the way. Other members of my dissertation committee besides Dr. Hall who offered valuable input included Peter Filene, Chuck Stone, Ruth Walden, and, especially, my committee chair, Margaret Blanchard. Thanks are due to Meredith Morris-Babb for finding this book a home and to the staff at the University of Tennessee Press for turning the manuscript into a good-looking book.

Several scholarships enabled me to delve deeper into my research to make this a better work. Thanks are due to the Freedom Forum and to the Minnie Rubinstein Graduate Research Scholarship awarded by the School of Journalism and Mass Communication at UNC in Chapel Hill.

I also would like to thank staff members in the microform departments at Davis Library at UNC, Perkins Library at Duke University, Special Collections at the Dartmouth College Library, and the Library of Congress.

Many friends listened to me talk about the book—or offered a pleasant diversion from it. They include Karen and Brian Delaney, Liza Frenette, Claire and Bob Jentsch, Julia Knaub, Doris Pereske and Jeff Platsky, Linda Petrella, Georgann Roche, Jeanne Steele, Mei-ling Yang, and my aunt, Patricia Walker.

My parents, Lennox and Margaret Lumsden, and my sister, Laurie Kamuda, never flagged in their interest and support. Most of all, I want to thank my children, Jessalee Landfried and Samuel Landfried, for being the best daughter and son in the whole, wide world.

Linda J. Lumsden
Bowling Green, Kentucky
December 1996

Women and Freedom of Expression
before the Twentieth Century

When the thick rain clouds draping New York City's harbor split apart on the afternoon of October 28, 1886, the veiled Statue of Liberty loomed before the steamer *John Lenox*. "New York State Woman Suffrage Association" read a long, white banner spanning the ship's prow, and about two hundred women crowded its deck. Two warships flanked the *John Lenox*, which was among the first of some three hundred ships steaming down the North River to celebrate the statue's unveiling on Bedlow's Island. After ten thousand rounds of gunfire signaled President Grover Cleveland's arrival, whistles shrilled and the horde of onlookers cheered in Battery Park.[1] When the hoopla ebbed, the women descended to the *John Lenox*'s lower deck for their own ceremony: speeches decrying the hypocrisy of personifying liberty as female when American women were denied that most fundamental democratic right, the vote. As historian Sally Roesch Wagner noted, "The Statue was the ultimate metaphor of the pedestal of powerlessness on which all American women were placed."[2]

Just as the voiceless statue symbolized women's lack of voice in government over the previous century, the women's gathering aboard the *John Lenox* foreshadowed the instrumental role the First Amendment right to assemble peaceably would play in the campaign for woman suffrage in the next century.[3] Perhaps American women would not have the vote today if their predecessors had not taken to the streets. Americans would have ignored the suffragists if they had not delivered their message so publicly. During the decade before Congress approved the Nineteenth Amendment in 1919, suffragists were innovators in soapbox speaking at "open-air" meetings, outdoor pageants, petition drives, picketing, civil disobedience, and the use of symbolic expression, all manifestations of their exercise of the right of assembly.

The suffrage movement exemplified how the right of assembly can effect change in a democracy. Arguably the most ancient and basic principle of a free society, the right of assembly served suffragists well during the 1910s.[4] As a disfranchised class with limited resources, suffragists took their message to the streets—that most public and accessible forum—forced their ideas upon an indifferent public, and gradually won over a significant portion of the public and politicians, who also were besieged by suffrage assemblies in male political bodies. Suffrage only became a national issue when women publicly agitated for the vote. If they had not taken to the streets—to soapbox, solicit petitions, parade, or picket—the suffrage movement never would have gotten off the ground, because no one was eager to listen to suffragists' ideas, much less act upon them. The right of assembly provided the foundation for every step of the suffrage campaign.

Suffragists also challenged beliefs about how women should behave when they took to the streets to speak, march, and picket. This book analyzes both the role the First Amendment right to assemble peaceably played in the twentieth-century suffrage campaign and the reciprocal, little-known role the suffrage protests played in the development of twentieth-century conceptions of the right to assemble.[5] Among the minorities that fought for freedom of expression by staging a broad range of demonstrations during the tumultuous decade that encompassed World War I, suffragists indirectly helped prod the legal system to establish protections for dissidents exercising their First Amendment rights.

The right of assembly protects people meeting together or the communication of ideas among people to accomplish various common purposes.[6] It is the foundation for all other forms of freedom of expression, because ideas must be shared before they can have an impact upon society. "The important political right of assembly and petition is rather the original than a derivation from freedom of speech," explained constitutional law scholar Frederic Jesup Stimson in 1908.[7] According to a pair of later legal scholars, "An assembly of two or more people is a necessary basis for the exercise of the right of freedom of speech and a multitude of other privileges."[8] Speech is meaningless if unheard: "Without that right of assembly, guarantees of free speech are empty gestures; for if no public forum is available, then the right to speak freely is of little value."[9]

The role of outdoor meetings in self-governance has been respected by free societies throughout history. "Wherever the title of streets and parks may rest, they have immemorially been held in trust for the use of the public and, time out of mind, have been used for purposes of assembly, communicating thought between citizens," asserted the United States Supreme Court in a landmark case involving the right of assembly.[10] The leading nineteenth-century Court case on the right of assembly simply stated: "It is found wherever civilization exists."[11] The concept of a right of assembly was first set down on paper in 1215 in the Magna Charta, from which all Anglo-Saxon civil liberties flow.[12]

Colonial Americans engaged in myriad street assemblies, including mobs, reflecting the Whig belief in the people's right of resistance. "Extralegal groups and conventions repeatedly sprang up to take public action into their own hands," according to historian Gordon Wood.[13] Revolutionary mobs characterized as "surprisingly humane and orderly" tended toward responsibility and purposefulness and arose out of the republican ethic that the people should rule.[14] Colonists drew heavily upon guidelines for direct action defined by English radical writers who justified extralegal action when all established avenues for change had failed.[15] The nation's founders, in fact, prominently placed a clause in the First Amendment of the Bill of Rights specifically guaranteeing the people's right to assemble peaceably.[16] This right was considered so basic that Representative Theodore Sedgwick of Massachusetts found including it "derogatory to the dignity of the House to descend to such minutiae" and wanted to strike the phrase from the proposed bill. Others, who foresaw the threat of governmental suppression, defeated his motion.[17] In republican America, mobs lost much of their respectability because domestic turbulence was viewed as reflecting poorly on the new nation's experiment in democracy.[18] By the 1830s, the occasionally lethal violence of anti-abolition mobs had made street meetings anathema to most Americans.[19]

Because of the disruptive potential of street assemblies, the Bill of Right's rhetorical homage to the right of assembly was not matched by legal protections for assemblies. For one thing, the First Amendment was not considered applicable to state laws prior to 1925.[20] Courts ruled erratically on all First Amendment freedoms until well into the twentieth century and were especially hostile to gatherings of politically radical groups.[21] Prior to the 1920s, the United States Supreme Court with one minor exception ruled against the few free-speech defenses it heard.[22] It would take the courts half a century to catch up with pioneering legal scholar Thomas Cooley's declaration in 1868 that freedom of expression was "essential to the very existence and perpetuity of free government."[23]

Courts seldom considered First Amendment issues prior to the late nineteenth century. From 1791 to 1889, the United States Supreme Court heard only twelve cases involving speech and press issues. Between 1890 and 1917, the Court heard fifty-three such cases, still an average of just two a year. Partly because of its unfamiliarity with free-speech issues, "the Court's opinions often were illogical or inconsistent," noted legal historian Michael Gibson.[24] Most nineteenth-century First Amendment cases never even went to court, partly because of extrajudicial factors such as threats of violence and economic and social pressures.[25] And greater emphasis was placed upon the police power to protect the public's health, safety, and morals.[26]

Police power was "the power of promoting the public welfare by restraining and regulating the use of liberty and property," according to a turn-of-the century legal scholar.[27] Judges deferred to police power when occasional cases involving the right of assembly reached the courts. Municipal authorities deemed police powers essential to protect the public welfare against unorthodox methods of expression, such as street meetings and parades.[28] That meant a mayor could ban any outdoor gathering he believed might stir unrest. Only a handful of pioneering legal scholars decried this police power as a pernicious threat to individual liberties.[29]

The right of assembly suffered a blow in 1897 when the Supreme Court decided a Massachusetts minister had no right to preach on Boston Commons—hallowed ground of the Sons of Liberty. In *Davis v. Massachusetts*, the Court ignored free-speech issues in upholding a Boston city ordinance prohibiting speeches on public grounds without a permit from the mayor.[30] When minister William Davis asserted his First Amendment rights of religion, free speech, and assembly to preach on Boston Commons, the Court rejected his argument: "For the legislature absolutely or conditionally to forbid public speaking in a highway or public park is no more an infringement of the rights of a member of the public than for the owner of a private house to forbid it in his house."[31]

Davis demonstrated the nineteenth-century legal system's overreliance upon property law as well as the nineteenth-century view of parks as common property.[32] The legal system's view that public property was for the use of the entire public rather than a disgruntled minority continued into the twentieth century.[33] The Georgia Supreme Court in 1905, for instance, sustained the conviction of a Socialist professor for speaking on an Atlanta street corner without a permit because "the primary object of streets is for public passage."[34] It said no man has a constitutional right to "make the most necessary demands of his nature in the public streets."[35]

The right of assembly fared better in parade cases. The Salvation Army won an 1886 case vindicating its right to parade peaceably without a permit. The Michigan Supreme Court invalidated a city ordinance that gave officials "unregulated official discretion" to control parades through a permit system.[36] The court alluded to the social value of parades: "It is only when political, religious, social or other demonstrations create public disturbances or operate as nuisances or create or manifestly threaten some tangible public or private mischief that the law interferes."[37]

Such liberal court rulings "reflected a new sensitivity to the public's interest in peaceful expression," as one scholar put it, but that sensitivity evaporated when courts considered assemblies of radicals.[38] State courts routinely suppressed speech threatening violence out of fear of anarchy and socialism, especially after the fatal 1886 Haymarket riot was linked to anarchists. The public cheered when the codefendants were found guilty of conspiracy to commit murder because their speeches inflamed the crowd.[39] The 1901 assassination of President William McKinley by an avowed anarchist fanned further repression. After anarchist lecturer Emma Goldman was refused a public hall in Philadelphia, a Pennsylvania court rebuffed her free-speech defense.[40] The court held that the government's right of self-preservation overrode the "abuse" of the right to free speech.[41]

Despite such limitations and infringements, the right of assembly was instrumental in helping nineteenth-century American women acquire a feminist consciousness. No disempowered group can organize without assembling. Street meetings were the simplest, cheapest, and most effective way for such groups to gather to discuss and/or protest their plight. Public assemblies also enhance group cohesiveness as well as attract the public's attention, a prerequisite for social change.[42]

Given the chilly reception nineteenth-century courts accorded freedom of expression, it probably was lucky for women that courts addressed no cases involving women and freedom of expression in the nineteenth century.[43] The main reason for the absence of such cases, however, was that extralegal cultural proscriptions denied women the right of assembly among other constitutional rights.[44] In eighteenth-century America, freedom of expression was linked to politics, and politics belonged in the public sphere, which remained taboo for women. Women had to fight to assert their right to assemble peaceably. "If today women can be said to have obtained freedom of expression in the United States," noted colonial historian Mary Beth Norton, "they have achieved that goal through their own efforts, not because a 'great man' of the past sought to extend them the right of free speech."[45]

The Founding Fathers spoke literally when they declared all men are created equal.[46] Women lacked basic civil rights, such as the vote, control over their property and wages, custodianship of their children, and access to the professions and education.[47] They were confined to duties in the home, whereas men controlled politics.

This public-private split claims ancient roots in Aristotle's theory of citizenship, which elevated the *polis,* or public life, as the public domain in which the highest good could be attained through "perfect association" among citizens. Citizenship, however, was limited to free men; women, slaves, and children could not participate in the polis. Their private sphere was considered inferior to men's public sphere. Transported and transformed over centuries to eighteenth-century America, this Aristotelian public-private split eventually came to mean that men represented rationality and assumed responsibility for politics, commerce, and other aspects of the amoral public sphere. Women represented the inner emotional life and assumed responsibility for the home, where their most pressing duty was to nurture and preserve morality.[48]

That deeply ingrained dichotomy justified restricting women from the public sphere to prevent them from being tinged by immorality. This internalized belief system served as a highly effective form of social control; any woman who dared inject herself in public affairs in even the mildest manner jeopardized her most valuable cultural currency—her reputation. In contrast to the civic virtue associated with the "public man," a "public woman" was vile and sexually suspect, a whore.[49] Prostitution laws, in fact, were just one form of social control that hindered women's participation in the public sphere, as when the mayor of Pittsburgh in 1869 ordered the arrest of any woman on the street after nine o'clock.[50]

Social custom further encroached upon independent women. Women who wanted to attend public balls in the mid-nineteenth century, for instance, could not without a male escort.[51] Independent women who avoided the appellation "whore" risked the indignity of their womanhood denied. Labeling as unsexed or mannish any American woman who ventured even onto the fringe of politics, the epitome of the modern polis, was a powerful silencing technique. It was no coincidence that an editorial denouncing Belva Lockwood's doomed 1884 presidential bid appeared under the headline "An Unsexed Monster."[52]

The public-private split not only sabotaged women's participation in the public sphere but, even more invidiously, denied women their humanity, as political philosopher Hannah Arendt observed, for the public sphere is the space in which human beings use words and deeds to discuss and make decisions on matters of common interest.[53] As a result of excluding women from political life, observed political scientist Susan Moller Okin, "the great tradition of political philosophy consists, generally speaking, of writings by men, for men, and about men."[54]

American patriots continued that tradition. "The ideological climate of the postrevolutionary decades seems to have reinvigorated, rather than undercut, an already established, popularly based misogyny," according to historian Christine Stansell, because republicanism linked civic (public) virtue to independence, a state denied women.[55] The language of republicanism, in fact, was suffused in cultural norms of masculinity such as individualism and self-reliance, as Paula Baker has pointed out. She added, "'Feminine' attributes—attraction to luxury, self-indulgence, timidity, dependence, passion—were linked to corruption and posed a threat to republicanism."[56]

Tied to their families and isolated from other women, American women rarely congregated in public before 1800.[57] From the nation's earliest beginnings, the male-dominated political atmosphere did not bode well for female public assemblies. One of America's earliest political disputes centered around a woman, Anne Hutchinson, who assembled women at her home to study religion in the 1630s. Her challenge to Puritanism compounded by her gender provoked Massachusetts Bay Colony authorities to banish her.[58]

Colonial women's assemblies largely occurred in the home and centered on family. Laurel Thatcher Ulrich has analyzed the central role women's gatherings played well into the republican era through domestic rituals surrounding birth, illness, and death. "This was the era of 'social childbirth' when female relatives and neighbors, as well as midwives, attended births," she wrote.[59] Such intense events drew women into physically and emotionally supportive associations.[60] Yet even these domestic gatherings attracted male interference, so that male doctors had usurped midwives by the end of the nineteenth century.

A few women took tentative first steps toward public protest. In 1733, property-holding women in New York protested their disfranchisement in a letter to the *New York Journal* rather than in the streets.[61] Four years before the Boston Tea Party, some three hundred Boston women joined in league to boycott tea.[62] The Revolution sanctioned some female public assemblies that combined domestic traditions with support for the war. Public spinning bees involving dozens of women, part of a campaign to substitute homespun clothes for imported British goods, became ritualized patriotic functions that attracted hundreds of spectators and pages of favorable press coverage. The *Boston Evening Post* wrote of a Long Island spinning bee, "The ladies, while they vie with each other in skill and industry in their profitable employment, may vie with the men in contributing to the preservation and prosperity of their country and equally share in the honor of it." As historian Mary Beth Norton observed, such praise "must have been exceedingly attractive to any eighteenth-century woman raised in an environment that had previously devalued both her and her domestic sphere."[63] A rarer assembly that exposed women's potential for violence occurred in 1783, when a group of women helped drag an alleged British sympathizer off to be hanged before George Washington intervened.[64]

Nascent feminists may have found their concerns articulated in two tracts published at the close of the eighteenth century. Judith Sargent Murray's essay *On The Equality of the Sexes* argued for educating women in 1790, followed the next year by English feminist Mary Wollstonecraft's revolutionary *Vindication of the Rights of Woman.*[65] The embryonic feminist consciousness partly reflected the natural rights philosophy that infused the American and French Revolutions. "It is not surprising that in so marked a transition period from the old to the new, as seen in the eighteenth century, that women, trained to think and write and speak, should have discovered that they, too, had some share in the new-born liberties suddenly announced to the world," observed the editors of the *History of Woman Suffrage*, itself a six-volume testament to how women's powers of expression expanded over the next century.[66]

Women's ability to express themselves increased in the republican period because the male establishment deemed education for women necessary so they could instill civic virtue in their husbands and sons.[67] An unanticipated consequence was that literacy created an awareness of injustice among women through reading as well as the ability to counter injustice through writing—activities that could be practiced at home. "Ever since there have been women able to make their sentiments known by their writings (the only publicity which society permits to them), an increasing number of them have recorded protests against their present social condition," John Stuart Mill wrote in 1870.[68] Still, Victorian doctors blamed reading for destroying the reproductive functions of young women, whom they admonished to abstain from intellectual effort during adolescence and menstruation.[69]

Women faced greater opposition when they tried to assemble or speak, because these activities occurred in the inviolable public sphere. Assembling proved less formidable than speaking. Although the earliest women's club dates back more than two thousand years, when the Greek poet Sappho gathered women to study the arts, the United States was nearly two decades old before women began assembling in clubs. The handful of voluntary associations that comprised women's first public assemblies in the late eighteenth century preceded a flood of women's associations between 1800 and 1820.

Early organizations, bearing names such as the Female Association for the Relief of Women and Children in Reduced Circumstances, restricted their scope to missionary and charitable work. These domestically oriented forays into social services helped spawn the more aggressive reform associations during the 1830s that moved beyond meeting the private needs of impoverished individuals to tackling more public problems. An example was the New York Female Moral Reform Society's campaign against prostitution, in its time a radical departure for women into unspeakable corners of the public sphere.[70] Voluntary associations offered women a way to exercise the public influence otherwise denied them, according to historian Anne Firor Scott, by tying their purpose to domestic needs.[71] These associations initiated women in speaking and assembling in public.

In response to this challenge to the male domain, the creation of male public space became more formalized and sexually exclusive between 1825 and 1840, according to historian Mary Ryan, with the construction of public halls such as Tammany Hall and creation of male sanctums such as theaters, restaurants, and merchants' exchanges.[72] The "cult of true womanhood" arose at about the same time, seductively sentencing middle-class women to their parlors with blandishments about their moral superiority.[73] This exclusion of women from the public, political sphere was so complete that Paula Baker has argued gender—not class or race—was the "most salient political division" in nineteenth-century America.[74]

Women learned to swaddle their desire to gather in the language of domesticity. Members of the first club organized to improve women's intellect in Bloomington, Indiana, in 1841 defused criticism their Edgeworthalean Society chapter was "too masculine" and immodest by responding that carefully policed mental inquiry helped women in their quest to make "home the seat of happiness."[75]

Cultural taboos prohibiting women from speaking in public remained the most daunting. The mere act of women speaking on a public platform violated the entrenched gender roles that anchored virtually all social organization.[76] Social sanctions against women who dared violate their assigned social role comprised part of the spectrum of "extralegal" means free-speech historian Thomas Tedford has pointed out historically prevented women from exercising their constitutional rights of freedom of expression.[77] The harassment endured by Fanny Wright of Scotland when she began delivering the United States' first public lectures by a woman in 1828 epitomized these extralegal forms of censorship. Wright's way was not eased by her advocacy of free love and racial unity. After Philadelphia's mayor banned her speech in 1829, Wright waged the first woman's battle for the right of assembly, pleading her case at nearby fairs and other sites. Rowdies once destroyed her stand, and another time several listeners were slightly wounded after boys hurled stones through the windows of an abandoned factory where she spoke as disinterested police looked on. Attacks upon Wright's womanhood foreshadowed the viciousness of verbal attacks upon suffrage speakers. Prominent educator Catharine Beecher fumed, "I cannot conceive anything in the shape of a woman, more intolerably offensive and disgusting."[78] Three years later, critics hounded African American abolitionist Maria Stewart out of Boston after she delivered the first public lecture by an American woman.[79] Violence against women speakers "made the gender limits of the public sphere emphatically clear," historian Mary Ryan observed.[80]

The enforced silence was all-encompassing. Even after Oberlin College became the first American college to admit women in 1833, it forbade them from speaking in class.[81] A male minister conducted all business at meetings of the Female Cent Society, the first female missionary society, as women were forbidden to read their reports because it was considered unladylike to raise their voices in public.[82] When abolitionist Abby Kelley challenged a resolution to exclude women from the Connecticut Anti-Slavery Society, the rebuke she drew from its chairman revealed the subterranean fears that percolated whenever women dared speak out in male assemblies: "I will not sit in a meeting where the sorcery of a woman's tongue is thrown around my heart. I will not submit to PETTICOAT GOVERNMENT. No woman shall ever lord it over me. I am Major Domo in my own house."[83]

The abolition movement proved the crucible for women who dared speak their minds. The key role abolition played in creating the woman's rights movement is undebatable. "As abolitionists they first won their right to speak in public, and began to evolve a philosophy of their place in society and of their basic rights," said suffrage historian Eleanor Flexner.[84] Abolition also honed women's experience in wielding the right to petition, which would figure prominently in the twentieth-century suffrage movement.

Lucy Stone, the nation's first full-time woman's rights speaker, was just one leader who emerged from the abolition movement. At times she was peppered with coins, dried apples, fish, beans, tobacco, and even a hymnal hurled so hard it stunned her.[85] When Abby Kelley launched her antislavery lectures in 1838, she endured slurs such as "nigger bitch," "man woman," "Jezebel," and "infidel." "During two decades of public speaking she dodged rotten eggs, rum bottles, and the contents of outhouses," wrote her biographer.[86] "The appearances of the antislavery women on the platform were praised as angelic and excoriated as diabolical," concluded historian Jean Fagan Yellin, "but in and through their public presence they dramatized the possibility of female freedom on a human level."[87]

Because women abolitionists had to fight to meet and speak, freedom of assembly and freedom of speech were indelibly linked with the woman's rights movement from its genesis in the abolition movement. Nineteenth-century woman's rights activists recognized the link between their second-class status and their inability to speak up for themselves. "Woman is taught to refrain from any public expression of speech or intellect, from a religious principle, as a tribute of adulation to man's superiority," Paulina Davis told the first national woman's rights convention in 1850.[88] Women's experiences on the abolition trail vividly demonstrated to them the connection between the freedom to assemble and to speak with other civil rights.

Trailblazers in the fight for women to speak and meet freely were South Carolina abolitionists Sarah and Angelina Grimké. Angelina Grimké's words in the 1830s on the link between slavery and women's status sowed the seeds for nineteenth-century feminism. She defined freedom as engagement in significant action and characterized significant action as public speech. In other words, she recognized that free speech was a precondition for women to be free. She wrote, "If we have no right to act, then may we well be termed 'the white slaves of the North'—for, like our brethren in bonds, we must seal our lips in silence and despair."[89]

Numerous encroachments upon the Grimké sisters' right to meet and speak characterized their antislavery speaking tour before "promiscuous audiences" (containing men and women) across Massachusetts in 1837. Officials often denied them meeting places. Critics called them names. The venom spewed at the Grimkés and the women who followed them was part of a larger public antipathy toward the abolitionist movement that sparked an assault upon fundamental American values such as free speech, a free press, and the right to assemble peaceably.[90]

In the Grimkés' case, a Massachusetts newspaper editor not only censored Angelina's speech, part of the first public debate between a man and a woman, but Congregational pastors wrote a letter to their congregations condemning the Grimkés for violating New Testament injunctions against women participating in public life.[91] Sarah Grimké responded in a series of landmark articles in which she asserted that the Bible merely reflected the patriarchal society that produced it. "I ask no favors for my sex," she wrote. "All I ask our brethren is, that they will take their feet from off our necks, and permit us to stand upright on that ground which God designed us to occupy."[92] Her sister also replied, saying: "If we surrender the right to *speak* in public this year, we must surrender the right to petition the next year, and the right to *write* the year after, and so on. What *then* can *woman* do for the slave, when she is herself under the feet of man and shamed into *silence?*"[93]

Abolition provided the impetus for the first woman's rights convention, in fact, when the World's Anti-Slavery Convention in London in 1840—presumably comprising the planet's most egalitarian-minded men—forced eight American women delegates to sit behind a curtain in a gallery and forbade them to speak.[94] The injustice and indignity spurred Lucretia Mott and Elizabeth Cady Stanton to organize the Woman's Rights Convention in Seneca Falls, New York, on 19–20 July 1848. From that moment, woman's rights conventions, predicated upon the right to assemble peaceably, formed the core of the woman's rights movement.

Unfamiliar with how to run a convention, the women perused male productions. "The reports of Peace, Temperance, and Anti-Slavery conventions were examined, but all alike seemed too tame and pacific for the inauguration of a rebellion such as the world had never before seen," recorded the *History of Woman Suffrage*.[95] Finally, they adopted the Declaration of Independence as the model for their Declaration of Sentiments seeking improved property and child custody rights, better professional and educational opportunities, and the most radical demand—the vote.

Why so radical? As historian Ellen DuBois observed, feminists' focus on citizenship called for a new kind of power for women not based in the family; a nonfamilial role for women in the public sphere challenged the male monopoly on the public arena. "This," wrote DuBois, "is what gave suffragism much of its feminist meaning."[96]

This helps explain why men found woman suffrage so threatening. The vote symbolized female autonomy. It threatened the social order, because full citizenship for women implied a revolutionary change in the conception of woman. The vote also implied parallel changes in men's role, which helps explain why so many antisuffrage articles and cartoons caricatured men pushing baby carriages, washing dishes, or performing other female tasks. The idea of women imposing their morality and values upon the male political system caused many cigar-chomping, whiskey-swilling, epithet-spewing backroom politicos to eye them as a "Puritan scourge incarnate."[97] But men were not the only Americans unsettled by the idea; most women also opposed suffrage and the changes it portended for women's well-defined role.

Why did a handful of women so covet the vote that they defied such well-entrenched legal and cultural authority? The ballot conferred citizenship upon its holder, and citizenship conferred humanity. As suffrage historian Eleanor Flexner wrote, the vote represented for women "a vital step toward winning human dignity, and the recognition that they too were endowed with the faculty of reason, the power of judgment, the capacity for social responsibility."[98] The symbolism was so tied up with humanity that innumerable suffrage talks and essays sought to answer the question "Are Women Human Beings?"[99]

The women assembling in Seneca Falls had embarked upon a radical course. The mere act of women assembling on their own behalf without cover of offering charity or studying meekly to improve their mothering was so radical that even the bold convention organizers shrank from leading discussions. James Mott chaired the Woman's Rights Convention. "The proceedings were extensively published, unsparingly ridiculed by the press and denounced by the pulpit," the *History of Woman Suffrage* recorded.[100] The ridicule prompted women to vigorously exercise their right to a free press by launching several suffrage newspapers, another important First Amendment tool of the woman's rights movement.[101]

The right of assembly figured prominently as women convened in Ohio, Indiana, Pennsylvania, and Massachusetts. The first National Woman's Rights Convention in Worcester, Massachusetts, on 23–24 October 1850, attracted a thousand persons from as far away as California.[102] Women soon gained the confidence to run their own rights conventions. "Not a man was allowed to sit on the platform, to speak, or vote," the *History of Woman Suffrage* recorded of a convention in Salem, Ohio. "*Never did men so suffer.*"[103]

The radical nature of woman's rights conventions occasionally prompted the abrogation of their rights of assembly. Ohio women were denied use of the local school and church for a rights convention. The women found shelter on the threshing floor of a barn filled with more than three hundred farm families: "The farmers' wives brought huge boxes and pans of provisions. Men and women made speeches, and many names were added to our memorial. . . . It was no uncommon thing in those days for Abolitionist, or Methodist, or other meetings, to be held under the trees, or in large barns, when school-houses would not hold the people. But to shut up doors against women was a new thing."[104]

Men also employed harassment and ridicule to abort women's public gatherings. Hecklers turned an 1853 woman's rights convention into a riot at the Broadway Tabernacle in New York. "Gentlemen and ladies alike who attempted to speak were interrupted by shouts, hisses, stamping, and cheers, rude remarks, and all manner of noisy demonstrations," the *History of Woman Suffrage* reported. Speaker Wendell Phillips told the crowd, "You prove one thing to-night, that the men of New York do not understand the meaning of civil liberty and free discussion."[105] The uproar forced the convention to close.

Instead of criticizing the disruptive audience, the *New York Herald* ridiculed the women, a typical press reaction to woman's rights assemblies. "The assemblage of rampant women which convened at the Tabernacle yesterday was an interesting phase in the comic history of the nineteenth century," its editorial began, launching into a lampoon of the women's goals. The newspaper used a timeworn tactic for silencing women: questioning their womanhood. It asserted that participants in the "gathering of unsexed women" at the "Women's Wrong Convention" were "entirely devoid of personal attraction."[106] The ridicule was yet another example of the extralegal pressures that stymied women's expression of the right of assembly. Twentieth-century suffragists, however, would proudly appropriate the label "rampant women."[107]

African Americans were among the "rampant women" prominent in the movement in the nineteenth century. They played an integral role in early woman's rights conventions, in contrast to the ostracism by white suffragists they endured after the turn of the century. Stanton's radical resolution calling for woman suffrage at Seneca Falls, for instance, seemed doomed until Frederick Douglass vigorously endorsed it.[108] Suffrage was a joint goal of black and white activists who together created the American Equal Rights Association (AERA) after the Civil War. Nineteenth-century woman's rights assemblies engaged in a dialogue about race and privilege absent from the twentieth-century suffrage movement. Frances E. W. Harper, the black poet, novelist, and civil rights activist, won cheers when she told the AERA: "I do not believe the white women are dewdrops just exhaled from the skies. . . . You white women speak here of rights. I speak of wrongs. I, as a colored woman, have had in this country an education which has made me feel as if I were in the situation of Ishmael, my hand against every man, and every man's hand against me."[109]

Neither did Sojourner Truth, who delivered her rousing "Ain't I a Woman?" speech at the 1851 woman's rights convention, mince words when she addressed middle-class white audiences about suffrage.[110] The former slave once chastised a well-dressed crowd in Providence, Rhode Island: "What kind of reformers be you, with goose-wings on your heads, as if you were going to fly, and dressed in such ridiculous fashion, talking about reform and women's rights?"[111]

Black and white cooperation fell apart, however, during debates on the Fourteenth and Fifteenth Amendments concerning voting rights, which pointedly denied women the vote. The former inserted the word "male" into the U.S. Constitution for the first time.[112] Some of the racism that pervaded the later woman's rights movement can be traced back to Stanton and Susan Anthony's resentment over the perceived treachery. The question of whether women should defer to the "negro's hour" split the woman's movement.

Stanton and Anthony created the National Woman Suffrage Association (NWSA) in 1869 to seek a sixteenth amendment granting women suffrage. As their newspaper, the *Revolution*, made clear, theirs was a radical organization that in addition to the vote also addressed taboo women's issues such as prostitution, birth control, working women's unions, marriage, and the Bible. More conservative suffragists, led by Lucy Stone and her husband Henry Blackwell, organized the American Woman Suffrage Association (AWSA) in 1870. AWSA believed women should step aside so that African American men could at least gain the vote, and it opposed associating votes for women with the inflammatory issues trumpeted by Stanton and Anthony. The schism existed until 1890, when the two groups merged to form the National American Woman Suffrage Association (NAWSA).[113]

During NWSA's two decades, Anthony and a handful of other suffragists broke new ground by experimenting with symbolic expression and civil disobedience, both of which would play an important role in twentieth-century suffrage demonstrations. Symbolic expression is the use of objects, movements, words, or graphic expressions that express the hidden meanings of a culture to communicate ideas. "Symbolic conduct is an exceptionally vivid means of communication," according to one scholar.[114] Woman's rights activists first used that vivid means in Vineland, New Jersey, on 19 November 1868, when women set up a table across from one where men voted in the presidential election. One hundred seventy-two women, including four African Americans, cast their symbolic ballots, vividly drawing attention to their disfranchisement.[115] Anthony employed civil disobedience when she tried to vote in 1872 in Rochester, New York. After she was arrested, she stumped upstate New York to plead her case at public meetings.[116] Her conviction under federal law and one-hundred-dollar fine inspired a protest meeting by Rochester women at which an upside-down flag draped over the rostrum symbolized their mourning.[117]

Suffragists also refused to pay taxes, a form of civil disobedience usually associated with Henry David Thoreau. Lucy Stone stopped paying property taxes in 1857.[118] Abby Kelley labeled her refusal to pay taxes on her Massachusetts farm a "Bunker Hill battle" for woman's rights. Echoing the patriots, "no taxation without representation" became a rallying cry for nineteenth-century feminists. Women activists also learned the value of publicity when newspapers across the nation picked up the story of seven cows seized by tax collectors from elderly Connecticut sisters Julia and Abby Smith, who refused to pay taxes because they could not vote for the Glastonbury town budget.[119]

Protesters grew bolder. More than seventy women marched to the registrar's office to sign up as voters in the District of Columbia only to be turned away.[120] The New York Woman Suffrage Association called a mass meeting on the Boston Tea Party centennial on 16 December 1873, to protest taxation of women without representation. The Woman's Tax-payers Association of the city of Rochester routinely sent memorials to Albany to demand from the legislature either representation or relief from taxes. To commemorate the centennial of the Battle of Lexington, New York women assembled at the Union League Theatre on 19 April 1874, where activists compared the women's fight with that of the patriot soldiers.[121]

Suffragists began to assert their constitutional rights. When Washington, D.C., police appeared at NWSA's annual convention in 1876 to demand it pay for an entertainment license or be shut down, presiding officer Matilda J. Gage informed the police the Constitution guaranteed the right of the people to assemble for redress of grievances. The crowd cheered wildly when she threatened to hold a perpetual woman's rights convention if she were jailed. "We of this Centennial year, must not forget that this country owes its birth to disobedience to law," Gage said. The police left.[122]

NWSA's radicalism was a forerunner of the radicalism of the National Woman's Party (NWP) in the 1910s, just as Anthony became a role model for NWP chair Alice Paul. Anthony's most radical demonstration occurred when she disrupted the 1876 centennial festivities in Philadelphia to present the Declaration of Rights for Women. The rebuffs NWSA experienced during earlier attempts to participate in the centennial typified how extralegal factors hampered women's rights of assembly.

First, the owners of Carpenter Hall refused to rent it to NWSA for a women's exhibit. Then Gage arranged to rent rooms from a woman only to have her husband rip up the lease when he discovered the tenants' identity. Eventually they found some first-floor rooms on Chestnut Street, but because none of the married women legally could enter a contract, only Anthony could sign the lease. Finally, centennial officials refused NWSA's request to present their Declaration of Rights for Women to dignitaries during a gala ceremony at Independence Square.

Anthony resorted to civil disobedience. She wangled five seats in the press section, and the women joined more than 150,000 persons who jammed the square and surrounding streets on a sizzling 4 July morning. After a grand military parade, the dignitaries sat on a speaker's stand in the center of wooden scaffolding that seated four thousand people. As a speaker finished reading the Declaration of Independence, the five women rose and hurried down the aisle to the speaker's stand while the band prepared to play its next number. Anthony handed the speaker a three-foot-wide scroll. "Mr. [Thomas] Ferry's face paled, as bowing low, with no word, he received the declaration, which thus became part of the day's proceedings; the ladies turned, scattering printed copies, as they deliberately walked down the platform," recorded the *History of Woman Suffrage*.[123]

Once outside the square, the five women climbed a platform in front of Independence Hall, where Anthony read the Declaration of Rights for Women before a large and enthusiastic crowd. The impromptu gathering predated the "open-air" meetings that would figure so heavily in the 1910s suffrage campaign. Later, the women moved to a church to hear five hours of speeches. Similar declarations were read by women that day in protests in places as far flung as Olympia, Washington, and Maquoketa, Iowa.[124]

Anthony's civil disobedience in Philadelphia moved the middle-class suffrage movement into the streets, a venue already familiar to working-class women. They marched during the nation's first strikes in the 1820s and 1830s.[125] In 1825, New York City seamstresses protesting poor pay and working conditions staged the first all-woman strike. After Lowell, Massachusetts, textile workers walked off the job in 1834, one of the strike leaders "mounted a pump, and made a flaming Mary Wollstonecraft speech on the rights of women."[126] Women began to mount the public podium at workingmen's outdoor meetings. At a New York labor rally of ten thousand people on 5 July 1886, three-quarters of the crowd clustered around the suffrage platform, one of four set up in the corners of Union Square. Labor's inclusion of the suffragists formalized the union between feminists and labor, which would further influence suffrage protests in the 1910s.[127]

Temperance was another nineteenth-century women's movement that profoundly influenced twentieth-century suffragists. The Woman's Temperance Crusade during the winter of 1873–74 was the nation's first women's mass movement, enlisting hundreds of thousands of women in hundreds of towns who marched to liquor outlets to sing and pray in what a historian called a "spectacular nineteenth-century version of street theater."[128] The crusade deployed the right of assembly in mass meetings outdoors, parades, and picketing, all new forms of female public protest that swept temperance women into civil disobedience.[129] The crusade truly was militant: Delegations not only prayed on saloon floors and blocked shipments of liquor with picket lines but also occasionally destroyed casks of liquor with hatchets.[130] As historian Ruth Bordin has pointed out, middle-class women excused their indecorous protests by tying their militant movement to the home. They claimed they were protecting the domestic sphere by ridding society of the evils of alcohol.[131] These exercises in civil disobedience also helped awaken women to their entitlement to civil liberties. The cask smashers, for instance, defended their actions with analogies to the Boston Tea Party.[132]

But these experiments in public protest still posed danger. Beer and sausages rained upon temperance protesters in Ohio, and a mob with dogs set upon militant crusaders in Cleveland.[133] Marchers were convicted of disturbing the peace in Portland, Oregon, ordinances aimed at banning the marches were enacted in Cleveland and Cincinnati, and an injunction blocked women from singing and praying in an Ohio beer garden.[134] "The crusaders' marches, undertaken in the face of hostile crowds and violent resistance by liquor dealers and their supporters, represented an attempt to exercise the right to participate in public affairs," noted historian Jack S. Blocker Jr.[135] They succeeded within months in dropping the nation's malt liquor production by five and a half million gallons.[136]

The crusade's true significance was far broader. The mass movement served as "one of the most powerful instruments of women's consciousness-raising of all time," Bordin concluded.[137] Many leaders of the fledgling suffrage movement launched their activism in the Woman's Christian Temperance Union (WCTU), including Anthony and future NAWSA presidents Dr. Anna Howard Shaw and Carrie Chapman Catt. Anthony organized the first state woman's temperance organization in 1852 after the Sons of Temperance banned women from speaking at their convention.[138] In turn, the inaugural convention of the WCTU excluded male members.[139]

Anthony later uncharacteristically objected to temperance protests' "desecration of womanhood," but most female crusaders came away with a new appreciation for the power of assembly and association. The crusade impressed upon women the power of public protest. "It really seems to me that nothing short of the street praying movement will arouse the apathy and indifference among men," wrote one crusader.[140] In the twentieth century, a handful of militant suffragists would come to similar conclusions when they defied society to picket the White House in wartime. By the end of the nineteenth century, women had gained considerable expertise and confidence in expressing their demands through the right to assemble peaceably.

Rampant Women

⚜ ONE ⚜

THE RIGHT OF ASSOCIATION
Mass Meetings, Delegations, and Conventions

The right of association lay at the heart of the woman suffrage movement, as it does with all political and social movements. Individuals who gather to achieve common aims exercise the right of association, which encompasses the right to belong. Almost every aspect of the suffrage movement employed the right: When a woman paid dues to her local suffrage association, swapped stories at a suffrage tea, signed a petition, gathered listeners at her soapbox, marched down Fifth Avenue, voted for new officers at a national convention, joined the White House picket line, or helped form a political party, she exercised her right of association.

The right of association evolved from but is broader than the right of assembly, with which it is inextricably entwined. Alexis de Tocqueville observed during his travels across America in the early 1800s that the right of association formed the foundation of American society: "The most natural privilege of man, next to the right of acting for himself, is that of combining his exertions with those of his fellow-creatures, and of acting in common with them. I am therefore led to conclude, that the right of association is almost as inalienable as the right of personal liberty."[1]

Although America was founded on the right of religious association, the Bill of Rights ignored other associational rights, perhaps because the right was so basic it seemed self-evident.[2] As a result, the United States was slow to develop formal recognition of associational rights, even though these rights were deeply rooted in the American and British experience. Voluntary associations got their earliest legal recognition in the common-law right of contract. Later, tradesmen were free to associate for socializing or for education, but the advocacy function of the modern labor union remained unlawful until the mid-nineteenth century. Courts rigidly circumscribed union activities, applying criminal conspiracy laws to union efforts to compel members to unite for better wages or working conditions. No law guaranteed workers the right to organize in associations until the National Industrial Recovery Act of 1933.[3] The United States Supreme Court finally ruled in 1958 that freedom to associate for "political, economic, religious or cultural matters" was a constitutional right protected by the First Amendment.[4] Like other facets of freedom of expression, however, the limits of its protections continue to be subject to legal tugs of war.[5]

Although suffragists faced no legal challenges to their right to organize, authorities infringed upon suffragists' rights of association when those authorities refused the women meeting permits or hall rentals. Only rarely did violence disrupt women's conventions, as when rowdies shut down the 1853 woman's rights convention in New York. Women at the 1913 Tennessee state suffrage convention evacuated the proceedings, however, when someone tossed a container of vile-smelling chemicals into the meeting hall. Women faced considerable censure from family, employers, the media, and men on the street when they participated in the suffrage campaign.

Suffrage was both a part and a product of the urge to join that infected women throughout the nineteenth century, first in charities, then in reform associations, most notably the abolition movement. In the late nineteenth century, women had other options for associating. Women's colleges, by then proliferating, fostered female autonomy, self-esteem, and sorority. Settlement houses in poor urban neighborhoods gave many of these idealistic, intelligent young women a home and a career.[6] The Woman's Christian Temperance Union helped stir a feminist consciousness. Historian Susan Dye Lee noted the power of association that surfaced in the temperance movement: "It brought thousands of women out of their homes and into the community. It gave many their first opportunity to speak publicly, to lead groups, to formulate plans, and to execute goals. Unity in a cause women could identify with gave the crusaders a chance to express shared feelings of sisterhood. And, having learned the power of association, they began to organize beyond the local level."[7]

All of these voluntary associations bridged private and public life, culminating by the end of the nineteenth century in the massive women's club movement. Hundreds of thousands of women joined the thousands of clubs united under the auspices of the General Federation of Women's Clubs and the National Association of Colored Women (NACW). Women's clubs served as training grounds for the activist, articulate reformers who steered the suffrage movement in the 1910s.[8] "Women saw [clubs] as vehicles for training themselves about public issues and for making an impact on the world," according to historian Glenna Matthews.[9] Suffrage study groups numbered among the clubs' many reforming activities. Club women applied the experience they had gained in organizing and legislative work to suffrage in the 1910s.[10] By then, suffrage finally had evolved into a mass movement, probably the first of the twentieth century.[11]

Women found many ways to associate with the suffrage movement. At the most basic level, they exercised the right of association simply by joining the National American Woman Suffrage Association or any of its hundreds of local affiliates. The rise in NAWSA membership in the 1910s indicated the snowballing strength of the movement: it increased from one hundred thousand women in 1915 to about two million in 1917, in contrast to some forty-five thousand members in 1907.[12]

The creation of a Denver suffrage league illustrates the reach of women's informal associational ties. While campaigning in South Dakota to remove the word "male" from the state constitution, Matilda Hindman traveled to Denver to raise funds. She persuaded local friends to form the Colorado Equal Suffrage Association Education Committee. Louise Tyler, recently moved from Boston to the territory, encouraged the group to formalize itself with a constitution, bylaws, and regular meetings. She also brought the local group an invitation to affiliate with NAWSA. Thus a nineteenth-century prototype of networking expanded the suffrage movement.[13]

As suffragists banded together, they discovered the power of association, a power that becomes apparent when large numbers of people share a common purposeful identity. In the suffrage movement, the power of association first became visible in the three earliest forms of suffrage assemblies: mass meetings, delegations, and conventions.

Mass Meetings

Mass meetings were the least formal and most easily organized political assembly, with a long heritage in American politics. American men had traditionally gathered en masse in political parties or in trade unions, in halls or in the streets. Polemics and inspiration characterized the numerous speeches that were the hallmark of mass meetings. A popular strategy for citizens to protest unpopular legislation, mass meetings were sometimes called "indignation meetings" by suffragists. When rowdies disrupted a 1913 suffrage parade in Washington, D.C., for example, leaders that evening called an indignation meeting, where they called for—and won—a congressional investigation.[14]

The sight of hundreds and then thousands of women assembled to espouse suffrage made mass meetings an effective visual technique for women to show the public the extent of interest in their cause. Women in Utah Territory won the vote in 1870, for instance, partly because Mormon women's mass meetings across the state won legislators' attention and sympathy.[15] The Mormon women's gatherings predated even the widespread mass prayer meetings of the WCTU later in the decade. The site of many Mormon mass meetings was the temple, which provided a safe, respectable venue for women venturing into politics. African American women also turned to the church when they used mass meetings as a mobilization tactic. When the Maryland legislature proposed an amendment in 1909 that would exclude black men from the polls, black women organized a mass meeting at a Baltimore church. The amendment died.[16]

As suffrage sentiment expanded in the East in the twentieth century, mass meetings grew larger and more frequent. Popular indoor venues such as Cooper Union and Carnegie Hall began overflowing with suffrage crowds by the 1910s, so that eventually only the Metropolitan Opera House could house major assemblies of suffragists in New York City.[17]

Delegations

After assembling together, the next step for woman's rights activists was to place their demands before legislators. Suffrage speakers and delegations ventured at risk beyond the portals of male political power. They had as their role model Angelina Grimké, the first woman to address any legislature. Grimké spoke in 1838 before the Massachusetts legislature on behalf of antislavery petitions presented by women. The disapproval of most New England abolitionists exacerbated her "fear and trembling," yet politicians and the press roundly praised Grimké's speech.[18]

Elizabeth Cady Stanton delivered the first speech on woman's rights to a legislature in 1855, addressing the Joint Judiciary Committee of both legislative houses of New York on women's legal disabilities; in 1860, her speech to the legislature specifically centered on suffrage.[19] The legislators failed to act on her proposals, but Stanton's appearance paved the way for what by the 1910s would be a flood of women's delegations to governors' homes, state houses, the United States Congress, and the White House.

In Wyoming Territory in 1869, for instance, a small group of suffragists appeared at Governor John Campbell's home, making it clear they would stay until he signed a suffrage bill. He did.[20] Nearly half a century later, the Women's Political Union (WPU) in New York also marched on legislators' homes, where they serenaded them with suffrage songs.[21]

Beginning in 1868, suffragists attended every national political convention.[22] More important, the National Woman Suffrage Association annually convened in Washington, D.C., so suffragists could present suffrage arguments to congressional committees. African American activist Mary Ann Shadd Carey, for instance, addressed the House Judiciary Committee on suffrage in 1871.[23] Zerelda Wallace of Indiana told the Senate Judicial Committee in 1880, "We are no seditious women, clamoring for any peculiar rights," before she invoked women's responsibility for home life as a reason to give them the vote. "We find ourselves hedged in at every effort we make as mothers for the amelioration of society."[24]

Even women from the South, where sentiment against suffrage flowed strongest, chanced social censure back home by asking the Senate for the vote. "Voting will never lessen maternal love," Helen Morris Lewis of North Carolina promised the Senate Committee on Woman Suffrage in 1896. A South Carolina woman advanced the white supremacist argument that formed the foundation of the southern suffrage movement: southern white women voters with property and educational requirements would outnumber African American voters. The speaker argued suffrage would curb rapacious blacks and stop lynchings by whites.[25]

Suffragists also visited state legislatures, for much of the early suffrage movement focused on persuading individual states to let women vote. Texas women converged on a state legislative committee weighing a suffrage amendment to the state constitution in 1907.[26] The Equality League of Self Supporting Women in New York jolted legislators awake at the annual suffrage hearing in Albany that same year by introducing two working-class speakers whose moving personal accounts debunked the homily that woman's place was in the home.[27] The effect was so invigorating that by 1909 the league arranged for special trains to carry whole carloads of speakers to enliven the annual hearing. Hundreds of women packed the hearing room, crowding out the legislators during the four-hour debate.[28] Suffragists started to camp out at suffrage hearings in other states, such as Pennsylvania and Maryland.[29]

These group appearances were among the earliest demonstrations of the new assertive, public nature that would characterize suffrage assemblies in the 1910s. In 1909, two hundred women in Chicago boarded a special suffrage train that whisked them to Springfield. Twenty-five speakers, including Jane Addams, lectured the legislature for seven hours. The suffrage newspaper *Woman's Journal* became giddy over the female presence: "All day long the State House was in possession of the fair visitors. There corridors were a-flutter with spring millinery and gay frocks, the air was filled with soft laughter and dulcet-keyed arguments."[30]

The *Journal*'s overwrought tone cloaked the radical, unfeminine nature of the women's ventures. Despite the *Journal*'s frilly prose, women's appearance in previously all-male sanctums threatened men. The headline of an account by the *Boston Herald* of a similar demonstration conveyed their unease with the suffragists' demonstrations. "Women Suffragists 2,000 Strong Stormed the State House Today," announced the paper in 1909 after women marched from Beacon Hill to a legislative hearing.[31] The crowd spilled out from the meeting rooms onto the State House steps and sidewalks, where the women conducted "great, orderly, inspiring" meetings. "Never was there such a demonstration," boasted *Progress*, the NAWSA journal.[32]

Such displays empowered and inspired participants. "I realized solemnly that we had embarked on a new phase of our movement," said one woman after witnessing the Boston demonstration.[33] That new phase was characterized by an unapologetic recognition by women that they possessed the right to stand up and speak up in American politics. Marches upon state houses bordered on the militant and demonstrated a new confidence among suffragists in public. They were less fearful of being labeled unwomanly and more assured about taking their places in the corridors of male power, which had seemed so foreign and intimidating. The appearance of large numbers of women worked no overnight miracle on male legislators, but women's persistence began to get men's attention.

Women's presence also occasionally raised men's ire. In 1910, fifty automobiles deposited at the Senate hundreds of women carrying a mammoth national petition for a constitutional amendment solicited by NAWSA.[34] Women filled the Senate to hear their representatives present suffrage petitions from their districts. The women clapped and laughed during the proceedings, sparking a confrontation that indicated male discomfort when a bold group of women challenged their authority: When the women ignored his gavel for order, Senator Kean of New Jersey warned them that Senate rules prohibited any displays of emotion. But after Senator Robert LaFollette of Wisconsin delivered a particularly potent appeal, the women laughed again, and Senator Kean slammed down his gavel, threatening to clear the galleries. Silence ensued. "Dare to Laugh in Senate," said the *New York Times* subhead.[35]

The spirit of confrontation escalated following the creation in 1913 of the scrappy Congressional Union for Woman Suffrage (CU) headed by Alice Paul. A hint of the flamboyant CU protests to come occurred when the CU's Mabel Vernon sneaked a big yellow suffrage banner into the Senate gallery during Wilson's address to Congress in 1916. Vernon unfurled the banner, pages grabbed it, and police escorted her out.[36] In a more serious vein, the CU sent numerous delegations to President Woodrow Wilson beginning in 1913. The presence of women assembled in the White House to make political demands signified a new daring and seriousness in the movement. Dozens of CU deputations to Wilson over four years represented a broad cross-section of American women that included delegations of working women, college women, CU members, New Jersey women (Wilson's home state), and women from all of the states.[37] In June of 1914, for instance, five hundred members of the General Federation of Women's Clubs marched to the White House, where spokeswoman Rheta Childe Dorr futilely pressed Wilson to support the federal suffrage amendment.[38]

These deputations were treated as rude and bothersome by both the president and the press.[39] "The President of the United States is not to be bothered or made a defendant," the *New York Times* wrote of Dorr's defiant tone.[40] "From [the headlines] it might have been supposed that an Army of Amazons was going to brandish a hatchet over his head," the *Woman's Journal* reported of newspaper coverage about a 1913 deputation.[41] The press seemed annoyed simply by the women's belief that they were entitled to a hearing from the president. Even when a group of Pennsylvania women waited in vain for days to see Wilson in 1915, the press blasted them for "heckling" him.[42] Such rebuffs began edging Alice Paul closer to more confrontational tactics, which culminated in the picketing of the White House in 1917.

Yet highly visible assemblies of women worked some effect upon Washington. One sign of the growing influence of NAWSA was an unprecedented appearance by three members of the Cabinet at a prosuffrage reception hosted by Senator LaFollette in 1913.[43] And in 1915, Wilson and his daughter hosted a White House reception for suffragists during the 1915 NAWSA convention. "You ladies have a pretty strong clasp," he said upon shaking hands with Anna Howard Shaw. "Yes," she replied. "We hang on."[44] Wilson went to Atlantic City the following September to address the NAWSA convention.[45] A visit from the president of the United States to a female convention signaled a significant shift in suffrage sentiment. Wilson's appearance also underscored the centrality of conventions to the suffrage movement.

Conventions

Suffrage conventions formed the heart of the movement and epitomized the power of association. Suffrage conventions helped women discover a shared ideology and work toward social change to reflect that ideology. Conventions imbued the suffrage movement with a group identity that affected both participants and observers and created the "spark of life" deemed the key ingredient by sociologist Jo Freeman in the making of a social movement.[46]

The first spark was ignited in 1848 at the Woman's Rights Convention at Seneca Falls, where the radical Declaration of Sentiments contained the first formal call for woman suffrage. National woman's rights conventions held annually from 1850 to 1861 (except 1857) continued in that radical vein. Delegates cheered Lucy Stone when she exhorted members of the 1851 convention, "Instead of asking, 'Give us this, or give us that,' let us just get up and take it." The next year she urged convention delegates to refuse to pay taxes: "One such resistance, by the agitation that would grow out of it, will do more to settle this question of rights, than all the Conventions in the world." Woman's rights conventions helped legitimize the movement and the demand for the vote, because suffrage resolutions became routine calls at these gatherings that were dutifully (if derisively) reported by the press. Conventions thus provided an important forum for articulating suffrage demands. When conventions resumed after the Civil War in 1866, the annual suffrage resolution for the first time demanded a federal constitutional amendment granting women the vote because "it is the crowning right of citizenship; it is dignity, protection and power; it is civil and political life."[47]

Conventions fulfilled several key functions for suffragists that demonstrated the instrumentality of the right to associate. They were the forum at which suffragists could gain confidence and skills as they hammered out policy, devised strategies, approved resolutions, gained publicity, raised funds, and elected officers. Less tangible but vital services included exposing members to new ideas, reaffirming old ideals, and lending the movement a sense of sorority, history, continuity, and progress. One attendee of NAWSA's 1916 convention remarked upon how the gatherings linked women: "The union of generations is shown by second, third, sometimes fourth generations of women seeing each other with new sight and new friendship because they are all working together for what they believe to be good and beautiful and to be greatly desired."[48]

Suffragists blossomed as they became more practiced in the art of the large public meeting. Conventioneers in the 1910s exuded a confidence in the public sphere practically unheard of in the previous century as a result of women's immense strides into traditional male turf, which included universities, factories, offices, and the professions as well as the streets.[49] Suffrage conventions contributed to and benefited from the trend of women moving into the public sphere. The *Woman's Journal* praised the "psychological impression" as "victors and conquerors" that suffragists made when groups of conventioneers wearing yellow badges bustled along Manhattan streets during the 1911 NAWSA convention.[50] The newspaper's choice of language indicated how suffragists were shedding their passivity.

By the mid-1910s, women began to feel absolutely cocky about their potential. One self-congratulatory NAWSA delegate said of the Atlantic City convention in 1916: "The great assembly represented the best of American womanhood: women of ability, women of education, women of achievement were gathered together in a spirit of consecration and determination." The contrast between that spirited gathering in 1916 and NAWSA conventions just a decade earlier prompted one veteran to exclaim, "How times have changed!"[51] Signs that more change lay ahead arose the next year, when the first female member of Congress, suffragist Jeannette Rankin of Montana, addressed the convention.

Conventions nurtured the political skills responsible for that progress. "Not Used to Voting?" is how a newspaper headlined a report that confusion clouded the election of NAWSA officers in Minneapolis at the turn of the century.[52] But by 1916, NAWSA women wielded considerable prowess in parliamentary procedure, staging a three-cornered debate after which they approved a major policy shift to focus on a federal amendment.[53] The press in the 1910s praised both the efficiency and idealism of women's conventions. "Their meeting was positively the most intelligent gathering in Chicago," the *New Republic* wrote after the formation of the Woman's Party of Western Voters in 1916.[54] The *New York Post* said NAWSA managed its Atlantic City convention in 1916 twice as well as the major political parties and pointed to how suffrage conventions in themselves molded good citizens: "[Suffrage conventioneers] have gained poise, a knowledge of public speaking, experience in Parliamentary procedure, and training in executive management, besides demonstrating their ability to debate clearly, logically and right to the point."[55]

Such analyses were in stark contrast to the sexist stereotypes that had dominated press reports a decade earlier. A press notice of the 1905 convention noted of the week-long proceedings, "It must be borne in mind that it is a woman's affair, and there will be much talking."[56] Women complained to editors in 1906 that what the press termed an "argument" by men became a "plain fuss" when indulged in by women.[57] By the 1910s, more women journalists were covering suffrage and the tone of coverage changed. "In questions of dull procedure they are petty," said an article in *McClure's Magazine* coauthored by a suffragist. "In manners of humanity they are enormously big."[58] Suffragists were dependent upon such magazines and newspapers to cast their movement in a positive light.

Newspapers played a key role in disseminating suffrage convention news, and they began to accord more respect to suffrage conventions as the century progressed. The *Woman's Journal* noted that the press gave the 1908 convention in Buffalo "full and unusually respectful reports."[59] By 1918, newspapers in forty-four states had covered the annual NAWSA convention. The *Woman Citizen* estimated coverage added up to more than half a million words.[60] Speeches and resolutions made news, and convention planners scheduled special events to get even more publicity.[61] Suffragists recognized that publicity was their lifeline.

Suffragists became adept at orchestrating their gatherings to coincide with the major political party conventions or other events where press and public would already be on hand. The gavel for the first Woman Voters Convention sponsored by the Congressional Union, for instance, sounded with the opening of the Panama Pacific Exposition in San Francisco in 1915. "It is doubtful if any assembly of women called together in this country ever reached such a high intellectual level in its personnel," the *Washington Post* editorialized. "[It] marks an epoch in the history of the country of more than passing importance."[62]

Suffragists became more attentive to the press and sophisticated about currying its favor. As early as 1906 NAWSA conventions urged local suffrage clubs to work more closely with the mainstream press, and a 1913 session discussed the importance of publicity.[63] A 1917 convention resolution even thanked the press.[64] Both NAWSA and the National Woman's Party, founded in 1917, operated large press departments that were leaders in the emerging field of public relations. By 1919, NAWSA's National Woman Suffrage Publishing Company had produced fifty million pieces of literature in the five years of its existence.[65]

Suffrage organizations also kept members apprised of convention proceedings through their own newspapers. Innumerable accounts in the *Woman's Journal* found conventions conducted weekly in every corner of the nation, and they appeared to be the main, if not sole, undertaking of many organizations.[66] The suffrage newspapers themselves promoted associational ties by keeping suffragists informed of each other's activities and heartening readers that women elsewhere shared the same values.

Resolutions proved to be an easily digestible item for the press, and passing resolutions proved the most tangible way conventioneers could deliver their message to the public. The scope of convention resolutions over the years showed that the suffragists' agenda extended beyond merely obtaining the vote. In 1913, NAWSA's resolutions included a call for world peace, denunciation of white slavery, excoriation of child labor, and commendation of political economics studies by the General Federation of Women's Clubs.[67] But suffrage resolutions predominated. In 1915, the Congressional Union staged simultaneous conventions in 212 congressional districts that churned out hundreds of resolutions backing the federal amendment that the women then delivered to their representatives.[68]

Besides passing resolutions, conventions expended much energy upon conducting most of the particular organizations' business. Mundane chores such as the election of officers or revising the group's constitution took up some time.[69] More important, members debated policies that often were decided far from them but that carried serious consequences for local work. At the NWP's 1917 convention, for instance, a discussion on the controversial White House picketing concluded that it had achieved its intended effect of drawing attention to the federal amendment.[70]

Fund raising was another crucial piece of convention business. Associations raised most of their annual budget by pledges made at conventions. In 1913, NAWSA started its own invaluable publishing company by selling more than eleven thousand dollars in shares at ten dollars apiece in less than four minutes during its New York convention.[71] The NWP collected fifty-one thousand dollars at its inaugural convention.[72] Convention fervor so inspired at least one teacher at NAWSA's 1914 convention in Nashville that she wrote a novel in her spare time, published it at her own expense, traveled and sold it while giving speeches in the South, and gave the proceeds to NAWSA.[73] State groups also raised considerable sums at conventions, such as the $8,693 that the New York State Suffrage Association collected in 1913.[74] Because all of its members were under one roof and usually flushed with the success of the movement's progress, real or imaginary, conventions proved invaluable for organizations to solicit funds to carry out their suffrage work during the remainder of the year.

The most important business NAWSA leaders ever conducted occurred after Carrie Chapman Catt unveiled her secret "winning plan" in 1916 at a preconvention meeting of state association leaders. The plan was pivotal because it called for dropping the states' rights approach to the amendment.[75] After agreeing to switch to campaigning for a federal amendment, NAWSA delegates immediately pledged $818,000 toward its $1-million goal for the new campaign.[76] Conventioneers who approved the plan cheered Catt's most famous speech, "The Crisis," which ended on a militant note: "WILL to be free. Demand the vote. WOMEN ARISE!"[77]

Conventions helped instill this sense of female destiny by making space on every program for celebrations of suffrage history. Celebrating a common history created a group identity. "The Spirit of 1848" was the topic of a convention speech in Buffalo in 1908, and eighty-two-year-old Eugenia Farmer read a paper titled "A Voice from the Civil War" at Minnesota's 1917 convention.[78] New Hampshire's state convention in 1913 feted the sole survivor of its first meeting of sixty women forty-five years earlier, and the oldest speaker at a 1913 "Octogenarian Suffrage Meeting" in Oregon was ninety-seven years old.[79] NAWSA, in fact, moved its conventions from winter to early fall beginning in 1908 so that older members could avoid travel in winter (another reason was so that conventions would not interfere with spring housecleaning).[80] The presence of these suffrage relics seemed not to remind the women of the apparent futility of their cause. Fittingly, a lunch honoring the pioneers at NAWSA's 1920 victory convention in Chicago enabled them to finally celebrate the fruits of their lives' work.[81] Both NAWSA and the NWP scheduled their 1920 conventions celebrating passage of the suffrage amendment in 1919 on the centennial of Anthony's birth on 15 February 1820, suffragists' favorite holiday.[82] Annual Anthony birthday celebrations ranged from teas to a special Susan B. Anthony Day on the White House suffrage picket line featuring banners that quoted her. Suffragists' reverence for their history satisfied more than nostalgia; it placed their current actions in the context of making history. Possessing a history helped them envision the possibility of a future. Conventions helped them work toward that future by offering a forum for new ideas and techniques.

Conventions sowed, spread, and tested new ideas and campaign techniques. Newly enfranchised women voters from Idaho in 1897 told NAWSA conventioneers how to organize in precincts to conduct door-to-door canvasses to educate voters, a technique to which many later attributed the success of the 1917 suffrage referendum in New York state.[83] Kentuckian Laura Clay introduced her highly successful idea of recruiting through parlor meetings at the 1904 convention.[84] The 1908 NAWSA convention vetoed conducting a controversial open-air, or soapbox, meeting, but 1910 conventioneers hit the Washington, D.C., streets after a how-to workshop on soapbox speaking.[85]

A look at the 1911 NAWSA convention program shows the explosion of new campaign ideas. Susan FitzGerald illustrated the new open-air propaganda techniques with one of the latest advances in technology, a lantern slide show.[86] "Three of the most renowned women in the world"—NAWSA president Anna Howard Shaw, Hull House founder Jane Addams, and Emmeline Pankhurst, leader of Britain's militant suffragettes—shared a dais.[87] Talks in 1911 included "The Working Woman's Interest in the Ballot," "What Woman Suffrage Means to College Women," and "The Effect of Suffrage Work Upon Women Themselves."[88]

NAWSA's rank and file heard a variety of important speakers. Subjects included a 1912 address on the evils of white slavery and a critique of child labor in cotton mills in 1914.[89] Russian-born Socialist Rose Winslow spoke in 1913 along with laundry worker Margaret Hinchey, whose working-class experience was far removed from that of NAWSA's mostly middle-class membership. "They bring vital, vivid arguments that carry weight and conviction," the *Journal* reported.[90] Elizabeth Robbins, president of the Women's Trade Union League (WTUL), in 1916 was among four experts in the social sciences who argued suffrage would help mothers, child laborers, working women, and public morality.[91] A 1917 panel featured French and British women discussing their war work, and a debate by Americans that same year asked, "Should We Work for Woman Suffrage in Wartime?"[92] Booths stacked with pamphlets and books provided much more information on suffrage campaigning.[93]

Ideas were disseminated not only at NAWSA's annual meeting but also at hundreds of smaller conventions organized by the many state and city suffrage leagues. Attendees of Pennsylvania suffragists' forty-fifth annual gathering in 1913 came away full of new ideas, such as raising money by setting up suffrage stores or selling suffrage stamps. They even inspected a model of a county fair suffrage booth.[94] Conventions were the "most spectacular function" of Tennessee's suffrage association, according to historian A. Elizabeth Taylor. "New converts were won at conventions, and confirmed suffragists returned home with renewed enthusiasm."[95]

Exposure to new speakers and ideas expanded suffragists' horizons while validating their own work and beliefs. The exposure showed women the progress being made in other parts of the nation and helped them develop campaigns in their communities. The dissemination of ideas and beliefs accelerated after Kentucky suffrage leader Laura Clay in 1895 persuaded NAWSA to convene outside of Washington. NAWSA met in seventeen other cities, from Portland, Oregon, to Atlanta, Georgia.[96]

Perhaps the most critical feature of conventions was the sorority they provided suffragists. Meeting in large numbers fortified women who often fought lonely battles in small towns, where they were isolated and perhaps considered eccentric. Dinners and receptions always followed floor business. Songs and skits held a place on every program. In 1911, Inez Milholland enacted a sketch called "If Women Voted," and two other women delivered suffrage monologues.[97] Inez's sister Vida Milholland sang a "Women's Marseillaise" at the NWP's inaugural meeting in Chicago in 1917.[98] The

"Susan B. Anthony" pageant debuted during the CU's convention in Washington in 1915.[99] Special events such as Men's Night and College Night lent the proceedings thematic unity.[100]

One of the most sentimental convention tributes occurred when Catt succeeded Shaw as NAWSA president in December 1915. Each of the more than five hundred delegates passed by and threw a rose on the platform where Shaw sat before presenting her with a gift of thirty thousand dollars and a wreath of gold leaves. "Men say we are too emotional to vote," said Shaw, visibly moved, "but I am very sure that when we compare our emotions in political conventions with the kind they show in theirs, I prefer ours."[101]

Despite this sense of sorority, NAWSA conventions were no sea of tranquillity. Another important convention function was debating policy and strategy, and it sometimes seemed as many suffrage factions existed as there were suffragists. Suffrage conventions often were fractious gatherings that mirrored the many ideological and regional factions within the movement. "The Convention was chaotic from the start," wrote Maud Wood Park in 1912, complaining about several disputes over policy and personnel at the Philadelphia gathering.[102] The perennially upbeat *Woman's Journal* saw a silver lining in discord: "Even the marked differences of opinion in the Convention were encouraging," it stated in 1913, "as they showed that the delegates thought for themselves and had convictions of their own."[103]

Discord also had a dark side. Conventions became the battlefield for key decisions regarding racial issues. As suffrage historian Aileen Kraditor observed, white suffragists equated the capacity to exercise political liberty with Anglo-Saxon ancestry.[104] White suffragists' relations with black suffragists were fraught with contradictions and the racism that pervaded the era. The ostracism African American women experienced was one manifestation of the role privilege played in the suffrage movement. The mostly white, middle-class suffrage movement often did not work for equality for all women. A look at the record shows twentieth-century movement leaders invariably placed race loyalty above gender solidarity.[105] "Even the more radical suffragists appealed to racist attitudes to win support for woman suffrage," said historian Kay Sloan.[106] Northern white suffragists found it easier to practice racial tolerance in the abstract.[107] Susan B. Anthony, for instance, declined in the name of "expediency" to help African American women form a local branch of NAWSA in Atlanta.[108] Historian Paula Giddings has characterized white suffragists' attitude toward their African American counterparts as one of "patronizing arrogance."[109]

Black women generally were excluded from the decision-making body of NAWSA and were not recognized as a group to be included in general deliberations.[110] Adella Hunt Logan, a former assistant principal of the Tuskegee Institute and lifelong member of NAWSA, for instance, was not allowed to attend suffrage conventions in the South.[111] Suffrage newspapers advised southern readers on how white supremacy could be maintained despite woman suffrage.[112] To appease the South and its powerful politicians, NAWSA officially embarked upon a policy of racial discrimination at the 1903 NAWSA convention, when members implicitly endorsed white supremacy by passing a resolution endorsing a states' rights approach.[113] In addition to sanctioning racism, the states' rights policy derailed the movement by axing the more expeditious campaign for a federal constitutional amendment. Even long after ditching the states' rights approach, NAWSA president Carrie Chapman Catt in 1919 asked Mary Church Terrell, president of the National Association of Colored Women, to encourage the black National Association of the Northeastern Federation of Women's Clubs to withdraw its application for admission to NAWSA because she feared the pending federal amendment would lose southern support if NAWSA accepted the black clubs. "White women simply were willing to let black women go down the proverbial drain to get the vote for themselves," observed Giddings.[114]

Ironically, NAWSA welcomed prominent African American speakers even as it rejected African American members. Terrell addressed several NAWSA conventions beginning in 1898 and delivered a tribute to Frederick Douglass at the sixtieth anniversary of the Seneca Falls convention in 1908.[115] Crisis editor W. E. B. Du Bois also addressed NAWSA conventions several times.[116] More typical was the condescending snub Anthony handed Hunt Logan when the Atlanta University graduate asked to address the 1897 NAWSA convention. Anthony replied that an appearance by an "inferior speaker" would hurt both Logan's race and the suffrage movement.[117]

Despite such rebuffs from white groups, African Americans worked for woman suffrage because they saw the vote as integral to racial uplift.[118] Perhaps because their heritage of slavery and segregation made them especially sensitive to the need for political power, southern women led the black suffrage movement. The most influential black suffrage leaders—

Terrell, Hunt Logan, Mary Ann Shadd Carey, Ida Wells-Barnett, and Frances Harper—all were natives of the South. Long before most of their white southern peers worked for the vote, southern black women worked for suffrage in nineteenth-century organizations such as the Phillis Wheatley Club of New Orleans. As late at 1908, the *Woman's Journal*'s only subscribers in Alabama were African American women or organizations.[119]

Many of the myriad African American women's organizations in every corner of the nation supported suffrage—temperance unions, church organizations, fraternal societies, and women's clubs.[120] Many African American suffragists found sorority in the largest and most influential African American women's club, the forty-thousand-member NACW, which included a large suffrage department.[121] Shadd Carey had organized the first African American organization devoted solely to woman suffrage, the Colored Woman's Progressive Franchise Association in Washington, D.C., in 1880. In the twentieth century, African American journalist Ida Wells-Barnett formed the Alpha Suffrage Club in Chicago in 1913, and at least twenty black women suffrage organizations or groups existed by the mid-1910s.[122]

Other Suffrage Assemblies

Conventions, delegations, and mass meetings were integral to giving shape and form to the suffrage movement. They all, however, mirrored traditionally male forms of political assembly. As the movement began to coalesce, a wide range of innovative suffrage assemblies surfaced in new shapes. What set them apart from the initial suffrage assemblies was that they usually bore a distinctively feminine touch, indicating a burgeoning sense of self and confidence in their sponsors. A "banner meeting" of the New York Woman Suffrage Party to celebrate its new headquarters included singing, recitations, and a social half-hour.[123] New York suffragists sponsored a "Hopping for Suffrage" contest.[124] The Women's Political Union sponsored a "Votes for Women" ball at which women from the United Garment Workers Union mingled with society matrons.[125] Suffrage swimming races and potato sack races enlivened an open-air campaign across Long Island.[126] Determined to win recruits, suffragists in the 1910s went all out to imbue their assemblies with conviviality. Some suffragists touted their social political style as evidence of women's political superiority. "We began to dance about our cause at great balls," said suffrage leader Harriot Stanton Blatch of the New York campaign. "Men's idea was different. They could not ask for the vote for village constables without getting into a brawl over it. Their democracy grew by riots, revolutions, wars. Women conquered in peace and quiet, with some fun."[127]

Suffrage assemblies also attempted to meet the special needs of women. A baby rest tent at a Tennessee chatauqua provided free baby care. "In this way the first impression of our cause received by many a tired mother was that it meant to help her," noted one of the organizers. Suffrage baby shows in upstate New York attracted mothers to talks about children's health care. In Nashville, suffragists operated a sewing room in winter for unemployed women.[128] These assemblies seemed more earnest than simply an attempt by suffragists to prove citizenship and domesticity were not mutually exclusive. Even as critics heaped criticism upon suffragists for their "unwomanliness," suffragists celebrated feminine skills.

The work of the New York Woman Suffrage Party in the 1910s demonstrated the breadth of assemblies sponsored by suffrage organizations. The "What is Going On" column in the *Woman Voter* newsletter listed twenty-three suffrage activities in the boroughs in a month. The East Side Equal Rights League, for instance, offered programs for its numerous immigrant residents every day of the week: on Tuesday, a social gathering; Wednesday, a suffrage history lecture; Thursday, physical culture and dancing; Friday, a class for young women; Saturday, a discussion of current events; and Sunday, a concert and dance.[129] The hallmarks of suffrage gatherings were their creativity and sensitivity to the need or desire to imbue them with a sense of community.

Suffragists frequently found community in the traditionally feminine venue of preparing and sharing food. Sharing meals gave women emotional sustenance. While canvassing for petition signatures in 1913, Syracuse women eased that lonely, frustrating task with a picnic supper at a solicitor's home at the start of their evening, returning at nine o'clock to compare notes.[130] Tennessee suffragists added a regional flair by sponsoring suffrage barbecues.[131] A suffrage banquet proved the highlight of the anniversary celebration of the Woman's Era Club, an African American woman's club in Boston.[132] The Massachusetts Woman Suffrage Association suffrage store lured visitors with colorful window displays; once inside, they found petition forms and literature alongside the tea and cakes, and speakers discussed suffrage daily at noon.[133] Later, the "Sunflower Lunch" room of the

Boston Equal Suffrage Association for Good Government served up suffrage sorority along with sandwiches, as did the "Grated Door" at the NWP's headquarters in Washington, D.C.[134]

Teatime proved a congenial assembly for marshaling ideas or recruiting members, partly because the parlor was a safe, familiar gathering place for women just beginning to consider joining the movement. At age 104, suffragist Sylvie Thegson reminisced about conducting parlor meetings: "You had these little afternoon gatherings of women, maybe six or eight women. You had a cup of tea. A little social gathering. While we were drinking tea, I gave a little talk and they asked questions about what was going on. . . . It was a lot better, I thought at the time, than to have a lecture. Because a lot of them wouldn't go to a lecture."[135]

The militant NWP probably sponsored more teas than pickets as well as a Christmas card party, dance, and ball.[136] New York City suffragists and the female reporters who covered them became close after gathering daily for years to trade news over tea at suffrage headquarters.[137] No matter what form they took, suffrage assemblies always included opportunity for restorative sorority.

Suffrage Novelties

One way women showed their association with suffrage even when alone was to buy, display, or wear the many novelties spawned by the movement. Pins, sashes, and other regalia served as icons that expressed more powerfully than words a woman's support for suffrage. "Wearing the Suffrage badge implies courage and enthusiasm when the cause is unpopular," wrote Alice Park of California, who collected 178 pins. "It is one of the easy ways to advertise votes for women among strangers."[138] Souvenir seekers could find many more whimsical items that announced their support for votes for women at suffrage stores that opened their doors in cities. Novelties included suffrage soap, crackers, pin cushions, umbrellas, notepaper, gold-edged china stamped with "Votes for Women," jugs, and a doll wearing a suffrage-yellow sash and hat.[139] The *Woman Suffrage Cook-Book* featured seven hundred recipes; the College Suffrage Calendar contained a suffrage quote for every day of the year; a Chicago club's postcard displayed a girl clad in yellow; a suffrage jigsaw puzzle targeted children, and the Women's Political Union's purple, green, and white playing cards cost twenty-five cents. "A good suffragist will hardly play bridge without her own cards," said the *New York Times*.[140] NAWSA sold music sheets for the many suffrage songs that also united women, such as "For Women," sung to the tune of "Dixie," and the "Suffrage Song" to the tune of "America."[141] A Pennsylvania woman showed her colors by planting a suffrage garden filled, of course, with yellow flowers.[142]

The feminine cast of many suffrage articles and activities masked the revolutionary nature of the social movement that spawned them. The suffrage movement threatened many men and women who feared women's entrance into politics would upend the social order. Suffrage baby tents and suffrage cookbooks could help divert opposition by their link to mothering and the home, but less domestically endowed assemblies provoked outright antagonism.

The Woman's Party

Shock waves reverberated through the male political establishment when the Woman's Party of Western Voters organized in 1916. The Woman's Party convention marked the first time women organized their own political party, one of the most powerful forms of the right of association. By 1916, women were voting in thirteen states. Almost immediately, Republican and Progressive men also convening in Chicago came to curry the women's political favor, a "refreshing sight" in the view of the *New Republic*.[143]

Yet the specter of women forming their own political party sent chills up many men's spines. The *New York Times* castigated "the influence of sex for political blackmail." It feared the Woman's Party would rip apart the social fabric of the nation. "The Woman's Party has lighted a firebrand," an editorial warned.[144] Indeed, the WP immediately began campaigning against all Democratic candidates in the Western states where women voted to protest the Democratic administration's failure to act on suffrage. Although relatively unsuccessful, the campaign enraged politicians as well as many suffragists, principally the leaders of NAWSA, who believed it counterproductive.[145]

Male fear of assemblies of independent women spiraled to near-hysterical heights when a prominent suffragist called upon New York City women to strike for one day in 1915 to show how essential women had become in the public sphere. Her theory was the city would grind to a halt if women abandoned their jobs in offices and factories or as teachers, nurses, servants, telephone operators, sales clerks, and settlement workers.[146] Although representatives of the Woman's Trade Union League, social clubs, suffrage organizations, and settlement houses met to discuss the plan, it was abandoned because it drew so much ire. "A promise by everybody never to say again that woman's place is home would be a small price to pay for the escape from the effects of such a strike," the *Times* wrote.[147] The overreaction to the suggested strike revealed fear that chaos would occur if women rebelled against their assigned supportive roles in American society. It also acknowledged the potential power of women in association.

It is inconceivable that the woman's suffrage movement could have coalesced into any kind of political or social force without the right of association, the basic building block of a social or political movement. Until at least two people join forces to promote an idea, any effort to convert others to that idea or to effect change is no more than agitation by an individual. The more individuals who associate for a cause, the more significant the social movement, until it achieves critical mass. The associational ties that develop among followers as a movement grows increase individuals' devotion to a cause and their sense of possibilities for it. Associating with other women who shared their belief that they should vote reinforced suffragists' sense that they had been wronged by federal and state governments and that they had a right to demand a role in their government.

Suffrage associations in clubs, mass meetings, delegations, and conventions bore some fruit in the nineteenth century. A joint resolution for a federal suffrage amendment was introduced in Congress in 1878 and voted upon in 1887 in the Senate, where it fizzled, sixteen to thirty-four. By 1896, however, women were voting in Colorado, Idaho, Utah, and Wyoming.[148]

Then suffrage hit a wall. The problem was that conventions preached only to the converted, so that contrary to their rebellious roots, conventions by the turn of the century had become staid, insular affairs populated by white-haired women and neglected by the press. Radcliffe College student Maud Wood Park was appalled when she discovered that the 1900 NAWSA convention consisted of roughly one hundred older women meeting in the basement of a church. The first speaker presented a state report in rhyme.[149]

Procedural minutiae dominated convention agendas. Prayers, welcoming speeches, and the reading of letters, for instance, filled most of the first night of the 1906 NAWSA convention in Baltimore, Maryland. The greeting from the state association president set the tone: "Conservative—what a sweet-sounding word—what an ark for the timid soul!"[150] Reports from the states, a round of pleasant club receptions, and a "lively discussion" on whether to use the NAWSA label on its stationery nearly completed the program.[151] The insular atmosphere of conventions ensured that they made a rather limited impact upon politicians and the public. Before conventions could resume their role as dynamic fulcrums for suffrage activism, suffragists had to discover the power of taking their message to the streets.

Near the end of the first decade of the new century, a new breed of suffragist emerged willing to take the movement from the safety of convention halls to the unpredictable streets. It was time to test a new facet of the right of assembly, a facet that planted suffragists in the rollicking public sphere.

⚸ TWO ⚸

THE OPEN-AIR CAMPAIGNS
Suffragists Take Their Message
to the Streets

Open-air meetings played a pivotal role in pushing suffrage into the public consciousness. Countless street meetings conducted by soapbox speakers across the nation beginning in 1908 educated hundreds of thousands of Americans about suffrage. Once people recovered from the shock of seeing women speaking on the streets, they usually listened. The suffragists' open-air campaign exemplified classic arguments on the paramount importance of the right of assembly: Street meetings were cheap, easily arranged, attracted publicity, and forced the issue upon indifferent audiences.

"No rent, no paid speakers . . . no notices to be sent to members," said a Philadelphia open-air speaker. "Also, the audiences we reached on the street were largely persons who would not have taken the time to go to an indoor suffrage meeting, but who would listen to our appeal when presented without any inconvenience to them."[1] The open-air meetings demonstrated what one constitutional scholar described as the "considerable value in the mental nudges which the more conservative groups of our society receive from the unpopular and unorthodox views" that are often confined to street-corner advocacy.[2]

More than any other factor, open-air campaigns fertilized public opinion so that Americans finally began to seriously consider the merits of woman suffrage. A generation after the Nineteenth Amendment was first introduced in Congress in 1878, the suffrage movement was static; open-air meetings revived the movement beginning in 1908.[3] All future tactics of all suffrage factions grew out of the experience and confidence women gained during the open-air campaigns, and acceptance of the movement stemmed from the education and good will speakers dispensed from the soapbox. Open-air campaigns not only pushed suffrage into the public conscious-ness but also helped force authorities to recognize their duty to safeguard the right of assembly.

Two kinds of restrictions affected suffragists' exercise of the right of as-sembly. One set of objections was legal, and the other was cultural. Legal barriers faced by suffrage speakers consisted of restrictions placed upon public meetings under the prevailing legal rationale that rated public order as more valuable than the airing of minority opinions. Suffrage soapboxers launched their street meetings in the middle of a heated debate among legal scholars on the meaning of free speech. That debate helped expand protections for freedom of expression for minority viewpoints. Suffrage soapboxers contributed to the debate by asserting their right to speak in the streets at a time when protections were inconsistent and narrower than today.

Cultural barriers involved restrictions upon women's behavior in the public sphere and rigidly held beliefs about what constituted feminine ac-tivities. Any discussion about women's exercise of the right of assembly must be placed in the context of broader extralegal factors that erected internal and external restrictions upon women's ability to assemble together in public. The move into the streets by privileged women, who comprised the bulk of suffrage soapboxers, is a vital link in the story of how women emerged from the private domestic sphere into the public sphere. Ameri-cans could possibly overlook the expanding presence of women in facto-ries, universities, and the professions, but they could not avoid the signifi-cance of ladies in the street.

Origins of the Open-Air Campaigns

One or two American suffrage pioneers spontaneously addressed crowds outdoors during western suffrage campaigns of the nineteenth century. At least one historian placed Susan B. Anthony on a soapbox when she toured Colorado in the 1870s, and her biographer described Anthony speaking at railroad stations and mining camps, which may have involved speaking in the streets. When no public hall was available to suffrage lecturer Carrie Chapman Catt in a small South Dakota town in 1893, she reportedly spoke in the street in front of the post office.[4] Aside from these isolated incidents, nineteenth-century suffragists restricted their suffrage talks to speeches in halls and at parlor meetings.

Twentieth-century American soapboxers got their inspiration from British suffragists. Both the English militants in the Women's Social and Political Union (WSPU) and the more conservative constitutionalists in the National Union of Women's Suffrage Societies (NUWSS) influenced the American suffrage movement during its decade of vigorous and innovative protests from 1908 to 1919.[5] American suffragists adopted virtually every one of their campaign techniques from English methods, including not only soapbox speaking but also parades, torchlight processions, pageants, petition pilgrimages, banners, and picketing; the one British method Americans did not import was the violence of the WSPU "suffragettes," who eventually turned to smashing windows, burning buildings, and destroying other property.[6]

The British militant campaign began when aristocrat Emmeline Pankhurst led the first WSPU protest on 12 May 1905.[7] That October, her daughter Christabel and a comrade interrupted a speech by future prime minister Sir Edward Grey, shouting, "Will You Give Votes for Women?"[8] After police dragged the pair outside of the hall, they convened an "indignation meeting" before they were arrested, convicted, and sentenced to three days in jail, becoming the first of more than a thousand British women to be imprisoned before they won limited female suffrage in 1918.[9] "We threw away all our conventional methods of what was 'ladylike' and 'goodform,'" Emmeline Pankhurst wrote, "and we applied to our methods the one test question, will it help?"[10]

The core of the Britons' campaign was the open-air meeting. London's first open-air meeting attracted seven thousand listeners in Trafalgar Square on 19 May 1906.[11] In Hyde Park, up to a dozen suffragettes at a time played cat and mouse with police, carting soapboxes onto which they stepped, unfurled the WSPU's banner, and spoke until an officer arrived, his chase subverted by sympathetic crowds into which the "Votes for Women" speakers vanished like fish in the sea.[12]

The most striking spectacle of the suffragettes' colorful open-air campaign was "Women's Sunday" on 21 June 1908, when half a million people surged into Hyde Park for a "monster" mass meeting at which eighty women spoke from twenty wagons. Seven processions totaling thirty thousand marchers converged in the park as bands played and the WSPU's purple, white, and green "Votes for Women" banners flapped overhead. A week later the House of Commons refused another suffrage delegation; that night, frustrated that their awesome demonstrations left Parliament unmoved, one hundred thousand persons massed at Parliament Square, and two WSPU members hurled rocks through windows.[13]

Over the next six years, suffragettes smashed many more windows, chained themselves to Parliament gates, disfigured museum paintings and sculptures, and eventually burned empty buildings.[14] Because the British Highway Act of 1835 made it illegal to use the highways for purposes other than travel, anyone attending a street meeting could be convicted of obstructing the streets.[15] Convicted suffragettes were arrested and sentenced to Holloway Jail, which became infamous for force-feeding hunger-striking suffragettes through gastric tubes. British women's resistance roused American suffragists. "Never before, except among a few enthusiasts, had there existed any feeling that suffrage was a thing to fight for, suffer for, even to die for," wrote Rheta Childe Dorr, an American journalist and suffragist.[16]

Rising suffragette militancy stirred considerable debate in American publications, and newspapers kept Americans well apprised of London developments.[17] All of the most visible suffragists had ties to the British suffragette movement. Harriot Stanton Blatch, instrumental in introducing open-air meetings and parades to the United States, married a British man and lived with him many years in England, where she befriended Emmeline Pankhurst.[18] Inez Milholland, the "most beautiful suffragist," who starred in American parades and pageants, sailed to London to study suffragette methods.[19]

Alice Paul, the "heart and brains" of American suffragists' most radical demonstrations, was a twenty-three-year-old doctoral student at the London School of Economics when she was first arrested after marching upon Parliament.[20] Later, she was imprisoned thirty days and force-fed after she and another woman sneaked into a banquet, rose up from a staircase, shouted "Votes for Women" and hurled a shoe through a stained-glass window.[21] The suffragettes' colorful and symbolic aesthetic sense would inform every aspect of the stirring demonstrations staged years later by Paul, a plainly dressed Quaker, as head of the militant National Woman's Party.

Carrie Chapman Catt, head of the larger and more conservative National American Woman Suffrage Association, watched suffrage soapboxers dodge police in Hyde Park, and her handbag was searched for bombs when she visited the gallery at the House of Commons. Like most Americans, Catt found the arson and window smashing appalling, but she admired the suffragettes' spirit.[22]

American suffragists also were influenced by the example of a handful of women labor organizers who had mounted soapboxes. In late 1905, Helen Marot and Leonora O'Reilly of the Women's Trade Union League launched daily street meetings at noon and closing time near factory gates in New York City.[23] Elizabeth Gurley Flynn, the labor movement's best-known female orator, was first arrested at age sixteen in 1906 for conducting a street meeting with her father.[24] Previously, street missionaries in the Salvation Army were the only women to conduct street meetings. Women labor leaders endorsed suffrage in the early 1900s, and Blatch, an admiring member of the WTUL for whom working women epitomized female independence, served as a link between the two groups. In 1907, Blatch formed the Equality League of Self-Supporting Women, a coalition of wealthy reformers and working women dedicated to suffrage.[25] The Vassar College alumna was instrumental in the proliferation of open-air meetings, parades, and other dramatic assembles to agitate for the vote. "We all believed that suffrage propaganda must be made dramatic," Blatch wrote.[26]

Blatch belonged to a new generation of suffragists frustrated with NAWSA, which in contrast to the animated Britons had reverted in the early 1900s to "near-paralysis" because of attrition, poor organization, and a vacuum in leadership.[27] "It bored its adherents and repelled its opponents," she wrote.[28] The number of suffrage states had remained frozen at four since 1896, and the federal suffrage amendment appeared moribund.[29] News of the British militants spurred a few American suffragists to consider daring new techniques such as street speaking. "There is a middle ground between marching into the Capitol at Washington and standing mute at our firesides," ventured *Progress* in January of 1907.[30]

American suffragists finally conducted the nation's first open-air meeting for suffrage on 31 December 1907.[31] Several hundred men gathered around a woman standing atop a small bench in Madison Square in New York City. "You have made woman believe that politics is something that she cannot understand," she said in a clipped British accent. "We can understand it quite easily, and we are determined to have a hand in the legislation. We are going to make a vigorous struggle, and this is our first effort."

Several mounted police officers and others on foot looked on but did not interfere. The speaker turned to oblige the photographers hanging out of a handful of delivery wagons that had pulled up. She asked the audience if women could make a worse mess of politics than men had. "No! No! No!" shouted the crowd.[32]

Twenty-one-year-old Maud Malone, co-organizer of the open-air meeting and one of four women who participated, had ignored the opposition to the meeting of her colleagues in the Harlem Equal Rights League, of which she was president.[33] Malone's boldness foreshadowed the more militant tactics she alone among American suffragists adopted later. Mainstream suffrage leaders including Catt, then a leader in the New York suffrage campaign, refused Malone's invitation to speak at the open-air meeting.[34] They were unwilling or unable to cross the cultural breach that found women soapboxers improper and undignified.

Newspapers labeled the soapboxers "suffragettes," in reference to the British militants. Bettina Borrmann Wells, the English woman who opened the Madison Square meeting, had organized the National Progressive Woman Suffrage League in New York in 1907; members called themselves suffragettes and shouted their message from soapboxes across the city. Borrmann Wells advocated militancy and had served time in Holloway Jail in London.[35] The Madison Square open-air meeting probably also was inspired by a 13 December speech at Cooper Union by convicted London suffragette Anna Cobden-Sanderson sponsored by the Equality League of Self-Supporting Women. Some men were so worried that Cobden-Sanderson would incite New York women that they debated denying her permission to speak, and Cooper Union was packed with men and women anticipating a ruckus. "Nothing happened," the *Times* lamented, and the imagined militant ogre turned out to be a "gentle little woman."[36]

Malone's legacy was the open-air campaigns she helped pioneer. That May, she helped Blatch popularize open-air speaking during a two-week trolley tour across upstate New York to commemorate the sixtieth anniversary of the Seneca Falls Woman's Rights Convention. It was the heyday of the trolley, the affectionate nickname for the electric street cars tethered to power lines above thirty thousand miles of tracks that revolutionized urban mass transit.[37] Blatch and Malone, among the close to ten billion passengers trolleys carried in 1908, launched a smaller revolution on their unprecedented journey.[38]

Blatch's bearing, wit, and humor held crowds and cowed authority. "There is no man orator alive who can hammer a thought home with more force than can Mrs. Harriot Stanton Blatch," a reporter once wrote.[39] Shrewdly, she and Malone always asked for a permit where the Salvation Army usually spoke, knowing the street missionaries picked the choicest locations. When the president of Vassar College refused student Inez Milholland's request that the women's school host the tour's concluding rally, Milholland moved the meeting to an adjoining cemetery. The trolley tour revolutionized American suffrage campaign techniques. "I am grateful for all it taught me about the open-air meeting, that ideal auditorium for those who are trying to push an unpopular cause, who have in their pack no drawing cards, and lack money to 'go hire a hall,'" Blatch wrote later.[40]

Over the next decade, suffrage soapboxers swarmed city street corners before radio or television could deliver a personal appeal to voters. "In those days every evening in every city the downtown street corners were all occupied by soapboxes," Boston suffragist Miriam Allen DeFord reminisced. "Literally sometimes, and sometimes we just called them that when they were little platforms with a flag."[41] DeFord and other suffragists vied with missionaries, Socialists, or politicians for choice street corners, speaking fifteen to twenty minutes about other aspects of woman's rights, such as controlling earnings or guardianship of children, fielding the occasional jeer before addressing suffrage, soliciting questions, and passing out petitions. DeFord recalled: "The audiences would be people going along the street. . . . They were just the same kind of people you'd find if you had an auto accident on the corner. . . . Some of them went from one to another speaker, just to spend an evening listening to conversations. . . . That was the day of the soapbox. Every evening when you went downtown, every corner was occupied."[42]

Suffrage soapboxers could be heard in any corner of New York by 1910. A free speakers' class sponsored by the National Progressive Woman Suffrage League groomed open-air recruits.[43] "It is no longer considered bad form to hold street meetings," stated the *New York Times* at the end of 1908. "On the contrary, it is considered bad form not to."[44] Suffragists toured the Erie Canal by boat from Albany to Buffalo, speaking at small towns along the way beneath large, fluttering yellow suffrage banners.[45] Four suffragists in 1913 galloped off on an upstate "Horseback Crusade," speaking to one thousand people in the Catskill Mountain village of Liberty; they were followed the next year by an oxen-driven prairie schooner tour as well as a traveling tent city.[46] Alva Belmont and Milholland conducted an open-air meeting aboard the *Lusitania*.[47] Cartoonist Lou Rogers abandoned her Times Square soapbox to set up her easel at state fairs, where she lectured while she sketched.[48] Soapboxers visited longshoremen on the docks and trolley conductors at the car barns, climbed rooftops, and sold "Votes for Women" buttons at a Fourth of July baseball game.[49] NAWSA convention-eers in Washington in 1913 conducted nightly open-air suffrage meetings at six locations for a week.[50] In New York City, women marched to legislators' homes in the middle of the night and serenaded them with suffrage songs.[51] At one point during the frenetic New York state referendum campaign of 1915, two hundred street meetings were conducted simultaneously across the state.[52]

Open-Air Meetings across the Country

Open-air campaigning techniques spread across the nation. In the West, soapboxers formed the vanguard of several spirited—and successful—state campaigns. In South Dakota and Nevada in 1914, lawyer Antoinette Funk rode stagecoaches across the desert and plains to speak several times daily inside mines, at butchers' homes, and before meetings that wound into supper and a dance. Funk spoke outside whenever possible. "I found that the small audiences which would assemble in [halls] were made up of women and men already interested and that the uninstructed voter would only listen when you caught him on the street," she said.[53]

Anne Martin and Mabel Vernon also traversed Nevada in 1914, often speaking in the street or in a church, because the saloon was many towns' only public meeting place.[54] "Men have not made [suffrage] the subject of mockery or jest at a single street meeting," wrote Vernon, one of NAWSA's ablest speakers. "Without a doubt the open-air meeting is to play an impor-tant part in the Nevada campaign."[55] Long distances between outposts of civilization made speaking tours grueling. Once Martin and Vernon trav-eled a hundred miles in one day to visit seventy voters. Campaign recruit Margaret Foley of Massachusetts wore out three pairs of shoes visiting eight mines, attending fifty dances, and making a thousand speeches.[56] "I'm hav-ing the time of my life," wrote Laura Gregg, who crisscrossed Arizona on horseback and by stagecoach to address remote settlements. "When I think of those long, winding mountain roads that have to be traveled in lumber wagons in the dark, I wonder at the audience I have," she wrote.[57] Audiences returned that respect, and personal admiration transformed into winning ballots on election day. After Vernon drew a crowd onto a dark street in a snowstorm in Elko, the local newspaper reported: "She has a silver-toned voice that carries a remarkable distance in the open air. There is now no doubt of her courage; and it is due to such women that victories are won."[58]

The automobile expanded the impact of open-air campaigning in the West and Midwest. Driving was yet another symbol of women's independence and her invasion of a male domain. Women at the wheel gained a new sense of self—more mobile, more active and more public—as cars gave them greater freedom. The automobile played as important a role in expanding the suffrage campaign as it did in revolutionizing the major parties' political campaigns.[59] By 1907, every upper-class American who desired an automobile owned one, including 62,660 New Yorkers in 1910, the year Henry Ford opened his first Model T mass-production line.[60] Cars (and paved roads) were less common farther west, but motor vehicles proved indispensable for suffrage open-air campaigners on the hustings. "Suffrage auto campaigners seized the practical advantages of automobility with regard to both travel and spectacle in the name of personal and political emancipation," observed historian Virginia Scharf.[61]

In 1910 and 1911, the automobile carried Washington state and California suffragists to victory. The Northern California College Equal Suffrage League affectionately dubbed its seven-passenger Packard the "Blue Liner," in which members barnstormed the state with speeches and songs, delivering talks from the back seat of a colorfully decorated vehicle.[62] Auto tours sped open-air speakers across Connecticut, Massachusetts, Maryland, New Jersey, Iowa, Kansas, Illinois, and Wisconsin.[63] "The sight of cars and women passengers alike festooned in 'suffrage yellow,' careening from town to town, drew many an onlooker," wrote historian Genevieve McBride. NAWSA sent two women on a propaganda tour of the entire nation in 1916 in the "Golden Flier," which racked up more than ten thousand miles. Dr. Anna Blount delivered fifty-two talks in twelve days on her 250-mile trip across Wisconsin. Sometimes unusual events created unplanned recruiting opportunities, as when suffrage speaker Jane Olcott enlisted her vehicle to drive firemen to a burning house in upstate New York—and then hung around to deliver a suffrage talk after they doused the flames. "The usefulness of auto tours in suffrage is now generally recognized," noted the *Woman's Journal.*[64]

Open-air meetings even arrived in the conservative South. Southern white women who dared speak in the streets risked greater censure than did their peers in other parts of the nation. As a northern movement rooted in abolition, woman suffrage was anathema to most southerners. Politicians viewed feminism as a "hostile alien force, invading the South," according to historian Marjorie Spruill Wheeler.[65] Still smarting over the loss of state sovereignty implied in the Fourteenth and Fifteenth Amendments, southerners disliked northerners and westerners trying to force another federal amendment upon them. Most of all, southern politicians feared white supremacy, the foundation of southern culture, would fall apart if African American women voted. Southern women's behavior was further circumscribed by the powerful symbolism of the modest "Southern Lady" as the guardian of southern civilization. Southern suffragists took great pains to make themselves and their cause appear as nonthreatening as possible.

So it was remarkable that by the mid-1910s, white, middle-class suffragists spoke in the streets of Virginia, South Carolina, North Carolina, Louisiana, Georgia, Alabama, and Arkansas, where in Little Rock "a curious and conservative crowd was changed into a sympathetic one."[66] Southern suffragists debated the desirability of the new methods. "Get all the fun out of the thing there is in it," urged Kentucky leader Madeline Breckinridge, who encouraged suffrage hikes and auto tours against the advice of her predecessor, Laura Clay.[67] When the Nashville Equal Suffrage League invited British suffragette Sylvia Pankhurst to the city in 1912 to give her first speech in the South, a letter to the editor protesting Pankhurst's visit to a local woman's college revealed the threat her views presented: "Could it have been right that these girls should have been allowed to listen to a woman who holds lightly all the virtues our southern girls are taught to cherish[?]" The next year, the league refused to endorse a visit by Sylvia's even more notorious mother, Emmeline Pankhurst.[68]

By then, open-air campaigns had sowed suffrage seeds across the nation. The streets became an effective forum for disseminating the suffrage creed despite—or in some respects because of—the controversy they stirred. "We don't mind them hooting and jeering at us so long as we know we are right," said New York soapboxer Mary Ting. "And all of them will go home and talk to their families about the great gathering we had, and our cause will get great advertising."[69] Even more important, the open-air meetings forcefully announced women's presence in the public sphere. The successful campaigns gave women confidence in speaking out in public. The experience literally helped women find their voice in American civic life. "It was in the broadest spirit of democracy that we went out into the streets inviting all passersby to listen to our arguments and offer their objections or ask questions," soapbox pioneer Maud Malone wrote later.[70]

A key aspect of that spirit was the women's willingness to confront male authority. Time after time on the soapbox, they battled not only hecklers but also police and city officials. The suffragists' forceful assertion of their right to assemble and speak prodded officials to ponder their obligation to protect those rights.

Legal and Cultural Obstacles

During the days of the open-air meetings, police possessed more power to restrict assemblies than today.[71] Police power gave officials great leeway to protect citizens' health, welfare, and safety. That included banning assemblies officials believed might stir trouble. Given the xenophobic nativism that thrived in the 1910s, any challenge to social homogeneity and national unity fell into that category. The nation reacted to the upheaval created by industrialization, urbanization, and immigration by trying to suppress ideas and individuals it deemed threatening. Tremendous power lay vested with officials and police in determining whether a group could hold a street meeting. "Under the police power," wrote free-speech historian Margaret Blanchard, "governments were permitted to engage in a wide range of repressive functions."[72]

The meeting permit was the official mechanism for regulating street meetings. When Malone checked with authorities on street-meeting regulations, for instance, she learned that a telephone call to the local station the day before would suffice for a written permit required for all public gatherings.[73] The relative ease with which suffragists got their first open-air permit exposed the arbitrary nature of the permit system. Permits were routinely denied to groups delivering undesirable messages. Chicago police in 1907–8 banned speeches by anarchist Emma Goldman.[74] Officials in Tarrytown, New York, forbade labor organizers from speaking in its streets.[75]

Two freethinkers were arrested for delivering antireligious speeches in 1915.[76] The following year, birth control pioneer Margaret Sanger was refused halls in Akron and Chicago, arrested and jailed in Portland, Oregon, and locked out of her speaking hall in St. Louis because of pressure from the Catholic church.[77] "Movement toward opening up public facilities to minority interests depended almost entirely on the social acceptability of the group seeking permission to communicate," Blanchard concluded.[78] Sometimes suffragists were among those denied halls.[79]

Further, twentieth-century safeguards for speaking in streets or parks remained mired in nineteenth-century notions about public property. The majority's right to enjoy public property overrode dissidents' right to speak. In the contemporary judicial view, neither free speech nor the right of assembly gave citizens the right to speak on public property dedicated by the public to other uses. The Supreme Court ruled in 1897 that a municipality could prohibit the use of its parks to public speakers unless they secured a permit.[80] State courts made similar rulings, routinely upholding the police power to limit the right of assembly. A Massachusetts court, for example, found no violation of the right of assembly when it validated park regulations forbidding orations, harangues, and loud outcries.[81] A Michigan court upheld a Detroit ordinance forbidding public addresses within half a mile of city hall without a license from the mayor.[82] And the Appellate Division of the New York Supreme Court rejected the First Amendment claim of two Socialists who challenged an Amsterdam ordinance forbidding street gatherings.[83]

Labor organizers and political radicals such as anarchists fared the worst under the arbitrary permit system. As late as 1928, the American Civil Liberties Union reported that 74 percent of cities responding to a survey required street-meeting permits and that in 70 percent of those cities, radical meetings were "not freely held"; half of the cities had refused at least one street-meeting permit in 1927.[84] Perhaps the most repressed radicals were the "Wobblies," members of the Industrial Workers of the World (IWW), a militant working-class movement whose goal it was to overthrow capitalism. The public and politicians associated the IWW with violence and anarchy, and between 1909 and 1917, thousands of Wobblies were imprisoned and/or beaten during prolonged but often successful free-speech fights against ordinances preventing street speaking, the lifeline for their recruiting and propaganda.[85]

In contrast to the Wobblies, suffragists fared much better when they tried to exercise their right of assembly. Many suffragists' standing in the upper-middle class and their respect for social order made them less threatening than the radicals. Suffragists, who prided themselves that theirs was a "bourgeois movement," wanted to realize and further the Founding Fathers' goals, not overthrow them.[86] Nonetheless, suffragists recognized the connection between radicals' free-speech battles and their own. "The question of free speech is of more than passing interest to suffragists," a suffrage newsletter said. It concluded: "If public meetings are subject to official scrutiny, street meetings prohibited, and citizens arrested for expressing an honest opinion with regard to the government, the hope of progress towards true democracy is indefinitely postponed."[87]

An editorial in the *Woman's Journal,* the weekly NAWSA newspaper, protested violations of labor leaders' rights of freedom of speech and freedom of assembly. "Suffragists should value both," wrote editor Alice Stone Blackwell. Lucy Stone's daughter offered a sophisticated First Amendment analysis well ahead of her repressive times when she said speakers should not be arrested nor meetings banned out of fear their words would incite violence.[88]

The only violence that arose at suffrage soapbox speeches was directed at the speakers. They routinely risked assault. A suffragist in Brooklyn was pelted with pebbles, and a Harlem soapboxer was knocked down and kicked.[89] An antisuffragist beat a drum throughout labor organizer Rose Schneiderman's street speech on suffrage, and hooligans dumped a bag of water on another suffrage soapboxer.[90] A speaker who crossed the Ozark Mountains on horseback to bring the suffrage message to remote churches and schools once was accosted in the street at night by a man who grabbed her throat. This attack followed letters that threatened, "Stop this campane or yiu [*sic*] will wish you had."[91]

Wall Street was the most hostile site soapboxers visited. Bettina Borrmann Wells and others once were pelted with apple cores, wet sponges, miles of ticker tape, and bags of water by men perched in windows. "Every word was greeted by roars of laughter or cheers," the *New York Times* reported. Police officers struggled to keep the raucous crowd away from the speakers' carriage. "They'd better go home. They'll be murdered," muttered an observer. Finally, the driver whipped his pair of black horses and the suffragists sped off.[92] "Wall Street was not much loved before by the general public," the *Woman's Journal* noted dryly. "It will not be loved the more for this exhibit of chivalry and respect for free speech."[93]

Outside New York City, authorities were even less sensitive to civil rights, again reflecting the arbitrary nature of enforcement. Borrmann Wells and six others were kicked out of a Staten Island park because they lacked a written street-meeting permit.[94] Massachusetts' first open-air meeting was conducted from an automobile parked in the street because park commissioners denied the speakers a meeting permit on Lynn Commons.[95] In Los Angeles, city ordinances that barred discussions of politics in public parks forced suffrage open-air meetings to private grounds.[96] In Massachusetts, the Leominster police chief forbade open-air campaigners to distribute suffrage literature, and the Fitchburg police chief confined suffrage soapboxers to standing in the street.[97] In the shadow of reports of arson and window smashing by London suffragettes, the press dismissed the First Amendment implications stemming from suffrage open-air assemblies with almost as much hostility as it viewed labor and political radicals. "There is no room in our busy thoroughfares for the meetings of agitators," said the *New York Times* of suffragists. "Let them hire halls."[98]

Sometimes suffrage soapboxers paid the price when listeners misbehaved, reflecting the judicial doctrine that held speakers responsible for the effect their words might work upon their audience. An officer stopped women from addressing a rowdy crowd of two thousand stockbrokers on Wall Street.[99] Another threatened to arrest a speaker when a shoving, taunting crowd surrounded her in New York's City Hall Park. "If you only had sense to get a permit we'd protect you," said the officer, demonstrating the power of that piece of paper.[100] A police officer arrested a doctor's wife after she called him drunk when he grabbed her arm and shook her at an open-air meeting for which she had a permit.[101] Helen Schloss was charged with violating a city ordinance regarding littering streets with handbills when a patrolman ordered her to stop passing out suffrage handbills in Harlem.[102]

Police occasionally failed to offer soapbox suffragists the "positive protection by responsible officials against hostile groups" that one scholar maintained the Constitution requires.[103] Suffragists futilely called the police for forty-five minutes when a mob howled down Emmeline Pankhurst.[104] Two soapboxers in Hell's Kitchen assailed with garbage bags and water and chased up the street said five phone calls to the police were answered "languidly and impertinently."[105]

But suffragists spoke up for their civil rights and in the process performed a service for the free-speech rights of all Americans. The imperious Blatch complained to police when crowds interrupted soapbox speeches. She blamed inadequate police protection when she and Borrmann Wells were kicked and thrown down during one of the first open-air meetings, which attracted some two thousand people who blocked trolley traffic. "Get the hook!" screamed one youth at the suffragists. Numerous officers accompanied the women back to the corner a week later.[106] Blatch used the same technique after Pankhurst was howled down, giving police notice that she would return to the spot in a week "as we did not propose to be deprived of free speech." That meeting succeeded.[107]

Suffrage soapboxers often emerged victorious in confrontations with authority. When Emmeline Pankhurst filled Carnegie Hall in 1909, four women began speaking to the overflow crowd outside. Police demanded a meeting permit and ordered the speakers to the station. When lawyer Helen Hoy Greeley challenged the chief, he backed down.[108] In one remote western town, suffragists successfully threatened the mayor with an injunction when he removed billboards advertising an open-air suffrage meeting in the park, for which the city had refused a permit. The meeting went on.[109] When the antisuffrage mayor of Albany, New York, assigned two soapboxers to a deserted square, they confronted him and got a permit to speak on bustling State Street.[110]

The well-connected husbands of upper-class suffragists also afforded them protection. After the police commissioner refused to hear suffragists' complaints about harassment in Hell's Kitchen, the women visited the precinct captain, who lackadaisically advised that street speaking was unsafe. But after wealthy banker James Laidlaw, husband of a prominent suffragist, complained to the commissioner, sufficient police surfaced at the next Hell's Kitchen open-air meeting so that it proceeded uneventfully.[111] After Mrs. Pankhurst was howled down on Wall Street, Blatch, other suffrage soapboxers and their prominent husbands complained, and the next week the department sent ten uniformed officers and thirty plainclothesmen to protect the suffragists while they addressed several thousand listeners without incident.[112]

Soapboxers grew adept at handling hecklers, as when Borrmann Wells tickled the crowd with her rebuke to a Bronx drunk, "There stands an example of your superior masculinity."[113] Lawyer Mary Coleman hauled a heckler to court, where he was fined five dollars and locked up, after she was mobbed during a "small riot" at the same uptown corner where Borrmann Wells and Blatch were manhandled.[114]

A willingness to deploy so-called feminine wiles to unravel officialdom also helped women to negotiate their way through traditionally male turf. In Schenectady, New York, for instance, the police chief rescinded his refusal of a street-meeting permit for suffragists following, as Blatch recalled, "patience on the part of everyone, and particular pleas on the part of Alberta Hill, our very able and beautiful secretary."[115]

Suffragists' response to police harassment of their "Voiceless Speech" in a Fifth Avenue shop window demonstrated their willingness to resist authority. The speech involved volunteers who slowly turned over about thirty large cards on an easel bearing large black letters that formed a continuous message advocating suffrage.[116] When police finally charged a card turner with causing a crowd to block the sidewalk, her colleagues protested the ban and staged another voiceless speech on Wall Street. The voiceless speech resumed unhampered on Fifth Avenue.[117] Meanwhile, the officer on nearby Sixth Avenue never interfered with the voiceless speech on that street, more evidence of the inconsistency of assembly laws.[118]

Sometimes, anticipated police interference failed to materialize. On 25 July 1911, Alice Paul led six other women who, fearful Philadelphia police would reject their unprecedented meeting-permit request, plotted aboard an open trolley car. Paul told them, "If the police threaten to arrest us and we offer no resistance, it will mean the end of open-air suffrage meetings in Philadelphia." One of the conspirators recalled years later, "The policeman on the beat near our corner appeared to grow taller and taller and bigger and bigger the closer we got to him." The police officer ignored the gathering, however, and the women had no trouble obtaining future street-meeting permits.[119]

In fact, police often endeavored to protect suffrage soapboxers. Manhattan police once dispatched fifty officers on foot and horse to control a "howling crowd" that followed a small suffrage automobile procession to the mayor's office. One woman was carried aloft by the mob. "You had better take off those [suffrage] sashes, ladies; they might throw something at you," warned an onlooker before their taxis sped off with several officers clinging to their sides as they fought off the crowd.[120]

Police became friendly and supportive as suffrage soapbox orators became more common. When six "sandwichettes" bearing sandwich-board messages paraded on Broadway, officers grinned and left them alone.[121] The suffragists returned the favor by buying a box at the police department carnival fund raiser for widow relief.[122] Washington, D.C., police who protested soapboxers selling "Votes for Women" buttons without a street vendors' license ended up wearing them.[123] New York police were sufficiently won over so that by 1915 both the New York State Association of Police Chiefs and the Patrolman Benevolent Association endorsed suffrage.[124]

Suffragists argued forcefully for their rights of freedom of expression. But in addition to legal obstacles, they had to overcome even more formidable cultural barriers to speaking in the streets.

The sight of suffragists speaking in the streets was just one manifestation of the revolutionary changes wrought in America by the rise of the city, capitalism, and a flood of immigrants in the decades cradling the turn of the century. Those changes created the climate for the Progressive era, whose name bespoke its adherents' conception of civilization as sustained improvement of the human race. Through reform and legislation, Progressives worked to eradicate social evils brought on by the modern industrial state, including conditions in industry, education, government, race relations, urban life, the family, and woman's role.[125] Mostly middle-class, Anglo-Saxon Protestants, Progressives believed with evangelical fervor that individuals could improve their lot through hard work and personal morality. Because they also believed society bore an obligation to create an environment in which individuals could prosper materially and spiritually, Progressives were righteously reform-minded. Nativism and racism infected their zeal, because they equated progress and morality with Protestant morality.

The woman suffrage movement was both a part and a product of the Progressive era. Progressives' emphasis upon morality and reform created a special role for women, as they were long imagined the keepers of morality. "They were the mothers of those whose strength and character the future of the human race depended," wrote one historian.[126] Women believed they could clean up the mess men had made of society with a bit of what has been called public housekeeping.[127] Women threw themselves into reform between 1890 and 1920.

Women were fleeing the domestic sphere in droves. More than five million women were working outside of the home by 1900, and they comprised almost a fifth of the nation's work force.[128] Most were young, single, white, and lived in cities. The emerging field of clerical work in the 1910s employed many women, but most women toiled under more brutal conditions in factories or as domestics.[129] All were underpaid. The number of women attending college, however, more than tripled to 283,000 between 1900 and 1920, and by 1920 professional women comprised 11.9 percent of the female work force, more than doubling their numbers between 1890 and 1920.[130] Only 5 percent of Americans attended college in 1910, yet 40 percent of college students were female, creating what historian Nancy Woloch called a "new elite."[131] Women's ties to the home unraveled further as the birth rate fell to 3.5 children per mother, the divorce rate doubled between 1900 and 1920, and about 10 percent of all women never married. In fact, more single women were at the peak of their careers in the Progressive era than at any other time.[132] The emerging "New Woman"—young, well educated, independent, and often self-supporting—also was a suffragist. If married, she enjoyed a companionate rather than patriarchal relationship with her spouse.[133]

Women voting was just one among many radical notions about female behavior astir in the 1910s; the New Year's Eve open-air meeting in Madison Square, for instance, received less attention than did the Cafe Martin nightclub's decision to allow women revelers to smoke cigarettes.[134] "Sex O'Clock in America" struck in 1913 according to one magazine, and another asked, "Where Is Your Daughter This Afternoon?"[135] Authorities in 1914 confiscated copies of the first issue of Margaret Sanger's aptly titled birth-control newspaper, the *Woman Rebel*.[136] Clergy condemned the turkey trot in 1913, and public dancing required licenses.[137] The rising suffrage tide, however, came to signify for many Americans women's apparent abandonment of the domestic sphere.[138]

In the early years of open-air campaigns, suffragists debated among themselves the propriety of women speaking in the streets, a venue so long associated with prostitution. The newspapers labeled the soapboxers "suffragettes" after their British models, and most speakers happily equated the term with modern and effective methods that distinguished them from the more conservative suffragists who gathered at teas. "The Suffragette is conscious of the necessity of converting the masses—all the people, and therefore goes to the people direct, in the streets, on the highways and byways, and holds open-air street meetings with able speakers to address the crowds," wrote Sofia Loebinger, editor of the *American Suffragette* newspaper.[139]

Woman's Journal editor Alice Stone Blackwell argued that soapboxing won attention. "Let any impartial person compare the attention which is given the equal suffrage question today and what it was receiving this time last year," she wrote.[140] Yet the *Journal* felt compelled to assure its readers, "An open-meeting is neither illegal nor per se unladylike."[141] Blatch's WPU in 1910 chose the British suffragette colors of purple, green, and white to serve notice of its new, politicized methods.[142] On the other side of the debate stood traditional suffragists, who tellingly described the upstarts as representatives of the "active" suffrage movement.[143]

Women at NAWSA's 1908 convention in Buffalo spurned a suggestion they mount a soapbox on a street.[144] When the subject of militant methods came up at the New England Woman Suffrage Association meeting in 1909, discussion became so prolonged a janitor finally asked the women to leave. But at that year's NAWSA convention, objections had softened sufficiently to make space for a speech on the "Conditions That Create Suffragette Methods," by Clara Colby, who concluded, "Let us emulate the spirit, if not the methods, of our English sisters."[145] Even sixty-three-year-old Dr. Anna Howard Shaw, NAWSA president from 1905 to 1916, had a change of heart. Shaw had bristled that the rise in suffrage interest was solely attributable to the "unwearied service" of suffrage veterans.[146] But after attending seminars and seeing an open-air meeting at the 1910 NAWSA convention in Washington, D.C., she declared them the cheapest and most effective way to reach audiences. "We might as well follow the example of our English sisters and utilize our entire vacation in holding out-of-door meetings," she wrote before sailing to England to march and address a mammoth rally.[147]

A sense of propriety kept many suffragists off the streets, and soapboxers comprised only a small but significant segment of the movement. "Many women had been so thoroughly socialized to believe in the rules of etiquette that they did not find the public meetings acceptable even within the suffrage movement," observed sociologist Marjory Nelson.[148] Jibes like those of a heckler at the first soapbox speech in Madison Square garden— "The place for the wimmins is in the home, and to cook the dinners!"— were enough to keep many women off the soapbox.[149] In fact, the women's unconventional behavior formed the true source of antagonism toward suffragists rather than their call for votes. As sociologist Rosamund Billington said of antipathy directed at British suffragists, any deviation from the idealized view of pacific woman threatened the family and the organization of social life. "It was as much the behaviour of feminists—such as speaking on public platforms—as their demands for reform, which implied gender changes," she wrote.[150]

Many American suffragists hesitated to challenge those roles. Connecticut women who toured rural hills by automobile in 1911 spoke in halls because they worried residents would be so outraged by soapboxers that "the suffrage cause would lose more than it could possibly gain if open-air speaking were allowed."[151] Others found the experience liberating, such as the New York teacher who had worried street speaking was unladylike. "I felt more like crawling under the box than standing on it," she said. "Then I stood there and looked down on those expectant faces and I realized they were human beings, and the rest was easy."[152]

Joining the open-air campaigns intensified women's commitment to the movement. "Militants expected that overstepping the boundary of respectability would etch suffrage beliefs on women's souls," wrote historian Ellen DuBois.[153] Soapboxers' consideration of gender roles was honed to a "razor's edge" because they participated in norm-defying behavior, pointed out historian Nancy Cott, inclining them to challenge other constraints upon women's behavior. "If one norm were crossed," she wrote, "why not another?"[154]

Suffragists remained vulnerable to charges they acted like men, because that charge defiled their basic sense of themselves. The popular press depicted suffragists as "unattractive, selfish, and rowdy."[155] The cultural breach caused by women speaking in the streets was so wide even the militant *American Suffragette* assured its critics of soapboxers' femininity and allegiance to men. "We love our husbands as much as do the women who do not belong to our movement, . . . and we all love to be fondled and petted just as much as you do," its editor wrote.[156] This attitude helped neutralize attacks on suffrage soapboxers, but it also subverted the radical nature of the suffrage creed because it clung to constricted images of female humanity.

Even convention-flouting soapboxers were initially hesitant to be associated with the shocking new term "feminism." In the late nineteenth century, "feminism" was a medical term describing a "tendency to degeneracy"—the development of female characteristics in the male.[157] Although by the 1910s, it generally meant the body of ideas and motives at the root of the modern women's movement, confusion existed about what exactly those ideas and motives were.[158] Antisuffragists equated feminism with easy divorce and the abandonment of motherhood; in short, the destruction of the family. Carrie Chapman Catt countered that feminism was "a world-wide revolution against all artificial barriers which laws and customs inter-pose between women and human freedom."[159] Suffragists remained defensive about the term; in fact, many were not feminists, whose agenda was broader and more radical than simply attaining the vote. In 1909, even the supposedly radical *American Suffragette* decried feminism: "Women do not want to ape men, but wish to remain true women, good daughters, sisters, mothers, and we claim emphatically that none if [sic] the attributes of ideal womanhood will be sacrificed to the ballot."[160]

Suffrage soapboxers tried to deflect attention from their behavior by emphasizing their womanliness. Open-air meetings in Los Angeles featured baking contests in which suffragists talked while listeners ate.[161] A Rochester suffragist challenged antisuffragists to a cooking contest; none responded. That night, after reporters sampled suffragist Jane Thomsen's southern hot biscuits and chocolate cake, she addressed five hundred men on a street corner to prove that "cookery and civics do not interfere with each other."[162] Southern suffragists in Virginia, Georgia, and Tennessee sold home-baked cakes and fancy needlework to demonstrate their domestic capabilities.[163] Cleveland women staged a fair featuring food booths, dancing pavilions, and sewing and embroidery exhibits as a "practical demonstration of the deftness of suffragists in the housewifely arts." But after the domestic displays closed, the fair ended with a "rousing suffrage speech."[164] Suffragists staged baby shows to prove they were good mothers.[165] The organizer of a Long Island baby health show explained, "I want to overcome the notion suffragists are not good mothers."[166] A *Woman's Journal* advertisement plugged a cracker called "The Suffragette": "Just Sweet Enough to Be Fascinating."[167] Some New York suffragists canvassed door-to-door with a washing machine in tow, promoting suffrage while doing the wash in their hostess' sink. "It is such a nice, womanly, feminine way of working, too," said Elizabeth Morton.[168] Delivering their suffrage message in such a domestic fashion enabled women to ask for the vote without appearing unfeminine.

Women suffrage cartoonists who began to work in the 1910s also altered the public image of the dour suffragist depicted by male cartoonists. She became younger, slimmer, and prettier. A 1915 *Woman Voter* cover, for instance, showed just such a woman on a soapbox: Well dressed, she speaks confidently into a megaphone, head tilted back and one hand on her hip in an assertive posture that commands attention.[169] "Women who were attractive and feminine were used to allay fears of the unwomanly," explained art historian Alice Sheppard.[170]

Besides their womanliness, suffrage soapboxers emphasized their place in the middle to upper class. The primacy of class in the open-air campaign cannot be overstated. Ironically, the usefulness of street meetings, the forum of the oppressed, was biased toward the elite because the sight of working-class women in the street was less startling. "The wealthier its proponent was—the more ladylike she was supposed to be—the greater the effect of her subversion of the norm," observed Cott.[171] While labor organizers such as Rose Schneiderman sometimes shared suffrage podiums, and the Women's Trade Union League actively supported suffrage in the 1910s, suffrage soapboxers usually were upper-class white matrons or young, college-educated, professional women.[172]

Class, Race, and Suffrage Soapboxers

Reality dictated that the novelty of upper-class, white women on soapboxes attracted publicity. "A society matron on an open-air platform made page one while a working girl did not, because society women were obliged by conventions and could outrage by flouting them," noted historian Ellen DuBois.[173] Her point was demonstrated by a *Progress* account of how Borrmann Wells addressed a Long Island open-air meeting: "People arrested in passing by the sound of a low, cultured voice uttering strange truths, stopped and listened; presently automobiles stopped and carriages stopped that the occupants might hear what was said."[174] An Illinois suffragist noted the impression upon the press made by open-air speakers during a cross-state auto tour. "The ability and dignity and social standing of the parties amaze the newspapers," she wrote.[175] Southern newspapers emphasized the beauty and femininity of suffrage leaders, who encouraged ladylike behavior among their followers.[176] Suffrage journals were as guilty as the mainstream press of being fixated with class, in part because the women were so bent upon proving their respectability. Thus the *Woman's Journal* gushed about a crew of open-air speakers on Cape Cod, "The speakers are young, earnest, refined—several of them are college graduates—intelligent, well dressed, and of pleasing personality."[177]

Despite their tentative partnership with working women, wealthy suffrage leaders also had mixed emotions about the poorer segments of their constituency. Press praise of the "smartly dressed" speakers at a New York City street meeting presided over by Blatch demonstrated how class influenced the suffrage campaign. Although those soapboxers supposedly represented the movement's radical segment, that rally ended with lunch at the tony Colony Club.[178] Open-air pioneer Maud Malone quit the Progressive Woman Suffrage Union to protest its elitism three months after it criticized the New Year's Eve open-air meeting in Madison Square. "Speakers and audience alike were condemned as not being up to the required standard, and it was emphatically declared we must attract a well-dressed crowd," Malone wrote to the *Times*. "To me, the movement to be truly progressive should recognize no prejudices of race, color, difference in clothes or creed."[179]

The racism that infected the suffrage movement underscored how daunting extralegal factors could be for minorities trying to exercise their constitutional rights such as freedom of assembly. Yet African American suffragists did exercise their right of assembly. Despite hostility from fellow suffragists and their vulnerability when participating in public political activities, at least one African American woman led open-air meetings. Miss A. L. T. Waytes of Milwaukee was "one of the most inspiring speakers we have had . . . and knows how to carry an audience with her, especially if it is made up of her own people," the *Woman's Journal* reported in 1912.[180]

But the suffrage movement remained largely a white, middle-class mainstream movement. The experience of America's most militant suffragist illuminated the limits of both the American legal system's tolerance for the right of assembly as well as the narrow scope of suffrage cultural radicalism. Clad in a chin-to-knee yellow suffrage placard that triggered much ridicule, "lone suffragette" Maud Malone was arrested and fined several times for speaking solo off Broadway or for heckling candidates in the manner of the militant Britons.[181] "When there's a situation in politics that just seems to call for attention, she just puts on her war bonnet, pins her yellow banner across her breast, and sallies forth alone against the political machinery of New York," the *Woman's Journal* wrote of the originator of suffrage open-air meetings in America. "They say that political public speakers dodge her as they would a bomb in an open meeting."[182]

One of those speakers was presidential candidate Woodrow Wilson, who visited Brooklyn on 19 October 1912 to address the local Democratic Party. In the middle of his speech, Malone arose from her seat and called out, "You have just been talking about monopolies, and what about woman's suffrage? The men have a monopoly of the suffrage."[183] When Wilson demurred, Malone persisted and was hauled out of the meeting, arrested, and fined five dollars after being convicted of willfully disturbing a meeting.[184] An appeals court rejected her First Amendment defense. "There is no question of free speech or of oppression involved in the case, and it does not bulk large with incidental questions of liberty," the court said.[185] The *Times* also derided her methods. "However high her aim might be, she has missed her mark," an editorial said.[186]

Malone posed a "perplexing problem" for suffragists who strived to separate their cause from escalating British militancy. Although sympathetically describing her as a "quiet, well-mannered little woman, well-born, well-bred," the *Woman's Journal* could not bring itself to endorse her methods.[187] Malone was too odd and her methods too strident to win favor with either the public or her suffrage peers. She won no suffrage followers. Newspaper references to her disappeared after the 1913 appeals court ruling.

In contrast, Beacon Hill matron Susan FitzGerald, who led a trolley tour across Massachusetts in 1909, represented the ideal open-air campaigner.[188] The former Bryn Mawr College graduate student had been head social worker at the West Side Branch of the Union Settlement of New York City. After marrying a lawyer in 1901, she defied convention by continuing to work as a city truant officer, showing herself streetwise but somewhat blind to the compromises poverty induced. Her efforts sent twenty youths to truancy school and resulted in fines for more than twenty-five parents. By 1908, the FitzGeralds had moved to Boston, where she cared for three young daughters and served as secretary of the Boston Equal Suffrage Association for Good Government.[189]

The mainstream press seemed awed by FitzGerald and her elite colleagues aboard the trolley, including Radcliffe College student A. P. McClure, lawyer Edith Haynes, and Mary Ware Dennett, another wealthy Boston matron. "The quartet are well bred, and possessed of that ease and confidence characteristic of educated persons," reported the *North Adams (Mass.) Herald*. The *Clinton (Mass.) Courant* wrote, "They proved themselves refined, cultured women, able to speak intelligently upon their pet theme."[190]

The praise that suffragists also heaped upon FitzGerald illustrated the homage they paid to the tenacious cult of true womanhood, which in the nineteenth century had defined women as pure and pious domestic creatures submissive to husbands and fathers.[191] Even suffragists internalized the dominant ideology that portrayed women as nurturing caretakers of the most sacred cultural institution, the family. It was important to *Journal* readers that FitzGerald embody the ideals of true womanhood despite her suffrage work; the attractive young mother's persona not only soothed male qualms but also bolstered suffragists' self-esteem. As sociologist Rosamund Billington observed of the British suffragettes, the American suffragists needed to remain ladylike because their opponents emphasized the unwomanliness and abnormality of the demand, and this attack upon their gender assaulted their most basic sense of self.[192]

Some suffragists responded by linking their work with the responsibilities of motherhood. When soapboxers returned to Hell's Kitchen to successfully speak a week after they were chased out of the neighborhood, for instance, the *Woman Voter* claimed they "upheld their principle that they will not be shut out of any part of New York where women and children are living."[193] The *Buffalo Sun Times* ran a full page of photographs of babies with their suffragist mothers. "These beautiful children have suffrage parents and grandparents," it said.[194] Dennett framed voting as a responsibility of motherhood, and the *Journal* ran a photograph of a serene FitzGerald ringed by her daughters, whom it lauded as better behaved than most children.[195] The newspaper later attributed the successful Massachusetts trolley tour "to the fact that the leader of the expedition was a woman not only capable and intelligent but beautiful, dignified and every inch a lady."[196]

Rigors of Open-Air Campaigns

To give them their due, these ladies also were troupers. FitzGerald's uppercrust band of trolley-car speakers mastered the legal and social dynamics of an open-air campaign while conducting ninety-seven unannounced meetings in seventy-nine towns, covering sixteen hundred miles in twenty-eight days.[197] The *Journal* called FitzGerald a "genius of outdoor campaigning."[198] The suffragists wrote each police chief of the towns where they stopped to notify them of their expected arrival time and to request a speaking permit; if he refused, they collared the mayor.[199] The suffragists also kept the press apprised of their schedule and were accompanied part of the way by two Boston women reporters. Always on the lookout for human-interest stories, the press quickly warmed to open-air meetings. As the *American Suffragette* noted, "[The] press finds no more interesting subject."[200]

Once they found a town's busiest street corner, FitzGerald's band unfurled a brilliantly inscribed "Votes for Women" banner.[201] "I want to tell you why we are so anxious to have what this banner stands for," FitzGerald would begin.[202] While one woman spoke, the others distributed suffrage posters, sold "Votes for Women" buttons, and urged a suffrage petition upon listeners.[203] The first day began at 8:30 A.M. and ended thirteen hours later, after open-air meetings in Clinton, Leominster, and Fitchburg.[204] "One cool day left me wilted despite the fact that I did not, of course, do any speechmaking," wrote *Boston Traveler* reporter Phoebe Dwight after accompanying the Bay State trolley car tour.[205] The women visited a socialist club in Springfield and spoke at the Worcester loom works.[206] An escaped white rooster twice interrupted their talk in Attleboro; a dog fight raged during another talk elsewhere; and the quartet was mistaken for the Salvation Army in North Attleboro. "They never lose their audience," observed a reporter, "no matter what happens."[207]

FitzGerald listed requirements for successful open-air meetings at a symposium during the 1910 NAWSA convention. Speakers needed stage presence and the ability to speak with "spirit and rapidity" to make very practical, definite, and simple points, as well as a strong voice, sense of humor, the instincts for sizing up a crowd, and the determination to speak under any circumstances. She advised speakers to carry a banner to capture public and press attention and to stand on a chair to be seen and heard.[208] The well-attended symposium culminated in a live demonstration, marking Washington's first open-air suffrage meeting.[209]

As FitzGerald's savvy attested, the seeming spontaneity of soapbox orators often was well rehearsed. The WPU in 1912 offered voice lessons for soapboxers at which women picked up tips, such as saying "anti" so it sounded insignificant or strengthening their tonsils to drown out unruly crowds. "Don't minimize the value of the effect on a crowd of the way you mount your soapbox or stool," their instructor advised. "Gracefulness is not to be despised."[210] The suffragists' ingenuity channeled male ridicule into curiosity. Upstate New York organizer Laura Ellsworth Seiler's surefire method for enticing audiences was to park her convertible, its rear end draped by a huge green, white, and purple "Votes for Women" banner, in front of the local bar: "My mother, who was small, and charming, and utterly Victorian, and convinced that all good things started with the favor of the male, would go through the swinging doors and say, 'Gentlemen, my daughter is going to talk about suffrage outside, and I think you would be interested. I hope you'll come out.' And just like the Pied Piper, they would all dump their drinks on the bar and come out and make the nucleus of the crowd."[211]

By 1915, soapboxers had driven home the legitimacy of the suffrage cause, and suffragists could concentrate on legislative work.[212] Suffragists had won the vote in twelve states by then.[213] In 1917, New York suffragists stopped street speaking so that they would not conflict with World War I military recruiters.[214] By then, parades, pageants, and even picketing had overshadowed suffrage soapboxers. But the suffrage cause owed a huge debt to open-air meetings.

By exercising their rights of assembly in creative ways and forthrightly asserting those rights when challenged by authority, women had delivered the suffrage message to much of the nation. Suffragists never could have forced the public to consider votes for women if they had not taken their message to the streets; otherwise, it would have gone virtually unheard. The suffrage open-air campaigns are an excellent example of how the right of assembly is supposed to serve democracy: Suffragists forced the issue upon an indifferent audience. Possessing a minimum of resources besides their intelligence, fortitude, and passion for their cause, they argued their unpopular case on street corners across the nation. Their poise, spirit, and logic won supporters nationwide—or at least stirred debate.

The act of gathering together and addressing assemblies also unified and galvanized the suffrage movement, fulfilling another important function of the right of assembly. The crucible of street speaking empowered soapbox orators and bonded them as if they were soldiers who fought in the trenches together. Those women who faced down hecklers, stood up to the police officer on the beat, or received the cheers of the crowd discovered new strength within themselves. Speaking on the streets changed their identity and helped them cast off the internal restrictions that prevented so many women from exercising their right of assembly. Soapboxing demonstrated that women could gather and speak and not disappear into a hole in the ground. Instead, the heady experience of serving as street missionaries for suffrage often infused women with a crusading spirit that rose to a spiritual plane.

Open-air speakers also recognized that women deserved a place in the public sphere, and on that most public forum, the street-corner soapbox, they began to feel at home with speaking up for themselves. The open-air campaigns gave them the confidence to push harder for suffrage in places and by means that were foreign to women, such as marching in parades, buttonholing politicians in legislative hallways, and picketing the White House. On a more basic level, skills women learned in the unpredictable art of the soapbox—resourcefulness, humor, flexibility, and persuasion—steeled them for the next tumultuous decade of working for suffrage.

The open-air meetings also advanced arguments for enhancing protections for all Americans to exercise the right of assembly. Suffragists prided themselves in their knowledge about the workings and rhetoric of democracy, largely as a defensive reaction to charges women were incapable of participating in governing themselves. They especially were cognizant of the role of freedom of expression in a democracy, in light of their own self-interest in serving up their message to the public. Whenever male officials challenged their right to speak on the streets, suffragists asserted their right to assemble and address crowds. They also defended freedom of expression for political radicals and labor organizers.

But the success of the suffrage soapboxers masked the malleable nature of early-twentieth-century protections for the right of assembly. Class and chivalry combined with suffragists' reformist rather than revolutionary agenda insulated the women from the beatings, imprisonment, and censorship that silenced some speakers whose ideas were deemed revolutionary. Suffragists did not challenge capitalism as did labor and Socialists, and suffragists paid homage to the democratic system. They perhaps represented the outer limits of unconventional speakers considered safe enough to be heard unmolested by authorities. For instance, the Washington, D.C., police chief made an exception to a rule limiting street speakers to a single site and gave suffrage orators permits to speak through the city.[215]

Suffragists seemed unbothered when arbitrary enforcement silenced their foes. NAWSA president Shaw wondered if there was a way to prevent antisuffragists from distributing literature during a NAWSA parade.[216] It pleased the *Woman's Journal* that Asbury Park, New Jersey, officials refused antisuffragists a meeting hall.[217] In Atlantic City, suffragist Mary Brennan crowed that the prosuffrage mayor made an exception by giving her permission to speak on the Boardwalk: "No one else has this privilege."[218]

Suffrage soapboxers were more radical in the cultural sense than in a political or economic sense. Their blatant presence on street corners—making obvious their absence from the home—formed a tangible symbol of the revolutionary changes in women's role. It is not surprising that many Americans in the 1910s found the appearance of middle- and upper-class women speaking on street corners so threatening, because the challenges arising from women's move from the domestic to the public sphere continue to vex Americans. Although most municipal officials felt unthreatened by suffrage soapboxers in terms of preserving public order, the women's fellow citizens—male and female—felt terribly threatened by the social message announced by the suffragists' presence on a soapbox.

Women tried to swaddle this radical behavior in the most conservative dressing by linking soapboxing for suffrage to motherhood and emphasizing their womanliness. That strategy often worked, although women would not realize the implications of knotting their civic self to traditional female roles until after they won the vote. The feminine aspects of suffrage soapboxing, however, also had positive ramifications. Their style marked women's outdoor assemblies as distinctively female as they staked this new cultural territory for women.

Even the elitism of open-air meetings served a purpose; many of the soapboxers were part of the first generation of American women college graduates, and their intelligence and articulateness impressed many of their listeners. Once they heard such women, listeners no longer could confidently pronounce women incapable of understanding politics. Finally, the winsome soapboxers themselves were proof that women could join the public sphere without abandoning that important part of themselves they considered feminine. Open-air meetings literally and figuratively gave the campaign a breath of fresh air.

⚜ THREE ⚜

PETITIONS

The Power and Limits of
Women's Sole Political Tool

Carrie Chapman Catt once wrote that between 1868 and 1920 suffragists solicited millions of names on petitions during 480 campaigns seeking state amendments to grant women the vote. Their efforts secured referenda in only seventeen states, and suffrage lost all of them except Colorado and Idaho.[1] Suffragists also collected over many years more than a million names on various petitions asking Congress for a federal suffrage amendment. Although petitions worked no overnight magic upon politicians, they helped women win the vote. They provided suffragists with a tangible way to demonstrate their commitment to suffrage, raising morale and their sense of achievement, and they publicized the movement through picturesque petition presentations that further won at least nodding recognition from legislators that a demand existed for woman suffrage.

The petition's glacierlike effect may have frustrated suffragists, yet it was disfranchised women's sole political tool. As Catt told the New York state legislature when suffragists petitioned its Judiciary Committee in 1908, "No matter how insignificant a man may be, or how absurd his petition, he may feel reasonably certain that through his representative in the legislature or congress, his plea will reach the law-making body."[2] American women's earliest attempts to express their needs in the public political sphere were through the First Amendment right to petition the government for redress of grievances. The oldest of rights, the petition is closely tied to the right of assembly. Petitioning was inextricably linked with street meetings, parades, conventions, and other suffragist exercises of the right of assembly. Because of its symbiotic relationship with the right of assembly and because of the unique role the petition played in American women's political history, it is useful to explore its origins and how women wielded it prior to the twentieth century to understand the petition's significance in the final decade of the suffrage campaign.

Origins of the Right of Petition

The right of petition is ancient and forms the cornerstone of the Anglo-American constitutional system.[3] Justice William Douglas once wrote that it lies at "the heart of the democratic philosophy."[4] One survey of U.S. Supreme Court cases found that the right of petition helps protect the right of the people to make peaceful public protests for a redress of grievances.[5] In a sense, any political act can be characterized as a petition—sit-ins, demonstrations, litigation, lobbying, and boycotts—because all of these activities seek a redress for grievances.[6] The essential elements of a petition are preparing a written communication and sending it to the government.[7]

The right of petition has been closely tied to the right of assembly since the signing in 1215 of the Magna Charta.[8] Legal scholar Norman Smith argued that petitioning instigated a recognition of the right of public assembly in eighteenth-century England, because regulations of public assemblies originated as a response to meetings held to frame and sign petitions as well as to present them to government.[9] Legal scholars have pointed out that during the suffrage era the right of assembly was viewed as simply a byproduct of the right to petition, and the U.S. Supreme Court described it that way in *United States v. Cruikshank*, the leading nineteenth-century case involving the right of assembly.[10]

Historically, direct petitioning of government was a central feature of democratic government "because it was a means of publicizing issues and setting the legislative agenda, as well as an avenue for aggrieved parties to seek relief unavailable through other channels," wrote scholar Anita Hodgkiss.[11] The right to petition in colonial America was an affirmative, remedial right that required colonial governments to consider and respond to any citizen's petition. Some scholars argued the framers intended that the right of petition required a corresponding governmental duty to respond, but by the time twentieth-century suffragists wielded the petition its value lay solely in arousing public opinion.[12] By then, the right of petition had been subsumed by the other free-expression clauses, and government officials no longer felt obliged to respond to petitions. This relegated the major value of petitions to the publicity generated by their solicitation and presentation.

Women Petition

The earliest example located for this book of women petitioning occurred in London in 1641, when a delegation of English "gentlewomen and brewers' wives" stood at the House of Commons doors to petition Parliament for the same rights to petition as men.[13] Its form was as significant as its message, because the women's presence at the portals of authority served as their petition. The first English suffrage petition was delivered to Parliament in 1866 by John Stuart Mill as women were forbidden from attending its sessions, and in 1910 the National Union of Women's Suffrage Societies gathered 280,000 signatures on a petition to the House of Lords.[14] Northern British textile workers launched their mammoth suffrage petition drive with an open-air meeting, indicative of how these two forms of agitation would complement each other in Britain and the United States.[15] The British militant campaign became violent when Parliament refused suffrage petition delegations, and the women stoned its windows.[16]

In colonial America, petitioning meant that no group in colonial society was totally without political power.[17] "Slaves, women, and various reform societies had petitioned since colonial days," noted historian Gerda Lerner.[18] Connecticut women petitioned to replace an indiscreet minister as early as 1658, and fifty-one women in Edenton, North Carolina, signed a petition in 1774 supporting the tea boycott.[19] After American soldiers in 1782 expelled loyalist wives and children from Wilmington, North Carolina, the bond between women proved stronger than politics. Local patriot women, earlier themselves expelled by the Tories, petitioned patriot military leaders to rescind the order. "It is not the province of our sex to reason deeply upon the policy of the order," they began, reflecting their self-consciousness over stepping outside gender roles by venturing into politics.[20]

The abolition movement in the 1830s developed women's experience in wielding the right to petition. Abolition petition drives significantly strengthened women's ability to express themselves and organize. From 1834 to the early 1840s, women in local abolition societies undertook door-to-door canvassing for signatures on antislavery petitions to Congress. The experience gave women practice in political organizing and in improving their verbal skills of persuasion; it also demonstrated to them the power of the corresponding rights of association and assembly. Angelina Grimké pointed out in her *Appeal to the Christian Women of the South* that petitioning was particularly appropriate work for women, as they could not vote.[21] Historian Jean Fagan Yellin has argued that Grimké viewed the right to petition as an affirmation of selfhood, because it was the "only significant action" allowed women. Denied a say in her governance, Grimké grasped the petition as women's only avenue toward freedom. She wrote to Catharine Beecher, "The *very least* that can be done is to give [women] the right of petition in all cases whatsoever; and without any abridgement. If not, they are mere slaves, known only through their masters."[22]

The act of petitioning required a willingness to violate considerable cultural restrictions; women in a Massachusetts antislavery society encouraged each other not to "shrink before scorn and ridicule."[23] As historian Eleanor Flexner observed: "It took the same kind of courage as that displayed by the Grimké sisters for the average housewife, mother, or daughter to overstep the limits of decorum, disregard the frowns, or jeers, or outright commands of her menfolk and go to her first public meeting, or take her first petition and walk down an unfamiliar street, knocking on doors and asking for signatures to an unpopular plea."[24]

Susan B. Anthony, Elizabeth Cady Stanton, and Lucretia Mott were among feminist leaders who sharpened their communications skills as petition solicitors in the 1830s. More than half of the signatures on the annual flood of antislavery petitions to Congress throughout the decade belonged to women. As the number of antislavery petitions rose, the House of Representatives passed its infamous "gag rule," which automatically tabled without discussion all antislavery petitions. The outraged reaction expanded the abolition campaign into a broader debate about free speech.[25] Abolition historian Gilbert Barnes said the exercise of the right of petition inaugurated a new era for women: "Upon that right, which woman's 'physical weakness renders so peculiarly appropriate that none can deny her its exercise,' the women of the new era built a mighty organization, the first corporate expression of women's will in American history and the first organized stage in their century-long struggle for civic freedom."[26]

The petition campaign angered Congress, partly because the flood of abolition petitions clogged its operations and partly because the women's political involvement offended male politicians. Senator Benjamin Tappan of Ohio expressed the sentiments of many Americans when he refused to present abolition petitions collected by women. "The field of politics is not her appropriate arena," Tappan said. "The powers of government are not within her cognizance, as they could not be within her knowledge unless she neglected higher and holier duties to acquire it."[27] A Maryland congressman expressed "sorrow" over women petitioners' "departure from their proper sphere."[28] Many women agreed petitioning was beyond woman's sphere, such as educator Catharine Beecher, who lectured Angelina Grimké: "Men are the proper persons to make appeals to the rulers whom they appoint, and if their female friends, by arguments and persuasions, can induce them to petition, all the good that can be done by such measures will be secured."[29]

Woman's Rights Petitions

The earliest recorded woman's rights petition was filed by Mary Ayres to the New York legislature in 1834.[30] Although nineteenth-century woman's rights activists began to petition only after the power of petition waned, they grasped the petition because it remained their only political tool. The main purpose of many woman's rights conventions, for instance, was to organize petition drives articulating their members' grievances. Petitioning remained closely tied to the right of assembly because solicitors naturally sought crowds. When the Albany woman's rights convention in 1854 resolved to annually petition the state legislature for suffrage, it also urged activists to hold public meetings across the state to educate the public about their movement.[31]

During the Civil War, Anthony and Elizabeth Cady Stanton channeled fledgling female political activism through the petition, organizing the Woman's Loyal National League to collect a million signatures urging a constitutional amendment forbidding slavery. The league gathered some four hundred thousand signatures, representing approximately one signature for every fifty Americans in the northern states, on petition rolls that were carried into the Senate in huge bundles by two African American men on 9 February 1864.[32] Such ceremony would also play an integral role in twentieth-century suffrage petition campaigns.

The women's efforts on slaves' behalf spurred ratification of the Thirteenth Amendment freeing the slaves, followed by the Fourteenth Amendment that in part protected voting rights—for men only. The amendment for the first time inserted the word "male" into the Constitution. Anthony and Stanton futilely turned to the petition to deal with this blow, a bitter lesson to voteless women on the limits of the petition's power. When petition drives to strike "male" from the amendment failed in 1865 and 1866, Stanton and Anthony unsuccessfully petitioned in 1867 and 1868 to include women in the Fifteenth Amendment protecting voting rights. Finally, they petitioned Congress in 1868 and 1869 for adoption of a Sixteenth Amendment that would specifically guarantee women the vote.[33] By 1872, nearly five million signatures had been collected on petitions for women's rights.[34] But Stanton and Anthony vowed to appeal no more because the petitions only piled up in Congress, "unheeded and ignored."[35] Lacking any other recourse, however, they launched a "mammoth petition" they believed too big for Congress to ignore. Obtaining ten thousand names a day during the first ten days of 1877, they pinned high hopes on the process, as they recalled in the *History of Woman Suffrage*: "In view of the numbers and character of those making the demand, this should be the largest petition ever yet rolled up in the old world or the new; a petition that shall settle forever yet the popular objection that 'women do not want to vote.'"[36]

It too failed, but female activists clung to the petition as their only political recourse. The petition proved a mainstay of the temperance movement and other women's reform campaigns. One of the first political acts of the Woman's Christian Temperance Union involved submitting to Congress forty thousand signatures on a petition requesting the establishment of a committee to investigate the evils of alcohol.[37] Intense petitioning by the WCTU, concerned about the sexual exploitation of girls, pushed more than a dozen states to raise the age of consent in the late 1800s (it was as low as ten years in many states).[38] Louisiana women in 1879 petitioned a state constitutional convention to enlarge their civil rights, and Oregon women petitioned Congress to revise homesteading laws.[39] In 1882, twelve hundred persons signed a petition requesting that women be allowed to enter Columbia College.[40] African American women wielded the petition to protest encroaching Jim Crow laws and the convict-lease system at the turn of the century.[41] Such petitions were a "sure link between women and politics," noted historian Mary Ryan.[42] Although women knew the petition was a weak political tool, they optimized its utility as an educational and propaganda tool.

Nineteenth-century suffragists scored some success with petitions. Although the Colorado legislature denied suffrage petitioners a referendum in 1891, when women petitioned again, in 1893, they won a referendum—and the vote. Historian Beverly Beeton credited petitions to state political leaders with winning Utah women the vote in 1896. So many women crowded into the legislature to deliver a petition one day that they spilled over from the guest seats into the delegates' seats.[43] Suffrage campaigner Laura Clay oversaw the distribution of 1.5 million tons of petitions and leaflets prior to the unsuccessful Oregon suffrage referendum in 1906.[44] The National Association of Colored Women included a suffrage resolution in its petition to Congress demanding more equitable treatment of African American women.[45] Circulating a petition was a prime function of the American suffragists' first open-air meeting on New York City's Madison Square on 31 December 1907. While her three companions spoke, Mrs. L. C. A. Volkman solicited signatures.[46]

Twentieth-Century Suffrage Petitions

The first significant American suffrage petition campaign of the twentieth century began in 1908 with the call from the National American Woman Suffrage Association for a giant petition drive to Congress for a federal suffrage amendment. By then, suffragists harbored no illusions that Congress would act upon their petition. As Carrie Chapman Catt explained years later, the "chief benefits of petitions [are] the education which their circulation carries into homes, clubs, churches, and all varieties of community gatherings."[47] The 1910 suffrage petition was suggested "chiefly for its agitational value," and its ambitious goal was to obtain a million signatures.[48]

NAWSA offered suffragists' guidelines for fulfilling their quota of 100 names, such as setting the petition on a table near their doorway and having a pencil handy.[49] *Progress*, the NAWSA newspaper, published blank petition forms and apprised readers of the petition's progress. Three "colored" church women solicited signatures, it noted, one of white suffragists' few references to African American women.[50] Texas suffragists settled for asking each member to obtain at least 2 signatures.[51] Massachusetts suffragists gathered 678 signatures on Cape Cod and set up a petition counter at the suffrage booth at October's popular New England Food and Home

Furnishings Exposition.[52] They wheedled and charmed to get names. When one potential signer protested he had no address because "I am a wanderer, as free as a bird of the air," a suffragist replied, "Then why not put the place where you will light tonight?"[53] Women at the Minnesota State Fair obtained 1,288 signatures in their suffrage tent, gratified by the class of people signing—"thoughtful, progressive people." Many farm couples dropped by to pick up suffrage literature, but when they returned, only the husband signed. Wives refused, the suffragists ruefully noted, because they said they lacked time to read the literature.[54]

"The petition work is fascinating," wrote Emma Gillett. "I could easily get a thousand names if I only had time."[55] Soliciting signatures could also be maddening, as a Boston woman reporter discovered while covering the Massachusetts trolley tour described earlier. "I had to leave my camera in the drugstore for fear I should hurl it at the next man who said, 'Ain't no place for them. I want my wife to do my stockings,'" she wrote.[56] The National Petition Committee performed clerical work such as providing blanks, counting petitions, and rolling them up.[57] By April, NAWSA had collected 404,825 signatures.[58]

The campaign culminated in a procession of automobiles gaily decorated in NAWSA yellow to deliver the petitions to the Senate on 18 April 1910, exemplifying the petition's effectiveness as a public relations tool. Three carloads of newspaper reporters occupied an honored position just behind the NAWSA officers' vehicles and ahead of fifty cars lined up in Arlington for the drive up Pennsylvania Avenue to the Capitol.[59] The press prominently featured the procession in articles and photographs. Behind the reporters rolled the rest of the convoy, each car carrying two envoys from each state, its name on yellow banners on the cars' sides, the envoys' laps piled high with neatly rolled petitions tied in yellow ribbons.[60] An applauding crowd and an honorary committee of representatives greeted the women. After several speeches, the women split up to deliver petitions to their respective representatives.[61]

The petition had served as a valuable mechanism to enable women to enter the heart of male political power. Newspaper headlines revealed how threatening many men found the women's unabashed appearance. "Mile-Long Line of Suffragists Invades Senate," said the *New York World;* "Woman Suffragists Storm Congress With Petitions for Votes," blared the *New York Herald.*[62] The 1910 petition procession marked a suffrage mile-

stone: Decades after first raising the suffrage question, suffragists had finally seized Congress' attention. "The petition, the procession, and the
speeches made woman suffrage the most talked of theme for days," said the
Woman Voter.[63]

The 1910 petition procession occurred at the same NAWSA convention
that featured its first symposium on conducting open-air meetings, and it
preceded the nation's first big suffrage parade by less than a month. These
events revealed a growing confidence and assertiveness among women in
the streets. They pointed to the aggressive new direction in which the 1910s
suffrage movement was headed, a direction steeped in the historical ante-
cedents of the right to assemble peaceably as well as its related rights of
association and to petition.

State suffrage organizations turned to the petition with renewed vigor,
focusing on petitions to state governments for suffrage referenda or amendments to state constitutions. Soliciting petitions went hand in glove with
open-air campaigns: Connecticut suffragists gathered eight thousand signatures on a 1912 trolley tour; Nebraska suffragists announced a Petition
Day, when they descended upon vacationers to get sixty thousand signatures; Tennessee women petitioned their governor and legislature; Wisconsin suffragists collected tens of thousands of signatures; and Alabama suffragists handed state legislators ten thousand signatures. In 1908, the Equal
Suffrage League of the National Association of Colored Women petitioned
Congress to give women the vote.[64]

Exemplifying the petition's symbiotic relationship with open-air meetings, Atlanta soapboxers spoke for two hours from an automobile while
their comrades circulated petitions at a 1916 street meeting. Labor orator
Maggie Hinchey collected signatures at street meetings when the Woman
Suffrage Party sent her to Rochester, New York, to agitate for the vote.[65]
When twenty Maryland suffragists walked from Baltimore to Annapolis
bearing petitions, they concluded their pilgrimage with a soapbox rally in
front of the Maryland state house.[66] Petition pilgrimages became a dramatic way for especially dedicated women to demonstrate their commitment to winning the vote.

The concept of petitioning as a pilgrimage originated with a handful of
New York City suffragists who hiked 170 miles to Albany in the winter of
1912 to give the governor a parchment petition signed by leaders of the city's
several suffrage societies.[67] The women called the trek a pilgrimage, denot-

ing the sacredness with which they approached the undertaking.[68] In fact, the sole reporter to march the entire route admitted, "I became imbued with a religious devotion to suffrage."[69] At the head of the marchers departing Yonkers on 16 December 1912, strode organizer Rosalie Jones, twenty-one, of Brooklyn, an open-air veteran who had toured Long Island and Ohio aboard a pony cart the previous summer. Wearing a yellow hat and carrying a five-foot wooden staff, Jones fancied herself the "general" of an army that hiked to "get close" to the people—attracting unprecedented national publicity along the way.[70]

Open-air meetings and informal processions punctuated their arrival in upstate villages. Jones's comments to the *New York Tribune* underscored the relationship between the petition and the right of assembly. The immediacy of the hikers made an impression on villagers that would be unattainable if the women sped through them aboard trains. "When we march through with banners flying and leave suffrage literature for them to read in the long winter evenings," Jones explained, "suffrage comes to have a definite meaning for them."[71]

Because of its novel nature, the pilgrimage won priceless publicity—the *Woman Voter* somehow estimated its value at three million dollars' worth of advertising. "Probably a whole series of orthodox suffrage meetings would not have received the same amount of publicity in seven seas, as did this simple expedition on the open road," said the *Woman Voter and the Newsletter.*[72] Even the antisuffrage *New York Times* conceded that the pilgrimage was effective propaganda.[73]

The unprecedented amount of favorable press coverage the pilgrims captured for nearly three weeks highlighted the inestimable value of the petition as a public relations tool, especially when combined with novel approaches to delivering it. Ten reporters representing all of New York City's major dailies accompanied the party at least part of the way, half of them "front page gals" such as *New York Tribune* star reporter Emma Bugbee, whose pilgrimage stories often made page one.[74] Their participation showed how suffrage benefited women reporters, as editors saw the movement as a "woman's story" that required a female perspective. The presence of women reporters also benefited suffrage, because most supported the cause and pleaded with their editors to cover suffrage stories.[75]

Their sex, however, did not prevent women reporters from adopting the jesting tone that characterized most newspaper coverage until late into the campaign. "Stories were done in a jocular vein," wrote reporter Ishbel Ross, who published an expansive history of women in journalism in 1936, of the Albany pilgrimage. "No one took suffrage seriously at this stage, except the suffragists themselves."[76] The Albany pilgrims bristled at stories depicting them in a pitiful vein. "The modern newspaper reporter is a rapid fire fiction artist," wrote Jessie Hardy Stubbs, the pilgrims' "war correspondent" (press spokeswoman).[77]

News accounts often revealed the arbitrariness of legal protections for outdoor assemblies: Yonkers police fetched their mayor when the pilgrims showed up without a street-meeting permit, and the Rensselaer mayor denied them a meeting permit.[78] Finally, four survivors who marched the entire 170 miles (including reporter Sibyl Wilbur of the *New York American*) arrived in Albany after dark accompanied by four others. As they followed their police escort and a band single file up the street, onlookers cheered and fell in behind them until the line grew to two blocks before reaching the governor's mansion, where the women received a warm welcome.[79]

Within weeks, the NAWSA Congressional Committee announced a nationwide petition pilgrimage to deliver a new demand for a federal suffrage amendment to Congress. Under the stewardship of dynamic new committee chair Alice Paul, pilgrims crisscrossed every state to snare signatures aboard all manner of conveyance—by cars, trains, trolleys, canal boats, and foot. The New York delegation, which lumbered from Buffalo to Long Island aboard a 1776 caravan, offered the town that gathered the most signatures a special position in the fall suffrage parade.[80] Massachusetts open-air speakers collected four thousand signatures while barnstorming fifty towns, and future congresswoman Jeannette Rankin drove from Montana to Washington to deliver petitions she picked up across her state.[81]

NAWSA stressed that the pilgrimage's purpose was educational. "Automobiles bearing the suffrage flag and pennant will roll into town after town along the various routes," the *Woman's Journal* explained. "Their coming will have been heralded by the eager press; the pilgrims will explain their mission, unroll their petitions, and the crowd will be ready to hear and sign as healthy schoolboys are to roll up a snowball."[82]

Much of the petition's appeal lay with its personalized nature. The act of extending and signing a piece of paper gave both solicitors and signers a concrete way to demonstrate their support of the cause. At one chatauqua, the entire audience stepped forward to sign.[83] Part of the petition's appeal may have been that the act gave Americans coping with an increasingly impersonal society a chance to participate directly in democracy. Solicitors were also keenly aware that part of the petition's potency stemmed from its centuries of association with democratic principles. "They do not need to believe in suffrage," a Kentucky solicitor said of potential signers, "but merely in democracy."[84] Soliciting petitions not only demonstrated women's ability to comprehend democratic principles but their willingness to agitate for change within the system, in contrast to Britain's brick-throwing suffragettes. The *Times* contrasted the peaceful pilgrimage of the Albany suffrage pilgrims to British militant tactics.[85]

The 1913 campaign's value was considerably magnified by the publicity surrounding the ceremonious presentation of the petition's two hundred thousand signatures. NAWSA intended the demonstration to impress upon the Senate the popular demand for woman suffrage.[86] As in 1910, a gala automobile procession preceded the presentation on 31 July 1913. This time, however, some senators traveled to Hyattsville, Maryland, to welcome the pilgrims and send off the procession. "They usually barricade the doors and call out the troops," the *Woman's Journal* gloated. "But, then, no class ever made so picturesque or so determined a fight for freedom as women are making."[87]

Picturesque it was. Rankin's vehicle joined eighty decorated autos that roared up Pennsylvania Avenue to the Capitol, where 531 petition bearers delivered the documents to their respective senators.[88] Their efforts "showed the tremendous strength of the suffrage cause," the *Journal* contended.[89] Twenty-two senators spoke in favor of suffrage (three spoke against it), marking the first time Congress debated suffrage since 1887.[90] This milestone indicated the petition packed some political punch when wielded aggressively and creatively. Further, Catt believed signatures gave politicians tangible proof of wide support for suffrage. She believed petitions offset the "fatal effect" of hostile legislators' argument that women did not want the vote. "The only answer is a petition signed by a sufficient number of women who wish to vote," she wrote.[91]

The most aggressive suffrage petition occurred when members of the National Woman's Party picketed the White House in 1917, which will be discussed later. After some pickets were imprisoned, the NWP protested the infringement upon its right to petition the government for a redress of its grievance.[92] The pickets demonstrated the breadth of the forms a petition may take. But a judge hearing the cases of some of the arrested pick-eters said the president was "not the one to petition for justice." He sen-tenced them to thirty days for allegedly obstructing the sidewalk. "It was not the fashion to petition Congress in that way, to stand in front of the White House, the President's mansion, to petition somebody else, a mile and a half away," the judge reasoned.[93]

The most colorful and successful of the suffrage petition campaigns was the five-thousand-mile, transcontinental automobile odyssey undertaken by Sara Bard Field in the fall of 1915. The journey sponsored by the Con-gressional Union for Woman Suffrage incorporated many of the elements related to the right of assembly that eventually made suffrage succeed: petitioning, street meetings, parades, pageantry, and a convention. It also won unprecedented nationwide publicity. The expedition began at the Panama Pacific International Exposition in San Francisco, ending three months later at the White House, where Field presented President Wilson with a four-mile-long petition supporting the suffrage amendment.

The first signatures were obtained from visitors to the CU exposition booth, lavishly decorated in the union colors of purple, gold, and white. Two years earlier, Paul had created the CU to concentrate on the federal amendment. The cross-country suffrage petition was just one in a series of her grandly staged protests to force attention upon the suffrage question. Its purpose was to demonstrate the voting power of four million voting western women in support of their eastern, disfranchised sisters.

Field, Frances Jolliffe (who dropped out ill before they reached Sacra-mento), and two Swedish women who volunteered to drive their Overland touring car were waved off from the exposition palace amid great pageantry at the climax of the first Women Voters Convention. On the evening of 16 September 1915, ten thousand people gathered amid myriad gold lanterns, ubiquitous purple, gold, and white flags and banners, and women in native dress from nations where women voted—including China, Finland, Swe-den, and Norway. After a flurry of speeches, all formed a huge chorus that sang "Song of the Free Women," composed by poet Field. The crowd surged to the exhibition gates to send off the envoys and the half-million signa-tures they bore to Wilson.[94]

Suffragists appeared more eager to wave off the envoys than join them; the *New York Times* had reported that a hundred women in automobiles would carry the petition to Washington.[95] No one could be faulted for backing out of such an arduous undertaking. At the beginning of the decade, more than 90 percent of the nation's roads were dirt, and mostly gravel covered the remainder. That did not stop the first three transcontinental auto journeys in 1903, however, which inspired thousands of cross-country auto vacations the following year.[96] Field waxed less enthusiastic about the trip, and she implored the unflappable Paul, "Do you realize that service stations across the country are very scarce, and you have to have a great deal of mechanical knowledge in case the car has something break down?"

"Oh well," Paul replied, "if that happens, I'm sure some good man will come along to help you."[97]

Field and her companions were preceded by train by capable CU organizer Mabel Vernon, who rounded up the press, public officials, bands, and suffragists at dozens of stops to greet Field with suitable fanfare. Before the envoys entered a town, they decorated their car with the CU flags and the huge "Great Demand Banner," which read, "We Demand an Amendment to the U.S. Constitution Enfranchising Women."[98] Response was enthusiastic throughout the western states where women voted. In Reno, Nevada, a crowd pressed against the car to sign the petition during the first of dozens of impromptu street meetings.[99] Ten autos escorted the Overland to the state capital steps in Salt Lake City, where the mayor, governor of Utah, and a congressman welcomed them. Denver topped that when twenty autos carried the women to Colorado's gracious governor. The warm welcome extended into the disfranchised states as the car bounced through parades and receptions in Nebraska and Iowa. In Kansas City, Missouri, large street crowds listened to Field's speeches with a "peculiar kind of earnest curiosity."[100] Fifty cars formed a parade to the Art Institute of Chicago steps, where yet another suffrage chorus serenaded Field. Field conducted the largest street meeting ever held in Indianapolis.[101]

The journey was not all pomp and glory. The car got mired in mud on the Kansas prairie in the middle of the night, and throughout another frigid night the mapless trio wandered lost in a six-hundred-mile desert. "The utter desolation of the whole country and the fear that we would not have enough gasoline to get to a filling station kept us agitated and in a good deal of physical distress," Field recalled.[102] Antisuffragists heckled her in Chicago; a snowstorm blanketed their open-air meeting in Cleveland; one of the Swedish women turned out to be a recently released mental patient who threatened to kill Field, and the Overland's axle snapped in upstate

New York. They persevered, eventually rolling through Detroit; upstate New York; Boston; Hartford, Connecticut; and Providence, Rhode Island. The battered car was shipped by boat to New York City, where it followed a hundred gaily decorated cars that blazed a "path of purple and gold" down Fifth Avenue before Field addressed a huge assembly of suffragists in the Sherry-Netherland Hotel ballroom.[103]

The petition's transcontinental odyssey ended in Washington with a grand petition procession to the Capitol on 5 December, the day before the Sixty-fourth Congress opened. The Overland carrying Field, Vernon, the Swedish drivers, and the recovered Jolliffe led the parade, which featured twenty women carrying the first hundred feet of the petition, unfurled from the huge spool holding the 18,333-foot document. The petition bearers followed women on horseback from the suffrage states and women marchers from the thirty-seven disfranchised states, all clad in long purple capes trimmed in gold and bearing purple, white, and gold pennants.[104] A large delegation of congressmen awaited Field at the top of the Capitol steps. As she climbed them, the long petition borne majestically behind her stood out as a symbol of western women's political power, according to historian Amelia Fry.[105] Later, the procession headed to the White House, where Wilson had invited three hundred suffragists to an East Room reception. Field asked him to inspect the petition. Among the five thousand names added to the four miles of signatures since the Overland chugged out of San Francisco were those of ten governors and innumerable congressmen and mayors.[106] After Wilson inspected a portion of it, he said, "This visit of yours will remain in my mind, not only as a very delightful compliment, but also as a very impressive thing which undoubtedly will make it necessary for all of us to consider very carefully what is right for us to do."[107] "Oh, the women went out jubilant," Field recalled half a century later. "They thought he was going to back the amendment in Congress."[108] Wilson did—three years later.

Wilson's lack of action illuminated the limits of the petition; the president might flatter the women, but he did not have to respond to them. On the other hand, the suffrage petitioners' presence in the East Room signified the civic progress women had made since the days when senators refused to present their abolition petitions. The publicity and good will the petition stirred during its cross-country odyssey—in tandem with the petition's utility as a springboard for staging street meetings, parades and other media events—demonstrated its strengths. Together, all of these manifestations of the right of assembly and petition were a powerful force for suffrage agitation. As Field later wrote of her feat: "The national awakening was in a sense accomplished. Never has any suffrage activity had the press at its feet. Locally and nationally, this little gasoline flight across country and the message of loyalty to women which it bore has appeared in the papers in every form and in every guise."[109]

The petition scored markedly less success at spurring concrete political action, as proved by the meeting with Wilson. Senator Robert LaFollette expressed how implicitly demeaning petitioning was in his speech presenting Wisconsin's suffrage petitions in 1910. "I hope the day will come when it shall not be necessary for a great body of intelligent people to petition the Congress for rights of equal opportunity which ought to be permitted in this free country," he said.[110] Writing half a century later, even Justice William Douglas was moved to note of the petition, "Its futility may make martyrdom attractive."[111]

Suffragists had firsthand knowledge of how easy it was for politicians to ignore petitions from voteless women. One writer in the *Woman Citizen* noted that nineteenth-century woman's rights petitions always ended, "for this your petitioners do continuously pray." She added, "This continuously praying business has been overdone."[112] A remark by Carrie Chapman Catt after women won the vote revealed not only the resentment that smoldered for decades but the suffragists' acknowledgment that the petition was the province of second-class citizens. "We are no longer petitioners," Catt wrote in 1920. "We are not wards of the nation but free and equal citizens."[113]

Although one can empathize with how petitioning frustrated Catt, her bitterness should not mask its value as a public relations and lobbying instrument even throughout the final stages of the suffrage campaign. In her vaunted "winning plan" for a federal suffrage amendment, Catt required county suffrage chairwomen to circulate petitions to arouse public opinion and then to arrange for women's delegations to present them to state legislatures.

Catt had earlier orchestrated the largest individually signed petition ever created—1,030,000 signatures asking that the New York legislature schedule a 1917 referendum on woman suffrage following the state's crushing 1915 referendum defeat. Canvassers systematically combed the city for signatures. "They climbed stairs, descended into cellars, found their way into the homes of the rich and the incredibly poor, walked country lanes, left no section untouched," Catt recalled.[114] New York suffragists presented the petition with their usual aplomb, hosting press parties in Albany and New York City to verify the signatures. They carried the petition in the nation's last great suffrage parade on 27 October 1917, in which a line of twenty-five hundred women marching two abreast, each pair holding a placard bearing the signatures, stretched half a mile.[115] After the suffrage referendum passed by a margin of one hundred thousand votes, Catt surmised that Tammany Hall did not tamper with the vote because of the impression made by the huge petition, a service of no small value.[116]

Even the radical National Woman's Party relied upon the petition. NWP chair Alice Paul broke new tactical ground by staging pickets and other symbolic protests (all of which she viewed as a form of petition), and she continued to petition the Senate after the House passed the Nineteenth Amendment in 1918.[117] The contrast between the timorous petitions of nineteenth-century abolitionist women and the NWP pickets pointed out the distance women had traveled in the public sphere.

After the Senate approved the Nineteenth Amendment, NAWSA again turned to the petition to secure its ratification by the thirty-six required states. NAWSA ran a contest awarding one thousand dollars to the first state affiliate to reach its petition quota. Instructions to state leaders set out how to procure petitions to speed ratification in state legislatures.[118] Each county required an "alert, energetic" petition chair. "She must arouse the indifferent, awake the slackers and keep her workers on the job until it is completed," Catt wrote. She suggested women use the canvassing technique that worked so well in New York. Solicitors should obtain a map and list of enrolled voters as well as meet the political party leaders and key men and women in their election district. "Go to every house," she wrote. "Ten women can canvas an entire election district in 2 days."[119]

The petition's true value lay with its tremendous publicity value. Reporters relished colorful petition presentations that gave them a fresh angle for their stories. The suffragists recognized how the press lent weight to their petitions. "Remember that one of our most powerful allies is the press," Catt told petitioners. "Make friends with your editors."[120] Petition presentations by women in the halls of politics also reiterated how assemblies of women augmented the signatures' impact. Had suffragists mailed in the petitions, their effect would have been largely diluted. NAWSA recognized the importance of making an event of petition presentations. Catt instructed state leaders to stage a "Demonstration Day" after reaching their quota for petitions asking states to support the Nineteenth Amendment in 1918. State organizers were to exhibit the signatures in a vacant store or similar site to which they should invite the mayor and other politicians to inspect the document. Then they should carry the petitions "colorfully" to the governor so he would publicly recommend ratification.[121]

The petition's special role throughout the suffrage campaign was highlighted when Catt chose the activity as a metaphor to describe women's reaction to Wilson's unprecedented address to the 1916 NAWSA convention in Atlantic City: "Silent, unmoving, the audience stood, a spellbound living petition to the most influential man in the nation."[122]

The petition gave suffragists a much-needed forum for making their political demands. Laborious, frustrating, and as impotent as petitioning sometimes seemed to suffragists, they choreographed the most expansive and successful exercise of the right of petition in American history. It was no coincidence that so many petition campaigns of the 1910s ended with parades. Suffragists saw how petition processions made an impression that a piece of paper simply could not, no matter how many signatures it bore. As one placard read in a suffrage demonstration at the 1916 Republican convention, "One Marcher in Line is Worth Ten Petitions in the Waste Basket."[123]

⚥ FOUR ⚥

PARADES
Shoulder to Shoulder, Women March

In 1908, a handful of suffragists challenged a New York City ban against Sunday processions by marching in the United States' first suffrage parade.[1] By 1915, when more than thirty thousand suffragists strode up Fifth Avenue sandwiched between a quarter of a million onlookers, parades had impressed the nation with the seriousness and extent of the suffrage movement.[2] The spectacle of women marching down the streets was a powerful form of public assembly, and parades gave the movement its first national exposure. In the nine years between the first tentative march and the final suffrage parade in 1917, American women made the streets their own. The suffragist moved from a figure of curiosity to a recognized actor on the political stage, thanks largely to her exposure in parades.

Parades affected participants and onlookers alike. A sense of solidarity and idealism rubbed off on the women who marched shoulder to shoulder in vibrant, color-coordinated costumes, bearing exquisitely stitched banners of velvet and silk, or who rode opulent floats, costumed as goddesses or historical figures as bands stirred the air with marching music. "I think every woman who marched or rode in that parade felt herself near the border of the enchanted Land of Heroism," said one participant in a Louisville, Kentucky, parade.[3]

Parades also awed onlookers, impressing by their numbers, dignity, and pageantry. They helped debunk the stereotype of the suffragist as a hatchet-faced, desexed harridan by displaying a broad range of women, including professionals, factory workers, and mothers who appeared no less womanly for marching. The scale of the parades demonstrated women's organizational abilities and flair for spectacle and symbolism. Suffrage parades attracted reams of favorable publicity and provided editors with colorful fare for popular newspaper photograph sections. The nation could see that suffrage was something to be taken seriously—and that, if nothing else, would-be women voters knew how to put on a fantastic show.

Marching suffragists also experienced the dangers of taking their message to the streets. A 1913 debacle in Washington, D.C., erupted into a national scandal following charges that police stood by laughing while mobs spat upon, knocked down, and cursed women marchers. That parade was the most blatant example of extralegal factors that hindered suffragists' exercise of their right to assemble peaceably. Those cultural barriers stemmed from opposition to a female public assembly visibly more assertive—and supposedly more masculine—than even soapboxing.

Parades were a popular form of civic ritual that embodied the essence of American civic culture in the antebellum era. Patriotic and ethnic holidays became vehicles for unifying Americans through elaborate street parades in which politicians, militias, fire departments, ethnic clubs, and other fraternal groups united amid banners and bands. The Fourth of July parade was an "ingenious method of displaying a diverse social structure and a heterogeneous culture," noted historian Mary Ryan.[4]

Women remained in the background, sewing banners for parades (a skill they would put to excellent use in the twentieth-century suffrage struggle), decorating meeting halls, and preparing food for male gatherings. A rare exception occurred when sixteen young women led a local memorial parade in 1800 commemorating George Washington's death. Clad in white dresses, black hats and cloaks with white scarves fastened on the right shoulder with a black and white rosette, the women represented the sixteen states and led a procession of militia men, dignitaries, and a fife and drum.[5] Although early in the nineteenth century women sometimes attended rallies, they appeared in parades only as symbols. Female allegories had begun to represent political authority in eighteenth-century European ceremonies, and the female Liberty was seen as the antithesis of the venal monarch/patriarch. In antebellum parades, statues of female figures represented virtues such as justice or liberty or ethnic qualities. By the 1860s, real women enacted the allegories, like the Maid of Erin astride a horse in New York City's St. Patrick's Day parade in 1866 or the girl who sat atop a brewery wagon in an 1877 New York carnival draped in the American flag with an eagle and shield at her feet. "[Women] were easy game for incorporation as ornaments, dependents, or pawns of other identities," according to Ryan.[6]

Courts Protect Parades

Nineteenth-century court rulings protected parades for the most part because of their well-established legal and cultural roots. As the Michigan Supreme Court said in 1886: "It has been customary, from time immemorial, in all free countries, and in most civilized countries, for people who are assembled for common purposes to parade together, by day or reasonable hours at night, with banners and other paraphernalia, and with music of various kinds."[7]

Nineteenth-century court rulings also recognized parading as a form of expression, although the U.S. Supreme Court did not specifically state that parading was an activity protected by the First Amendment until 1969.[8] The Michigan justices denounced statutes that granted individual officials too much power to quash processions representing views with which they disagreed.[9] The Kansas Supreme Court emphasized the role parades played in democratic debate when it held lawful a Salvation Army parade staged without a permit.[10] An Illinois appellate court also tucked parades into the cradle of democracy when it threw out yet another municipal parade permit system contested by the Salvation Army. The ruling said: "Ever since the landing of the Pilgrims from the Mayflower the right to assemble and worship according to one's conscience, and the right to parade in a peaceful manner for a peaceful purpose, have been fostered and regarded as among the fundamental rights of a free people. The spirit of our free institutions allows great latitude in public parades and demonstrations."[11]

Legal protections in the 1910s appeared stronger for parades than for meetings partly because, as one scholar suggested, parades attracted a less disreputable crowd than street meetings.[12] Nineteenth-century courts demonstrated a great antipathy for requiring licenses for parades.[13] The courts' aversion toward license schemes was rooted in William Blackstone's *Commentaries,* a popular attempt to codify the common law of England that was influential on both sides of the Atlantic. Blackstone argued that censorship encompassed only prior restraints. Prior restraint occurs when a speech or publication is suppressed before it is uttered or published. If a parade permit were denied a group, for instance, that would comprise prior restraint. In the Blackstone view, sanctions against speech or publications after the fact were justifiable to preserve public order.[14] So if that same group paraded but unsympathetic observers rioted, according to Blackstone, the marching group could be punished for any damage caused by the observers.

Courts proved less sympathetic to Salvation Army marchers convicted under nuisance statutes that did not involve prior restraints. The California Supreme Court rejected a petitioner's request for the daily right to beat his drum and parade, for instance, and the Illinois Appeals Court rejected drum-beater Eliza Mashburn's First Amendment argument that her rights of religion and speech were violated when she was convicted under a city anti-noise ordinance.[15]

Parades by radical organizations were more susceptible to suppression than those by the Salvation Army, especially after an alleged anarchist assassinated President William McKinley in 1901. In New York, a member of the Industrial Workers of the World was arrested after leading a march to protest unemployment in 1914.[16] In 1908, judges on the Michigan Supreme Court upheld the conviction of Socialists for carrying a red flag in a parade on the ground that the marchers knew their symbol's display would "provoke violence and disorder."[17] The rulings reflected the courts' deference to police powers. For instance, when the Supreme Judicial Court of Massachusetts held it constitutional to forbid the use in a parade of any flag "which may be derogatory to public morals," the court explained that personal rights may be curbed for the common good.[18]

So although courts generally protected the concept of parades in the 1910s, rather rigid standards existed concerning the purpose or content of parades. The less threatening their message, the more confident groups could be that they would be allowed to march. Radicals and labor groups could expect obstacles.

Female factory workers became the first American women to parade in a handful of nineteenth-century labor disputes. On 7 March 1860, for instance, eight hundred striking women shoe workers withstood a blizzard while parading through Lynn, Massachusetts, accompanied by a band, musket-bearing militia, and male strikers.[19] The woman's temperance movement took to the streets a decade later. Otherwise, women marched only in the annual May Day parades of Socialists and labor groups.

New York suffragists committed a major cultural breach and faced uncertain legal protection when they first paraded in New York City on 16 February 1908.[20] At the head of the first American suffrage parade strode Maud Malone and British suffragette Bettina Borrmann Wells, last seen together launching the nation's first open-air meeting at Madison Square Garden that New Year's Eve. Borrmann Wells defied the police commissioner's denial of a parade permit when she, Malone, three other women, and one of their husbands set off on foot from the Progressive Union for Woman Suffrage headquarters on West Fourteenth Street to Union Square, where a dozen police officers and a crowd of one thousand men awaited them.[21]

When Malone stopped to speak to the crowd, police ordered her to move on. She then invited the crowd to follow her to a meeting hall on East Twenty-third Street. The indoors meeting was a concession to police, who had banned a planned open-air meeting in Central Park; the absence of music and banners was another concession to police.[22] Like the piper of Hamlin, the six suffragists walked up Broadway trailed by more than one thousand men and twenty-three women with police bringing up the rear. After they entered the hall, Malone elicited cheers from the largely Socialist crowd when she began, "So you see this law against a parade of this sort and an open-air meeting is to be the only Sunday law enforced in New York City today."[23] But police arrested no one, and the *Woman's Journal* later cheered American authorities' tolerance in contrast to British suppression of suffragettes.[24]

Borrmann Wells probably was inspired by her countrywomen's bold, colorful processions. As historian Lisa Tickner has explained, between 1907 and 1913 British suffragists developed a "new kind of political spectacle in which they dramatized the cause by means of costume, narrative, embroidery, performance, and all the developing skills of public entertainment at their disposal."[25] All of these techniques coalesced around the novelty of women marching in the streets, which was meant to impress the government with the magnitude of support for votes for women. The visually lush and symbolically rich British processions culminated in the Women's Coronation Procession on 17 June 1911, when forty thousand women in a seven-mile sea of banners, bands, costumes, and floats took over the London streets. British suffragette parades became characterized by oversized, embroidered symbolic banners of velvet and satin carried by contingents of women grouped by occupation, each with their own colors and uniform.

"For the time some of the pageantry of the Middle Ages came back to the London streets," said a participant.[26]

Their American counterparts were slower to take to the streets. As late as 1909, suffrage leader Carrie Chapman Catt remained opposed to parades, as did many suffragists who hotly debated their propriety. "We do not have to win sympathy by parading ourselves like the street cleaning department," Catt said.[27] Catt's reluctance to march mirrored most women's aversion to occupying public space in so assertive a manner.

In fact, when Harriot Stanton Blatch and her Equality League of Self-Supporting Women (later the WPU) organized the first sizable suffrage parade on 21 May 1910, to protest legislators' failure to approve a suffrage referendum, most participants rode in ninety automobiles rather than dare march down Fifth Avenue. The Equal Franchise Society and Political Equality Association declined to march, for instance, and both the National American Woman Suffrage Association and the New York State Suffrage Association warned that a parade would set back suffrage fifty years.[28] But NAWSA president Anna Howard Shaw overcame her misgivings and rode in one of the cars, and a new era in suffrage campaigning roared down Fifth Avenue.[29]

Several thousand women who chose to march behind the automobiles represented every profession and trade in which women worked. Forty banners with slogans such as "New York denies the vote to lunatics, idiots, criminals—and women" added more color to the procession, as did a band with women buglers.[30] The parade publicized suffrage on an unprecedented scale; in addition to ten thousand onlookers, many more New Yorkers read about the procession in all of the newspapers.[31] The parade served notice that Empire State women no longer would be silently resigned to legislative inertia, noted Catt.[32] She was converted to parading after witnessing a London suffrage procession whose marchers spanned a social spectrum from university women in academic regalia to chainmakers in overalls. According to her biographer, Catt returned to the United States "burning with desire to reproduce it in New York."[33]

The success of the 1910 parade spawned six more Fifth Avenue suffrage parades over the next seven years. On 6 May 1911, approximately three thousand suffragists marched; on 4 May 1912, ten thousand; on 9 November 1912, twenty thousand; on 3 May 1913, ten thousand; on 23 October 1915, as many as fifty thousand; and on 27 October 1917, twenty thousand.[34] The paraders' "public confession of faith" earned even their foes' respect for the suffragists' courage in standing up for their beliefs. "We now know that there is an army as well as Generals, and that it isn't afraid to stand up and be counted, and to take places in the firing line," a 1911 *Times* editorial said.[35]

By 1913, the success of New York suffrage parades inspired smaller processions across the nation from Bartlesville, Oklahoma, to Baltimore, Maryland.[36] In many cities, where suffrage contingents were a part of larger festivities, their effect remained powerful. "I never knew how necessary suffrage was until I saw the faces of the people who cheered for us and the faces of those who jeered," commented one suffragist in Louisville's centennial parade.[37]

Even usually decorous white southern women got caught up in the spectacle of parading. Arguing there was "no reason we should make a funeral of it," Madeline Breckinridge, a Kentucky suffrage leader, encouraged women to try colorful new campaign techniques. Louisville hosted the South's first suffrage parade in 1913. These bold public displays bothered other southern suffrage leaders, such as Laura Clay. "I find parades, 'hikes,' etc. are not popular with the main body of the people," she wrote. "I am afraid the suffragists are doing too much of those things to please the judgment of the plain people." But suffragists went on to march down streets in Waco, Texas; Johnson City, Tennessee; Lexington, Kentucky; and other southern towns. Even Kate Gordon of New Orleans, one of the movement's most conservative leaders, confessed to finding suffrage parades and similar demonstrations "exhilarating experiences."[38]

It is difficult to grasp today what a huge step it took for women to march. Women marchers had to overcome not only external disapproval but also internal injunctions against appearing in the streets. Parading signified a revolt against cultural restraints regarding female public behavior, especially for middle- and upper-class women. The 1910 dispute over automobiles in parades illustrated how huge a step it was.

The Woman Suffrage Party's reliance upon automobiles drew the scorn of parade organizer Blatch. "Riding in a car did not demonstrate courage; it did not show discipline; it did not give any idea of numbers of 'marchers'; it did not show year-by-year growth in adherents," she wrote.[39] The auto parade's effect was further diminished when the drivers sped off so fast they forced the mounted police accompanying it to a gallop.[40] In fact, women on foot trudging behind the cars made the greatest impression. Next year, Blatch barred automobiles to demonstrate the magnitude of women's power and unity. The only carriage allowed was reserved for suffrage pioneers such as ninety-year-old Antoinette Brown Blackwell.[41] Blatch's Women's Political Union sponsored classes in the art of walking, and marchers pledged in writing to complete the route.[42] An editorial praising a Boston parade that banned automobiles explained the appeal of petitioners on foot: "Walking is the primal, elemental means of getting anywhere. It is the poor man's method of moving about. Paraders in carriages or automobiles look too well conditioned to be needing anything. Their pleas lack the sympathetic touch. On foot all men, and women, too, are equal and on a level. They are in a position to ask for all their rights."[43]

Parades only began to gain acceptance when suffragists realized they could not forfeit the phenomenal publicity and visibility parades afforded their movement. Since suffrage predated the opinion poll, the only way women could impress upon politicians and the public the widespread popularity of suffrage was through demonstrations such as big parades or delivering long petitions, a form of protest that was much easier to ignore. Parades were great vehicles for showing the influential press that suffragists were womanly, serious in purpose, and existed in large numbers.

Enthusiastic front-page stories and special photograph sections indicated how pivotal a role newspapers played in the parades' success. Newspapers reigned as the most influential mass medium in the 1910s, and more general-circulation dailies—twenty-two hundred—existed at the beginning of the decade than at any other time in American history.[44] Suffrage parades forced the press to take notice, and suffragists owed much to parades for "the new seriousness with which they are regarded," according to the *Times*, which opposed suffrage.[45] "We may almost conclude that the parade marks a new era in the suffrage work," another article stated.[46] The *Woman Voter* marveled that the "facetious and semi-sarcastic tone" of previous newspaper coverage had disappeared by 1911.[47]

Thanks to parades, the press for the first time gave suffragists a national forum for carrying their message to the public. "Probably no group of persons ever secured so much advertising at such low rates," wrote one admirer of the 1915 Fifth Avenue parade, which cost fifteen thousand dollars.[48] Even the *Times* inadvertently advanced suffrage arguments when it quoted speechmakers at the mass meeting at the end of the 1910 parade.[49]

Press comment that the *Woman's Journal* culled from the major dailies spouted dozens of piquant details about that parade.[50]

The press played an instrumental role in transforming a Washington, D.C., parade that began as a debacle into the suffrage movement's greatest publicity coup to date. The inaugural-eve parade fiasco on 3 March 1913 showed how vulnerable women were if the state chose not to protect their right of assembly. It also showed how skilled suffragists had become in orchestrating publicity, without which the effect of even the largest demonstrations was moot.

Alice Paul chose a national parade and pageant for her first project as newly appointed head of the NAWSA Congressional Committee to demonstrate "in numbers and beauty" how badly women wanted the vote.[51] The official program's statement of purpose set forth Paul's radical agenda: "We march in a spirit of protest against the present political organization of society, from which women are excluded."[52] She believed a national suffrage parade in the nation's political center on the eve of President Woodrow Wilson's inauguration would dramatically announce women's political presence.[53] The first national suffrage parade featured seven divisions, including twenty-six floats, ten bands, and at least five thousand marchers representing women from all nations, occupations, and social strata.[54] Bringing up the rear of the parade marched a small contingent of hikers from New York led by "General" Rosalie Jones and "Colonel" Ida Craft, who previously had led the petition pilgrimage from Albany to New York.[55] The parade culminated in another first, a pageant held on the Treasury Building steps to be discussed later.

From the beginning, police appeared hostile. Police superintendent Major Richard Sylvester refused Paul's request for a permit to march down Pennsylvania Avenue as "totally unsuitable for women" on the afternoon before the inauguration.[56] After a public uproar arose when he tried to relegate the women to Sixteenth Street, Paul enlisted the suffragist wife of Connecticut congressman Ebenezer Hill to get a permit to march from the Capitol past the White House.[57] The women's success in obtaining a permit indicated the arbitrary nature of protections for exercising the right to assemble peaceably.

Federal authorities had refused similar parade permit requests, most notably Jacob Coxey's 1894 request to march through the city with his army of unemployed workers. Coxey had called the unemployed from across the nation to rally in the capital to dramatize their plight. After his parade permit was denied, Coxey declared his right to speak and to petition, assembling his followers on the Capitol grounds on 1 May. Police charged the self-made businessman and two followers with trampling the grass. The peaceful protest disintegrated, and the unemployed workers went unheard. "Their ideas were too disruptive of the status quo to be considered, and their presence was too frightening to be evaluated clearly," observed historian Margaret Blanchard.[58] The suffragists received their permit twenty years later at least in part because their ideas were less explosive, their presence less threatening, and their social connections more impressive than those of Coxey's Army.

When the police seemed unconcerned about protecting the women during the parade, for instance, Paul used another political connection. She and Elizabeth Selden Rogers, sister-in-law of Secretary of War Henry Stimson, visited him to request a military escort to help the police.[59] He agreed to put a cavalry unit on watch on the outskirts of the city, even as special trains from as far away as Chicago and Boston dropped off thousands of marchers at Union Station.[60] As Paul feared, police protection proved wholly inadequate to control the boisterous throng of half a million spectators, and men broke past ropes and surged onto the street. "Looking down the avenue the paraders saw an almost solid mass of spectators," said the *New York Times*.[61] The marchers had to elbow their way through the "solid wall of humanity."[62] White-clad Inez Milholland, astride a white horse at the head of the parade, cut a swathe through the crowd, and Paul commandeered an auto to make way.[63] In 1971, one participant still remembered her horror as the float she rode approached the din: "There was no division between the parade and the crowd, and the crowd was a seething mob of men who surged around the struggling marchers, shouting obscenities. There were few police in sight, and those who were in sight were making no effort to control the crowd. It was an obscene spectacle, and it lasted from one end of the avenue to the other; that is, it lasted for hours."[64]

Men spat upon women, slapped them in the face, tripped them, pelted them with cigar stubs, pulled them off floats, tore off their skirts, and cursed them. Crushed and trampled onlookers kept two ambulances busy for six hours carting between one hundred and two hundred victims to the hospital. Among the injured filling the cots placed in the corridors to handle the overflow was a seventy-seven-year-old man with a crushed hip, a three year old who suffered head wounds, and the child's father, who broke both his real and his cork leg.[65] "The police stood by and did nothing," charged the

New York Post, and the *Woman's Journal* agreed they "stood by with folded arms and grinned."[66] When Blatch appealed to an officer to check the abuse, he scoffed, "Oh, go home!"[67] "They would have taken better care of a drove of pigs being driven through the streets by some farmer than they did of us," said one marcher.[68] The Fifteenth Cavalry galloped up the avenue to break up the crowd, but the harassed marchers took hours to reach the Treasury Building, where the chaos delayed the pageant.[69]

Widespread indignation about the fiasco prompted the formation of a Senate investigating committee that on the heels of the parade heard 150 witnesses during four days of testimony about maltreatment of the marchers and police officers' failure to stop it. Paul charged that unnamed higher officials ordered police to allow "roughnecks" to break up the parade.[70] Senator Miles Poindexter listed twenty-two badge numbers of negligent officers he had recorded.[71] Major Sylvester blamed the fiasco on a manpower shortage. Although the seven-hundred-page Senate committee report largely absolved the police, Sylvester retired within a year.[72] Blatch's sophisticated critique of the fiasco sounded surprisingly similar to radical feminist analyses of the state a half-century later. "The women's procession at the National Capital was broken up and the participants insulted," she wrote, "because the State taught lack of respect for the opinion of women, for the affairs of women, and the unthinking element, the rough element in great crowds, reflected the State's opinion of its women citizens."[73]

One positive ramification of the mayhem was the sympathy it won suffragists. Newspapers across the nation roundly criticized both the mob and the police.[74] The *New York Times* denounced the "abominable ill-treatment" suffragists received while attempting to exercise a right "the legality and legitimacy of which [is] beyond question."[75] The suffragists' dignity under duress won them thousands of unexpected converts, dramatically disproving the antisuffragists' predictions the parade would boomerang. Their nonviolent resistance won the marchers favorable comparisons to the British militants in the press.[76] Not all press comment was favorable: The *Birmingham (Ala.) Ledger* blamed suffragists for failing to anticipate that "men are not always considerate in expressing their disapproval."[77] The antisuffrage journal *Woman's Protest* also absolved the perpetrators: "Washington is sufficiently far south for the existence of a feeling that the public streets are not a proper place for women and young girls to make themselves conspicuous."[78]

Although NAWSA president Shaw had reservations about the parade and believed the money spent on decorations and floats could be better spent elsewhere, the blizzard of positive press won her over. "All the papers throughout the country, even the most anti-suffragist papers, are keen and strong in their denunciation of the whole affair," she wrote.[79] Catt, who later as president of NAWSA disavowed Paul's increasingly militant tactics, also acknowledged the public response to the inaugural parade. "It taught many suffragists the world around that special events carried suffrage messages to the masses of the people as suffrage appeals to reason never could," she said.[80] Paul never forgot how the perception of suffragists as martyrs boosted the cause. The parade aftermath sealed Paul's future policy to always "keep the people watching the suffragists."[81]

Spectacle, Symbolism, and Solidarity

Hundreds of thousands of Americans watched suffragists as they paraded throughout the 1910s. Although processions were a powerful political tool for voteless women, the emphasis upon spectacle also risked the loss of the political significance of parades once the novelty of women in the streets wore off. To maintain interest, suffragists tried to make each parade unique.

A salient point of the parades was the number of professional and working women who marched. In 1917, for instance, twenty thousand women nurses, doctors, teachers, farmers, lawyers, actors, musicians, editors, factory workers, and others marched.[82] The appearance of working-class women alongside professional women and society matrons underscored the universality of the demand for votes for women. Blatch said the 1911 parade was a milestone because it replaced the notion that only an elite few women favored suffrage with the realization that suffrage enjoyed wide-based support. "The procession will not only move the public to a belief in our cause, but it will demonstrate that the supporters of our cause form a vast army," she wrote the next year.[83] The broad cross-section of women who participated drove home how women had assimilated into all aspects of American society save politics. In the 1911 Fifth Avenue parade, the participation of professional women, philanthropists, factory workers, the first woman civil engineer, and the most prominent woman mountain climber all advertised the modern woman's widespread sphere.[84]

One vital outcome of the parades was the solidarity forged among women marching side by side. "The march is a demonstration of the solidarity of womanhood," Blatch wrote on the eve of the 1912 Fifth Avenue parade. "Women of all ranks stand shoulder to shoulder, thus feeling the profound influence of democracy."[85] The Woman Suffrage Party described the 1912 procession as an "ocular demonstration that women are to be found in every walk and industry of life, and also that they are bonded together with serious determination."[86] The press responded enthusiastically to the cross-class spectrum in the ranks. The *Times* said in 1912: "There were women of every occupation and profession, and women of all ages. . . . There were nurses, teachers, cooks, writers, social workers, librarians, school girls, laundry workers. There were women who work with their heads and women who work with their hands and women who never work at all. And they all marched for suffrage."[87]

Beauty imbued all aspects of suffrage parades. The *Times* conceded a "keener appreciation for form and color" among women.[88] As historian Michael McGerr noted in his study of women's political styles, the suffrage parades "reflected a fascination with color coordination" unparalleled by male parades.[89] Contingents of women wore the same colors and/or uniforms to enhance their impact: women doctors wore green; wage earners, blue; artists, pale rose; actresses, deep rose, and so on.[90] Parade floats, gowns, sashes, streamers, and banners created a kaleidoscope of color.

Ubiquitous banners and flags flashed a rainbow bearing messages ranging from cute to combative. Slogans in 1912 included, "The feeders of the world want votes to lower the cost of food" and "We prepare children for the world. We ask to prepare the world for our children."[91] As the world edged closer to war, banners portrayed women as peacekeepers and nurturers. "More Ballots, Less Bullets" and "Government is Housekeeping and Homekeeping," said some of the hundreds of big banners in the 1913 Fifth Avenue parade.[92] In the 1917 parade, a month after the United States entered the world war, American flags predominated, along with patriotic slogans such as "My Country, I Am at Your Service" and "Our sons are fighting for democracy." Other banners quoted President Wilson's recent avowal of personal support for the federal suffrage amendment.[93] Catt's biographer said, "There were so many instructive banners the effect was like a walking speech."[94]

The 1912 parade was the first in which many women wore white dresses, which came to symbolize the suffrage parades and was copied by women marching for the Equal Rights Amendment in the 1970s.[95] Women trimmed dresses with yellow ribbons or their suffrage club colors. Parade organizer Blatch refused to make the white uniform mandatory, linking her decision to women's promise as responsible voters. "Any regret some may feel for lack of uniformity in their fellow marcher, should be outweighed by the thought that distaste for conforming may be but the promise of independence in the future," Blatch wrote.[96] Militant suffragists transformed the Victorian image of the woman in white from passive innocence to a symbol of militant activism, observed sociologist Marjory Nelson: "The woman in white became the heroic Joan of Arc fighting for Justice and Freedom."[97]

That woman in white most often was Inez Milholland, who epitomized the beauty and idealism embodied in suffrage parades. Most famous for portraying a radiant herald on horseback in parades in New York and Washington, D.C., in 1913, Milholland also portrayed the suffragists' ideal woman in several guises in a string of parades and pageants.[98] NAWSA touted Milholland as the "most beautiful suffragist," which combined with the lawyer's education and humanitarian politics made the Vassar graduate the perfect representative of the modern woman.[99]

Symbolism as well as aesthetics informed suffrage parades. A woman carried in a sedan chair in 1911, for instance, represented the helpless, old-fashioned woman. No one could have missed the stark symbolism in the 1915 parade of a band of shackled women in black representing the disfranchised states and a blindfolded woman in white representing Justice, her arms bound by a rope held by three masked men in black labeled "Vice," "Ignorance," and "Prejudice."[100]

By 1915, the press had ceded to women superiority in staging parades. "The female marchers and riders, as always, showed the hopeless feminine superiority in grace, decorative effect, art of representation," wrote the *Times* after as many as fifty thousand marchers tramped up Fifth Avenue. "American men seem to be rather shamefaced, at least self-conscious, in political processions."[101] Police commented after the 1912 parade that only soldiers were better disciplined in line.[102]

Blatch, the driving force behind popularizing suffrage parades, recognized how powerful an argument the spectacles delivered for the cause. "The stirring of our feelings, rather than an appeal to our reason, carries us to high convictions," she wrote.[103] Blatch and her successors strived to make their demonstrations assault the senses. As she explained the plans for 1910: "We wished to make the procession a great emotional appeal. The enemy must be converted through his eyes. He must see uniformity of dress. He must realize without actually noting it item by item, the discipline of the individual, of the group, of the whole from start to finish. He must hear music, as must each marcher, too, music all the time, if the beat, beat of the feet were to be kept in time and tune with the beat of the heart."[104]

Part of the suffrage parades' emotional appeal was the dignity with which women marched. Suffragists had struggled for decades to be taken seriously and used parades to point up their dedication to the cause. Organizers in 1912 cautioned marchers, "Remember you are marching for a principle," and they later congratulated themselves because no "frivolity" colored the parade.[105] "Be dignified, imposing and memorable," the *Woman's Journal* counseled marchers in a 1913 parade in Washington.[106] Plans to pair Uncle Sam with Columbia in 1915 were dropped at the last minute for fear "something grotesque" might be implied.[107] As marching lost its novelty, organizers worried women would drop their reserve and spoil the mood by relaxing, laughing, and talking. "We must march as crusaders with seriousness and dignity," they said.[108]

Suffrage marchers' dignity was most severely tested during the 1916 Republican Convention in Chicago, when more than five thousand women marched through high winds and driving rain from Grant Park to the coliseum.[109] From hotel windows, the women appeared to form a sea of bobbing umbrellas and soaking yellow banners. "There have been bigger and more beautiful suffrage parades, but never one that commanded so much respect," said the *Woman's Journal*.[110] One Republican delegate said to another, "I watched it from a window where men stood eight to ten deep and many had tears in their eyes."[111] The appearance of the first wet and bedraggled women pouring into the hearing room deflated the pronouncement of an antisuffragist who at that moment was assuring the Resolutions Committee women did not want to vote.[112] The next day the party adopted a suffrage plank.[113] A couple of weeks earlier, the Democrats also adopted a suffrage plank after NAWSA staged a photogenic, mile-long "golden lane" of four thousand suffragists at their convention in St. Louis, filling the convention galleries and cajoling convention crowds at nightly street meetings.[114]

Before experiencing such heady victories late in the campaign, most marching suffragists took their first step in line nervously. "Many of [the paraders] had never taken part in anything of the kind before, and were resolute, but a good deal scared," the *New York Times* reported in 1910.[115] The Woman Suffrage Party newsletter acknowledged that older suffragists found marching "degrading and undignified." Unfortunately, suffragists needed to shock the public to get its attention, it concluded: "They will not march because they want to, but because they must."[116]

It became easier for women to join the line as suffrage parades became less of a novelty. Suffrage leader and society matron Mrs. Frederick Nathan, for instance, who refused to march in 1910, joined the line in 1911.[117] The *Woman Voter* wrote after that parade, "When we march next year, as we shall, thousands who were kept from the ranks by conservatism or fear, will be found in line; other thousands will be there too, who were won by the spirit and enthusiasm of the parade."[118] They included millionaire Alva Belmont, who in 1912 capitulated and authorized her Political Equality Association to march.[119] Women marchers grew so confident that they violated the cultural taboo against women appearing in the streets at night in a torchlight procession that November.[120] Police were out in force when twenty thousand marchers carrying orange, pumpkin-shaped lanterns formed a "river of fire" that flowed down Fifth Avenue to Union Square, cheered by a crowd estimated at close to half a million people.[121]

Organizers knew the greater the number of marchers, the greater their impression. "The significance of the parade depends upon the number in line, and upon the geographical extent of the interest evidenced," said a recruiter who urged women to sign pledges to march in a Boston parade.[122] Recruiters also appealed to women's guilt. "We know that you will be ashamed when we march on," said the 1912 *Woman Voter* parade number. "We know that you will wish you had the courage of your convictions."[123] Veterans assured newcomers that the euphoria of marching in a great body of women united in a cause would quickly transcend their self-consciousness: "You have a sensation of being the only spectator present. It is as though everybody else were there in the flesh, but you were disembodied. And presently the sunshine, the clear air, the music, the forest of snapping banners creates a strange mental exhilaration."[124]

Religious references also infused women's statements about demonstrating for suffrage, and paraders frequently likened marching to a crusade. Borrmann Wells spoke of the "inner spirituality" achieved by women participating in public demonstrations—"a nobility which puts their actions on a higher plane."[125] Perhaps elevating suffrage to a sacred cause salvaged marchers' dignity and steeled them to take to the streets. Marchers needed courage, as ridicule was only one sanction they risked.[126]

Many Americans remained opposed to women demonstrating in the streets. "I hope the sidewalk falls thro' and you all go to HELL," one anonymous correspondent scribbled on a blank marching pledge form for the 1912 parade.[127] Miriam DeFord, who marched in 1910, recalled half a century later: "We got a lot of jeering from the sidelines, but we didn't retort."[128] Teenagers routinely hectored marchers. One suffragist contrasted the jibes shot at suffragists to the respect accorded fraternal organizations that marched wearing silly fezzes or behind an elk. "When, however," she wrote, "women impelled by earnest convictions resort to the unconventional method of a street parade by way of arousing public interest, they are subjected to the most denunciatory criticism."[129]

Pressures against women marchers were sizable. One company threatened to fire any woman who marched in 1911, and a Catholic school teacher was fired for setting a bad example after she marched in 1912.[130] A New Jersey community parade banned suffragists from its procession (they circumvented officials by trailing the parade in six automobiles filled with speakers who took advantage of the crowds).[131] Antisuffragists also indirectly threatened a boycott against Fifth Avenue merchants who decorated their shops for the 1917 parade, but virtually all festooned their shops anyway with yellow streamers and banners and put yellow chrysanthemums on mannequins.[132] The city board of alderman targeted suffragists when it attempted to ban daytime Fifth Avenue parades except for military, city, and longstanding processions, but it backed down when the WPU protested.[133] Cartoons belittled parades; the *Memphis Commercial Appeal* published one that depicted marching suffragists bearing banners demanding "More Mirrors in the Subway" and "Give Us Municipal Manicure Parlors."[134]

Parading remained linked to the specter of British suffragette militancy; even the admiring *Harper's Weekly* described the 1911 parade as a "cleverly contrived advertisement of a militant campaign," although it was perfectly peaceful and legal.[135] Many women abstained from marching at the insistence of fiancés, husbands, or parents. The blossoming genre of suffrage plays examined the domestic conflicts marching brewed. Two marching sisters in the one-act "The Parade," for instance, are startled to discover their mother joined the line unbeknownst to their disapproving father. "He has never worried particularly about the number of steps I take around the house every day," the mother tells them, resolving to announce her transgression.[136]

Women's looks and demeanor were of endless fascination to the public and press, an inevitable risk of placing themselves so prominently before the male gaze. Marching women found themselves trapped in the conundrum of trying to appear womanly but not too womanly. Although marchers initially had to dispel the myth that parading desexed women, it was not long before they had to counter charges they flaunted their sex appeal.

A 1911 *Times* editorial stated, for instance, that marching "by all the established conventions was distinctly unfeminine and therefore obnoxious and ridiculous."[137] Even admirers condescended, such as this *Boston Transcript* reporter: "Women naturally have a keen sense of rhythm, but Nature has fitted them to sway with the waltz rather than swing with the march, and many of them were called up to valiant, almost heroic effort to step to time."[138] A *Times* reporter noted without irony in 1912, "It was a very feminine procession, though some of the women marched uncommonly well."[139]

Because parading and voting were associated with masculinity, parade organizers worked to demonstrate the participants' feminine and maternal virtues. A wagon full of babies joined a small torchlight parade on New York's First Avenue in 1915 to show that suffragists were devoted mothers. Because their femininity was under so much scrutiny, individual marchers also took pains to appear feminine. One Grecian herald in the 1912 parade cooked dinner for her mother before marching to prove that she could be both feminine and a suffragist.[140] The press dependably latched onto parades' "distinctly feminine points," such as the pretty girls who tossed a crowd candy wrapped in suffrage messages.[141]

Parading Themselves a Double-Edged Sword

The emphasis upon femininity proved to be a double-edged sword. Press fascination with pretty suffragists focused the parade away from politics to physical appearances, as when a California newspaper reported of an early parade: "Judging from the delegation, the square-jawed, short-haired suffragist is a mere creature of a comic weekly, while the real thing is a vision of loveliness."[142] Popular parade herald Milholland endured questions about the relationship between beauty and voting and once said she wished NAWSA emphasized her intellect over her looks—"as that is much more essential."[143]

The press idealized women's femininity, but the very femininity that won praise also risked being patronized. Feminine marchers contributed to other stereotypes that equated a woman's worth with her looks and/or her class. The *Times'* description in 1912 of marchers as "well dressed, intelligent women" was typical and inferred that poorly dressed or uneducated women were less deserving of the vote.[144] Although the cause was aided by observations such as the one in the *Washington Post* that predicted the "thousands of clever and pretty women in line" in a 1913 parade would make people consider the merits of votes for women, the press's obsession with looks reinforced the message that women's sole value lay in their appeal to men.[145] The antisuffrage *Woman's Protest* was not totally off the mark when it noticed that the suffrage movement appealed to the "aesthetic or sensuous side of men, which in our opinion is even more dangerous [than militancy]."[146] Marching in parades subjected women to public scrutiny, and they were judged by male criteria. The gist of press coverage indicated women marchers could not escape categorization as sex objects.

The dangerous dilemma this created for marchers trying to please the male-dominated press and voting men who controlled their fate was that the women risked the damaging accusation they flaunted their sex. Usually paraders skillfully skirted the issue, but an antisuffragist stirred a small scandal in 1913 when she charged that marchers' flimsy Grecian gowns were intended to appeal to sex and not to the reason of men. "The sex appeal was flagrant and the dominant note in the parade," said a statement disseminated by the National Association Opposed to Woman Suffrage (NAOWS).[147] Women marchers dressed in a shocking manner that would have been prohibited five years earlier, another said.[148]

The antisuffragists probably were not merely imagining an erotic undercurrent between pretty female marchers and their admiring male onlookers. The dynamic probably was similar to that described by historian Jacquelyn Dowd Hall in her analysis of the erotic and playful nature of women's labor protests in North Carolina.[149] The revealing suffrage parade and pageant costumes, however, also reflected changing fashion standards more suitable for the more active women of the era. Women shucked off or loosened restrictive undergarments in the 1910s, and an unprecedented display of the female figure and limbs showed how women had begun to abandon passivity.[150] NAOWS president Mrs. Arthur (Josephine) Dodge was among Americans perturbed by this development. She charged that revealing parade costumes offered more evidence that a "sex disturbance" lay at the heart of the suffrage movement, and the *New York Times* parroted her concerns that the "so-called sex freedom" was associated with the suffrage creed.[151]

They were partially correct, as sexual freedom figured prominently on the radical agenda of the feminist movement that coalesced in the 1910s.[152] Most suffragists, however, had a much narrower agenda for social change than did true feminists. The exchange over paraders' dress was an expression of the tension that percolated about changing sex roles in the 1910s. During the years women marched down streets for the vote, for instance, Margaret Sanger among others stirred another controversy as she battled for women's right to birth control.[153]

As Dodge's protest demonstrated, some of the most vocal opponents of marching women were other women. Many women opposed the suffrage movement because they believed women's entrance into the political sphere spelled changes for women's well-defined role in the home. Some antisuffragists were public activists themselves (notably Dodge) who believed women's nonpartisan status enabled them to lobby more effectively for reform. These antisuffrage reformers feared women would lose their "distinctive public realm" if they voted.[154] Their criticism of suffrage parades went beyond flimsy costumes. They claimed suffragists selfishly succumbed to the allure of pageantry instead of tending to the more mundane business of social reform, as articulated in an essay in *The Woman's Protest*: "It is more exciting to attend suffrage meetings, speak to street crowds, walk in parades, and easier to believe in the fallacy that the vote will change all the evils in the world, than it is to give hours, days, thought and energy to quiet, persistent, unheralded work toward the amelioration of the condition of women, children, and the unfortunate."[155]

Although numerous, well organized, and well funded, antisuffragists found themselves at a disadvantage in countering the suffrage media blitz because they were on record as condemning public displays by women.[156] Antisuffragists also proved less adept at symbolic expression. They adopted wearing red roses as a "quiet, dignified" way to make their protests, for instance, apparently unaware red was worn by Socialists, their other nemesis.[157] One antisuffragist at the inaugural-eve parade stood on Pennsylvania Avenue in a black gown with a large scarlet *A* sewn on its front, for "Anti," she said, apparently oblivious to the literary allusion.[158] Suffragists capitalized on the antisuffragists' opposition to marching women by chiding their failure to participate in a 1916 New York war preparedness parade, an event that gave suffragists an opportunity to flaunt their patriotism.[159] Those antisuffragists who did march were denounced as hypocrites.[160] Suffragists joked that the antis' diatribes advanced their cause, and the Woman Suffrage Party newsletter ran a regular feature called "With Our Allies— the Antis."[161]

Among suffrage supporters, working-class women perhaps lent the greatest support to the parades. The Equality League of Self-Supporting Women, which organized the 1910 Fifth Avenue parade, was a coalition of wealthy reformers and factory workers that under Blatch's leadership had promoted open-air campaigning. Historians differ over the extent of the women's labor movement's influence upon the suffragists' increasingly assertive public demonstrations in the 1910s, but there is no doubt that working women were well versed in the power of women's public assemblies before suffragists took to the streets.[162] Many of the one hundred thousand women who walked out of factories in strikes between 1905 and 1915 participated in labor open-air meetings, parades, and picketing.[163] Months before the 1910 suffrage automobile parade, nine thousand women shirtwaist makers had marched to New York's City Hall to deliver a petition to the mayor asking him to stop police intimidation and abuse of picketers, a protest that combined several forms of assembly.[164] Twenty thousand women formed a third of the marchers in the 1910 May Day parade, at the time the largest number of women ever taking part in a New York parade.[165]

Double Jeopardy for African Americans

African American women also marched for suffrage in the 1910s. Racism required even more courage of black women than of white women to put themselves before the public eye. Perhaps the first African Americans to take that risk for suffrage marched down Fifth Avenue in 1911 when four black women joined the real estate division.[166] In 1912, African American women formed their own division and marched in black frocks with yellow sashes, and in 1913, a contingent of twenty-five black women "attracted wide attention" as they brought up the rear of the parade.[167] African American women were especially vulnerable to harassment when they participated in public demonstrations. A division marshal brandishing a flagpole chased away men who harassed a black girl in line in 1912.[168] African American suffragist Estella Hall Young avoided Baltimore parades because she claimed police harassed black women even more than white women.[169] Worse, white suffragists sometimes tried to block black marchers.

The maltreatment African American suffragists received when they tried to participate in the 1913 inaugural-eve parade in Washington, D.C., underscored the moral confusion and contradictions that riddled white suffragists' dealings with them. It illustrated the extralegal obstacles black women faced to assert their rights to assemble peaceably. In the case of the Washington parade, their biggest obstacle was white suffragists. Alice Paul and others worried that black marchers in the segregated capital would offend southerners and divert attention from suffrage. The *Woman's Journal* complied with the NAWSA Congressional Committee's request that it not publish letters raising the "negro question." "It will prevent the parade, ruin us and do nobody the least little bit of good—and least of all the negros," a committee member wrote.[170]

The heavy recruiting the committee did of women from all strata of society—including college women, professional women, and even Socialists—contrasted markedly to its pointed refusal to invite African American women's groups to join the parade. The Congressional Committee rejected a contributor's offer of fifty dollars if the committee recruited one hundred African American marchers.[171] "The feeling against them is so strong we must have a white procession or a negro procession, or no procession at all," Paul wrote. While declining to ban blacks to avoid a scandal, Paul instructed that the committee do nothing to encourage African Americans to march. Paul and others viewed their ostracism of blacks not as racist but pragmatic, proclaiming themselves "unbiased" in the same breath that they rejected black women marchers.[172] The only leading suffragist who objected to the racial discrimination was NAWSA secretary Mary Ware Dennett. She wrote Paul from New York headquarters, "The suffrage movement stands for enfranchising every single woman in the United States."[173] But although national headquarters wired Paul to welcome African American marchers, NAWSA president Shaw later told Paul she endorsed her position on race.[174]

Paul's plans to scatter among northern contingents the handful of African American women she expected to participate dissolved when the Alpha Kappa Alpha sorority of Howard University offered to march. "We do not wish to enter if we must meet with discrimination," sorority President Nellie Quander wrote, requesting a "desirable place in the colored women's section." The committee ignored the letter, but when Quander persisted, Paul invited her to headquarters.[175] Civil rights leader W. E. B. Du Bois later charged that the Howard women received a chilly reception, a point Paul privately conceded.[176] Marcher Ida Wells-Barnett, an African American journalist and founder of the first black suffrage club, experienced another ugly nugget of discrimination. The head of the Illinois parade delegation announced to members as they assembled to march that she had acceded to parade organizers' request that Wells-Barnett march with the "colored delegation" to avoid offending southerners, according to the *Chicago Tribune.*[177]

Despite these obstacles, dozens of African American women marched. According to the *Crisis,* black women were represented by "one artist, one musician, two professional women, one teacher, twenty-five students, three homemakers, one nurse, and one mammy."[178] Two white women offered to join Wells-Barnett in the black delegation, but when the parade started, all three stepped in line with the Illinois delegation farther down the line and completed the route.[179] Accounts differ of how the dispute was resolved between Paul and Alpha Kappa Alpha, but the *Washington Post* reported that a delegation of Howard University students marched behind women physicians and pharmacists in the "Education" section.[180]

African American women continued to persevere for the vote and their right to demonstrate on public streets. The following spring, fifteen African American Howard University students joined a smaller procession to the Capitol.[181] In 1917, a number of African American women in line marched in New York, including an elderly woman who trekked on crutches from Washington Square to Fifty-ninth Street.[182]

White suffragists' snub of black women marchers contrasted to the warm welcome they extended to men who marched in suffrage parades. The number of male marchers on Fifth Avenue swelled from 94 in 1911 to 619 in 1912 to 2,500 in 1913.[183] Hecklers hooted at them, "Go home and wash the dishes."[184] Governor James Brady of Idaho fortified his peers at a Fifth Avenue pre-parade rally in 1911 by bolstering their sense of masculinity. "You will find that the manly men are not afraid," he said.[185]

Slurs slung from the curbside were softened by the female gratitude showered upon male marchers. "It took moral courage for those men to get into line, and we owe them thanks," one suffragist commented in 1911.[186] By 1912, according to their grand marshal, the men received applause "from one end of the parade to the other."[187] As the men's division brought up the rear of the 1915 Fifth Avenue parade, thousands of women who had already completed the march waved and cheered them.[188] The press lavished almost as much attention upon male marchers as it did upon pretty young women in line.[189] That attention also served the cause, however, by making suffrage as well as marching for suffrage more respectable.

By 1915, the tinge of scandal that surrounded marching in suffrage parades had faded. Husbands marched alongside their wives that year, and young couples pushed children in carriages or carried them papoose-style in baskets on their backs, reflecting how respectable marching for suffrage had become. The cause had made so much progress that one observer noted it would "never again be necessary to make another such demonstration to show that the women were really in earnest in their desire to vote."[190]

They were wrong, as were suffragists in Pennsylvania and Massachusetts, where other big parades and a flurry of other suffrage activities heralded approaching referenda.[191] All failed, demonstrating the overwhelming opposition to votes for women that countered the enthusiastic shows of support engendered by the parades.[192]

Parades accomplished many things for suffragists and deeply affected both participants and observers. Marchers gained a sense of their numbers, a unity in purpose, and a pride in their organizational abilities as well as the realization they possessed the courage to defy cultural conventions and stand up for their beliefs. Like delivering one's first soapbox speech, marching in one's first suffrage parade became a kind of crucible. Marching down the street chipped away yet one more obstacle to women's participation in public life. Once women marched and realized they did not turn to stone, their sense of possibilities expanded both for the movement and themselves as individuals.

Parades demonstrated to onlookers the broad-based support that existed for votes for women, the women's dignified dedication to their cause, their executive ability, and their sense of grandeur that made the big parades successful spectacles. Staging demonstrations required considerable organization. The parades showcased women's organizational abilities. That helped to dispel assumptions about their limitations in participating in public life and emphasized the contributions they could make. Even though the *Times* opposed suffrage, for instance, it attributed the 1912 parade's success to the suffragists organizing and leadership abilities, desirable qualities in any citizen.[193] Parades forced the public and politicians to take suffrage seriously and won innumerable converts. After the parades started, suffrage became front-page news for the first time.

The parades also exposed suffragists to public ridicule and physical harm, drawbacks they succeeded in overcoming. The inaugural-eve debacle in 1913 showed how dependent women were on the good auspices of the state to exercise their right of assembly. But the women also discovered resourcefulness and inner strength as they verbally struck back at the state and won public support in unprecedented numbers. Suffragists, creatures of ridicule a few years earlier, became transformed in the public mind as courageous and dignified heroines. The suffragists' fear and physical discomfort seemed a small price to pay for the positive publicity that flowed out of the inaugural-eve incident.

The dangers of taking to the street were also compensated by the near-religious sense of solidarity many marchers described. The *Woman Voter* attributed the 1910 parade's success to the "nearness and dearness of the marchers, our own women all of them . . . marching bravely on the dusty street for a cause that they held high and holy."[194] The transcendent state suffragists experienced of belonging to a movement larger than one's self also stood as powerful testimony to the power of the parade as a political statement, spectacle for the senses, and as a form of the right to assemble peaceably.

Parades even added a splash of glamour to the cause, best personified by the "ideal woman," Inez Milholland. But the glorification of Milholland and similarly well-endowed young suffragists also pointed up the limitations of a movement based on sex. Marching down public streets placed women precariously under male scrutiny. Suffrage parades encapsulated the dilemma of the modern women's movement: Marchers tried to demonstrate they were the same as men and thus deserving of full citizenship. On the other hand, women had to demonstrate their difference based on sex to appease men. But calling attention to their sex was rife with risk for women. Although they appreciated being labeled feminine, femininity was associated with passivity and frivolity. Further, when their public displays of femininity overstepped the bounds of decorum, marchers risked an association with harlotry, as when antisuffragists criticized the Grecian gowns.

The emphasis upon appearances also revealed how little space existed in the suffrage community for women who did not meet cultural standards of appearances, class, or color. The most blatant example of the limits to suffrage solidarity was the ill treatment African Americans received in the 1913 inaugural-eve parade, discrimination that was replicated in every aspect of the suffrage campaign. The spectacle also masked the ephemeral quality of the solidarity achieved marching in line. Sisterhood dissipated after the vote was won in 1920, and women would not experience the solidarity of marching together for women's rights in such numbers for another half-century.

Parades had other shortcomings. The emphasis upon spectacle risked diverting attention from their political purpose. Even though hundreds of thousands of onlookers turned out and enjoyed the suffrage parades in New York and other states in 1915, for instance, male voters still rejected woman suffrage in major state referenda. No one can say for sure how parades affected those votes. Perhaps enjoying an afternoon of banners and bands did not translate into voting for woman suffrage; more likely, the opposition to suffrage was so overwhelming that even the grandest of suffrage spectacles could not overtake it.

Parades at least had placed suffrage on the political agenda, no small thing after more than forty years of stymied lobbying. They were a logical step after open-air speaking, in which individual women took to the streets to try to sway crowds. Parades, composed of large numbers of united women, possessed a different dynamic. Parades made suffrage sound more like a demand than a request, as it tended to be seen when a single woman argued the case before a crowd. Women, however, would learn it would take even more aggressive and elaborate assemblies to win the vote.

One thing is sure: The parades exposed the nation to the ideas of the suffrage movement and gathered momentum for passage of the federal amendment. They changed the suffrage image from dour to daring. The beauty, dignity, and scale of the parades provided suffragists with a distinctively feminine yet effective way to get across their message that women wanted and deserved the vote. Parades showed suffragists that combining pageantry with politics forged a winning combination.

PAGEANTS
Acting Onstage and Offstage

Twentieth-century suffragists used pageants to glorify female wisdom and strength and to project their vision of a future in which women would be equal partners with men. The allegorical extravaganzas inspired and empowered participants and mesmerized their audiences, relying upon emotion rather than logic to deliver the suffrage message. Just as the suffrage movement never would have gotten off the ground unless women had taken to the streets, certainly suffragists' appearance on the stage hastened public acceptance of the idea of votes for women. Suffragists also indelibly left their imprint upon this short-lived civic phenomenon because they were the first group to use pageants to agitate for social change.

Pageants were a particularly interesting form of assembly because they united civic enterprise with art. Embodying both a refined aesthetic sense and an earnest belief in populist democracy, pageants provided the perfect vehicle for the idealistic, spectacle-smitten suffragists. Pageants usually were held outdoors in public spaces, necessitating the cooperation of public officials, which sometimes had proven elusive for other forms of political assemblies. Authorities rarely thwarted pageant plans, perhaps because pageants were so closely aligned to entertainment, were perceived as a wholesome form of expression, and were tightly orchestrated demonstrations that seemed to attract a better-behaved crowd than did unpredictable street meetings or even parades.

Pageants consisted of a series of separate and distinct episodes on a single theme, the most common being the history of the community or group sponsoring the pageant. The episodes often were linked by allegorical tableaus in which players in Grecian-style gowns froze in positions to represent abstractions such as Liberty or Truth.[1] Sometimes pageants actually were processions of floats. Pageants relied upon visual cues to tell their story; dialogue was minimal or nonexistent. "The spectacle is of vastly more importance than the dialogue," an observer wrote in 1916.[2] Background music or Grecian-style choruses, however, were important elements. The use of a Grecian chorus, costumes, and outdoor venues linked modern pageants to the ancient Greek theater.

The pageant was the most democratic of art forms because its purpose was to unite factions by involving everyone in the community. Its advocates called the pageant the art of democracy, and the assembly of common citizens in an artistic enterprise for the greater good of the community was thought to instill both unity and idealism in cast and audience.[3] "The purpose of pageantry . . . is to create a desire for community expression through the drama," wrote a pair of its champions in 1916. "The ideal of pageantry is to give the community self-expression through a beautiful art."[4]

Their creators saw in them the vestiges of participatory democracy and individualism, virtues threatened by encroaching industrialism and urbanization. Although their idealism seems painfully naïve today, pageant advocates held high hopes this form of assembly could improve society by melding diverse groups into a cohesive whole through the orderly, wholesome expression of community ideals. Pageants strived to tie a pastoral past to a bright future and avoided controversy. Its optimistic nature made pageantry the emblematic art form of the Progressive era.

Pageantry's roots stretched back to the religious processions of medieval Europe and Elizabethan England. Pageants resurfaced in the early twentieth century as successors to the historical orations and tableaux vivants increasingly used to commemorate civic holidays and anniversaries in the late nineteenth century.[5] Louis Parker of England became the father of modern pageantry with the ambitious scope of his first historical drama on the grounds of Sherbourne Castle in 1905. Parker directed six hundred players, almost the entire community, and enacted eleven episodes depicting twelve hundred years of Sherbourne history.[6] Three years later in Philadelphia, the first large United States pageant took shape as an hours-long procession of floats carrying costumed figures in sixty-eight scenes to celebrate the city's 225th anniversary. Hundreds of American communities, churches, clubs, and schools staged similar pageants to celebrate their past. Pageants became the first choice of organizations wishing to spread their principles and win adherents to their cause.[7] Ideally, the entire citizenry of a town would don historical dress to enact episodes from the town's past or appear in Grecian gowns to represent ideals such as Liberty, Peace, or Mercy. By the 1910s, the populist appeal of pageantry had swept across the nation.

In contrast to other live entertainment, the pageant's impact upon its participants was more important than that upon its audience. "Artistic guidance is good, of course," the president of the American Pageant Association (APA) wrote, "but in this pageant movement there is a strong and right instinct that citizenship is more important." This focus upon the participants' response made the pageant an unusual and powerful form of assembly. The APA president claimed grandiosely that participants "will themselves, every one, be artists and voice their own supremacy over circumstances and fate."[8] This was an especially appealing and important trait for suffragists, who were struggling to shed their traditional mantle of passivity.

Even before pageants became a recognized art form, suffragists had reveled in pageantry in the broadest sense of the word. As their parades demonstrated, they gave meticulous thought to color schemes, the design of banners, and the overall visual impact of their processions. In a sense, the suffragists saw their entire campaign as a huge pageant. They were extremely conscious that not only did they have to catch an indifferent or hostile public's attention but also that their entire movement would be judged on the success of their demonstrations. Demonstrations had to be beautiful and graceful, to prove the suffragists' femininity, and they had to impress, because they reflected upon women's abilities to do other things. In her history of the National Woman's Party, Inez Haynes Irwin wrote that Chair Alice Paul always "visualized her work in pageantry." Suffragists were extremely sensitive to the fact that they were on display. Irwin also described Sara Bard Field's cross-country petition pilgrimage in 1916 as a pageant: "The stage was the entire United States of America."[9]

Suffragists began to experiment with transforming this safe mode of public entertainment into a vehicle for social change. In the nineteenth century, historical tableaus had offered an expanded role for women in public celebrations, both as players and, more important, as directors. Women pageant directors sometimes slipped into community pageants images of women that defied stereotypes. Mary Livermore and Cora Scott Pound, for instance, included a procession of women in law, business, and medicine in a Hartford, Connecticut, historical pageant they created in 1889.[10]

Suffragists went a step further, using pageants' powerful imagery to demonstrate that suffrage was the next just, logical step in women's inevitable progress. Despite the egalitarian origins of pageants, the first suffrage pageants ironically were tools of the elite. The first suffrage tableau organized by socialite Catherine Mackay and her Equal Franchise Society consisted of eighteen scenes contributed by the varied suffrage groups in New York City. Mackay may be remembered for refusing to allow her society to march in the 1910 and 1911 Fifth Avenue parades. Mackay, however, had no qualms about narrating the tableaus staged at Maxine Elliott's Theatre in January 1911, an indication of the greater social acceptability of pageants. The tableaus deified maternity, as had other suffrage campaign techniques seeking to reconcile voting with traditional notions of womanhood. The description of "Motherhood," a favorite episode modeled on Raphael's portrait of the Madonna, featured a crying baby. Mackay read: "The pathos of it is poignant. Raphael could have paid no higher tribute to the woman who was the love of his life than to leave her face as a living symbol of the noblest joy and sacrifice of womanhood."[11]

Some of the evening's tableaus ventured into more controversial territory, heralding unconventional women such as Revolutionary War hero Molly Pitcher and feminist author Mary Wollstonecraft. The most radical tableaus were created by the Women's Political Union, headed by Harriot Stanton Blatch. One showed two healthy girls spinning and weaving in an eighteenth-century home; in contrast, a second offered a slice of social criticism when it depicted bedraggled women workers shivering outside a factory.[12] The evening concluded with "The Spirit of Liberty," the bluntest reference to the evening's purpose, winning votes for women. The pageant scored a "great success" with the *New York Times* in part because of its high-society cast; Mrs. William K. Vanderbilt, for instance, played Joan of Arc.[13] The tableaus delivered the suffrage message less directly but perhaps more persuasively than speeches, because they used powerful images. Pageants were orchestrated so that audiences left feeling neither intimidated nor nagged but uplifted by the cause. The entertaining tableaus not only attracted a more diverse crowd than would a more dogmatic program but they also, not inconsequentially, raised several thousand dollars for the cause.

The next suffrage production two months later was bolder—the "Pageant of Protest." Maternal virtue again held center stage when Uncle Sam, a suffragist, replied to doubts about whether "woman" would fight in a war: "Try to take her children away from her and see." The players depicted "Our Cause," "Toil," and "Indifference," as well as pioneer women in all fields. When called to the stage after the curtain fell, author Augusta Raymond Kidder tried to soften her pageant's chiding tone by pointing out how much she liked men.[14] Similar tableaus were staged in other cities, such as "A Dream of Brave Women," by Emily Sargent Lewis at Philadelphia's Broad Street Theatre.[15] In Boston, two hundred suffragists participated in "Everywoman's Road," a benefit for the *Woman's Journal* in which Everywoman arose from the audience to confer onstage with Truth as women bearing the burdens of the past filed by.[16] In Nashville, suffragists capped off a May Day celebration in 1915 featuring a parade and speeches with a performance of the "Everywoman" pageant.[17]

As "Everywoman" indicated, suffrage pageants essentially celebrated the powers and capacities of womanhood. Common themes arose: Women endured hard work, were victimized by societal ignorance or indifference, and were hobbled by discrimination. But the superior qualities of women—hope, courage, honesty—would enable them to transcend these obstacles. The scripts offered an insight into how suffragists perceived themselves. Although downtrodden (represented by allegorical figures such as Ignorance), women had contributed to society (represented by historical figures such as Florence Nightingale) and would ultimately triumph because of their inner resources and faith (represented by Hope or other attributes). Positive, powerful figures almost invariably were female, such as Truth and Justice. A popular figure was Columbia, who in the nineteenth century was more commonly associated with the United States than was Uncle Sam, who began to usurp her role in the twentieth century. Pageants often used a "dream" as a plot device and in titles to convey their hopes for the future. The future in suffrage pageants always looked luminous—sometimes literally.

Beyond the bathos of suffrage pageants can be discerned a crucial step in the evolution of the twentieth-century woman. Women in pageants perceived themselves as heroes, perhaps for the first time and certainly never so blatantly. Significantly, women portrayed in pageants were not heroines awaiting rescue but heroes forging their own destiny. By making Courage

or Justice female, pageants in effect told women they embodied these qualities. This was an important message to women challenging authority. Suffrage pageants imbued women with agency, the sense that they determined
their destiny, by giving them powerful role models.

Pageants also gave women, virtually excluded from history books, a past
by glorifying historical female figures. Catherine the Great and Joan of Arc
were just two of the female heroes who cropped up in suffrage pageants.
Pageant players were actors both on and off the stage. The agency that
women depicted onstage translated offstage into action to improve their lot
and that of society, which was a far cry from the stereotypical passive female idealized by the nineteenth-century cult of true womanhood.

"A Dream of Freedom" staged at the Metropolitan Opera House by the
New York Woman Suffrage Party in 1913 epitomized the leitmotif of many
suffrage pageants. Garlanded girls in Greek gowns danced as the "Palace of
Truth" and the "Mountain of Freedom" rose behind them. The ubiquitous
Inez Milholland materialized as New York State, and a dancer lighted a
torch at the altar of freedom that was then passed hand to hand.[18] The
public responded enthusiastically. The "elaborate and imposing" pageant-
tableau attracted the cream of society, made front-page news, and was labeled one of the suffragists' "most remarkable affairs."[19]

Hazel MacKaye's Pioneering Pageants

The most remarkable suffrage pageants were produced by Hazel MacKaye.
Pushing the pageant form further than anyone, MacKaye broke new
ground by using pageants to raise questions about the depth of sexism in
American society. "Her work represents an ambitious endeavor to invest
mainstream rituals with social change messages," wrote historian Karen
Blair.[20] MacKaye maintained, "For the purpose of propaganda, a pageant
can hardly be surpassed." She listed its uses as converting followers, gaining publicity, stimulating members' interest and cooperation, and raising
money.[21]

The daughter of well-known playwright Steel MacKaye, Hazel and her
brother, Percy, also a famous playwright and poet, were among the most
influential pageant authors and directors. Working independently, brother
and sister differed from other pageant creators because they felt that pageants should address current problems as well as review the past. Both

were idealists who were sure pageants held the antidote to modernity; they believed pageants could alleviate the alienation that afflicted more and more people as machines dehumanized society.

Hazel MacKaye's faith in the power of pageants as public assemblies in retrospect was poignantly idealistic: Pageants could make labor joyful, Hazel suggested, because they required not just actors but also designers and craftspeople who would be enriched by contributing to a creative endeavor. MacKaye explained that the pageant "offers an outlet for that universal desire for self-expression for which the people, now that they have more leisure, feel a growing necessity."[22] MacKaye saw the pageant as "a great social force welding together ill-assorted elements in the community into a harmonious whole with a common purpose and a common understanding."[23]

She combined beauty with a call for justice in four major women's rights pageants between 1913 and 1923. These unique assemblies are important for several reasons: They portrayed women as strong and good; they showcased a woman writer and director's talent at a national level; they piqued the public's curiosity and won its admiration; they forged unity among participants; they introduced innovations to the art form; and they demonstrated the potential for splendor when feminine sensibilities were applied to traditionally male civic rituals.

"The Allegory," MacKaye's first suffrage pageant, is also noteworthy as the first national pageant on any subject. One hundred women performed on the Treasury Building steps in Washington, D.C., as the climax of the infamous 3 March 1913 parade on the eve of President Woodrow Wilson's inauguration. The use of a federal building for pageantry was another first, thanks to the "persistence and finesse" of Alice Paul, newly appointed chair of the NAWSA Congressional Committee, sponsor of the pageant. "Never shall I forget the excitement of that day!" MacKaye recalled later.[24] The *New York Times* called the pageant "one of the most impressively beautiful spectacles ever staged in this country," one accolade among many in the expansive press coverage.[25]

The committee had aimed for no less, as its organizers shared the Progressive era's faith in pageants' potential to uplift and unify. "We feel that this new crusade of our pageant-procession," said one of "The Allegory" planners, "like those splendid religious processions of the Middle Ages, will have the power to convert, to encourage and to inspire."[26] The *Woman's*

Journal explained that the pageant was added to the parade, itself an un-precedented monumental undertaking, because only pageants possessed sufficient emotional power to convey the suffragists' message: "An idea that is driven home to the mind through the eye produces a more striking and lasting impression than any that goes through the ear. . . . Here is a chance . . . to show that a woman's method of accomplishing a purpose may be distinctively and instinctively her own."[27]

The pageant was distinctively the suffragists' own in content and style. MacKaye's "Allegory" script was the least innovative of her four suffrage pageants, but its lavish production and lofty symbolism were representative of contemporary pageants. The Treasury Building's Greek columns jutting above wide steps leading down to a plaza made it an ideal venue. MacKaye claimed later she sat on the Treasury steps nightly for inspiration while writing "The Allegory."[28] It is instructive to describe "The Allegory" to illustrate its grandiose symbolism, splendor, and scope:

Columbia, upon hearing two trumpets announcing the parade's approach, appeared among the building's Greek columns clasping a huge golden spear, twenty yards of royal blue velvet lined with crimson and white trailing behind her.[29] She descended the Treasury steps to the plaza as "The Star Spangled Banner" blared, followed first by Justice and her maids, all clad in purple robes; then Charity in pale blue, preceded by two girls strewing roses in her path; Liberty and attendants, dressed in red, while a selection from the opera "Aida" played; and Peace, in white, who released a dove from her hands during Wagner's "Lohrengrin Overture." Finally, Hope tentatively entered the stage in an opalescent gown followed by twenty children in rainbow-hued costumes who tossed golden balls as they ran down the steps accompanied by Mendelssohn's "Spring Song."[30]

All gathered around Columbia to review the coming parade of women, delayed by the chaos along Pennsylvania Avenue. MacKaye sent word of the delay to Hedwig Reicher, a well-known German actress who portrayed Columbia. With a nod and a word to the band leader, who struck up "America," Reicher encircled the troupe and explained the predicament. Then the cast, group by group, wheeled about and retraced their steps as if the retreat was rehearsed. When the parade finally neared, they repeated the entire pageant for twenty thousand viewers, including three thousand who paid five dollars each for box seats in a covered grandstand erected across from the steps.[31]

A key to the show's significance was that it portrayed women as powerful and wise and still was deemed feminine. MacKaye's pageant said that women not only were lovely and graceful but also strong and just, in contrast to common associations of femininity with weakness and frivolity. The success of the pageants must have helped change the women's perception of what femininity meant. Participants and audience alike remarked upon how feminine the "Allegory" players appeared despite their participation in public ritual, until recently associated solely with men. The suffragists also used the pageants' majesty to refute widespread claims that voting would desex women. As the *Woman's Journal* noted: "To those that feared that equal suffrage would make women less womanly, to those who feared that in becoming politically free we will become coarse and mannish looking, to those who fear the loss of beauty and grace, art and poetry, with the advent of suffrage, the pageant offered the final word, the most convincing argument that human ingenuity can devise."[32]

To some observers, however, the pageant's sensuality illustrated suffragists' willingness to pander to male carnality. The antisuffrage *Woman's Protest* lashed out against the "exploitation of young women" said to have danced barefoot outdoors.[33] Suffragists' increasing theatricality also opened the door to satire. "Will women apparelled as Ceres challenge Congress to settle tariffs on cereals?" posed the *Protest* about postsuffrage politics.[34]

Yet the contrast between the suffragist's artful pageant and the militaristic display produced by men the next day for Wilson's inauguration parade served as evidence of women's superiority as citizens in the eyes of Percy MacKaye, certainly no disinterested observer. "No more significant attestation could have proved, for women, their claim to citizenship," he wrote.[35] Percy also contrasted the suffragists' authorized performance at a federal building to the arson to which frustrated English suffragettes had resorted.

Suffragists' use of the Treasury Building was a good example of the subjective nature of regulations regarding public assemblies. In this case as in others, the suffragists appeared to benefit from the system's malleability. Their male connections smoothed their path. Committee member Elizabeth Kent, who obtained the District of Columbia parks commissioner's permission to use the federal building for the unabashedly partisan suffrage pageant, was married to a California congressman.[36] The parks commissioner also heard from the wife of Connecticut congressman Ebenezer Hill—whose daughter Elsie was among the young women who planned to dance barefoot on the Treasury steps.[37] The suffragists' reformist goal and respect for democratic institutions surely eased granting of the permit, as it is difficult to imagine the federal government allowing anarchists to stage a similar spectacle on the same site.

The symbolism of the nation's disfranchised citizens performing outdoors in the heart of the American government, however, offered some evidence that democracy worked at some level. Certainly British suffragettes received no comparable offer to perform on the steps of Parliament. The suffrage pageant exemplified how, ideally, the right of assembly served citizens. It showed that a dissatisfied minority could make its argument on the age-old forum of the streets, where it could win adherents by the strength of its argument. Percy MacKaye believed it politically significant that the suffrage pageant made "victorious order out of threatened rout," a reference to the chaos along the parade route just up the avenue.[38] Further, the pageant served as an orderly release valve for the suffragists' pent-up fervor. Suffragists—at least in 1913—came to the capital to make art, not war. Their assembly embraced grace, affirmed the democratic creed of equality and progress, and relied upon peaceful means to effect change, a winning combination in the eyes of the political establishment. Several years of governmental indifference would accumulate before militant suffragists resorted to less pleasing demonstrations.

But in 1913, the warm reception accorded "The Allegory" seemed to justify women's growing confidence in the public sphere. Contrasted to the apple cores and jeers that greeted nineteenth-century woman's rights conventions, which were far less public or flamboyant than pageants, the acclamation the pageant received was a barometer of women's progress in the public sphere. The pageant's florid paean to female potential may have obscured obstacles to sexual equality so evident in the riot further up the avenue, but the significance of women taking over the U.S. Treasury—even for an afternoon—was a tangible sign of change.

Because the arts, like all facets of American society, were dominated by men, MacKaye's accomplishment in itself was a breakthrough for women. The pageant advanced women's emerging competence in public demonstrations by the unprecedented fact that the nation's capital witnessed a major production written by a woman, directed by a woman, and enacted by women all for the advancement of women into American public life. The Congressional Committee played up that angle in its blizzard of news releases. The "entrancing" pageant signified to the mainstream press the "ability and common sense with which the women are directing their campaign."[39]

As was the case with parade coverage, such accolades, although condescending, nonetheless benefited the cause because they attributed to suffragists positive traits usually ascribed solely to men. In parades and pageants as well as in other assemblies, suffragists attempted the difficult feat of transforming the meaning of femininity. And also as in parades, players walked a fine line between appearing too sexy or too sexless. Suffragists won praise for exhibiting "male" traits such as executive ability in part because the lush spectacles exuded a feminine sensibility that obliterated any charge they were acting like men.

Few plum roles awaited men in suffrage pageants. The few men cast usually appeared as oppressors, such as politicians, factory owners, or spouses. In at least one instance, men were recruited on the basis of their good looks, giving them a taste of what it was like to be treated as sex objects. Dozens of men applied to appear as "perfect men" in "A Dream of Freedom." "Believing that I reach all the qualifications for the ideal man, as specified, I take the liberty to write," wrote one hopeful. "I am 6 feet 3 inches, weigh 212 pounds, broad shoulders, chest measurement 40, waist 35."[40] Other men proved less willing to be scrutinized like cattle, and the ensuing flap over the reverse sexism spurred the suffragists to deny the charge that only handsome men interested them.[41]

That incident aside, pageants offended men less than suffrage parades. Unlike marchers, women in pageants lost their identities in the message they conveyed, a fact that eased women's first big step onstage. Women found pageants a comfortable form of expression, the *Woman's Journal* suggested, in part because they conveyed big ideals in a simple, direct, and clear fashion.[42] The emphasis on splendor and dignity also eased women's move into the public forum. Pageants advanced women's participation in public rituals, and in particular women's appearance on the public stage, because they provided a respectable vehicle featuring impeccable characters or ideals, which helped mask the transgression of women flaunting themselves so publicly. At the time, actresses on the legitimate stage were just beginning to shed their stigma of immorality.[43]

Suffragists in fact had already appeared in the theater to plead their case. Pioneering free-speech scholar Theodore Schroeder for one recognized the theater as a powerful forum for disseminating social messages. In the face of "vigorous censorship" that plagued the theater during the 1910s, Schroeder argued that theater deserved free-speech protection.[44] American suffragists shared Schroeder's view and argued that linking their cause with drama embodied the "true conception of theater as a great public agency for the discussion of ideas."[45] The Actresses Franchise League first performed playwright Cicely Hamilton's "Pageant of Great Women" in 1909.[46] As independent professional women, stage and screen actresses enthusiastically supported suffrage. Actress delegations also marched in New York City suffrage parades.[47]

Suffrage plays helped win over the influential middle-class and upper-class segment of the suffrage coalition, which could afford theater tickets. The atmosphere at these events was congenial, not combative.[48] Wealthy and well-connected suffragists unwilling to soapbox or march, such as Mackay of the Equal Franchise Society, were more amenable to applauding suffrage plays in the comfortable surroundings of the theater or hotel ballroom. So were their influential husbands. Indifferent individuals also might be moved. "The drama is a particularly effective avenue for stirring to new consciousness the large group whose inherited emotional prejudice inhibits their power to think on the question," explained an article in a special drama edition of the Woman Suffrage Party's newsletter.[49] NAWSA promoted plays as propaganda and offered its affiliates more than a dozen suffrage scripts, with titles such as "A Suffrage Rummage Sale" and "Cinderelline."[50] The more radical Women's Political Union sponsored outdoors and indoors productions of "Lysistrata," the Greek comedy Aristophanes wrote in 412 B.C. in which women revolt against war by refusing their husbands sexual or other services until they make peace.[51]

Bettina Friedl, who collected dozens of suffrage scripts, said the plays developed into a genre of effective propaganda that retain today the "passion, energy, and moral fervor" of the movement.[52] Pageants and plays frequently appeared on the same bill; "A Dream of Brave Women" was paired with a British suffrage play to help publicize the 1912 Fifth Avenue parade. Suffrage assemblies such as open-air meetings and parades translated well onstage. In the popular operetta "Melinda and her Sisters," the heroine mounts a soapbox and converts the crowd to the cause; the operetta ends with a stirring suffrage parade.[53] In "A Suffragette Baby," four suffragists who adopt an abandoned baby wave a banner and shout "Votes for Women!"

on their way to a "monster suffrage parade."[54] The *Woman's Journal* found the romance in Elizabeth Robins's "Votes for Women" anticlimactic to the staging of a suffragette mass meeting: "In this scene, the mob was well drilled and the ensemble effective!"[55] The varied forms of suffrage assemblies had caught the public imagination, and suffrage plays cast their influence even further.

Suffragists also experimented with the new media of moving pictures. The infant film industry had mined the suffrage movement with a deluge of antisuffrage satires, comedies, and newsreels screened in the fourteen thousand nickelodeons that by 1915 had opened across the nation, the vanguard of a new form of public assembly. To counter the negative images of suffragists in the movies, NAWSA and Blatch's WPU became movie producers. They made three melodramas between 1912 and 1914 that showcased beautiful suffragist heroines. "Movie screens provided suffragists with a national forum from which to appease the public's anxiety over votes for women," one historian concluded.[56]

Suffragists fell back upon the pageant, however, to advance their most biting critique of sex discrimination. Hazel MacKaye's second suffrage pageant, "The American Woman: Six Periods of American Life," was her most innovative and daring production. It was important because it transformed the previously benign pageant into a vehicle for offering social criticism.

The progression of the pageant's six episodes from tragedy to triumph shared with previous pageants the suffragists' vision of steady progress toward a brilliant future. Sponsored by the New York City Men's League for Equal Suffrage, the production featured five hundred players at the Seventy-first Regimental Armory in 1914. The first episode showed an Indian chief trading away his daughter; in the second, Puritans carried off a witch to be hanged; then colonial women worked alongside men on the commons until a town meeting called the men away; next Uncle Sam freed the slaves before Susan Anthony stepped forward only to be derided; then the "Law" waved men past the state portals but barred women.

Finally, the women heard the suffragists, who marched in flying banners. "The women fall in behind the ranks of the marchers, and follow them as they proceed on their way to further conquests," MacKaye instructed. The stage dimmed and Justice emerged from a glowing light to summon the man and woman of the future, the latter portrayed by none other than Inez Milholland. Justice presented the couple with a law book they clasped together above their heads. The states entered bearing flags followed by the Spirit of Freedom, surrounded by girls in gold, who joined her to "dance the triumph that the Future holds for Womankind."[57]

By pageant standards, even this triumphal finale was insufficient to off-set the anger and criticism conveyed in the previous episodes. "The script was biting, not subtle, and bared centuries of sexism endured by American women," according to historian Blair. "Certainly no pageant before this one had presented so radical an analysis of a controversial matter."[58] Although Blair claimed "Six Episodes" was too bold and brutal to win acceptance because the public expected pageants to be joyous and affirmative, at least some newspaper reviews were positive.[59] MacKaye's innovations in pag-eantry inspired radical writers to imitate the way she confronted social problems.[60]

Although radicals adopted her confrontational technique, MacKaye abandoned it for what she believed was her most significant suffrage pag-eant, the inspirational "Susan B. Anthony." This pageant introduced an-other artistic innovation, because it was the first pageant to center around an individual.[61] "Anthony" was first produced for the Congressional Union's convention in Washington, D.C., on 13 December 1915, to coincide with the convening of the Sixty-fourth Congress.[62] Although MacKaye had light-ened her tone, she prided herself that her pageant portrayed Anthony not as a mild little Quaker but as a militant.[63] MacKaye spent a summer poring over three volumes of the *History of Woman Suffrage* to write its ten epi-sodes and five symbolic friezes. Actress Flora Keys Hanson aged from twenty to eighty years in the leading role. Four hundred supporting players required more than six hundred costume changes to illustrate key moments in the suffragist's life, the most dramatic of which was when Anthony dis-rupted the centennial celebration in Philadelphia.[64]

The significance of a major production about an individual woman's life was substantial. Anthony was a bona fide hero among suffragists and a role model for women who dared take to the streets or join other demonstra-tions. One episode, for instance, depicted Anthony's arrest for voting. The reaction of one viewer showed how the pageant's emotional appeal packed more punch than purely intellectual arguments. "I feel for the first time," he said, "the fervor of the movement."[65] Even curious antisuffragists at-tended the "Anthony" debut, although they rejected the mocking offer of an honor box.[66] The suffrage movement intensified around this time, and its growing popularity can be attributed at least in part to engaging pageants such as "Anthony." Successfully blending education and entertainment, the popular "Anthony" was produced in many other cities by local suffrage organizations, unlike "Six Episodes," which apparently never was staged again.

NAWSA also got into the pageant business. It staged a tableau as part of its "walkless parade" during the 1916 Democratic National Convention in St. Louis. The tableau was the focal point of a mile-long "golden lane" of more than four thousand women in white and yellow through which delegates had to pass to get from their hotel to the convention hall. The tableau relied upon heavy-handed symbolism to deliver its message, perhaps because frustrated NAWSA leaders believed that was the only way to elicit a response from the politicians. Liberty posed on a pedestal at the top of a pyramid of silent women against a yellow curtain background on the Art Institute steps. In the pyramid, women in gray gowns represented the eighteen partially enfranchised states, others in white the enfranchised states, and still others the disfranchised states in black, their heads bowed under black veils and their hands shackled.[67] The tableau was one reason the party for the first time added a suffrage plank to its platform.[68]

This tableau was also noteworthy because a later production was subjected to the only official interference of a suffrage pageant located during this research. NAWSA tried to restage the pageant in Central Park that September, but because city officials forbade propaganda in the park, the park commissioner banned the tableau and a planned speech by Carrie Chapman Catt, then head of the New York state suffrage campaign. Officials did approve a concert.[69]

Those restrictions did not go far enough for the *New York Times*, which said no political, religious, or artistic propaganda should be tolerated in a public park. "There is no public forum there," an editorial said. "It was not designed for public meetings of any kind, and if the woman suffragists are to be permitted to hold political meetings there the Republicans and Socialists will naturally demand the same privilege." The newspaper's insistence that Central Park was "everybody's pleasure ground" exemplified the prevalent attitude that parks were to benefit the majority rather than a minority.[70] The ban demonstrated the variations among legal regulations concerning assemblies, as it contrasted with the Treasury Department's acquiescence in the use of its building as a site for suffrage propaganda.

Suffragists responded to the ban with characteristic flexibility and humor, publicizing the "kaleidoscopic" event that would begin with the park concert, move outside of park boundaries for a legal street meeting to be addressed by Catt and conclude with the tableau to be held at no ascertained spot. "It will pleasantly proceed to any hospitable spot which comes within the law and there it will station itself," a press release said.[71] In the end, fifty banner-bearing women in Grecian gowns—including the unsettling shackled group in black—gathered in a semicircle around the grandstand while the band performed. They maintained they were simply enjoying the music in the clothing of their choice. An audience of about a thousand gathered, and the police left the suffragists alone.[72]

When suffragists finally won the vote, it was no surprise that they turned to the jubilant pageant form to celebrate. After Congress approved the Nineteenth Amendment in June 1919, NAWSA staged a "Living Procession of Victories" at its celebration convention in Chicago.[73] And when the amendment was ratified in 1920, MacKaye scripted a simple pageant local organizations could stage to celebrate the victory.[74]

MacKaye's final and largest woman's rights pageant in 1923 had two purposes: to commemorate the seventy-fifth anniversary of the Seneca Falls Woman's Rights Convention and to launch the campaign for the Equal Rights Amendment (ERA) proposed by the National Woman's Party.[75] The NWP threw itself into inaugurating the ill-fated ERA campaign with its customary pomp. The pageant enlisted one thousand women who depicted the history of the women's rights movement on the banks of Seneca Lake, where illuminated barges deposited players after a gala parade.[76] When the pageant was restaged that fall at the Garden of the Gods rock formation in Colorado Springs, the presence of three motion picture companies foreshadowed the even more powerful images that would soon help make pageants almost obsolete.[77]

The 1920s witnessed an explosion in mass communications that eclipsed the novelty of pageants. The prosaic message and static presentation of the vignettes that comprised pageants began to look plodding and predictable compared with the sophisticated visual and aural imagery delivered by motion pictures and radio. Feature films with a complex narrative and cinematic sensibility had blossomed after D. W. Griffith revolutionized the medium in 1915 with *Birth of a Nation*.[78] "Going to the movies" became a national pastime in the 1920s, with ninety million Americans visiting twenty thousand theaters weekly by the end of the decade. Radio soon offered more competition for Americans' leisure time, and 556 commercial stations existed just three years after the first station began operating in Pittsburgh in 1920.[79]

Americans also became jaded about pageant forecasts of glory and unity after World War I exploded the illusion of the twentieth century as a march of progress. The celebratory nature of pageants was alien to a postwar sensibility that one chronicler of the era described as "a landscape in which the past is not recoverable and the future offers no hope."[80] In Europe, the idealistic promise pageants once held for communal self-discovery regressed into mass demonstrations for fascism in the 1930s.[81] In the United States, historical pageants evolved into outdoor dramas that continue today as tourist attractions, mostly in the South.[82] Instead of uniting women, women's pageants began to pit them against one another. Beginning with the first "Miss America" pageant in 1921, women's pageants veered from showcasing women's strength and wisdom to exposing female bodies in bathing suits.[83] Ironically, the beauty pageants sparked some of the liveliest women's liberation protests of the 1960s.[84] Both suffrage history and pageant pioneer MacKaye suffered a final indignity when an obituary in 1944 credited MacKaye as producer of the pageant "Susan B. Whitney."[85]

Neither pageants nor woman suffrage fulfilled their champions' promise that they would solve the ills of society. But during the brief period when the pageant and the suffrage movement flourished in tandem, they proved well mated. Pageants were less confrontational than parades, less cerebral than open-air speeches, and less exhausting than petitioning. But they were more exciting and entertaining and probably won suffrage many converts.

Pageants as assemblies gave suffragists a lot. They gave women a relatively safe but glamorous new venue for entering the public sphere. They gave women as a group a sense of their contribution to history and as individuals a vision of themselves as heroes. Pageants associated women with positive virtues such as truth, justice, and freedom in an era when female traits were often denigrated. The symbolism of women holding center stage in pageants was far reaching. Both literally and figuratively, pageant participants announced they had moved from passive roles to become actors in their destiny.

As spectacles ripe with righteousness, pageants also fulfilled suffragists' desire to assert in majestic style their perception of woman's moral superiority. The most aesthetically rich of all forms of suffrage assemblies, pageants appealed to the senses and affirmed suffragists' sense of themselves as the vanguard of a new kind of public woman. She was a virtuous woman who would conduct herself and her state with courage and style. Pageants as a form of assembly offered suffragists a celebration of themselves as public citizens—and virtuous women. This helped close the divide between the positive associations of public men as civic-minded and negative associations of public women as sexually suspect.

Pageants as assemblies also conveyed that image to thousands of Americans who witnessed pageants, read about them in numerous newspaper accounts, or saw them depicted in motion picture newsreels. Suffragists in return contributed to the pageant form. Hazel MacKaye added a new edge to this melodramatic form of civic assembly by using it to critique social problems. When the Woman's Party chose to open its annual convention in 1915 in Washington, D.C., with the debut of MacKaye's "Susan B. Anthony" pageant, it used the oldest form of suffrage assembly to introduce the newest form of suffrage assembly.

The daring of a handful of suffragists who in 1917 embarked upon the most aggressive suffrage protests, picketing and lighting "watch fires of freedom," can be indirectly traced to their pageant experience. The ripening assertiveness of a small but significant militant minority of suffragists involved in flagrant and dangerous forms of protest was partially rooted in playing or viewing such roles onstage. It was a heady experience for a woman to appear onstage in productions such as "The Allegory" as no less than Truth or Peace. Unlike the criticism suffragists sometimes received for soapboxing or marching, women in pageants seemed to hear only accolades. Suffragists took more and more seriously their personification of women as justice and freedom. That identification helped embolden them to demand the government give them the vote, just as the resurrection of powerful female historical figures gave them a role model for challenging authority.

❄ SIX ❄

PICKETING
Women's First Battle
for First Amendment Rights

The White House pickets organized by the National Woman's Party accomplished several firsts. They fought women's first organized battle to exercise their First Amendment rights, they were the first group of Americans to demand political-prisoner status, and they initiated the nation's first organized hunger strikes.[1] They also may have been the first Americans to picket the White House.[2] More than one thousand women from all walks of life and from more than thirty states picketed, burned copies of President Wilson's speeches, or lighted "watch fires of freedom"; 500 were arrested and at least 168 were jailed.[3] As women, the suffrage protesters faced double enmity, because their foes reviled the pickets' wartime demonstrations not only as unpatriotic dissent but also as unwomanly public displays. Local pickets wore veils and asked newspapers not to print their names, for instance, so that their male relatives could not recognize them on District of Columbia Day on the picket line.[4]

Yet the NWP prided itself that its protests were feminine—peaceful and beautiful—in contrast to the world war, which they believed epitomized male violence. "The NWP always has beauty and a serious lesson to offer the onlooking public," one member wrote.[5] The women never resorted to violence despite the many attacks upon them.

In fact, the one truly original contribution Americans made to suffrage campaigning was their nonviolent political protests. The decision to invoke nonviolent protest was not only a canny publicity stroke but also a testament of faith and courage that gave the picketers unassailable moral strength. The Wilson administration learned the hard way about the moral invincibility of nonviolent protest, as would British colonialists in India and segregationists in the American South. The administration's repression of the NWP protests represented the nadir of official infringement upon American suffragists' right to assemble peaceably. At one point, authorities secretly locked Alice Paul into a prison psychiatric ward and nailed her windows shut.

The suffrage picketing had a precedent in that great woman's mass movement of the nineteenth century, the Woman's Temperance Crusade, according to historian Ruth Bordin, when some women picketed liquor outlets.[6] Both temperance and suffrage picketing occurred decades before the United States Supreme Court ruled the First Amendment protected picketing as a form of symbolic expression,[7] a way of communicating ideas and reaching the mind and the conscience of others.[8] Lower courts, however, had occasionally deemed picketing as protected free speech in more than fifty rulings, and most courts noted a connection between picketing and free speech even if they ruled against pickets.[9] Other judges agreed with the federal court in Iowa that ruled picketing per se illegal. "There is and can be no such thing as peaceful picketing, any more than there can be chaste vulgarity, or peaceful mobbing, or lawful lynching," the ruling stated.[10]

At the start of the 1910s, picketing sparked some of the decade's bloodiest battles between police and striking workers for whom the picket line was a favorite tool. Working women, who marched in the labor's first moving picket line, also experienced that violence.[11] Authorities turned fire hoses on picketing women strikers in Aberdeen, Washington, and picketing women were arrested with their children in Duluth, Minnesota.[12] Such battles instigated passage of the Clayton Anti-Trust Act of 1914 to protect the rights of union members.[13] The White House pickets believed the Clayton Act protected their protests.[14]

The harsh treatment the suffrage pickets faced fades in comparison to the fate of more than one thousand dissidents convicted during World War I under the federal espionage and sedition laws for protesting the draft, counseling conscientious objectors, or criticizing the government.[15] Many were sentenced to ten to twenty years in prison. The post office shut down the Socialist magazine *Masses* for criticizing the war, anarchist Emma Goldman was deported for making an antiwar speech, and Eugene Debs, who garnered a million votes for president on the Socialist Party ticket in

1912, was sentenced to two concurrent ten-year prison terms for making an antiwar speech.[16] "You can't even collect your thoughts without getting arrested for unlawful assemblage," complained *Masses* editor Max Eastman.[17]

One positive outcome of this dark period in American history was that the widespread repression forced many Americans for the first time to consider the practical meaning of free speech. Legal scholars opened the debate about free speech in the 1910s. Ironically, they began calling for broader First Amendment freedoms just before the war persuaded authorities to clamp down on free speech. The American Civil Liberties Union, created in 1920, grew out of the public's raised consciousness about civil liberties. It would take the United States Supreme Court more than a decade to catch up with the new, enlightened view of free speech.[18]

The Woman's Party contribution to the free-speech debate has been overlooked, although questions the pickets' imprisonment raised about the rights of free speech, assembly, and petition stirred debate across the nation. The pickets' gender and class proved to be a double-edged sword: their elite status offered them some protection from legal prosecution, but they were vulnerable to social sanctions. In this regard, they had more to lose than the anarchists and Socialists, because they enjoyed the privileges accorded educated members of the middle and upper classes. Outrageous public behavior could spell social ostracism. The suffrage pickets risked additional censure because they were women behaving unconventionally in public. People might get used to women speaking on soapboxes, but going to jail unquestionably exceeded the bounds (and bonds) of propriety. The women jeopardized not only their physical freedom but also their respectability. The *New York Times* underscored its disapproval of picketing, for instance, with the jibe that not even the reviled Industrial Workers of the World would pull such a stunt, because "there is something in the masculine mind that would shrink from a thing so compounded of pettiness and monstrosity."[19]

Suffrage historian Eleanor Flexner placed the pickets "among the earliest victims of the abrogation of civil liberties in wartime."[20] Historian William O'Neill agreed: "No other group of suffragists risked as much or suffered as much as they, nor demonstrated so much courage, resolution, and gallantry."[21] Yet free-speech scholars have virtually ignored the NWP.[22] The White House picketing has only recently been described in any detail by two sympathetic books that contend NWP militancy played a significant role in hastening approval of the woman suffrage amendment.[23]

The NWP, headed by Paul, was the product of the merger in March 1917 of the scrappy Congressional Union, an independent entity since the National American Woman Suffrage Association (NAWSA) cast it out in 1914, and the Woman's Party of Western Voters (WP), a political party of voting women the CU organized in June 1916.[24] The WP and CU campaigned in 1914 and 1916 against all Democratic candidates in the suffrage states, a strategy that further alienated the NAWSA. That strategy fared better in 1914 than in 1916, when peace candidate Wilson won all twelve suffrage states save Oregon and Illinois despite the deployment of a "Suffrage Special" train filled with the WP's best speakers that barnstormed fifty western cities in five weeks.[25]

The greatest loss of the western campaign was Inez Milholland. The thirty-year-old suffrage star collapsed on 22 October 1916, during a speech in Los Angeles, supposedly as she gasped, "Mr. President, how long must women wait for liberty?"[26] Milholland, who had been warned by her doctor not to travel because she was anemic, was rushed to a hospital, where she died a month later. She was mourned nationally as a martyr and continued to figure in suffrage protests even after her death.[27]

On 8 January 1917, the CU sent an Inez Milholland Memorial Deputation of three hundred women to call upon President Wilson.[28] The string of rebuffs of previous delegations had exhausted and frustrated CU members, and the death of Milholland, their vibrant symbol of triumphant womanhood, further darkened their mood. CU leaders had determined to intensify their protests so that Wilson could no longer dismiss them so easily.

The Milholland delegation was something of a ruse, because the CU executive committee had decided several days earlier to station pickets at the White House gates. It believed only such a radical gesture could keep the federal suffrage amendment before the public eye and keep pressure on Wilson.[29] It had become harder to gain priceless publicity as war news from Europe crowded suffrage off the front pages of newspapers. The CU leaders expected Wilson to rebuff them, and his intransigence opened the door for one of the most dramatic episodes of civil disobedience in American history.

The White House Picket Line

The small band of aggressive White House pickets broke from previous suffrage tactics. They no longer were interested in educating men, as soapbox orators attempted to do, or in pleasing men, as did beautiful marching women, or in impressing men, the intention of petition drives. Harriot Stanton Blatch expressed their changing mood when she earlier told Wilson that she, the driving force behind the open-air campaign, no longer "would stand on street corners and ask the vote from every Tom, Dick, and Harry."[30] The pickets came directly to the paramount symbol of American male power. They not only did not care if they were perceived as unwomanly but also hoped to offend and provoke the male political establishment.[31] The pickets represented a critical movement to male seats of power and a daring new militancy in suffrage tactics.

When the Milholland delegation returned to CU headquarters at nearby Cameron House, Blatch suggested that women stand at the White House gates with banners.[32] Blatch's WPU in New York had already borrowed the tactic from the Women's Freedom League in London, which stationed pairs of silent pickets at the door of the House of Commons for nearly all of 1909.[33] In 1912, the WPU had stationed two "silent sentinels" outside the legislature's Judiciary Committee room in Albany to protest its inaction.[34] Antisuffragists also had stationed silent protesters wearing their emblem of red roses in legislative galleries as a quiet, ladylike way to make their point.[35]

The most aggressive suffragists had been moving to more visible and brazen protests throughout the decade. A group of university women in caps and gowns sat in silent protest in a New York City naturalization court while about thirty immigrants received citizenship papers granting the vote.[36] New York City Woman Suffrage Party members held up placards at the polls the day of the unsuccessful 1915 suffrage referendum.[37] Just weeks before the White House picketing began, Tennessee suffragists marched into the state capitol to stage a silent demonstration at a farmers' convention after it refused their request to address the group. They hoisted banners and posters promoting their "tabooed cause" as they stood in a half circle in the middle of the men.[38] Clearly, women were determined to bring their message to the heart of the male political establishment. The CU and WP shifted gears from trying to sway authority to defying authority.

American suffragists' most radical use of the assembly clause began the morning of 10 January 1917. A dozen women marched from WP headquarters to the White House. Groups of three stood on each side of both the west gate and the east gate. Two women bore the organization's purple, white, and gold flags on either side of the third woman, who clutched a pole attached to a big banner.[39] One read: MR. PRESIDENT, WHAT WILL YOU

DO FOR WOMAN SUFFRAGE? The other repeated Milholland's final speech:
HOW LONG MUST WOMEN WAIT FOR LIBERTY?[40]

The "perpetual delegation" continued day after day, in snow and rain.
The *New York Times* labeled the protest silly, others called the pickets unwomanly, and the National Association Opposed to Woman Suffrage denounced it for inviting an assassination attempt upon Wilson.[41] But most
passersby offered good-natured encouragement, and the president politely
tipped his hat when his car drove by.[42] Other than the act of picketing itself,
the pickets behaved in a completely ladylike manner—"demure and silent,"
pointed out the *Suffragist,* the weekly newspaper published by the CU.[43]
The CU inaugurated special events such as state days to keep up interest.
College Day, Patriotic Day, Lincoln Day, Susan B. Anthony Day, and Voters
Day followed. Other days featured wage-earning women, teachers, doctors, and lawyers.[44]

Picketing bonded the women and was as cathartic for participants as it
was communicative. "There were twenty of us at that gate, all kinds of
women, business, society, professional, but all there for just one thing: to
make a demand for political freedom," one picketer said.[45] Mary Church
Terrell, president of the National Association of Colored Women, and her
daughter, Phyllis, were among the early pickets. The elder Terrell remembered standing on hot bricks to keep her feet warm.[46] Women from all races,
religions, and regions participated, including southerners Alice Cosu of
New Orleans and seventy-three-year-old Mary Nolan of Florida.[47] When
their shift ended, the women gathered at Cameron House for picket teas to
share stories.[48] Like earlier suffrage assemblies, this one also took on the
aura of a crusade. "I wonder if you realize the medieval spectacle you young
women present," said one woman caught up in the "truly religious spirit"
that pervaded the line on Susan B. Anthony Day. "You have made us realize
that this cause is a crusade."[49]

The legal status of the unprecedented protest was uncertain. Newspapers quoted unnamed District officials who offered inconsistent explana-
tions about the legality of the activity: Because the banners were not adver-
tisements, a permit was unnecessary; as long as the women kept moving
(which they did not), they would be unbothered; unless they caused a disturbance, they were within their rights.[50] District authorities grew more
agitated as war drew nearer and the picket line settled in. Friction increased
on 4 March, when at least four hundred banner-bearing women in an icy

rain marched four times around the White House to try to deliver resolutions to the president. Police officers every fifty feet guarded the building, all of the gates were locked, and guards refused the resolutions.[51] After Wilson declared war on 6 April 1917, relations deteriorated further as wartime hysteria poisoned the atmosphere.

The District of Columbia police chief warned Paul that future pickets would face arrest. Paul refused to stop the pickets, asserting that lawyers had advised her the women had a right to picket. The pickets also refused to bow to criticism they were bothering a chief executive preoccupied by world war.[52] Paul warned pickets to be prepared to go to jail. She recalled later, "That's when our militancy really began." [53]

On 20 June, two pickets sparked a small riot when they greeted the Russian envoy with a ten-foot-long banner that in part read "We women of America tell you that America is not a democracy."[54] A man in the crowd leaped at the banner, grabbed it, and shredded it, and the crowd closed in around the pickets. "One instant the banners were there," said a suffragist, "the next there were only bare sticks."[55]

Tearing the banners was like ripping out the suffragists' hearts. Rich in symbolism and political significance, banners held an essential place in the suffrage spectacle and argument. Banners were a medium familiar to women, who in the nineteenth century sewed the banners men carried in parades. Their slogans were the only way women could express female values in public rituals. San Francisco women, for instance, called for "Benevolence, Temperance and Libraries" in a banner they sewed for marching men to carry. Women's presentation of banners to men helped secure what historian Mary Ryan called a "symbolic foothold" in public life.[56]

Stitching banners was a labor of love for suffragists. The niece of pioneer woman's rights speaker Lucy Stone honored her by stitching a banner in white silk with gold letters spelling Stone's name and the word "Justice."[57] Banners also reinforced the movement's femininity. "Banners made for use in the parade," said one newspaper notice of the first parade, "may be hand embroidered by the women to show the entire femininity of the movement and support the contention that the suffragists are working for the good of the home."[58]

Yet banners possessed undeniable political symbolism, stretching back at least as far as when Joan of Arc rallied her troops with them. London suffragists found banners a potent medium for processions that were ablaze with tapestries as rich in symbolism as they were in color and texture.[59] One banner of orange silk with a broad arrow of blue velvet pictured Holloway Jail, where imprisoned suffragettes were force-fed. It read: "Stone Walls Do Not a Prison Make." One hundred banners, each bearing the name of a famous woman, added to the spectacle of a 1908 London parade.[60]

The NWP gave banners a new bite. "For the National Woman's Party," observed scholar Sidney Bland, "banners were the medium for reviling the system." Banners also bonded the pickets. As Bland explained: "The paraphernalia of ritual possessed by every social movement serves to fix loyalties and engineer sympathetic feelings among members. . . . [NWP banners] became objects of veneration and were a prominent part of rallies and commemorative ceremonies. Such use served as a constant reliving and reenforcement of the mutual feelings of the entire organization."[61]

After the crowds destroyed the Russian envoy banner, the women began inscribing their banners with quotations from Wilson's speeches. It proved a shrewd move that probably helped the pickets escape prosecution under federal espionage and sedition laws. A District judge then forbade the women from displaying any banners. But Lucy Burns and Katharine Morey returned to the White House bearing more banners quoting Wilson on 22 June 1917. Charged with obstructing the sidewalk, they became the first arrested NWP pickets.[62] The arrests marked a radical departure to uncharted and dangerous territory for the NWP. No women had ever taken on the federal government so brazenly. As the experience of other radicals showed, when the government decided to flex its legal muscle it could easily quash dissent. The suffragists were the first people to picket the White House by one account, and certainly no group ever attempted such a sustained protest against the federal government. By courting arrest, Burns and Morey launched the pickets' foray into civil disobedience.

Civil disobedience occurs when individuals or groups follow their conscience, disobey a law, and accept the penalty. As Henry David Thoreau wrote in his classic essay on the subject, "Under a government which imprisons any unjustly, the true place for a just man is also a prison."[63] Despite Thoreau's reliance upon the male pronoun, women committed civilization's first recorded act of civil disobedience in the Second Book of Moses, when Hebrew midwives refused to follow the pharaoh's edict to kill all male newborn babies. A woman also figured in the Greek prototype of civil disobedience: Antigone, who disobeyed King Creon and buried her brother, who had died a traitor. Both acts have in common a lack of violence and an appeal to the law of a higher authority than the rules they defy. As historian David Daube pointed out, women figured prominently in these ancient examples of civil disobedience because women are largely outside the power structure. "When we consider, furthermore," Daube wrote, "that women have neither the training nor the weapons for physical power struggle, the appropriateness of non-violent resistance becomes even clearer."[64]

The crucial principle of civil disobedience is that the violation of the law is justified because the law itself violates a higher, moral law. Mahatma Gandhi, who was inspired by British suffragettes, broadened the definition of civil disobedience to include opposition to a corrupt or tyrannical state.[65] The Gandhian tradition of civil disobedience "emphasizes strict nonviolence, submission to arrest, conviction and punishment, and a willingness to see opponents as moral persons to be persuaded of the justice of the disobedient's claim rather than forced into acquiescence," according to scholar Paul Harris.[66]

The suffragists practiced civil disobedience because they claimed the government persecuted them for their beliefs and did not represent them because it denied them the vote. Paul, in fact, insisted that all convicted pickets appeal their sentence while the NWP continued to send out weekly pickets to show that the NWP staunchly believed its actions were completely legal.[67] The pickets' civil disobedience included their refusal to cooperate with the courts because as a disfranchised class they refused to recognize the government's sovereignty over them. "We felt [Wilson] had neither political nor moral claim to our allegiance," wrote Doris Stevens, a jailed picket and author of the classic account *Jailed for Freedom*. Paul refused to make a plea for eleven pickets she represented at their sentencing in the fall: "We do not consider ourselves subject to this court, since as an unenfranchised class we have nothing to do with the making of the laws which have put us in this position." Other suffrage protesters arrested in 1918 remained silent in court.[68] The NWP even declined offers to picket from women who were willing to pay their fines instead of going to jail. "It might tend to break down the determination of others," Burns wrote a potential recruit.[69] Prison stood as dramatic testimony to the women's commitment. "Not to have been willing to endure the gloom of prison would have made moral slackers of all," explained one inmate.[70]

The initial pickets defending themselves in court in June 1917 argued from the start that the government was persecuting them. The charges were dropped against twenty-one women who were arrested over a period of several days, but six women arrested on 26 June were convicted and sentenced to pay a fine of twenty-five dollars each or serve three days in jail. In order to carry out the next step in their civil disobedience, they chose jail.[71] Eleven pickets convicted following a 4 July demonstration received three-day sentences, and by the end of the month, sentences were stretching to sixty days at Occoquan Workhouse in Virginia.[72]

The arrests wed the suffrage movement to free speech. First, the arrests awakened the women to the fact that they possessed constitutional rights. "We stand on the Bill of Rights," acting NWP chair Anne Martin said of the pickets.[73] Protester Sue Shelton White likened the protests to the Boston Tea Party.[74] Jailed picket Eunice Brannan noted how humiliation at the hands of officials failed to "stop our peaceful legal picketing."[75] The First Amendment figured integrally in the women's courtroom defense, especially the right to petition. "My presence at the White House gate was under the constitutional right of petitioning the government for freedom or for any other cause," said Florence Bayard Hilles.[76] Another woman lectured a judge: "We peacefully assembled and then proceeded with our petition to the President for the redress of our grievance of disfranchisement. The Constitution does not specify the form of petition. Ours was in the form of a banner. To say that we 'broke traffic regulations' when we exercised our constitutional right of petition is therefore unconstitutional."[77]

Second, a number of newspapers around the country, with their vested interest in free expression, protested the jailing of the suffrage pickets. Other scholars who have studied the pickets found a mountain of articles—mostly critical—on the picketing, indicating the picketing controversy was of the magnitude of the debate on the limits of abortion protests in the 1990s or of the protests against the Vietnam War.[78] Historian Aileen Kraditor noted that the abundance of newspaper articles and editorials she found on the picketing episode suggested it "was a much more important issue at the time than one would infer from most secondary works dealing with that period."[79]

Some segments of the press became stronger allies as infringements intensified upon the pickets' freedom of expression. "If the suffrage pickets were embarrassing, their power to embarrass has been doubled by their suppression," noted the *New Republic,* previously a critic.[80] The socialist

Masses predictably decried the unlawful assembly charges as an old standby "used in this country to throttle free expression for more than a century," but support also sprang from unexpected quarters. William Randolph Hearst's twenty-seven papers supported the pickets, for instance. The *Raleigh (N.C.) Times* was not alone in tracing a line from the Boston Tea Party to the White House pickets. "It blazes the trail," the paper said of the pickets' spirit."[81]

By cloaking their cause in the symbolism of venerated civil liberties, the suffragists broadened their base of support. The *Pittsburgh Press,* for instance, vindicated the pickets because "the right of petition is a sacred one in democracies, and our own constitution explicitly guarantees it." Other small-town editors also found the pickets heroic. "These ladies of Amazonian proclivities are the real stuff," said the *Utica (N.Y.) Herald Dispatch.* The *Lawrence (Mass.) Telegram* said, "If they have been sensational, they have also been brave and patient and self-sacrificing."[82] The federal government's heavy-handedness offended some editors. "Can't the disfranchised even ask for justice in a country so nobly going to the defense of oppressed nations?" asked the *Canton (N.Y.) Advertiser.* The *Fargo (N.D.) Courier News* scored treatment of the pickets as "a disgrace to the people of the United States." Even the critical *Washington Post* quipped on its editorial page, "Russia's death legion gives more support to the cause of equal suffrage than Occoquan."[83]

Yet most press coverage remained scathing. The *New York Times,* for instance, continued its opposition to the pickets as "idiotic" and "unlawful."[84] The *Washington Post* said, "Suffrage is rapidly becoming a reality in spite of the opera *bouffe* tactics of the militants, not because of them."[85] Whether publicity was positive or negative, however, the NWP protests succeeded in getting their message across to the public. Even such a vocal critic as the *Times,* for instance, to its credit offered generous and usually evenhanded coverage of the jailed pickets in its news columns.[86]

The NWP capitalized upon the publicity. "What splendid advertising we are getting from all of the papers," wrote executive board member Alva Belmont. "I never imagined the situation would be so brilliant."[87] The NWP expounded the Constitution and hammered home the infringement upon free speech in court and in the press, well aware that perceived infringements upon those sacred American values broadened their constituency. Paul knew the administration's repression increased sympathy for the arrested pickets.[88] The NWP's aggressive Press Department helped fuel the controversy by urging supporters to protest the arrests and disseminating press releases to the newspapers.[89]

The oppressive reaction the peaceful pickets provoked in the government did pose a real threat to freedom of expression. One bill introduced by a Texas senator would have allowed the president to ban any person from approaching or entering any place in the District of Columbia.[90] A Montana senator introduced another unsuccessful resolution to make suffrage banners and flags illegal in the District.[91] In court, judges were indifferent to the pickets' First Amendment arguments. Crowds, perhaps sensing the authorities' hostility toward the pickets, became more violent.

The peaceful pickets continued to pay the price for crowd violence against them. On 4 July a crowd of two thousand shouted, "Send them over to the Kaiser" as sailors charged NWP pickets and ripped banners from their hands in what the press termed a "comedy riot." Police smiled as they rounded up a dozen women, but eventually their tormentors became so violent police charged four men with disorderly conduct.[92] Another riot broke out on 14 August 1917, when the women unfurled their most inflammatory banner, which addressed the president as "Kaiser Wilson."[93]

That slur infuriated onlookers caught up in an anti-German hysteria so irrational that a movement was afoot to rename sauerkraut "liberty cabbage."[94] Servicemen and boys attacked the women and destroyed the banner and dozens of NWP flags while the police stood by. The mob followed the women back to their headquarters. Every time they emerged, the mob jumped them and destroyed their flags again. When Burns and another woman appeared on the balcony with another "Kaiser Wilson" banner, the men hurled stones, eggs, tomatoes, and apples at them. A shot rang out, just missing three women. One man was charged with disorderly conduct. "None of us went to bed that night," wrote picket Catherine Flanagan. "We were afraid that something—we knew not what—might happen."[95] Nonetheless, they marched back to the White House the next morning. Rampaging sailors knocked down Paul three times and hit other women.[96] "You took your life in your hands," picket Ernestine Hara Kettler recalled sixty years later. "When the crowd got too noisy and the police couldn't get rid of them, then they hauled us in."[97] Following the legal logic of the times, authorities punished the pickets for the violence their messages provoked.

Unlike their lawless British sisters, who turned to rock throwing and arson, the American militants remained nonviolent throughout their campaign despite the abuse heaped upon them. Paul's strategy of nonviolent civil disobedience was her one truly original contribution to suffrage campaigning. The Britons' violence was the only part of their suffrage campaign Paul chose not to emulate. Whether Paul based that decision on her Quaker faith, the more pragmatic conviction that violence would fail in America, or her awareness that victimization curried press favor, the NWP pickets' willingness to put their bodies and physical freedom on the line proved to be a brilliant stroke. The nonviolent protests won the pickets sympathy and support from diverse segments of the American population once they were perceived as victims of government repression. As historian Linda Ford noted, "Woman's Party feminists were America's first political dissenters to use the nonviolent resistance method, and they did it very well."[98] The women's uncompromising courage gave their protest its great moral imperative. Time after time they returned to the White House as sentences lengthened and their numbers dwindled.

Enduring Epithets and Prison

The pickets had to endure the enmity not only of many politicians, the press, and antisuffragists, but also of their peers. The Wisconsin Woman Suffrage Association spurned a campaign offer by the state movement's matriarch, Olympia Brown, after she was arrested on the NWP picket line.[99] The Nashville Equal Suffrage Association condemned the pickets as "profoundly hurtful to all American womanhood"; a statement issued by the Equal Suffrage Association of Virginia stated, "We utterly repudiate such methods."[100] Some members of the NWP also opposed wartime picketing, including Blatch, who abandoned suffrage work for war work.[101] State chapters were unable to organize protest meetings after the first arrests because sentiment against the pickets was so strong. "Ever since the picketing began we have been up against an intensely antagonistic public—both men and women," wrote the Minnesota NWP chair.[102] Members quit the NWP to protest picketing. When Burns sent a letter urging members to write Congress to protest the force-feeding of Paul and Winslow, one woman returned her copy with a note scrawled upon it: "*I will not*. Do not picket then you will not be force fed."[103] Paul admitted decades later that the most difficult aspect of picketing was coping not with violent crowds or jail but with "the general feeling over the whole country that you were the scum of the earth."[104]

One of the pickets' most outspoken critics was NAWSA. NAWSA president Catt's strategy centered around winning over Wilson by good works while building up political support in the states, a strategy that unquestionably was instrumental in the suffrage victory.[105] Unlike the NWP, NAWSA pledged its service to the war effort.[106] NAWSA called for woman suffrage as a war measure and blamed Congress rather than Wilson for the delay.[107] NAWSA believed NWP tactics to be the scourge of its efforts. The *Woman Citizen*, NAWSA's official newspaper, blasted the pickets as "absurd, illtimed, and susceptible of grave and demoralizing suspicion."[108] Catt urged Paul to stop the picketing after the war began, calling it an "unwarranted discourtesy to the President and a futile annoyance to the men of Congress."[109] Former NAWSA president Anna Howard Shaw also characterized the pickets as the "greatest obstacle" to the suffrage amendment.[110]

NAWSA went so far as to try to censor news of the NWP. First it implored the press to distinguish NAWSA from the NWP and then asked it to ignore the protests.[111] In fact, Maud Wood Park, head of NAWSA's Congressional Committee, and other NAWSA members in the summer of 1917 visited editors at the *Washington Post,* the *New York Evening Post,* and the three major wire services to request they drop the words "suffrage" and "suffragist" from all accounts of NWP activities. According to Park, all the editors were eager to stop publicizing the militant antics but generally believed her suggestion impossible. They agreed to do what they could to minimize publicity. *Washington Times* editor Arthur Brisbane offered to give the NWP space on the back page of the newspaper if the organization stopped picketing.[112] He also proposed a blackout of picket news to Wilson, who judiciously counseled keeping limited coverage as dull as possible.[113] Wilson's press secretary said he would consider Park's request to manipulate a news blackout.[114] This backstage maneuvering demonstrated what little regard some suffrage leaders (and newspaper editors) held for the rights of assembly and free speech they found averse to their agenda. NAWSA's willingness to sanction repression against fellow suffragists made the organization look morally lax in contrast to the NWP's stand for its beliefs.

The suffrage inmates' supporters made up in fervor what they lacked in numbers. The NWP won a few converts from NAWSA; the free-speech issues raised by their protests inspired Sue Shelton White to defect from NAWSA, of which she was recording secretary in Tennessee, and prominent Connecticut suffragist Mrs. Thomas Hepburn (Katharine's mother) resigned from NAWSA so she could speak out in favor of the pickets.[115] "They have the spirit of the martyrs, and stand for a magnificent conviction," one woman wrote of the pickets. "I would just like to see men have such undaunted courage."[116] A man wrote, "Kindly send these balsam branches and daisies to the BRAVE WOMEN who would rather go to jail for the cause of DEMOCRACY than pay a fine."[117] Financial contributions were another measure of the support the much-maligned pickets received from some segments of the public. Thanks to donors, the NWP ended 1917 in the black despite the nearly twelve thousand dollars it cost to feed and house the visiting pickets and pay their legal fees.[118]

Still, the sacrifice of going to jail exacted a toll. The dank Occoquan Workhouse created the "perfect setting for scandal."[119] The inmates soon realized that compared with the heroic poses suffragists enjoyed striking in suffrage pageants, the reality of jail lacked any hint of romanticism. "It was exciting in a frightening way but not exciting in a joyous way," Kettler said.[120] Rats and cockroaches scuttled over beds and across floors in the dark, and worms surfaced in the soup and oatmeal.[121] Prisoners shared one toilet, a bucket of wash water, and a single bar of soap—jarring conditions for the middle-class and upper-class women who comprised the bulk of suffrage inmates. To keep up their spirits, the jailed pickets sang suffrage songs such as "Shout the Revolution of Women."[122] Friendships sprang up with other inmates, mostly drug addicts or prostitutes whose lives were alien to the suffragists. "Especially the negroes are good to us," wrote one inmate.[123] The pickets' attitude toward African American inmates appeared to be a mixture of compassion and condescension.[124] Prison officials exacerbated racial tension by trying to shame the suffragists by assigning them to scrub the segregated bathroom floors used by the African American prisoners.[125] The prison superintendent once ordered black inmates to attack the white suffragists. "They beat the hell out of us," recalled Kettler.[126]

Wilson held the power to free the women and had in fact pardoned the first group of women sentenced to sixty days in July.[127] Wilson not only appointed District prison authorities but was made aware of prison conditions by friends.[128] For all of Wilson's pronouncements on the inviolability of democracy, his administration stands out as one of the most repressive in

American history. Wilson, a lawyer, must have known that the arrests of the peaceful suffrage pickets were unconstitutional. Luckily for the suffragists, his indifference to their constitutional rights was countered by his woeful underestimation of their resolve. That resolve eventually enabled the NWP to become practically the sole victor over the administration in its many free-speech battles during World War I.

The picketing suffragists did more than any group to expose the repressive qualities of the Wilson administration, because their maltreatment struck a chord that the suppression of male dissidents did not. Further, Wilson's hands were somewhat tied in his awkward attempts to silence the suffragists because of their gender. In this sense, the pickets' gender gave them an advantage in their defiance of the administration. If the White House pickets had been male Wobblies, for instance, the administration undoubtedly would have charged them under the much more severe federal sedition laws. The District would not have bothered with petty charges of blocking the sidewalk in dispersing male radicals. The public would have been less likely to protest such treatment than that accorded the suffragists because it was used to the arrests of male dissidents, but seeing middle-class women roughed up and jailed shocked them. The women also had protected themselves from the sedition laws partly because most of their banners quoted the president, which made prosecution problematic. And NWP banners never directly criticized the war or draft. For all of these reasons, the administration never tried to charge the picketers under the federal sedition laws.

The White House began to lose its battle against the NWP when the inmates demanded political-prisoner status.[129] The United States did not recognize political-prisoner status, although in Europe authorities distinguished between common criminals and those jailed for political acts. The demand marked another escalation in NWP tactics; it would require even more confrontations with yet another level of daunting male authority, the prison officials at Occoquan. Burns wrote a letter in her cell in solitary confinement in October stating that the suffragists should be exempt from work, permitted legal counsel, and receive food and writing materials from outside because they had been confined for their political beliefs. Inmates secretly signed it and passed it from cell to cell through coils of the building's steam pipes.[130] Doris Stevens deemed the letter a historic document because it represented the first organized group action ever made in

America to establish the status of political prisoners. The spirited defiance of Burns, the red-haired vice chairman of the NWP who was an alumna of both Vassar College and Holloway Jail in London, fortified the eleven women who signed it. Burns served six sentences and more time than any other American suffragist in addition to four sentences in England. Among the signatures was that of Maud Malone, the New York City suffragette who had led the nation's first suffrage open-air meeting and parade and was arrested for heckling Wilson. She had been sentenced to sixty days in September for picketing.[131]

Prison officials intensified their intimidation to quash the suffragists' protest. The worst incident became infamous as the "Night of Terror," when on 15 November 1917 eighty guards beat and terrorized thirty-three incoming suffragists who demanded they be treated as political prisoners. A Louisiana woman suffered a heart attack, a suffragist in her seventies injured a lame leg when guards dragged her upstairs, and another woman, isolated from the others, was implicitly threatened with rape until daylight. The suffragists believed the "unexpected ferocity" was part of the government's plan to suppress picketing. When the women were thrown in separate cells, Burns called out each one's name. After she refused to be quiet, guards handcuffed her wrists and fastened them above her head to the cell door for the remainder of the night, threatening to put her in a straitjacket and a buckle gag.[132]

The intimidation boomeranged and precipitated the suffragists' most dramatic demonstration, the hunger strike. The hunger-striking Americans emulated the British suffragettes, who in turn borrowed the technique from hundreds of recalcitrant Irish rebels imprisoned in British jails.[133] Hunger strikes originated in ancient Ireland, where an aggrieved party sat on the offender's doorstep and fasted until tradition and public opinion compelled the offender to make restitution before the visitor died on his doorstep. Hunger strikes became the "ultimate protest" of political prisoners against prison cruelty among Siberian exiles in nineteenth-century Russia, according to one source.[134]

American suffragists' hunger strikes, beginning on 5 November 1917, were the nation's first organized use of this extreme form of protest.[135] Other women had employed it earlier in individual protests, as the suffragists doubtless knew. Activist Becky Edelsohn attracted much publicity when she fasted in 1914 to protest her sentence for speaking on New York City streets on behalf of the unemployed.[136] The suffragists probably also knew that a hunger-striking female birth-control activist recently had been subjected to the first force-feeding in the American penal system.[137]

It took tremendous courage for the pickets to embark on the painful and potentially lethal hunger strike; unlike other protests, such as parades, no supporters would be around to cheer on the suffragists during this protractedly lonely form of protest. When the federal government reverted to the barbarous practice of force-feeding to get the obdurate suffragists back in line, it inadvertently made a glaring admission of its disregard for the right of assembly. The force-feeding revealed the depths of repression to which the United States could sink in times of national stress.

The Wilson administration's climactic mistake was to impose a draconian seven-month sentence for obstructing the sidewalk upon veteran hunger striker Alice Paul. No sooner was she sentenced than Paul instructed Congresswoman Jeannette Rankin to check out books on political prisoners for her from the Library of Congress.[138] On 5 November, Paul initiated a hunger strike in the District jail hospital, soon joined by Polish-born Socialist Rose Winslow.[139] Paul's willingness to die for the cause was a powerful weapon.

Paul has been called the sole charismatic leader of the suffrage movement, meaning her force of personality alone pulled in recruits.[140] As Katherine Mullen explained her motivation for joining the line, "Every generation and every individual has the opportunity to reject or recognize a prophet. My opportunity had come to believe."[141]

Paul was either a saint or insane, depending upon the perspective of those who judged her. Blue-eyed with auburn hair, Paul's ghostly complexion and ninety-five pound frame usually draped by a pale purple frock gave a deceivingly ethereal look to the thirty-two-year-old Quaker with a doctorate in economics.[142] An observer noticed how the eyes and face of suffrage's "Joan of Arc" lighted up with "exaltation of purpose" as she marched toward a sure prison sentence.[143] The NWP called her Joan of Arc "because she sees visions, because she stands alone, because she has led an apparently forlorn hope to victory."[144]

Paul also had detractors. One critic labeled her an "aneamic [sic] fanatic" who bordered on insanity. "She will be a *martyr*, whether there is the slightest excuse for it," wrote Ruth McCormick, Paul's successor as chair of NAWSA's Congressional Committee.[145] "She demands too much from the faithful slavish devotion of those about her," added a state NWP officer.[146] Yet one follower explained Paul was a great leader in part because she was willing to do whatever she asked of her followers—and more.[147] Paul's description of how five British prison guards held her down while a doctor pushed her head back to plunge a feeding tube down her throat summarized her entire career for women's rights: "I didn't give in."[148]

District and administration officials compounded the error of making a martyr out of Paul when they secretly transferred her to a psychiatric ward at the jail.[149] "This has taken a more serious turn than I imagined," Paul wrote in a note smuggled from prison. She explained that she had only planned to fast for a short time without publicity. "However, we see by the papers that it is known to the world so I suppose we are committed to the plan and must go forward!"[150]

Paul chose an odd time to embark on martyrdom. The day after she stopped eating, New York women began celebrating the suffrage referendum's landslide victory in that state.[151] "No militant methods were used," observed the *Washington Post*.[152] The New York victory even crowded war news off the front page of the *New York Times,* whereas Paul's hunger strike was relegated to a few paragraphs on page thirteen. As Paul endured the fourth day of her fast, NAWSA president Carrie Chapman Catt, former president Anna Howard Shaw, and others huddled at the White House with Wilson in a "heart-to-heart chat" about the federal amendment. That cozy scene revealed the need for Paul's melodramatic protest: At the end of the chat, the president still refused to support a federal amendment, even on the heels of the breakthrough victory in the East.[153] Friendly chats were insufficient methods to push through the suffrage amendment.

On the other side of the nation's capital, authorities took Paul's protest seriously. They labored valiantly to break her spirit, replacing her wooden door with a grated one so that mental patients peered in at her all day long, and during the night a nurse beamed a flashlight into her face hourly. They force-fed her three times a day.[154] After dozens of suffragists called news of the picketing up to her windows, a man climbed a ladder and boarded them up.[155] The inhumane treatment of the recidivist sidewalk-blocker made clear that the right of assembly was illusory by that point. Moreover, the abuse revealed how threatening authorities found Paul as well as their inability to grasp the futility and injustice of punishing her.

Authorities hit upon a last desperate scheme to silence the suffrage Joan of Arc that was just a few shades more humane than burning her at the stake. Soon after Paul stopped eating, authorities sent a psychiatrist (then called "alienist") to examine Paul in an attempt to declare her insane. "It appeared clear that it was their intention either to discredit me," Paul recalled, "as the leader of the agitation, by casting doubt upon my sanity, or else to intimidate us into retreating from the hunger strike."[156] NWP officials feared that prison authorities would institutionalize her to kill their movement. "Situation desperate," an NWP officer telegrammed members.[157] Paul remained forever grateful that the alienist, after listening to her discourse on suffrage for several hours, refused to classify her as insane. NWP lawyers located her after a week, and Paul returned to the prison hospital.[158]

The picketing movement was on its last leg, however, as the November sky turned grayer. Its leader was imprisoned incommunicado, perhaps dying, and the party's ranks were exhausted. Burns, just released from her grueling sixty-day sentence, beseeched supporters to bombard Congress and Wilson with protest telegrams and letters protesting Paul's treatment in prison.[159] From her cell, Paul sneaked messages directing her aides to organize one last picket line in a bravura act of defiance she felt sure would persuade Wilson and Congress they had no recourse but to pass the suffrage amendment.

Despite an all-out effort to recruit one hundred women from across the nation, only forty-one possessed the desire, resources, and/or courage to come to Washington to risk a months-long jail sentence during the final picket line on 10 November.[160] Spectators jammed Pennsylvania Avenue as police carted off all forty-one pickets in police vans, but charges against them were dismissed. They returned to the White House gates later that day and again the following day. This time police picked them up; most were sentenced to thirty days, but Burns got six months.[161] With virtually all of its activists locked up, the militant suffrage movement verged on collapse.

Inside prison, the suffrage inmates launched a hunger strike when they were refused political-prisoner status. "By the third day, I was rather nervous," wrote playwright Paula Jakobi of her hunger strike. "I could remember no names, and it was quite impossible to read."[162] Betty Gram dropped nineteen pounds.[163] Officials took the drastic step of force-feeding the fasting suffragists, which turned out to be a tactical error. The totalitarian image of force-feeding repelled many Americans. *Good Housekeeping,* for instance, had described the force-feeding of British suffragettes as "a rather ugly business, not quite human, a little too close to torture to fit in with Anglo-Saxon notions."[164] It was a dangerous procedure: Their captors forced gastric tubes down the suffragists' throats or nostrils and flooded their stomachs with a mixture of eggs and milk. A terse journal entry by Burns captured its terror: "I was held down by five people at legs, arms, and head. I refused to open mouth, [doctor] pushed tube up left nostril. I turned and twisted my head all I could, but he managed to push it up. It hurts nose and throat very much and makes nose bleed freely. Tube drawn out covered with blood. Operation leaves one very sick."[165]

The smuggled note from Burns was one of several that found their way onto the pages of the NWP newspaper *Suffragist,* which missed no opportunity to point up the women's martyrdom.[166] Paul wrote to an executive committee member from prison that force-feeding her and other harsh acts provided "excellent ammunition" against the administration. "The more harsh we can make the Administration seem . . . the better," she wrote. "It all depends on the publicity of course." She instructed her associates to make the most of such instances in the press and in the *Suffragist.*[167] The hunger strikers proved perfect propaganda fodder. "I am afraid this letter is not well written, as I am rather light headed from hunger," concluded an articulate, smuggled note from Mary Winsor printed by the *Suffragist.*[168] Such plaintive missives, along with numerous indignant, fact-filled articles churned out by the NWP's extensive Press Department, often were picked up by newspapers across the country.[169]

The NWP press-relations machinery began to work some effect by the end of November. Protests against the suffrage prisoners' treatment began piling up at the White House. The NWP obtained a writ of habeas corpus to move some thirty hunger-striking suffragists from Occoquan to the District jail, where they would join Paul and a handful of other fasting women.[170] The court ruled the haggard-looking pickets had been illegally removed from the District and had suffered cruel and unusual punishment, and District officials released all of the women on 27–28 November. "They tried to terrorize and suppress us," said a very pale, thin Paul upon her arrival at Cameron House. "They could not, and so freed us."[171] Miraculously and just barely, a handful of half-starved women had bested the United States government.

An illustration from the May 1912 issue of *Woman Voter* shows a confident, stylish soapbox speaker. Greenwood Press.

WHEN DR. SHAW SPEAKS

There is perhaps no other woman in this country who can stir and inspire an audience as can Dr. Anna Howard Shaw, the National President. It has been said that the most fascinating of intellectual treats is to watch the faces of her listeners.

Dr. Shaw is at present touring the campaign States. In Ohio she wound up the campaign with a two-hour address and held the crowded thousands spell-bound from the first to the last. Dr. Shaw reports her Ohio trip on the last page of this week's Woman's Journal.

NAWSA president Dr. Anna Howard Shaw holds a crowd in Ohio as she campaigns for the suffrage referendum in the summer of 1912. Schlesinger Library.

A speaker for the Congressional Union addresses a street-corner crowd. NWP Papers: The Suffrage Years, Library of Congress.

An illustration from the July 1916 issue of *Woman Voter* illustrates suffragists'
belief that women in the streets carried more political weight than petitions.
Greenwood Press.

The line marches down Fifth Avenue during the 1911 suffrage parade.
Schlesinger Library.

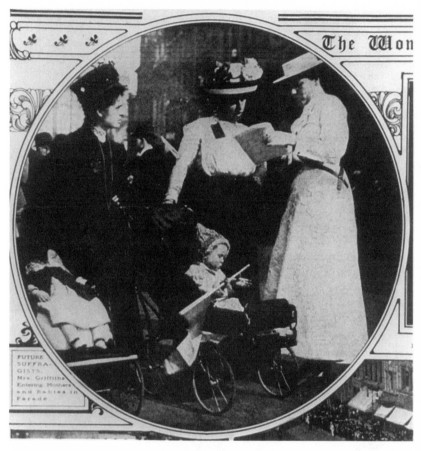

The Won

FUTURE
SUFFRA-
GISTS.
Mrs. Griffith's
Entering Mothers
and Babies in
Parade

Parades featured babies in carriages to show that suffragists were good mothers, as in the May 1911 parade on Fifth Avenue. *New York Times.*

Liberty and her attendants at the national suffrage pageant on the United States Treasury steps on March 3, 1913. Schlesinger Library.

WOMAN'S JOURNAL

OFFICIAL ORGAN OF THE NATIONAL AMERICAN WOMAN SUFFRAGE ASSOCIATION

VOL. XLIII NO. 19 — SATURDAY, MAY 11, 1912 — FIVE CENTS

GREAT SUFFRAGE PARADE

500,000 Crowd to See the Biggest Procession of Organized Womanhood Ever Held in this Country

ONE VIEW OF THE PARADE   REV. ANNA HOWARD SHAW AND HER BANNER

Reverend Anna Howard Shaw and her banner are highlighted on the *Woman's Journal*'s May 11, 1912, cover featuring the 1912 suffrage parade on Fifth Avenue. Schlesinger Library.

PLEDGE TO MARCH
— in the —
MASSACHUSETTS WOMAN SUFERAGE VICTORY PARADE
BOSTON

Saturday Afternoon, October 16th, 1915

Line forms 1.30 p. m.   Line starts promptly 2.00 p. m.
For information watch the Woman's Journal and the daily papers.
No automobiles or carriages will be included in the parade.
Complete instructions to those pledged will be mailed later.

All Suffragists from Everywhere are invited to march
Retain this slip, sign the one below, and send to

PARADE COMMITTEE
Massachusetts Woman Suffrage Association
585 BOYLSTON STREET - - BOSTON
TELEPHONE 8230 BACK BAY

- -

I will march in the MASSACHUSETTS WOMAN SUFFRAGE
VICTORY PARADE

NAME { Mr.
        { Mrs.
        { Miss _____

(Please do not use initials. Write name in full).

Address _____

City or Town_____

Section of parade, by { Home city or town _____
                 { Occupation_____

(Nurses, lawyers, social workers, etc.)

Although many women filled out this pledge to march in a Boston parade in October 1915, the suffrage referendum failed in Massachusetts. NAWSA Papers, Library of Congress.

Marchers in the largest suffrage parade in 1915, viewed by half a million spectators along Fifth Avenue. NAWSA Papers, Library of Congress.

NWP suffrage pickets attracted curiosity but little hostility when they began
picketing the White House with these signs in January 1917. NWP Papers: The
Suffrage Years, Library of Congress.

Lucy Burns leads a contingent of the "Prison Special," convicted suffrage pickets who in February and March 1919 toured the country telling the pickets' side of the story. They wore their jailhouse uniforms and sang songs from their days as inmates at Occoquan Workhouse. NWP Papers: The Suffrage Years, Library of Congress.

Suffragist cover after the Senate finally passed the Nineteenth Amendment in June 1919. NWP Papers: The Suffrage Years, Library of Congress.

Even better news arrived in March 1918, when a federal appeals court vindicated the NWP by ruling the picket arrests violated the Sixth Amendment provision that the accused be informed of the nature and cause of the accusation. "Unlawful assembly has a well-defined meaning," the court said. "The information is defective in that it fails to set out the acts committed by the defendants which constituted the crowding and obstructing of the free use of the walk by them."[172] As was common in similar cases of the era, the court ignored the First Amendment questions raised by the women's lawyers.[173]

The NWP kept up its pressure on Wilson even after he finally came out for the federal amendment 9 January and the amendment passed the House by a single vote on 10 January 1918.[174] The suffragists introduced even bolder demonstrations to protest Wilson's failure to push the Senate to a vote that fall. Dozens more women were arrested over the next year for climbing statues, speaking in parks, picketing the Senate, and lighting "watch fires of freedom." The most sweeping arrests came on 6 August 1918, the birthday of the late Inez Milholland, in a dramatic confrontation between police and one hundred NWP pickets at the Lafayette Monument. Police swarmed in when women began climbing on the statue to speak. They charged forty-eight women with meeting on public grounds and eighteen of those also with climbing on the monument. Sixty more women were manhandled and arrested over the next few days. The New York City Suffrage Party dismissed the protests as "foolish and futile," and the *New York Times* said jail was too good for the suffragists: "The place for them is the clinic of the pathologist or the psychiatrist."[175] The antisuffragist *Woman's Protest* called the women "fanatics."[176] But other segments of the press upheld the women's right to speak. Perhaps realizing that, as the *Washington Herald* put it, the police looked "puny and foolish" in these encounters, the District grounds superintendent permitted future meetings there. The administration backed down further when, after the women barraged the Senate with banners later that fall, the legal system again vindicated the NWP. A district court ruled illegal the arrests of one hundred and eighty-three protesters and the confiscation of their banners by Capitol police.[177]

The NWP turned to truly inflammatory measures. Protesters burned copies of Wilson's books and speeches on 16 September; the NWP probably was disappointed, however, when police deflated the protest by declining to interfere.[178] Weeks later, four hundred torch-bearing NWP protesters returned to Lafayette Monument and repeated the angry symbolism of burn-ing Wilson's words on 16 December, the anniversary of the Boston Tea Party. There were no arrests.[179]

In a ploy calculated to spark arrests and publicity, the NWP began stag-ing a series of "watch fires" on 1 January 1919. Members used a copy of Wilson's toast to the king of England to ignite its first watch fire in front of the White House, launching the final spate of suffrage protests. The suf-fragists understood that such dramatic symbolic expression packed more emotional punch than the spoken or written word, and they relied upon it to attract publicity. As one scholar noted of the power of symbolic expres-sion, "Its dramatic effect is a substitute for the protester's lack of access to the more traditional mass media."[180] In the case of the NWP watch fires, the drama intensified when police attempted to extinguish the fires and allowed onlookers to jeer the women, tear their banners, and throw buckets of water on the flame. After poring over statute books, police charged five women with setting fires in a public place after sunset.[181] Sentences of dozens more women over the next month never exceeded five days; threats of hunger strikes continued to be a powerful incentive for prison authori-ties to release suffrage protesters.

The most controversial NWP protest occurred when Sue Shelton White ignited an effigy of Wilson, mimicking patriots who burned a portrait of King George III during the American Revolution.[182] This act outraged not only antisuffragists but also some pickets, such as Lavinia Dock. The sixty-year-old founder of the visiting nurses in New York City tenements had soapboxed, marched, petitioned, picketed, and served forty days in jail for the cause. But burning Wilson's image went too far even for Dock; she found it a "frightful exhibition of barbarism" that resembled lynching.[183] When the suffrage amendment was defeated in the Senate by a single vote, the Christian Science Monitor said there was "general agreement" that the NWP was to blame.[184] White said lighting the effigy was "the greatest sac-rifice I have ever made, and nothing but the deepest conviction could have moved me to it."[185] Yet the burning of Wilson's likeness cut too close to physical violence and came closest to completely alienating the American public.

The hint of physical violence symbolized by the effigy burning, however, nowhere approached the level of real violence that marred the NWP's final two protests in northern cities in March 1919. The arrests of the peaceful pickets underscored the inconsistency of contemporary legal protections for public assemblies. In Boston, twenty-two women unfurled banners in front of a reviewing stand greeting Wilson on his return from the Paris Peace Conference. Sixteen were convicted and sentenced to eight days for loitering more than seven minutes.[186] In New York, officers clubbed twenty-five picketers who unfurled banners in front of the Metropolitan Opera House as Wilson spoke inside. Disorderly conduct charges against the women were dropped within an hour after they were hauled into the station.[187] They were the last NWP protesters to risk jail for their beliefs.

Meanwhile, the government erected other barriers to the NWP's exercise of its right of assembly when the suffragists deployed their best speakers across the nation to plead the pickets' case.[188] The most entertaining NWP propaganda was the "Prison Special," a railroad carload of twenty-six former picket inmates who traveled the nation in 1919 wearing replicas of their Occoquan-issue gingham dress and blue aprons, playing the comb and singing jail songs as they recounted their experiences. If the warm welcome the women received almost everywhere they stopped was any measure, the suffrage prisoners enjoyed support in every corner of the nation.[189]

The Secret Service was less enthusiastic. It not only kept tabs on NWP picketers but also followed speakers.[190] Meeting permits suspiciously were rescinded in four states, yet speakers refused to give in to the intimidation. When a Secret Service agent announced Anne Martin could not speak in Los Angeles, she read him the First Amendment assembly clause. When she persuaded a hotel to grant her a room in which to deliver her speech, agents sat on the platform and interrupted her, implying that Martin was violating the Sedition Act by telling her, "You've said enough about the President now." Martin replied: "If I've said anything seditious it's your duty to arrest me. Otherwise I'm going on with my speech." The audience applauded. Such acts marked the NWP as one of wartime's most audacious and effective standard bearers for the right to assemble peaceably and of free speech.[191]

Jail Forges a Lifetime Bond

The women's commitment extended to risking imprisonment. Going to jail had a profound effect upon the women. If picketing fostered sisterhood among them, jail forged a bond that lasted a lifetime.[192] For one thing, the act of going to prison sealed a public commitment to the cause that required great courage. "I had trembled all the time like a poplar leaf in a storm," wrote one picket of how she felt as she stood awaiting her arrest. But after having withstood the crucible of imprisonment, she exclaimed, "Picketing is glorious."[193] Another picket wrote, "It is so little to do for a great cause, just starve for a few days, put up with dirth [sic] and vermin, sleep on straw—any way lie on it."[194] Mary Winsor felt kinship with another political prisoner, Leo Tolstoi. "I have had a wonderful experience during these last two months," she wrote. "I have learned more of poor suffering nature than I could in two years at home."[195] Surviving the nerve-wracking experience instilled pride. Harriet Andrews wrote: "The morning I came out, the sense of air and light and space burst upon me like a shout. Along with that exhilaration there was another feeling. A feeling of something accomplished."[196] A reception for eighty-one jailed pickets at the Belasco Theatre on 6 December allowed them to bask in their shared travails; four thousand persons turned out to cheer the "jailbirds" dressed in white as they received silver pin replicas of the grated jail door.[197]

A long distance separated the barred doors at Occoquan from the first soapbox set up in Madison Square, both literally and figuratively. The NWP probably never would have undertaken its daring protests in 1917 had not American women ventured onto male turf in public assemblies for political ends nearly a decade earlier. When picketing got rough, their past successes in other public assemblies gave suffragists confidence that this latest form of protest also would eventually succeed. "There was a time when street parades and street meetings were assailed as bad suffrage tactics," said an article in *LaFollette's Magazine,* "but who now questions the valuable part they have played in the suffrage movement?"[198] The NWP also recognized that less aggressive forms of assembly had failed and the need for even bolder acts to win publicity during wartime. "For seventy years women had been attempting to 'concert public opinion' by mass movements, street meetings, and processions. They had rolled up huge petitions to Congress," an NWP press release said. "Who would be thinking of suffrage if no one picketed?"[199]

Picketing did publicize suffrage and prod politicians, but it was not enough to win the vote. Throughout the roiling drama of arrests and hunger strikes, both NWP and NAWSA lobbyists in Washington had worked less publicly but as diligently as the protesters. They buttonholed uncommitted senators in the Capitol halls and asked Wilson to call a special session of the new Congress in 1919. NAWSA especially, which claimed two million members to the NWP's forty-eight thousand, had argued politely—but persistently—for the federal amendment throughout the war.[200] Wilson, who enjoyed cordial relations with NAWSA, cabled crucial senators from the Paris Peace Conference and summoned a special session of the Sixty-sixth Congress on 20 May 1919. The House two days later passed the Susan B. Anthony amendment 304 to 89 (a new vote was required because it was a new Congress).[201] On 4 June the Senate passed it 56 to 25, two votes over the required two-thirds majority.[202] After Tennessee became the thirty-sixth state to ratify it, the Nineteenth Amendment became a part of the Constitution on 26 August 1920.[203]

Most historians believe the NWP protests hastened passage of the Nineteenth Amendment. As Stanley Lemon observed, "The militancy of the National Woman's Party only emphasized the reasonableness of NAWSA's position."[204] At the time, however, NAWSA president Catt was not alone in her belief that Wilson supported the amendment "in spite of" the pickets.[205] But the NWP received credit from some unlikely contemporaries. States' rights advocate Kate Gordon of Louisiana, an adamant foe of the federal amendment, blamed Wilson's eventual support of the amendment not on NAWSA lobbying but on NWP tactics, which she believed "got on his nerves" by embarrassing him.[206] Some suffragists who did not picket were still convinced the protests won suffrage faster, as did even a southern judge.[207] More evidence of support for the pickets was that by the end of 1917, the NWP treasury held $335,650, up 50 percent from the start of picketing.[208]

The picketing and hunger strikes were more than grandstanding. The protests enabled the NWP to elbow its way onto the front page of major newspapers; the federal amendment campaign would have been subsumed by war news if not for the sensational pickets.[209] The pickets also seemed to rouse Congress. It seemed an unlikely coincidence, for instance, that the Senate Committee on Woman Suffrage issued its first favorable report on the amendment on 15 September 1917, the day its chairman visited Occoquan.[210] Wilson came out for the federal amendment almost a year to the day after the pickets lined up at his gates.[211] And no sooner had Paul announced she would burn Wilson's words on 16 September 1918 than the president announced he would receive a delegation of southern and western suffragists on that same date.

A more important point than whether the White House pickets advanced woman suffrage is that they represented women's first organized and sustained battle to exercise their First Amendment rights. They waged that battle peacefully, beautifully, courageously, and intelligently. The pickets formed an elite that could claim it was the first organized group to fight the federal government for women's rights. This aggressive form of petitioning was far removed from the nineteenth-century style of silently mailing resolutions to a far-off Congress.

An important facet of the picketing and watch fires was that the suffragists won their battle on women's terms, never reverting to the violence or ugliness that characterized male responses to their peaceful, picturesque protests. The pickets' protest in a sense enabled them to claim as their own the Founding Fathers' egalitarian rhetoric that for so long had not applied to them. Because the picketing also marked the first organized women's fight to exercise their First Amendment rights, which so often had been denied them by extralegal forces, the successful civil disobedience proved the Bill of Rights also belonged to women. Another important result was the solidarity picketing forged among participants. The regalia, rallies, and rituals of NWP assemblies instilled a sense of shared purpose among members, and the symbolic expression of their banners evoked their shared history and vision for the future.

The picketing campaign epitomized how the right to assemble peaceably can effect social change. The women took their message to the streets, raised symbolic expression to new heights, garnered extensive media attention, and needled the political establishment into action. As the *Boston Journal* said, "The little band representing the NWP has been abused and bruised by government clerks, soldiers and sailors until its effort to attract the President's attention has sunk into the conscience of the whole nation."[212]

Yet the pickets came within inches of failure. The wartime climate in which the picketing occurred added a darker dimension to the NWP protests and accounted for most of the hostility they encountered. Women soapboxers and paraders had been able to counter caricatures of themselves as unwomanly by demonstrating their intelligence, commitment, and grace. But the picketers committed the unpardonable sin—in the eyes of the Wilson administration and much of the United States' citizenry—of indirectly criticizing the war and linking "Kaiser" Wilson to the enemy. War hysteria more than sex discrimination accounted for the federal government's repression of the suffrage message, although slurs upon their womanhood intensified the criticism they received. In fact, their gender probably insulated the women pickets from the harsher legal penalties handed down to male dissidents.

As Haig Bosmajian has noted, the fact that the women never were charged with violating the Espionage Act was an example of selective enforcement of the law.[213] Socialists and anarchists were convicted under those laws for uttering less offensive phrases than "Kaiser Wilson." The government undoubtedly viewed the suffragists as less threatening to the state than anarchists, which accounted in part for the women's more lenient treatment. But they also probably hesitated to make the more serious espionage and sedition charges against the White House pickets partly because they were women. Although federal authorities had been sufficiently whipped into war fever to charge the wives, mothers, and daughters of its leading classes with climbing statues and obstructing sidewalks, they could not bring themselves to accuse middle-class, well-connected women of treason and send them to jail for twenty years. That annoyed critics such as the antisuffragists, who labeled the pickets "cowardly." "The militant Suffragettes use the shield of womanhood, knowing well that behind it they will not be attacked as political offenders would be," said the *Woman's Protest*.[214]

Yet the peaceful pickets were persecuted by the government, and their gender also made the women's protests more susceptible to ridicule. The women's mistreatment at the hands of the government demonstrated the fragility of First Amendment protections in the early part of the twentieth century. Police tolerated the pickets for nearly six months before arrests began, and their erratic sentences ranged from twenty-five-dollar fines to seven months in jail. Charges against the suffragists were inconsistent and unconvincing. "I am only giving you thirty days because your banners were so harmless," a judge told them. "If any suffragists attempt to carry objectionable banners, the sentence will be longer."[215] As Agnes Morey said when Boston police arrested banner bearers, "Thousands loitered from curiosity on the day the President arrived. Twenty-two loitered for liberty, and only those who loitered for liberty were arrested."[216] These developments illuminated the extremes to which the government would go to maintain public order at the expense of civil liberties.

In the end, however, constitutional guarantees helped the pickets. If the government was quick to forget the meaning of the First Amendment, much of the public and the press was not. Invoking the rights to assemble peaceably and to petition called up something deep within the souls of some Americans. Some members of the press, appreciative that the First Amendment also granted them the latitude to criticize the government, ridiculed the administration for its treatment of the women. "To decry their pitiful little banners as seditious is ridiculous," said the *Richmond Evening Journal*.[217] Eventually the District ceded the women's right to assemble, and NWP street meetings occurred daily, undisturbed at Lafayette Monument throughout the fall of 1918.[218] The appeals court eventually vindicated the women under the Sixth Amendment.

It is a perverse law of publicity that, had governmental abuses not occurred, the NWP's protests would not have been nearly as effective vehicles for spreading the suffrage message. As picket organizer Mabel Vernon shrewdly analyzed it decades later, the picketing strategy involved "pursuing peaceful means to achieve a violent reaction."[219] But beneath the NWP's flair for publicity lay courage and principles. The women risked prison not just to make headlines but also to make their point that they had a constitutional right to protest peacefully. The contribution the White House pickets made toward helping sensitize the American public and officials about the sanctimony of First Amendment freedoms was impressive. The women were well informed about their rights of free speech and to assemble and petition. They also were bold and daring in asserting those rights, standing up to hecklers, police officers, judges, Secret Service agents, prison superintendents, senators, and even the president. The NWP pickets were considered so radical that they inspired proposals for repressive laws such as banning provocative banners or loitering and probably influenced passage of the Sedition Act of 1918.

They persevered and made an important contribution to laying the foundation for expanded protections for freedom of expression as the twentieth century progressed. In fact, the civil disobedience of the NWP suffragists influenced the epic civil rights protests that unfolded decades later in the American South. At least one American suffrage leader met with Mahatma Gandhi, who was deeply stirred by the civil disobedience of British suffragists he had witnessed in London. The suffragists' peaceful demonstrations inspired the civil disobedience with which Gandhi led India's fight for independence.[220] Gandhi's influence on Martin Luther King Jr. has been widely noted,[221] yet it is generally unknown that the marches, pickets, symbolic expression, and civil disobedience that formed the core of King's crusade all had precedents in the American suffrage movement.[222] In his famous "Letter from Birmingham Jail," King subscribed to the same creed articulated decades earlier by Alice Paul. He wrote: "I submit that an individual who breaks a law that conscience tells him is unjust, and who willingly accepts the penalty of imprisonment in order to arouse the conscience of the community over its injustice, is in reality expressing the highest respect for law."[223] Supreme Court justice Abe Fortas's analysis of civil rights and Vietnam War protesters in the 1960s could have applied to the unheralded suffragists' exercise of the right of assembly fifty years earlier: "It would be difficult to find many situations in history where so much has been accomplished by those who, in cold realism, were divorced from the conventional instruments of power. . . . They did not control political machines. They did not own vast newspapers or magazines or radio or television stations. But they have caused great events to occur."[224]

CONCLUSION

The Legacy of Suffrage Assemblies

A clearer picture of the suffrage movement emerges when viewed through the prism of the right to assemble peaceably.[1] Earlier histories of the suffrage movement have overemphasized the effect of behind-the-scenes lobbying by the National American Woman Suffrage Association and understated the effect of more public forms of suffrage assemblies.[2] Accounts that focused upon the picketing underestimated the influence of earlier suffrage protests upon the National Woman's Party pickets.[3] And the few articles that briefly discuss parades and the open-air campaigns pay scant attention to the First Amendment implications of those activities.[4]

The most striking and unexpected conclusion arising from my research is that virtually the entire suffrage story can be told through the prism of the right of assembly. This is perhaps not so surprising, because the right is so basic its workings are almost invisible. Perhaps for this reason most historians have lost sight of the significance of the very act of women banding together to fight for their rights. Suffragists also played a reciprocal role in helping safeguard the right of assembly at a time when it was jeopardized by officialdom's fear of social change. Suffragists repeatedly stood up to authorities and asserted their rights to gather and/or protest.

If Harriot Stanton Blatch and other soapboxers had simply retreated rather than complained to New York City police when mobs harassed them, the successful suffrage fight of the 1910s may well have ended there.[5] Freedom of expression also would have suffered. Blatch and other suffragists took to the streets at a time when legal scholars were debating the practical meaning of the right of assembly and other forms of freedom of expression. The suffragists' stand helped force authorities to recognize their responsibilities under the Bill of Rights. The women's stand was even more remarkable because First Amendment freedoms were so amorphous at the time. Legal protections for freedom of expression that today are incumbent upon authorities remained largely unarticulated in the 1910s. In fact, contemporary jurisprudence placed the onus of preserving the social order upon the speaker; a speaker could be blamed for the misdeeds of her audience. Suffragists, like other dissidents who took to the streets in the 1910s, were among the first Americans to demand a reinterpretation of the broad and vague clauses of the First Amendment that would afford them greater protection when they took their message to the streets.

The seeds of suffrage militancy displayed during the 1917 picketing originated a decade earlier when American suffragists first took to the streets. Suffragists beginning in 1908 escalated their use of the right of assembly in increasingly assertive modes. The success of those assemblies helped establish the climate in which the White House pickets could command attention and gave the pickets, old hands by then in the exercise of the right of assembly, the confidence to withstand yet another assault upon their alleged unwomanliness. A reiteration of the characteristics of the various forms of suffrage assemblies shows how each helped pave the way for suffragists to experiment with other forms of assembly.

Before women could work for the vote, they had to join together. They employed the right of association to gather in mass meetings and in suffrage societies. The Woman's Party of Western Voters employed the right of association when it conducted "every kind of meeting known to our civilization" during its campaign against the Democrats in the West during the 1916 election.[6] The right of association came into play across the entire spectrum of suffrage assemblies that demonstrated organizers' enterprise and ingenuity. Suffragists used the right of association when they gathered at teas, luncheons, stores, balls, baby shows, and tents at county fairs; in parades, tableaus, theaters, and the Senate gallery; on street corners; aboard the steamer *John Lenox*; on the White House sidewalks; and in conventions.

The thread that wound through the suffrage movement in its varied stages over fifty years was the suffrage convention. Conventions gave women experience working together and exposed them to new ideas and tactics. The associational ties women developed in conventions created a sense of unity and instilled in women a confidence that lifted suffragists to new heights of public activism.

The open-air campaigns beginning on the eve of 1908 launched the era of suffrage activism that by optimizing the right of assembly brought the moribund suffrage movement back into the public eye. The shocking sight

of suffragists speaking on street-corner soapboxes was just one manifestation of the revolutionary changes rocking women's role in a society besieged by change from all sides. The first step onto a suffrage soapbox may
have been a small one for Bettina Borrmann Wells, but it was a giant leap
for womankind.[7] It announced the presence of women in the public sphere,
and the generally genial reception Borrmann received was a far cry from
the riots Fanny Wright's speeches sparked in 1829.[8]

Soapboxing affected both orators and audiences: The act served as a
crucible that gave suffragists confidence in public speaking and helped
forge their sense of themselves as independent and capable freedom fight-
ers.[9] The medium itself often was the message, because the very presence
of spunky, articulate, middle-class and/or college-educated women on the
soapbox served notice that one way or another women were a force in
American civic life. Audiences took note, and whether or not listeners
agreed with the soapboxers, suffrage got a hearing and became a topic of
both conversation and the press.

The success of the open-air campaigns helped prompt the organization
of the first American suffrage parades, a more visible and assertive form of
assembly. The spectacle of women marching shoulder to shoulder achieved
many ends. One was that because of the press coverage parades attracted,
suffrage became a nationwide issue. Women also acquired organizational
and executive skills in the course of orchestrating extravaganzas featuring
tens of thousands of marchers, floats, and bands. Better yet, parades showcased women's skills in those areas and emphasized their numbers and
determination. Finally, and most crucially, marching together imbued
women with a sense of solidarity that lifted the movement to the status of
a crusade for many participants. "To this day," Carrie Chapman Catt recalled, "[women] close their eyes and hear again the thrill of martial bugles,
the tread of marching thousands, and see the air once more ablaze with the
banners of those spectacular years."[10]

The evolution of women's use of banners symbolized their emergence
from the domestic sphere into the political sphere. Originally stitched as
tokens of nineteenth-century women's support of male groups, banners
became standards women proudly bore themselves in parades and struggled
to prevent from being shred to pieces on the White House picket line.
Banners were the most ubiquitous example of the colors and regalia that
brightened all suffrage assemblies.

The lushest of all suffrage assemblies were pageants. Pageants provided the perfect vehicle for the aesthetically minded suffragists to make their case because they fused politics with art. They also offered a socially acceptable way for women to take the public stage. But pageants were more than pretty tableaus. Suffragists added new bite to civic pageants by tackling controversy and advocating social change in pageants such as Hazel MacKaye's "The American Woman: Six Periods of American Life."[11]

The most fundamental function of pageants as suffrage assemblies was that they placed women at the center stage of history and civic life. The pageant transformed women into actors and heroes, which was an important symbolic and pragmatic step toward shedding their passivity and invisibility. The opportunity to portray ideal women and goddesses in allegorical scenes empowered suffragists and reinforced their sense of themselves as crusaders. Suffragists needed that boost in the onslaught of criticism often directed at them for transgressing the bonds of female propriety.

In a sense, suffragists strove to make their entire campaign a pageant. The fusion of colors, symbolism, and spectacle that characterized suffrage assemblies helped feminize women's foray into political activism. Their style and symbolism stamped suffrage demonstrations as distinctively belonging to women. As Alice Paul said of even her most militant protest, "We always tried to make our [picket] lines as beautiful as we could."[12]

Women's increasing willingness to speak up for their rights was most dramatically illustrated by changes in the way they wielded the petition. In 1782, North Carolina women had apologetically petitioned patriot military leaders.[13] By the antebellum era, northern women began venturing from their homes to canvass door to door for abolition, an unprecedented female political movement that also opened the door for political activism for women's rights.[14] Twentieth-century suffragists solicited and presented petitions with a flourish their ancestors never would have dreamed of, yet the women chafed at the limits of this tool of second-class citizens.[15] Finally, the pickets in 1917 dared the most brazen form of petition when voteless women demanded redress by standing at the White House gates. This time, women sought apologies instead of offering them. As one arrested picket lectured a judge: "The Constitution does not specify the form of petition. Ours was in the form of a banner."[16]

The picketing of the White House was American women's Boston Tea Party. It symbolized their revolt against male tyranny. It marked their first organized battle to exercise freedom of expression, and the spoils of the NWP's legal and moral victory included proof that the Bill of Rights spoke to women as well as men. Women's demand for civil rights showed the progression of their conception of themselves as full-fledged citizens, a self-image that was nurtured by their participation in a broadening range of public demonstrations over the previous decade.

Further, the NWP's stand during perhaps the most repressive wartime experience in American history helped ensure that World War I did not totally obliterate freedom of expression. The picketing challenged the nation's commitment to free-speech ideals. Although the Wilson administration and much of the press and public proved lacking in that commitment, that does not mean the right of assembly failed the pickets. On the contrary, the pickets relied upon the First Amendment and the venerable traditions of the right of assembly and to petition to justify their actions. Ultimately, the American legal system vindicated the pickets, and the protesters won over a significant portion of the press and public.[17]

Surely the pickets' primary motivation for martyrdom was to win public sympathy for suffrage, but the fact remains that they were among the dismal era's most outspoken champions of freedom of expression. Their articulate insistence upon asserting their rights—and their willingness to endure prison—contributed to an intellectual climate in which Americans began to take stock of civil liberties. The specter of the suppression endured by the pickets as well as other dissidents helped move the United States Supreme Court toward finally beginning to articulate a legal philosophy of freedom of expression and to enact stronger legal protections for it.

Suffragists Challenge Laws and Cultural Limits

Even before some five hundred pickets and other NWP protesters were arrested, earlier and less aggressive forms of women's suffrage assemblies had been threatened by the malleable nature of contemporary legal standards regarding freedom of expression. The caprice of individual authorities and selective enforcement of the law meant that suffragists never were free from fear that their speeches, parades, or other gatherings would be suppressed, no matter how peaceful. As far back as 1876, for instance, District of Columbia police had tried to shut down the National Woman Suffrage Association's annual convention.[18] Even in the 1910s, a mayor's disapproval could cost open-air speakers a crucial meeting permit.[19] Police hostility or indifference to suffrage soapboxers' rights could mean crowds would be allowed to harass them.[20] Suffragists faced the gravest physical danger when authorities failure to protect marchers in the 1913 Congressional Committee parade in Washington, D.C.[21]

Suffragists were forced to confront authorities to exercise virtually every aspect of their right of assembly. They usually won these battles. The way suffragists circumvented or capitalized upon such obstacles, as when they transformed a forbidden pageant into a portable tableau to evade Central Park authorities, demonstrated their ingenuity and tenacity.[22] But the fact that they had to fight to exercise what has been called the most fundamental democratic right demonstrates the shortcomings of legal protections for the right of assembly during the Progressive era. Conversely, the privileged treatment authorities sometimes accorded suffragists also revealed the era's arbitrary nature of protections.

Because the suffragists' demand for votes for women fell just within the boundaries of palatable social change, authorities tolerated it better than calls for economic and political revolution by anarchists and Socialists. Suffrage was largely a reformist movement of middle-class women with more faith in and greater attachments to the American political system than the working-class and politically radical men and women who posed greater challenges to the social order. Suffragists did not want to topple the government but to join it.

Yet consternation over suffrage assemblies echoed throughout the decades-old woman's rights movement. Critics attacked each novel form of female assembly introduced by suffragists. An early example was the ridicule rained on "rampant women" after rowdies ruined their 1853 convention.[23] In the 1910s, male discomfort with independent assemblies of discontented women surfaced in speculation that American women would turn to violent British methods like arson and rock throwing.[24] Authorities who feared suffragists would resort to violence took steps to quash perceived subversives,[25] and American publications frequently debated the propriety of the British suffragette actions.[26] When a crowd cheered an Englishwoman's suggestion that Americans begin to throw bricks, it made front-page news.[27]

Suffragists labored to calm fears of impending violence. "This country is in no more danger of invasion by militant methods than of an invasion by an army of crocodiles from the banks of the Nile," the *Woman's Journal* editorialized.[28] Even the NWP declined to adopt the label militant until late in 1917, after hundreds of peaceful pickets had been arrested and dozens imprisoned.[29] In fact, the only violence committed throughout the entire American suffrage campaign was committed against the suffragists, although they often paid the price for their audience's misdeeds.

Suffragists resented being associated with violence and correctly objected to characterizations of open-air meetings and parades as militancy. "This is a very loose use of language," complained the *Journal* when New York newspapers described the 1911 Fifth Avenue parade as militant.[30] When the label persisted, NAWSA tried to make militancy respectable by applying the term to the actions of biblical female figures such as Mary and Ruth.[31] When Americans finally began picketing during World War I, Alva Belmont of the NWP scored critics. "Why all this tenderness and delicacy about 'militancy' in the form of banner-bearing when the Governments of all nations are conscripting their men, including our own nation, to be militant?" she asked.[32] Besides, Sylvia Pankhurst reminded an American audience, they owed their freedom to militancy. "If the men of America had not gone farther than persuasion there would have been no Boston tea party, and America would still be British colonies," she said.[33]

Charges of militancy were largely a manifestation of the powerful cultural taboos against women participating in public life, particularly in the rough-and-tumble venue of the streets. Out of those taboos stemmed extralegal mechanisms—a husband's refusal to let a wife march, a heckler's jibe about uncooked meals, a mocking editorial, men grabbing the ankles of young women on parade floats—that could be more effective censors than an unfriendly police officer patrolling the block on which suffrage soapboxers sought to speak.

Challenging the confines of the home and male authority constituted treason against dichotomized gender boundaries. One effective weapon wielded to bring dissident women back in line was to accuse them of tearing American family life apart at the seams, a refrain suffragists heard often. Only a handful of the most radical women, such as anarchist Emma Goldman, could withstand such criticism. Most suffragists deflected criticism by citing home and motherhood repeatedly as they edged into more public and assertive assemblies.[34] NWP stalwarts clung the most tenaciously and outspokenly to a natural rights argument for votes for women.

One fear that seemed to loom large in the male imagination was that changes in gender roles would be reciprocal, compelling them to assume the mantle of domesticity as women moved into the public sphere. These fears often surfaced in antisuffrage cartoons that depicted men in female roles, such as pushing baby carriages in a suffrage parade. It is hard to imagine today how men conjured a scenario in which the simple act of casting a ballot would leave women no time to cook or care for children. The explanation lies in how profoundly the symbolism of women voting portended seismic changes for male gender roles.

NAWSA sought to reassure men, even passing a resolution in 1915 that upheld the home as the foundation of the state.[35] "Suffrage is a bourgeois movement," maintained the NAWSA newspaper even as police hauled NWP pickets off to jail.[36]

Cultural taboos eased as the 1910s progressed, in part reflecting the changes affecting women's role throughout society and in part because suffragists helped extend the boundaries of female behavior in public. Among the accomplishments of suffrage soapboxers, marchers, and pickets was that they helped blaze a trail for all women to participate in public life, whether it be walking down a city street or serving in Congress, a female feat first achieved by Montana suffragist Jeannette Rankin in 1916.[37]

Remarkably, in light of the violence directed at them, American suffragists established their right to assemble publicly without ever resorting to violence. Several reasons explain why American suffragists never turned to violence. One reason was that Americans were more accepting of public assemblies than the British. *Woman's Journal* editor Alice Stone Blackwell, in fact, claimed that "nine tenths" of the Britons' supposedly militant tactics would be legal in the United States.[38] Americans also were less opposed to votes for women. This greater tolerance both for the suffrage message and the form in which it was delivered accounted for generally more congenial reactions to suffrage assemblies in the United States. As observed by a formerly imprisoned British suffragette who joined the American suffragists: "American women have free access to the State and Federal legislatures, and are received with courtesy and open arms. They hold street meetings unmolested and sell their papers as they like."[39]

In contrast to the rejection the British suffragettes faced when they brought their petitions to Parliament, for instance, twentieth-century American politicians accepted suffrage petitions with great fanfare.[40]

Whereas British soapbox orators played hide and seek with Hyde Park police, New York officers generally guarded suffragists after women asserted their right to speak and meet.[41] Two months after the inaugural parade fiasco in Washington, ten police officers per block lined Fifth Avenue to ensure that the suffrage parade of ten thousand marchers went off smoothly.[42] And a federal court soon ruled the pickets' arrests unconstitutional.[43] The suffragists' success in their legal confrontations helped persuade them to stay within the democratic system.

American women also believed American men and justice superior to England's. "In America, men would give women what women wanted without a struggle," is how Doris Stevens summed up their attitude prior to the picket arrests.[44] The mushrooming number of states in which women won the vote during the final decade of the campaign also increased women's faith in the system.[45] Women gained the vote in twelve states and Alaska Territory—a quarter of the nation—between 1910 and the end of 1917.[46] Thus the New York City Woman Suffrage Party newsletter concluded in 1913, fears about American violence were groundless. "We must continue, winning state by state, through the votes of men," the *Woman Voter* said.[47] After several years, of course, the NWP would feel the need to embark on a more drastic course of action.

Yet even the NWP abstained from violence. One of the main reasons all of its protests were peaceful lay within the psyche of NWP leader Alice Paul. Although Paul threw a rock through a London window, at home she drew the line at following the British suffragette example of violence against property.[48] This was partly because she fervently believed in democracy—as her words defending woman suffrage frequently attested.[49] Paul possessed great faith in the ability of her sex to attain its goal by political means, especially as the number of woman voters multiplied. Hence she created a woman's political party and marshaled her forces in political campaigns. Just as important, she was a Quaker and a pacifist. Further, by the time Paul launched the White House pickets, she had learned that women profited when they were perceived as victims, as marchers were perceived during the 1913 inaugural parade.[50] She was one of the first Americans to harness the power of organized nonviolent civil disobedience.

The press also played a role in keeping suffrage protests peaceful by publicizing them, a role the British press apparently failed to fulfill. Suffragists credited American press coverage with making unnecessary the desperate publicity-grabbing measures to which the British suffragettes resorted. One example was the generous if breezy coverage accorded the petition pilgrimage from New York to Albany in 1912. The *Journal* concluded the ample publicity proved Americans had "no need to be lawless for attention."[51]

Solidarity in the Suffrage Movement

Perhaps even more important than the effect of suffrage assemblies upon the press and public was their effect upon the women themselves. The strong feelings of group identity and solidarity that suffrage assemblies bestowed upon participants fulfilled another vital function of the right of assembly and its related right of association. Women seemed to feed off the energy and sorority of suffrage gatherings so that the movement gained momentum as a variety of suffrage assemblies proliferated. "There was a great feeling of cooperation and admiration among the women who were working together," said soapboxer Laura Ellsworth Seiler.[52]

Banding together and working for a common cause also raised women's consciousness about their entitlement to civil rights. They began to see themselves as a disfranchised class rather than as discontented individuals. As they conquered each new level of suffrage assembly—the petition, the convention podium, the soapbox, the line of march, the pageant stage, the picket line—they became more cognizant of themselves as a part of a social movement. Suffrage became a crusade, and the women crusaders. As their numbers grew, so did the women's sense of themselves as full citizens denied the basic right of citizenship.

Suffragists had their shortcomings, but the movement could claim the impressive feat of uniting for a few years diverse groups of women whose devotion to a cause transcended their many differences. All kinds of women worked for the vote—club women, Socialists, African Americans, college students, factory workers, millionaires, immigrants, Daughters of the American Revolution, doctors, actresses. It is not so odd that acrimony spiced their relations. Present-day feminists have only recently begun to wrestle with the thorny question of whether women share an experience that bonds them at a level that transcends differences of race, class, ethnicity, or sexual orientation.

The fissures in the suffrage movement hinted that women do not comprise a monolithic entity. A number of incidents, in fact, indicated that the solidarity the suffrage movement forged among women was fragile if not illusory. Class elitism tinged relations between suffragists of differing social stations, although working women were the first American women to soapbox, march in parades, and picket.[53] Rose Winslow, an immigrant working-class Socialist, had even joined Paul in the first suffrage hunger strike in prison. Yet the relations between working women and suffrage leaders were laced with condescension. Upper-class women such as Blatch or Catt and college-educated women such as Paul led the suffrage movement, and working women never entered the upper echelons of the suffrage campaign.

The most glaring example of the movement's exclusionary practices was the way white suffragists insulted and rejected African American women throughout the twentieth-century campaign, even though black women had figured prominently in the nineteenth-century woman's rights movement. The rejection of black women by both NAWSA and the NWP was a glaring example of just one of the extralegal factors that sabotaged attempts by African Americans to exercise their constitutional rights of assembly. It demonstrated how African American women were doubly burdened by sex and race in their attempts to function as full citizens. It also proved that the white suffragists who reveled in idealizing themselves as Justice or Truth in suffrage pageants or parades held no monopoly on such qualities offstage. White suffragists could be as indifferent to the constitutional rights of others as men were to theirs. Experiencing sexual discrimination failed to sensitize white suffragists to the injustice of racial discrimination.

Incidents of racism by white suffragists made a mockery of their movement's supposed egalitarianism. One example of the casual racism of the era was a *Suffragist* cover illustration of picket inmates captioned "Refined, Intelligent Society Women Act as Pickets and are Thrown into the Workhouse with Negroes and Criminals."[54] A more calculated instance of racial discrimination occurred when Paul schemed to prevent black women from marching in the 1913 inaugural-eve parade in Washington, or when Catt conspired to help keep black women's suffrage groups out of NAWSA in 1919.[55] Despite these obstacles, African American women throughout the 1910s risked the double jeopardy of sex and race prejudice to work for the vote; they convened, spoke on soapboxes, petitioned, marched in parades, and picketed.[56]

Suffragists could be as censorious as any official when it came to expression by antisuffragists, and more than once proved themselves more interested in making themselves heard than in guaranteeing freedom of expression for all.[57] When a suffragist critic of the NWP's anti-Democrat campaign unfurled an uncomplimentary banner in the Portland, Oregon, train station upon the arrival of the NWP delegation, the delegation called police. "Solidarity of Women!" sniffed Dr. Marie Equi. "Having me arrested was an example of it."[58]

Once women won the vote, the female solidarity that dazzled in parades proved as ephemeral as the glint of the sun that illuminated the suffragists' banners. "It really was an illusion; because Alice Paul has been fighting for equal rights ever since then," jailed picket Ernestine Hara Kettler said in an interview in the 1970s.[59] The superhuman "woman of the future" proved as mortal as the late Inez Milholland, who so often portrayed her, and American society did not seem to improve much after women voted.[60]

Although the advent of suffrage may not have lived up to some expectations, those expectations were unrealistically high. Most historians of the era have concluded that the woman's movement spearheaded by the suffrage campaign enjoyed some degree of success and continuity. The creation of the Women's Joint Congressional Committee initially joined ten women's reform organizations claiming ten million members that became known as "the most powerful lobby in Washington."[61] The biggest feather in its cap was the Sheppard-Towner Act to improve the health of children and mothers, the first federal program to allocate money for social welfare. Lapsed in the late 1920s, it was reborn as the Social Security Act of 1935. That is one example of how the continued work of female reformers throughout the postsuffrage decade lay the groundwork for many social issues finally addressed in the New Deal.[62]

The impressive public assemblies of women in the 1910s, however, dissipated after 1920. One reason may have been the dissolution of the separate, public women's sphere women had created in the Progressive era. The creation of women's clubs, women's colleges, the settlement movement, and the suffrage movement amounted to what Estelle Freedman called "female institution building," which reached its zenith in 1920. No sooner had those manifestations of female assemblies been erected than newly enfranchised women, believing them no longer necessary, allowed them to crumble as women naïvely attempted to assimilate into male-dominated institutions by adopting male values and devaluing female culture. "Women gave up many of the strengths of the female sphere without gaining equally from the man's world they entered," Freedman said.[63]

As Nancy Cott has astutely demonstrated, the 1910s and 1920s comprised the era in which the "woman's movement" became the "women's movement."[64] An important consequence of the suffrage movement's success was that women wanted to be viewed as individuals. That helps explain why virtually all female political leaders save Alice Paul eschewed a female voting block. But their emphasis upon individuality left women without an organizing base and vulnerable to pervasive external forces at work to dissolve the powerful associations of women that arose in the 1910s. Mainstream political parties condemned as sex war the notion of a female voting bloc and pressured women to join existing, male-dominated parties. So did the press, and the combined wrath of all of these powerful political forces contributed to the stalled agenda of the NWP, the only self-proclaimed feminist organization after 1920.[65] The *New York Times,* for instance, let loose its guns upon the "ugly portent" it saw behind creation of the Woman's Party.[66]

In contrast to the NWP, as suffrage edged closer to reality, NAWSA strived to appease male hostility to a female voting bloc. NAWSA opposed creation of a "sex segregated" party, and its newspaper assured readers suffrage did not mean a "massing of women against men."[67] NAWSA also changed its slogan from "Votes for Women" to the less threatening "Ballots for Both."[68] NAWSA president Catt reiterated, "There is no war, no conflict, no misunderstanding between the sexes."[69] NAWSA's conciliatory attitude, however, defused it as a political force after women won the vote. After NAWSA became the League of Women Voters in 1920, the organization unwittingly collaborated in quashing women's political voice by steering a lively yet nonpartisan course of educating women to work within existing parties. Women activists also fell victim to the ultraconservatism that swept the nation in the early 1920s.[70] The Red Scare brewed further repression of civil liberties that offered more evidence of the fragility of freedom of assembly and related rights.[71]

Women's emphasis upon individuality also was a product of Americans' fixation upon the self in the 1920s. Women's priorities accordingly changed from the collective struggle for the vote to individual struggles for careers. Emancipated women caught up in the entrepreneurial spirit of the 1920s "are now enduring liberty as interior decorators," noted Walter Lippmann in a lament for the end of the Progressive era.[72] The image of independent womanhood switched from a suffrage soapboxer to the flapper, whose self-indulgent individualism may have sounded the "keynote to modernity," as historian Nancy Woloch put it, but was antithetical to the suffrage creed.[73] Reformer Mary Heaton Verse ruefully noted upon returning home from Europe in 1928 that whereas youth in her day marched, the new youth danced. The younger generation's indifference to feminism, however, may in fact have reflected the success of their predecessors' agenda. "The new generation was free to move on to new issues and new challenges," noted historian Dorothy Brown.[74]

Yet as female assemblies receded, women's individualism "left them painfully alone in a world that continued to discriminate against women," historian Sara Evans observed.[75] The irony of suffrage's eventual success was that it spelled the end of the solidarity women had achieved during the fight for votes. Suffragists who celebrated in "jubilee meetings" across the nation in 1920 seemed unaware that ratification of the Nineteenth Amendment not only made them an anachronism but also cut the tie that bound them.[76]

Alice Paul alone among the former suffrage leaders retained her focus on a women's political block, training all of her energy on passage of an Equal Rights Amendment, which she believed would resolve women's legal and economic inequities. The blinders she wore concerning other women's issues alienated her from labor, leftist, and African American support. When Paul died in 1977 at age ninety-two, the ERA had yet to be ratified, although she succeeded in adding an equal-rights provision to the preamble of the United Nations charter.[77] The nearly dormant NWP today has head-quarters in Washington, D.C., in the basement of the national-landmark Sewell-Belmont House, where the party moved in 1929.[78]

Other leaders moved on to new interests, most notably world peace. Catt organized and chaired the Committee on the Cause and Cure of War.[79] Blatch worked hard for creation of the League of Nations and for world peace as well as for the ERA.[80] Pageant writer Hazel MacKaye retired from political themes, publishing pageants for schoolchildren, churches, and laborers before her health failed.[81] NWP firebrand Lucy Burns retreated to church and family in New York.[82] Mabel Vernon, the dynamic orator and NWP picket organizer, in 1935 shepherded the collection of four million signatures on a petition calling for world peace as director of the People's

Mandate to Governments to End War.[83] Newspaper accounts of Maud Malone, an enigmatic figure in the forefront of the spectrum of great suffrage assemblies in the 1910s, disappeared. Malone organized the first suffrage open-air meeting, led the movement's first parade, was arrested for interrupting a meeting addressed by Woodrow Wilson, picketed the White House, and signed the first document seeking political-prisoner status in the United States.[84]

Resurgence of Women's Protests

Women protesting in the streets also virtually disappeared for decades. The next time women protesters took to the streets in any numbers was during the civil rights movement in the 1950s and 1960s. During those decades, African American women were on the front lines of the dangerous forms of civil disobedience, such as sit-ins and freedom rides, which became the hallmark of the civil rights campaign. "Many of the protests that historians describe as led by ministers were initiated by women," historian Anne Standley wrote.[85] Jo Ann Robinson, for instance, was the "Joan of Arc" of the Montgomery bus boycott, according to a fellow member of the Women's Political Council, a group of black women who spearheaded the boycott after Rosa Parks refused to sit at the back of a city bus in 1955.[86] Diane Nash and Ruby Doris Smith became legends for their heroism on freedom rides and in prison in the early 1960s. Ella Baker, Septima Clark, and Fannie Lou Hamer were movement leaders.[87]

The effect upon young African American women engaged in civil disobedience seemed similar to that described by suffragists decades earlier when they ventured onto the street to soapbox, parade, or picket. Bernice Reagon, who was suspended from Albany (Georgia) State College for participating in civil rights demonstrations, said for her the most significant aspect of demonstrating lay with its liberating effect on her sense of self. "There was a sense of power, in a place where you didn't feel you had any power," she said. "The Civil Rights Movement gave me the power to challenge *any* line that limits me."[88]

Ironically, given the cold shoulder black women received from white suffragists in the 1910s, the example and leadership of African American women civil rights workers helped inspire the mostly middle-class, mostly white women's liberation movement of the 1960s and 1970s. "For the first time," said one young, white northerner of the black women activists she encountered in the South, "I had role models I could really respect."[89]

Many of these civil rights workers went on to participate in the protests of the second wave of feminism in the late 1960s and early 1970s. The aborted women's strike of 1915, for instance, finally took shape as the Women's Strike for Equality on 26 August 1970, in commemoration of the golden anniversary of the ratification of the Nineteenth Amendment. In New York on that day, fifty thousand women marched down Fifth Avenue in the largest demonstration ever by American women, many dressed in white like the suffragists who marched before them.[90]

The women's peace movement that arose during the Cold War also traced its history to suffrage protests. Leaders of Women Strike for Peace (WSP), born on 1 November 1961, when tens of thousands of American women took to the streets in a one-day peace protest, claimed kinship with suffrage protesters. WSP pickets and sit-in strikers followed in the footsteps of the White House pickets. As participant Catharine Stimpson wrote of a 1969 protest that fused the black civil rights movement, peace movement and feminism: "On a cold and snowy day, we marched through the streets of our capital, stamping our booted feet and exercising our First Amendment rights."[91] On 26 August 1995, two thousand American women again took to the streets to march down the same route along Pennsylvania Avenue as did suffragists on 3 March 1913 to commemorate the seventy-fifth anniversary of the ratification of the Nineteenth Amendment.[92]

One difference between the suffrage protests of the 1910s and the feminist protests of the 1960s was that the latter aimed to transform gender roles, a vastly more amorphous and threatening concept than the suffragists' single-minded campaign for the vote. Suffragists cloaked their social intransigence in pieties about the need for voting mothers to protect their children and homes. Women's liberation demonstrations attacked those values in demonstrations that sought to outrage onlookers. A particularly flamboyant symbolic protest in 1968 saw women toss "instruments of torture"—high heels, bras, girdles, curlers, and false eyelashes—into a "Freedom Trash Can" on the Atlantic City boardwalk outside the Miss America pageant.[93]

In contrast, the suffragists in the 1910s infused their protests with dignity and beauty. The suffragists wanted to impress male observers that they deserved the vote; women's liberationists took pains to reject male values.

Only the final protests of the militant NWP, most notably when protesters burned Wilson in effigy, came close to the angry symbolism used by protesters of the 1960s. Suffragists venerated democratic institutions; women's liberationists questioned them. A meeting between the two generations epitomized their philosophical and stylistic differences: When two radical women visited Alice Paul at NWP headquarters in 1972 to invite her to help burn voter-registration cards, the octogenarian "hit the ceiling."[94]

Another difference between women's protests in the 1910s and 1960s was that during the decades between them the judiciary had expanded protections for citizens' rights to assemble peaceably.[95] Although the debate continues on the limits of the right to assemble peaceably, protesters today have firmer legal ground to stand on when they demonstrate. Part of the impetus for rulings that solidified protections for the right of assembly was the influence that the suffragists in the streets had upon the American public and legal system.

American women owe the suffragists a debt for winning them the vote, but all Americans are indebted to the suffragists for the forthright way they insisted upon exercising their right to assemble peaceably.

APPENDIX I

Suffrage Organizations

Alpha Suffrage Club: First organization of African American women devoted solely to obtaining the vote. Founded in Chicago in 1913 by journalist Ida Wells-Barnett.

American Woman Suffrage Association (AWSA): Conservative suffrage organization founded in 1869 with Rev. Henry Ward Beecher as president; merged in 1890 with the National Woman Suffrage Association.

College Women's Equal Suffrage League: National organization incorporated in Buffalo in 1908; Radcliffe College alumnae Maud Wood Park and Inez Haynes (Irwin) had formed the first chapter in Boston six years earlier. Colors: violet, green, and buff. Members marched in parades in their academic caps and gowns.

Congressional Committee: The committee of the National American Woman Suffrage Association devoted to working toward a federal amendment. It galvanized the drive for a federal suffrage amendment beginning with its first meeting on 2 January 1913, under the leadership of new chair Alice Paul at its new headquarters at 1420 F Street in Washington, D.C. It sponsored the 1913 inaugural-eve parade and pageant in Washington, D.C.

Congressional Union for Woman Suffrage (CU): Washington, D.C.–based organization devoted to obtaining a federal suffrage amendment founded by Alice Paul and Lucy Burns in April 1913 to supplement the work of the NAWSA Congressional Committee. In March 1917, the union merged with the Woman's Party of Western Voters into the National Woman's Party.

Empire State Campaign Committee: Coalition of the New York City Woman Suffrage Party, College Equal Suffrage League, Equal Franchise Society, Men's League for Woman Suffrage, and the New York State Suffrage Association organized in November 1913 to lead the New York state referendum campaign. Carrie Chapman Catt served as chair until she resigned at the end of 1915 to become president of NAWSA.

Equal Franchise Society: New York City suffrage club headed by wealthy socialite Catherine MacKay. Colors: light blue, silver, and white.

Equality League of Self-Supporting Women: New York City suffrage club formed in 1907 that united working women with financially independent women, headed by Harriot Stanton Blatch. Its successor was the Women's Political Union, a leader in open-air meetings, parades, and other propaganda.

International Woman Suffrage Alliance: Organization of suffrage groups from around the world, headed by Carrie Chapman Catt for many years. Color: yellow.

Men's League for Equal Suffrage: New York City organization founded by Max Eastman, editor of the socialist magazine *Masses* and brother of feminist Crystal Eastman. Members marched in Fifth Avenue parades.

National American Woman Suffrage Association (NAWSA): Largest American suffrage organization with two million members by 1917, it was the product of the 1890 merger between the National Woman Suffrage Association and the American Woman Suffrage Association. Dr. Anna Howard Shaw was president from 1905 to 1915. Carrie Chapman Catt was president from 1900 to 1904 and December of 1915 to 1920, when it became the League of Women Voters. Published *Progress* newspaper until 1910; affiliated with *Woman's Journal* newspaper 1910–1917; published the *Woman Citizen* 1917–1931. Color: yellow.

National Association Opposed to Woman Suffrage (NAOWS): Antisuffragist organization headed by Josephine Dodge.

National Progressive Woman Suffrage League: Short-lived militant organization founded by British suffragette Bettina Borrmann Wells in New York City in 1907.

National Woman Suffrage Association (NWSA): Founded in 1869 with Elizabeth Cady Stanton as president; merged with AWSA into NAWSA in 1890.

National Woman's Party (NWP): Product of merger on 2–4 March 1917 between the Congressional Union for Woman Suffrage and the Woman's Party of Western Voters; chaired by Alice Paul and sponsor of the 1917 White House pickets. Colors: purple, white, and gold. Published the *Suffragist* weekly newspaper 1913–1921. First called for an Equal Rights Amendment in 1923 and continues to operate out of headquarters at the Sewell-Belmont House in Washington, D.C.

National Union of Women's Suffrage Societies (NUWSS): British organization of constitutionalists headed by Millicent Fawcett. Colors: red and white.

New York City Woman Suffrage Party: A coalition of city suffrage clubs organized in October 1909 by Carrie Chapman Catt, who was its first chair. Published the monthly *Woman Voter* newsletter 1910–1917. Colors: blue, white, and yellow.

Political Equality League: New York City suffrage club headed by wealthy socialite Alva Belmont, later a generous supporter of the National Woman's Party.

Woman's Party of Western Voters (WP): Political party organized by the Congressional Union in Chicago on 5–7 June 1916. Anne Martin of Nevada was its first chair.

Women's Freedom League: Founded in England by Charlotte Despard in 1907; favored symbolic demonstrations. Colors: green, white, and gold.

Women's Political Union (WPU): Successor to the Equality League of Self-Supporting Women in 1910 and headed by Harriot Stanton Blatch. Published monthly *Women's Political World.* Colors: purple, green, and white.

Women's Social and Political Union (WSPU): Militant British suffragette organization that advocated "Deeds Not Words," founded by Emmeline Pankhurst in 1903. Published *Votes for Women* from 1907 to 1912 and the *Suffragette* from 1912 to August 1914. Colors: purple, green, and white, inaugurated as a uniform by Emmeline Pethick-Lawrence on Women's Sunday at Hyde Park on 21 June 1908.

Prominent Suffragists in the 1910s

Alva Belmont: New York City millionaire (former wife of William K. Vanderbilt and widow of Oliver H. P. Belmont) who founded the Political Equality League and later was an executive board member and a generous financial supporter of the NWP.

Harriot Stanton Blatch: Founder of the Equality League of Self-Supporting Women, which became the Women's Political Union in 1910. A leader in innovations in suffrage assemblies, including open-air campaigns and parades. Daughter of Elizabeth Cady Stanton.

Lucy Burns: Vice chair of the NAWSA Congressional Committee and of the CU and executive member of the NWP. She requested political-prisoner status for jailed suffrage pickets in October 1917. One of the first two White House pickets arrested, she served more jail time during six sentences than any other suffrage protester.

Carrie Chapman Catt: President of NAWSA from 1900 to 1904 and from December 1915 to 1920. Credited with conceiving NAWSA's "winning plan." In the interim, she headed the Empire State Campaign Committee for woman suffrage in New York. She also was the prime mover behind the International Woman Suffrage Alliance from 1902 to 1923.

Rheta Childe Dorr: Prominent journalist and author of the influential feminist book *What Eight Million Women Want;* first editor of the NWP newspaper, *Suffragist.*

Crystal Eastman: Feminist, socialist, and pacifist who was one of five original members of the NAWSA Congressional Committee headed by Paul.

Sara Bard Field: Poet and activist who drove cross country in 1915 from San Francisco to Washington, D.C., to deliver to Congress a petition for a federal suffrage amendment sponsored by the CU and WP.

Susan FitzGerald: Leader of the Boston Equal Suffrage Association for Good Government who undertook a pioneering open-air campaign by trolley car across Massachusetts in 1909.

Inez Haynes Irwin: Cofounder with Maud Wood Park of the College Women's Equal Suffrage League. NWP historian and author of *The Story of the Woman's Party.*

Rosalie Jones: Led a suffrage petition pilgrimage by foot from New York City to Albany in December 1912.

Hazel MacKaye: Pageant writer and director; creator of major suffrage pageants, including "The Allegory" and "Susan B. Anthony."

Maud Malone: New York City woman who organized the first American open-air meeting for woman suffrage, led the first American suffrage parade, was arrested for heckling presidential candidate Woodrow Wilson, and served sixty days for picketing the White House.

Anne Martin: Vice chair of the NWP, chair of the WP, and head of NAWSA's victorious suffrage campaign in Nevada in 1914. She unsuccessfully ran for the United States Senate in that state in 1918.

Inez Milholland (Boissevain): Beautiful herald in 1913 suffrage parades in New York City and Washington, D.C., who also represented the "modern woman" in suffrage pageants. Graduate of Vassar College and New York University Law School. She died in November 1916 after collapsing while lecturing for suffrage; among the memorial services was one conducted by the CU in the Capitol Statuary Hall, the first there for a woman.

Katharine Morey: Along with Lucy Burns, the first American woman arrested for picketing the White House on 22 June 1917.

Emmeline Pankhurst: Founder and leader of the militant Women's Social and Political Union in England and mother of suffragettes Sylvia and Christabel. She was detained on Ellis Island when she visited the United States to speak.

Maud Wood Park: Cofounder of the College Women's Equal Suffrage League with Inez Haynes Irwin. Chair of the NAWSA Congressional Committee from 1917 to 1920. Graduate of Radcliffe College.

Alice Paul: As chair of the CU and the NWP, she orchestrated bold assemblies, including petition processions, parades, picketing of the White House, and watch fires of freedom. After she was sentenced to seven months in jail for picketing, Paul went on a hunger strike in November 1917 that forced the Wilson administration to abandon its battle with the NWP.

Dr. Anna Howard Shaw: President of NAWSA from 1905 to 1915 and one of the movement's most forceful speakers. She also was a physician and an ordained minister.

Doris Stevens: A NWP executive board member and jailed White House picket whose book *Jailed for Freedom* is a classic account of the experience.

Mary Church Terrell: First president of the National Association of Colored Women, she addressed NAWSA several times and picketed the White House with the NWP.

Mabel Vernon: Pioneer in suffrage open-air campaigns, advance person for Sara Bard Field's cross-country automobile pilgrimage, and organizer of the White House pickets. She created a stir when she unfurled a yellow suffrage banner from the Senate gallery in 1916.

Bettina Borrmann Wells: British woman considered the founder of the American suffragettes; founded the National Progressive Woman Suffrage League in New York City in 1907. She spoke at the first organized open-air suffrage meeting in the United States and helped lead the first American suffrage parade.

Maud Younger: The chief congressional lobbyist for the NWP. Dubbed the "millionaire waitress" because she was a wealthy young woman who almost single-handedly organized the Waitresses Union of San Francisco.

Chronology of Events
in the U.S. Suffrage Movement

19–20 July 1848: The first woman's rights convention at Seneca Falls, New York, issues a "Declaration of Sentiments" seeking improved rights and opportunities for women, including the vote.

23–24 October 1850: First National Woman's Rights Convention held in Worcester, Massachusetts.

19 March 1860: Elizabeth Cady Stanton addresses the New York State Legislature on woman suffrage.

1867–68: Susan B. Anthony and Elizabeth Cady Stanton unsuccessfully lead the first petition drive of Congress to include women in the Fifteenth Amendment protecting voting rights.

1868–69: Susan B. Anthony and Elizabeth Cady Stanton petition Congress for introduction of a Sixteenth Amendment to grant women the vote.

19 November 1868: One hundred seventy-two women cast ballots in a mock voting booth to demonstrate their desire for the ballot on election day in Vineland, New Jersey.

7 January 1869: Susan Anthony and Elizabeth Cady Stanton publish the first issue of the *Revolution* newspaper dedicated to winning the vote for women.

15 March 1869: Woman suffrage constitutional amendment proposed in a joint resolution to Congress.

15 May 1869: Creation of the National Woman Suffrage Association (NWSA) with Elizabeth Cady Stanton as president.

24 November 1869: Creation of the American Woman Suffrage Association (AWSA) with Henry Ward Beecher as president.

June 1873: Susan Anthony is convicted of trying to vote in a federal election in Rochester, New York.

29 March 1875: The United States Supreme Court rules in *Minor v. Happersett* that the Constitution did not confer the vote upon all citizens and that citizenship is not coextensive with voting.

4 July 1876: Susan B. Anthony disrupts centennial festivities in Philadelphia to present officials with a Declaration of Rights for Women.

10 January 1878: The joint resolution calling for the Susan B. Anthony amendment is first introduced in Congress by Senator A. A. Sargent of California.

11 January 1885: Alice Paul is born.

28 October 1886: Women conduct an alternative ceremony at the unveiling of the Statue of Liberty to protest their disfranchisement.

25 January 1887: Woman suffrage amendment first brought to a vote in the Senate, where it is defeated 16–34.

18 February 1890: AWSA and NWSA merge to form the National American Woman Suffrage Association (NAWSA).

19 May 1906: Seven thousand listeners appear at England's first open-air suffrage meeting in Trafalgar Square in London.

February 1907: Two working women address the New York State Legislature in Albany on the necessity of woman suffrage under the auspices of the Equality League of Self-Supporting Women.

9 February 1907: The "Mud March" of three thousand women becomes the first of London's sizable suffrage processions.

31 December 1907: First organized open-air meeting for suffrage in United States conducted by Maud Malone and Bettina Borrmann Wells in Madison Square in New York City.

16 February 1908: Maud Malone and Bettina Borrmann Wells lead first American suffrage parade from Union Square in New York City.

May 1908: Maud Malone and Harriot Stanton Blatch conduct a two-week open-air campaign via trolley across upstate New York to commemorate the sixtieth anniversary of the Seneca Falls woman's rights convention.

21 June 1908: "Women's Sunday" in London attracts half a million people to Hyde Park, the largest assembly in history.

8 December 1908: A mob howls down British suffragette leader Emmeline Pankhurst for forty-five minutes on New York City's Wall Street.

January 1909: Two thousand women march from Beacon Hill into the State House in Boston to ask the legislature to remove the word "male" from the state constitution.

27 June 1909: Painter Marion Wallace Dunlop begins the first British suffrage hunger strike in prison.

July–August 1909: Susan FitzGerald leads a month-long, statewide open-air campaign of Massachusetts aboard a trolley.

August 1909: NAWSA conducts its first workshop on how to conduct an open-air meeting.

31 October 1909: The New York City Woman Suffrage Party is founded with Carrie Chapman Catt as its chair.

April 1910: Women hiss President William Howard Taft at the NAWSA convention when he refers to suffragists as "hottentots."

18 April 1910: NAWSA automobile procession delivers to the Senate a national petition bearing 404,825 signatures in support of a suffrage amendment.

21 May 1910: Parade of ninety automobiles and several thousand marchers sponsored by Women's Political Union starts tradition of spectacular suffrage parades on Fifth Avenue.

17 January 1911: First suffrage-related pageant/tableau produced in New York City.

25 July 1911: Alice Paul leads six women in the first open-air meeting conducted in Philadelphia.

18 October 1912: Police charge Maud Malone with disturbing a meeting when she asks presidential candidate Woodrow Wilson in Brooklyn "What about woman suffrage?" and refuses to sit down when he refuses to answer.

16 December 1912: Pilgrimage of suffrage petitioners led by "General" Rosalie Jones departs New York City for Albany.

2 January 1913: The NAWSA Congressional Committee has its first meeting under the direction of new chair Alice Paul at its new headquarters at 1420 F Street in Washington, D.C. The other four new committee members are Vice Chair Lucy Burns, historian Mary Beard, Crystal Eastman, and Dora Kelley Lewis.

3 March 1913: The Congressional Committee of NAWSA sponsors a parade of five thousand women on Pennsylvania Avenue on the eve of Wilson's inauguration. The resulting melee prompts Senate hearings. The accompanying pageant, "The Allegory," directed by Hazel MacKaye on the steps of the U.S. Treasury Building, is the first national pageant.

17 March 1913: First suffrage deputation to President Woodrow Wilson organized by Alice Paul, then NAWSA Congressional Committee chair.

April 1913: Alice Paul and Lucy Burns form the CU to concentrate on a federal suffrage amendment; Paul continues to chair the NAWSA Congressional Committee.

31 July 1913: Five hundred thirty-one petition bearers representing the NAWSA Congressional Committee deliver petitions with two hundred thousand signatures to senators after an eighty-car automobile parade to the Capitol.

18 October 1913: WSPU leader Emmeline Pankhurst is detained for three days by immigration officials on Ellis Island.

19 March 1914: The Senate rejects a suffrage amendment thirty-five to thirty-four, far short of the required two-thirds majority.

17 April 1914: Hazel MacKaye's innovative pageant "The American Woman: Six Periods of American Life" debuts in New York City.

3 November 1914: The CU helps defeat twenty-three of forty-three Democratic congressional candidates in the Western states as part of its policy to oppose the party in power.

12 January 1915: The House defeats a suffrage amendment 174 to 204.

Summer 1915: The New York City Woman Suffrage Party conducts 5,225 outdoor meetings as a part of its Empire State suffrage referendum campaign.

16 September 1915: Ten thousand well-wishers send off envoy Sara Bard Field from the Panama Pacific Exposition in San Francisco on a cross-country auto tour to deliver to Congress a huge suffrage petition sponsored by the CU.

23 October 1915: As many as fifty thousand women march on Fifth Avenue in the largest American suffrage procession, cheered by half a million onlookers.

November 1915: Suffrage loses in New York State 553,348 to 748,332. Referenda also fail in Massachusetts, New Jersey, and Pennsylvania.

5 December 1915: Women march to Capitol steps bearing an 18,333-foot petition delivered by Sara Bard Field from Western women voters. President Wilson greets Field and three hundred other women in the White House.

13 December 1915: "Susan B. Anthony," Hazel MacKaye's most popular pageant, debuts during the annual CU convention in Washington, D.C.

9 April 1916: "Suffrage Special" train departs Washington, D.C., with twenty-three CU speakers on a four-week tour of the western states to recruit women for a convention to launch a woman's political party.

5–7 June 1916: At a Chicago convention, the CU organizes the Woman's Party of Western Voters (WP) in the twelve states in which women vote.

June 1916: Five thousand women march through wind and rain into the Republican National Convention platform committee hearings on woman suffrage. The GOP adds a suffrage plank to the platform.

15 June 1916: "Walkless parade" of four thousand women sponsored by NAWSA occurs at the Democratic National Convention in St. Louis. The party adds a suffrage plank to the platform.

16 September 1916: President Wilson addresses the NAWSA convention in Atlantic City, telling the women, "I have not come here to fight anybody, *but with somebody.*"

20 October 1916: Crowds attack WP members who unfurl a banner outside a Chicago hall where the president is speaking.

7 November 1916: Election day spells failure for the WP and CU's anti-Democrat campaign, in which peace candidate Wilson wins ten of twelve suffrage states.

25 November 1916: Inez Milholland dies four weeks after collapsing on a Los Angeles stage while delivering a speech for suffrage during the anti-Democrat campaign. Her supposed last words onstage, "Mr. President, how long must women wait for liberty?" become a rallying cry of the NWP.

25 December 1916: A memorial service for Inez Milholland in the Capitol Statuary Hall is the first for a woman held there.

9 January 1917: The Inez Milholland Memorial Delegation of three hundred women fails to extract a promise from Wilson to support a federal suffrage amendment.

10 January 1917: CU and WP begin picketing the White House with a perpetual delegation of "silent sentinels."

2–4 March 1917: CU and WP merge into the National Woman's Party (NWP). Founding officers are Alice Paul, chair; Anne Martin, vice chair; Mabel Vernon, secretary; and members of the executive board: Lucy Burns, Alva Belmont, Eleanor Brannon, Matilda Gardner, Abby Scott Baker, Elizabeth Kent, Maud Younger, Doris

Stevens, Florence Bayard Hilles, Edith Houghton Hooker, Allison Hopkins, and Dora Lewis. The convention culminates in a protest on 4 March in which one thousand women circle the White House four times in slashing rain on Inauguration Day.

6 April 1917: United States enters World War I.

22 June 1917: Lucy Burns and Katharine Morey become the first pickets arrested in front of the White House.

27 October 1917: Women carry a mile-long petition bearing the signatures of 1,013,531 women in the final Fifth Avenue suffrage parade of twenty thousand women.

5 November 1917: Alice Paul and Rose Winslow launch a hunger strike at the District of Columbia jail seeking political-prisoner status two weeks into their seven-month sentence for obstructing the sidewalk in front of the White House.

6 November 1917: Woman suffrage referendum succeeds in New York state.

15 November 1917: The "Night of Terror" at Occoquan Workhouse inspires two dozen imprisoned suffragists to begin a hunger strike.

20 November 1917: The British House of Commons passes a limited woman suffrage bill, allowing female property holders thirty years and older to vote. The House of Lords approves it on 10 January 1918.

27–28 November 1917: District of Columbia prison officials release all suffrage prisoners.

9 January 1918: President Wilson declares his support for a federal suffrage amendment.

10 January 1918: House approves Nineteenth Amendment exactly by the required two-thirds majority, 274 to 136.

4 March 1918: Federal appeals court declares unconstitutional the arrest and detainment of all White House pickets.

6 August 1918: NWP protest at Lafayette Monument results in the arrest of forty-eight women; twenty-six of them receive five- to ten-day sentences.

16 September 1918: The NWP burns copies of President Wilson's speeches and books in front of the White House. No arrests made.

1 October 1918: The Senate rejects the suffrage amendment, sixty-two to thirty-four, two votes shy of the required two-thirds majority.

2 December 1918: In his annual message to Congress, Wilson urges it to pass a suffrage amendment.

16 December 1918: The NWP again burns works by Wilson on the anniversary of the Boston Tea Party.

1 January 1919: The "watch fires of freedom" begin on the sidewalk in front of the White House.

9 February 1919: Sue Shelton White of the NWP ignites cartoon effigy of President Wilson in front of the White House. Thirty-nine of the protesters are charged with setting fires and sentenced to five days in jail.

10 February 1919: Senate vote of fifty-five to twenty-nine on the suffrage amendment falls one vote short of the required two-thirds majority.

20 May 1919: The House passes the suffrage amendment a second time, 304 to 89.

4 June 1919: The Senate approves the Nineteenth Amendment, fifty-six to twenty-five.

18 August 1920: Tennessee becomes the thirty-sixth and final state necessary to ratify the Nineteenth Amendment.

26 August 1920: Secretary of State Bainbridge Colby signs the proclamation that adds the Nineteenth Amendment to the U.S. Constitution.

2 November 1920: For the first time, women across the United States can vote.

When and Where Women Won the Vote

STATE	YEAR
Wyoming Territory	1869 (joined Union in 1890)
Colorado	1893
Utah	1896*
Idaho	1896
Washington	1910
California	1911
Arizona	1912
Kansas	1912
Oregon	1912
Alaska Territory	1913
Illinois	1913 (presidential)
Montana	1914
Nevada	1914
Nebraska	1917 (presidential)
New York	1917
North Dakota	1917 (presidential)
Rhode Island	1917 (presidential)
Michigan	1918
Oklahoma	1918
South Dakota	1918
Indiana	1919 (presidential)
Iowa	1919 (presidential)
Maine	1919 (presidential)
Minnesota	1919 (presidential)
Missouri	1919 (presidential)
Ohio	1919 (presidential)
Tennessee	1919 (presidential)
Wisconsin	1919 (presidential)
Kentucky	1920 (presidential)

As of 1910, women voted in school elections in Arizona, Colorado, Connecticut, Delaware, Kansas, Kentucky, Massachusetts, Michigan, Minnesota, Mississippi, Montana, Nebraska, New Hampshire, New Jersey, New Mexico, New York, North Dakota, Ohio, Oklahoma, Oregon, South Dakota, Vermont, Washington, and Wisconsin.

As of 1908, women voted on taxes and bonds in Iowa, Kansas, Louisiana, Massachusetts, Michigan, Montana, New Hampshire, and New York.

Kansas women also voted in municipal elections as of 1887.

*Utah had woman suffrage as a territory from 1870 to 1887, when Congress took it away.

Source: The National American Woman Suffrage Association, ed., *Victory! How Women Won It: A Centennial Symposium, 1840–1940* (New York: H. W. Wilson, 1940), app. 4, pp. 161–64.

NOTES

Introduction

1. "The Great Celebration," *New York Times*, 27 Oct. 1886, 2; "The Statue Unveiled," *New York Times*, 9 Oct. 1886, 2; and "World-Lighting Liberty," *New York Daily Tribune*, 29 Oct. 1886, 2.

2. Sally Roesch Wagner, *A Time of Protest: Suffragists Challenge the Republic, 1870–1877* (Carmichael, Calif.: Sky Carrier Press, 1988), 104.

3. "Congress shall make no law respecting an establishment of religion, or prohibiting the free exercise thereof; or abridging the freedom of speech, or of the press; or the right of the people peaceably to assemble, and to petition the Government for a redress of grievances." U.S. Constitution, amend. 1.

4. James Jarrett and Vernon Mund, "The Right of Assembly," *New York University Law Quarterly Review* 9 (1931): 1–38.

5. None of the major accounts of the twentieth-century women's rights movement analyze women's rights activists' protests in a free-speech context. See Nancy Cott, *The Grounding of Modern Feminism* (New Haven, Conn.: Yale Univ. Press, 1987); Alice Echols, *Daring to Be Bad* (Minneapolis: Univ. of Minnesota Press, 1989); Sara Evans, *Born for Liberty: A History of Women in America* (New York: Free Press, 1989); Eleanor Flexner, *Century of Struggle: The Woman's Rights Movement in the United States,* (Cambridge: Belknap Press, Harvard Univ. Press, 1959; rev. ed., New York: Atheneum, 1971); Linda Ford, *Iron-Jawed Angels: The Suffrage Militancy of the National Woman's Party, 1912–1920* (Lanham, Md.: Univ. Press of America, 1991); Aileen Kraditor, *The Ideas of the Woman Suffrage Movement, 1890–1920* (New York: Columbia Univ. Press, 1965); Christine Lunardini, *From Equal Suffrage to Equal Rights: Alice Paul and the National Woman's Party, 1910–1928* (New York: New York Univ. Press, 1986); and William O'Neill, *Everyone Was Brave: The Rise and Fall of Feminism in America* (Chicago: Quadrangle Books, 1969). Only two histories of free speech mention the jailed suffragists. See Margaret Blanchard, *Revolutionary Sparks: Freedom of Expression in Modern America* (New York: Oxford Univ. Press, 1992), 90–91; and Leon Whipple, *The Story of Civil Liberty in the United States* (New York: Vanguard Press, 1927), 312–17. Women's struggle for freedom of expression is omitted in Zechariah Chafee Jr., *Freedom of Speech* (New York: Harcourt, Brace

and Howe, 1920); Charles Goodell, *Political Prisoners in America* (New York: Random House, 1973); Nat Hentoff, *The First Freedom: The Tumultuous History of Free Speech in America* (New York: Delacorte Press, 1980); and Harry Kalven Jr., *A Worthy Tradition: Freedom of Speech in America* (New York: Harper & Row, 1988). Landmark court cases stemming from the civil rights movement are chronicled in the aggregate with no special attention to women's participation in Harry Kalven Jr., *The Negro and the 1st Amendment*, rev. ed. (Chicago: Phoenix Books, 1966). Neither do any of the above books discuss women's integral role in the free-speech battles that emanated from the abolition movement. Chafee's blanket description of abolitionists as "men whom we all honor to-day" is indicative of how women's contribution to American political culture has been overlooked by historians. Chafee, *Freedom of Speech*, 372.

6. Glenn Abernathy, *The Right of Assembly and Association* (Columbia: Univ. of South Carolina Press, 1981), 4.

7. Frederic Jesup Stimson, *The Law of the Federal and State Constitutions of the United States* (Boston: Boston Book, 1908), 43.

8. Jarrett and Mund, "Right of Assembly," 5.

9. "Public Order and the Right of Assembly in England and the United States: A Comparative Study," *Yale Law Journal* 47 (1938): 404.

10. *Hague v. CIO*, 307 U.S. 496 (1939).

11. *United States v. Cruikshank*, 92 U.S. 542, 551 (1875).

12. William Sharp McKechnie, *The Magna Charta: A Commentary on the Great Charter of King John*, rev. ed. (New York: Burt Franklin, 1958), 467. The charter implied a right of assembly in the portion granting delegations of four barons the right to petition the king for redress of grievances. Ibid.

13. Gordon Wood, "A Note on Mobs in the American Revolution," *William and Mary Quarterly*, 3rd ser., 23 (1966): 640.

14. Whipple, *Story of Civil Liberty*, 52.

15. Pauline Maier, "Popular Uprisings and Civil Authority in Eighteenth-Century America," in *Interpreting Colonial America: Selected Readings*, ed. James Kirby Martin (New York: Harper & Row, 1978), 372, 374.

16. George Smith II, "The Development of the Right of Assembly—A Current Socio-legal Investigation," *William and Mary Law Review* 9 (1967–68): 361.

17. *Annals of Congress*, 1st Cong., 1789–90, microfiche ed., 1, col. 731.

18. Maier, "Popular Uprisings and Civil Authority," 375.

19. A mob murdered abolitionist editor Elijah Lovejoy. Dorothy Sterling, *Ahead of Her Time: Abby Kelley and the Politics of Antislavery* (New York: W. W. Norton, 1991), 58.

20. The United States Supreme Court incorporated First Amendment protections into the Fourteenth Amendment in *Gitlow v. New York*, 268 U.S. 652 (1925).

21. Margaret Blanchard, "Filling in the Void: Speech and Press in State Courts Prior to *Gitlow*," in *The First Amendment Reconsidered: New Perspectives on the Meaning of Freedom of Speech and Press,* ed. Charlene Brown and Bill Chamberlin (New York: Longman, 1982), 26, 27, 40.

22. David Rabban, "The First Amendment in Its Formative Period," *Yale Law Journal* 90 (1980–81): 520. The Supreme Court only began ruling in favor of free speech in the 1930s, after a decade of dissents by Justice Brandeis and Justice Holmes that formed the basis of contemporary First Amendment jurisprudence. Ibid., 521.

23. Thomas Cooley, *A Treatise on the Constitutional Limitations Which Rest Upon the Legislative Power of the States of the American Union,* 7th ed. (Boston: Little, Brown, 1903), 59–60.

24. Michael Gibson, "The Supreme Court and Freedom of Expression from 1791 to 1917," *Fordham Law Review* 55 (1986): 270 n., 267.

25. Ibid., 268–69.

26. Blanchard, "Filling in the Void," 27.

27. Alexis Anderson, "The Formative Period of First Amendment Theory, 1870–1915," *American Journal of Legal History* 24 (1980): 67; and Rabban, "First Amendment in Its Formative Years," 524.

28. Blanchard, "Filling in the Void," 27–28.

29. See for example, Richard Byrd, "The Decay of Personal Rights and Guarantees," *Yale Law Journal* 18 (1907): 252–54. See also James Morton Jr., "Free Speech and Its Enemies," *Case and Comment* 22 (1915): 471.

30. 167 U.S. 43 (1897).

31. Ibid., 47, citing *Commonwealth v. Davis,* 140 Mass. 485 (1886). The words were written by Oliver Wendell Holmes, then a member of the Massachusetts Supreme Judicial Court.

32. Gibson, "Supreme Court and Freedom of Expression," 317. The operation of parks was not yet considered to be a government function, and their original use as pasture for community farm animals (hence the name "commons") meant that no single person had a right to control any particular part of a park. Ibid., 317–18 n.

33. Blanchard, "Filling in the Void," 28.

34. Rabban, "First Amendment in Its Formative Years," 570.

35. *Fitts v. City of Atlanta,* 121 Ga. 567, 570–71, (1905).

36. *In re Frazee,* 63 Mich. 396, 407 (1886).

37. Ibid., 405.

38. Anderson, "Formative Period," 69.

39. *Spies v. Illinois,* 122 Ill. 1 (1887); and Henry Adams, "Shall We Muzzle the Anarchists," *Forum* 1 (1886): 448–49.

40. *Goldman v. Reyburn,* 18 Pa. Dist. R. 883 (1909).

41. Ibid., 884.

42. Michael McGerr, "Political Style and Women's Power, 1830–1930," *Journal of American History* 77 (Dec. 1990): 866; and Abernathy, *Right of Assembly,* 55. Scholars also have argued the right of assembly serves another societal good by acting as a safety valve for disgruntled citizens. "Public Order and the Right of Assembly in England and the United States," *Yale Law Journal* 47 (1938): 431. This book will follow historian Mary Beth Norton's definition of feminists as women who, first, recognize that as a social group they face discrimination and inequality and, second, advocate a program to overcome those disabilities. Mary Beth Norton, "Freedom of Expression as a Gendered Phenomenon," in *The Constitution, the Law, and Freedom of Expression,* ed. James Brewer Stewart (Carbondale, Ill.: Southern Illinois Univ. Press, 1987), 42–64.

43. Gibson, "Supreme Court and Freedom of Expression," 269 n.

44. Thomas Tedford, *Freedom of Speech in the United States* (New York: McGraw-Hill, 1993), 28–29.

45. Norton, "Freedom of Expression as a Gendered Phenomenon," 45.

46. Linda Kerber, *Women of the Republic: Intellect and Ideology in Revolutionary America* (Chapel Hill: Univ. of North Carolina Press, 1980), 15.

47. Under the common-law doctrine of coverture, which persisted well into the nineteenth century, married women endured a civil death in which their husbands assumed total legal control over them. Susan Anthony, Matilda Gage, and Elizabeth Cady Stanton, eds., *History of Woman Suffrage,* 6 vols. (reprint; New York: Source Book Press, 1970), 1:14 (hereafter cited as *HWS.*)

48. This discussion of the public sphere is based upon Jean Bethke Elshtain, "Aristotle, the Public-Private Split, and the Case of the Suffragists," in *The Family in Political Thought,* ed. Jean Bethke Elshtain (Amherst: Univ. of Massachusetts Press, 1982), 51–65.

49. Glenna Matthews, *The Rise of Public Woman: Woman's Power and Place in the United States, 1630–1970* (New York: Oxford Univ. Press, 1992), 4.

50. Whipple, *Story of Civil Liberty,* 310.

51. Mary Ryan, *Women in Public: Between Banners and Ballots, 1825–1880* (Baltimore: Johns Hopkins Univ. Press, 1990), 81.

52. Beverly Beeton, *Women Vote in the West: The Woman Suffrage Movement, 1869–1896* (New York: Garland Publishing, 1986), 74.

53. Hannah Arendt, *The Human Condition* (Chicago: Univ. of Chicago Press, 1958), 178–79.

54. Susan Moller Okin, *Women in Western Political Thought* (Princeton, N.J.: Princeton Univ. Press, 1979), 5.

55. Christine Stansell, *City of Women: Sex and Class in New York, 1789–1860* (Urbana: Univ. of Illinois Press, 1987), 20.

56. Paula Baker, "The Domestication of Politics: Women and American Political Society, 1780–1920," *American Historical Review* 89 (June 1984): 624.

57. Jo Freeman, "On the Origins of Social Movements," in *Social Movements of the Sixties and Seventies*, ed. Jo Freeman (New York: Longman, 1983), 17.

58. See Gerda Lerner, *The Female Experience: An American Documentary* (Indianapolis: Bobbs-Merrill, 1977), 465–71.

59. Laurel Thatcher Ulrich, *A Midwife's Tale: The Life of Martha Ballard, Based on Her Diary, 1785–1812* (New York: Vintage Books, 1991), 12.

60. See Carroll Smith-Rosenberg, "The Female World of Love and Ritual: Relations Between Women in Nineteenth-Century America," in *Disorderly Conduct: Visions of Gender in Victorian America* (New York: Alfred A. Knopf, 1985), 53–76.

61. Wagner, *Time of Protest*, 35.

62. *HWS* 1:202.

63. Mary Beth Norton, *Liberty's Daughters: The Revolutionary Experience of American Women, 1750–1800* (Boston: Little, Brown, 1980), 167.

64. Matthews, *Rise of Public Woman*, 47.

65. Alice Rossi, ed., *The Feminist Papers: From Adams to de Beauvoir* (New York: Columbia Univ. Press, 1973; reprint, Boston: Northeastern Univ. Press, 1988), 18–24; and Mary Wollstonecraft, *A Vindication of the Rights of Woman* (London, 1792; reprint, New York: W. W. Norton, 1975). Murray was a poet, essayist, and the first woman playwright to have her plays professionally performed. Rossi, *Feminist Papers*, 16. *On the Equality of the Sexes* offered a feminist interpretation of the fall of Adam and Eve. Wollstonecraft argued for improved education and physical fitness for girls, rejecting Rousseau's claim that the chief goal of educating women should be to render them pleasing to men. Rossi, *Feminist Papers*, 48.

66. *HWS* 1:50.

67. See Kerber, *Women of the Republic*; and Norton, *Liberty's Daughters*.

68. John Stuart Mill, *The Subjection of Women* (New York: D. Appleton, 1870), 24.

69. Rosamund Billington, "Ideology and Feminism: Why the Suffragettes Were 'Wild Women,'" *Women's Studies* 5 (1982): 665. See also Carroll Smith-Rosenberg and Charles Rosenberg, "The Female Animal: Medical and Biological Views of Woman and Her Role in Nineteenth-Century America," *Journal of American History* 60 (1973–74): 332–56.

70. For a discussion of the reform society, see Carroll Smith-Rosenberg, "Beauty, the Beast, and the Militant Woman; A Case Study of Sex Roles and Social Stress in Jacksonian America," in Smith-Rosenberg, *Disorderly Conduct*, 109–28.

71. Anne Firor Scott, *Natural Allies: Women's Associations in American History* (Urbana: Univ. of Illinois Press, 1991), 177.

72. Ryan, *Women in Public*, 67.

73. See Barbara Welter, "The Cult of True Womanhood," in *Dimity Convictions:*

The American Woman in the Nineteenth Century (Athens: Ohio Univ. Press, 1976), 21–41.

74. Baker, "Domestication of Politics," 630.

75. Theodora Penny Martin, *The Sound of Our Own Voices: Women's Study Clubs, 1860–1910* (Boston: Beacon Press, 1987), 11–12.

76. Karlyn Kohrs Campbell, "Femininity and Feminism: To Be or Not to Be a Woman," *Communication Quarterly* 31 (1983): 106.

77. Tedford, *Freedom of Speech in the United States*, 28–29.

78. Celia Morris Eckhardt, *Fanny Wright: Rebel in America* (Cambridge: Harvard Univ. Press, 1984), 244, 247–50.

79. Dorothy Sterling, *We Are Your Sisters: Black Women in the Nineteenth Century* (New York: W. W. Norton, 1984), 157.

80. Ryan, *Women in Public*, 135.

81. Eve Cary, *Woman and the Law* (Skokie, Ill.: National Textbook, 1978), 5.

82. Caroline Katzenstein, *Lifting the Curtain: The State and National Woman Suffrage Campaigns in Pennsylvania as I Saw Them* (Philadelphia: Dorrance, 1955), 88.

83. Sterling, *Ahead of Her Time*, 108.

84. Flexner, *Century of Struggle*, 41.

85. Andrea Moore Kerr, *Lucy Stone: Speaking Out for Equality* (New Brunswick, N.J.: Rutgers Univ. Press, 1992), 52, 54–55, 86. As her biographer makes clear, Stone's marriage fell short of these ideals.

86. Sterling, *Ahead of Her Time*, 13–14.

87. Jean Fagan Yellin, *Women and Sisters: The Antislavery Feminists in American Culture* (New Haven, Conn.: Yale Univ. Press, 1989), 52.

88. "Proceedings," *Liberator*, 15 Nov. 1850, n.p., Reel 57, in National American Woman Suffrage Association Papers, microfilm edition, Manuscripts Division, Library of Congress, Washington, D.C. (hereafter cited as NAWSA Papers).

89. From *An Appeal to the Women of the Nominally Free States*, qtd. in Yellin, *Women and Sisters*, 35.

90. Clement Eaton, "Mob Violence in the Old South," *Mississippi Valley Historical Review* 29 (1942): 351.

91. The ministers expressed their displeasure in a *Pastoral Letter of the General Association of Congregational Churches of Massachusetts*. Gerda Lerner, *The Grimké Sisters from South Carolina: Pioneers for Women's Rights and Abolition* (Boston: Houghton Mifflin, 1967; reprint, New York: Schocken, 1971), 189–94. Abolitionist Maria Weston Chapman's poem poked fun at the pastors' disgust with women speakers: 'They've taken a notion to speak for themselves, / And are wielding the tongue and the pen; / They've mounted the rostrum; the termagant elves! / And— oh, horrid—are talking to men!" *HWS* 1:82–83.

92. Lerner, *Grimké Sisters,* 192.

93. Flexner, *Century of Struggle,* 48.

94. Lerner, *Grimké Sisters,* 296–97.

95. *HWS* 1:68.

96. Ellen DuBois, "The Radicalism of the Woman Suffrage Movement: Notes Toward the Reconstruction of Nineteenth Century Feminism," *Feminist Studies* 3 (Fall 1975): 64, 65.

97. Alan Grimes, *The Puritan Ethic and Woman Suffrage* (New York: Oxford Univ. Press, 1967), 83.

98. Flexner, *Century of Struggle,* xiii.

99. *Progress,* July 1904, 2.

100. *HWS* 1:73.

101. Woman's rights activists published dozens of newspapers, beginning with the *Lily,* published six months after the Seneca Falls convention. Linda Steiner has analyzed how suffrage publications identified, legitimized, and sustained a community of "new women" who challenged restrictive gender roles, fulfilling a key function of the right of association. Linda Steiner, "Finding Community in Nineteenth Century Suffrage Periodicals," *American Journalism* 1 (1983): 1–15. See also Sherilyn Cox-Bennion, "Woman Suffrage Papers of the West, 1869–1914," *American Journalism* 3 (1986): 125–41; Sherilyn Cox-Bennion, "The New Northwest and Woman's Exponent: Early Voices for Suffrage," *Journalism Quarterly* 54 (1977): 286–92; Sherilyn Cox-Bennion, "The Pioneer: The First Voice of Women's Suffrage in the West," *Pacific Historian* 25 (1981): 15–21; Sherilyn Cox-Bennion, "The *Woman's Exponent:* Forty-two Years of Speaking for Women," *Utah Historical Quarterly* 44 (1976): 22–39; Linda Lumsden, "*Suffragist,*" in *Women's Periodicals of the United States: Social and Political Issues,* edited by Kathleen Endres (Westport, Conn.: Greenwood Press, 1997); Marion Marzolf, "The Feminist Press Then and Now," in *Up from the Footnotes: A History of Women Journalists* (New York: Hastings House, 1977), 219–47; Lynne Masel-Walters, "A Burning Cloud by Day: The History and Content of the *Woman's Journal,*" *Journalism History* 3 (1977): 103–10; Lynne Masel-Walters, "Their Rights and Nothing More: A History of *The Revolution,* 1868–1870," *Journalism Quarterly* 53 (1976): 242–51; Lynne Masel-Walters, "To Hustle with the Rowdies: The Organization and Functions of The American Woman Suffrage Press," *Journal of American Culture* 3 (1980): 167–83; and Martha Solomon, ed., *A Voice of Their Own: The Woman Suffrage Press, 1840–1910* (Tuscaloosa: Univ. of Alabama Press, 1991).

102. Mildred Adams, "Rampant Women," in *Victory! How Women Won It: A Centennial Symposium, 1840–1940,* ed. National American Woman Suffrage Association (New York: H. W. Wilson, 1940), 43.

103. *HWS* 1:110.

104. Ibid., 118.

105. Ibid., 547, 573.

106. "The Last Vagary of the Greeley Clique—The Women, Their Rights and Their Champions," *New York Herald*, 7 Sept. 1853, 4.

107. Adams, "Rampant Women," 35.

108. Beverly Guy-Sheftall, *Daughters of Sorrow: Attitudes Toward Black Women, 1880–1920* (Brooklyn: Carlson Publishing, 1990), 95.

109. Proceedings of the Eleventh National Woman's Rights Convention, Church of the Puritans, New York City, 10 May 1866, Reel 57, NAWSA Papers. Born free in Baltimore, Harper became the first African American woman to publish poetry and novels. She also wrote and spoke on abolition. After the Civil War, she worked for women's rights. Sterling, *We Are Your Sisters*, 159, 414.

110. For an account of the speech, see *HWS* 1:115–17.

111. Sterling, *We Are Your Sisters*, 412.

112. Section 2 of the Fourteenth Amendment, which in part protected voting rights, for the first time inserted the word "male" into the Constitution: "When the right to vote . . . is denied to any of the male inhabitants of such State, . . . the basis of representation therein shall be reduced." Section 1 of the Fifteenth Amendment says the right to vote shall not be denied or abridged only "on account of race, color, or previous condition of servitude."

113. National Woman's Rights Conventions, Reel 57, NAWSA Papers.

114. Maurice Krout, "Symbolic Conduct," in Bosmajian, *Rhetoric of Nonverbal Communication*, 118.

115. Flexner, *Century of Struggle*, 165. Numerous such voting protests followed. For instance, Mary Ann Shadd Carey, former publisher of an abolitionist newspaper in Canada, joined sixty-four women who attempted to vote in the District of Columbia. Sterling, *We Are Your Sisters*, 414.

116. *HWS* 2:935.

117. Wagner, *Time of Protest*, 21.

118. Kerr, *Lucy Stone*, 103; and *Proceedings of the Woman's Rights Convention, Held at Syracuse, Sept. 8th, 9th, and 10th, 1852*, 34, Reel 57, NAWSA Papers.

119. Sterling, *Ahead of Her Time*, 367, 369–70.

120. Wagner, *Time of Protest*, 15.

121. *HWS* 3:411, 413, 414–15.

122. Wagner, *Time of Protest*, 50.

123. *HWS* 3:30.

124. Ibid., 38, 39 n.

125. Ellen Carol DuBois, *Feminism and Suffrage: The Emergence of an Independent Women's Movement in America, 1848–1869* (Ithaca, N.Y.: Cornell Univ. Press, 1978), 115.

126. Stansell, *City of Women*, 133, 134.

127. Wagner, *Time of Protest*, 97.

128. Susan Dye Lee, "Trampling Out the Vintage," in *Women in American Theatre*, ed. Helen Krich Chinoy and Linda Walsh Jenkins (New York: Theatre Communications Group, 1987), 19.

129. Ruth Bordin, *Woman and Temperance: The Quest for Power and Liberty, 1873–1900* (Philadelphia: Temple Univ. Press, 1981), 131; McGerr, "Political Style," 869; and Scott, *Natural Allies*, 94. See also Jed Dannenbaum, "The Origins of Temperance Activism and Militancy Among American Women," *Journal of Social History* 15 (1981–82): 235–52.

130. Bordin, *Woman and Temperance*, 31; and Scott, *Natural Allies*, 45.

131. Bordin, *Woman and Temperance*, 8–9.

132. Scott, *Natural Allies*, 45.

133. Bordin, *Woman and Temperance*, 24–25.

134. Ibid., 24; and Jack S. Blocker Jr., "Separate Paths: Suffragists and the Women's Temperance Crusade," *Signs* 10 (1985): 473.

135. Blocker, "Separate Paths," 471.

136. Bordin, *Woman and Temperance*, 26.

137. Ibid., 157.

138. Scott, *Natural Allies*, 45.

139. Bordin, *Woman and Temperance*, 36.

140. Blocker, "Separate Paths," 467, 470–71.

Chapter 1. The Right of Association

1. Alexis de Tocqueville, *Democracy in America*, 4th ed. (New York: Henry G. Langley, 1845), 1:209.

2. Melvin Rishe, Note, "Freedom of Assembly," *DePaul Law Review* 15 (1966): 339.

3. Abernathy, *Right of Assembly*, 173, 180, 187. The turning point came in *Commonwealth v. Hunt*, in which the Massachusetts Supreme Court said it was not a conspiracy for workers to associate or use their association's strength to agitate for better working conditions. Ibid., 182.

4. *NAACP v. Alabama*, 357 U.S. 449, 461 (1958). The U.S. Supreme Court implied freedom of assembly extended beyond a physical assemblage in *DeJonge v. Oregon*, 299 U.S. 353 (1937). It found political associations protected under the First Amendment in *Sweezy v. New Hampshire*, 354 U.S. 237 (1957).

5. The most raucous debates about rights of association have predictably involved controversial organizations such as the Ku Klux Klan, the Communist Party, and the National Association for the Advancement of Colored People at the

dawn of the civil rights movement. Rights of association generally end where criminal conspiracy begins, although the acceptability of a group's ideology has affected United States Supreme Court rulings. The Communist Party has fared particularly poorly in court battles over its members' rights of association. See *Albertson v. Subversive Activities Control Board*, 382 U.S. 70 (1965); *Barenblatt v. United States*, 360 U.S. 109 (1959); *Yates v. United States*, 354 U.S. 298 (1957); and *Dennis v. United States*, 341 U.S. 464 (1951). In contrast, the U.S. Supreme Court has been quite protective of the right of civil rights supporters to freely associate. See *NAACP v. Alabama*, 357 U.S. 449 (1958) (membership lists need not be publicized). The Court continued to allow states to compel disclosure of KKK membership lists because it was a terroristic organization, as established in *Bryant v. Zimmerman*, 278 U.S. 63 (1928).

6. See Nancy Woloch, *Women and the American Experience* (New York: Alfred A. Knopf, 1984), 276–83, 299–303.

7. Lee, "Trampling Out the Vintage," 24.

8. Meredith Tax, *The Rising of the Women: Feminist Solidarity and Class Conflict, 1880–1917* (New York: Monthly Review Press, 1980), 32. For discussions of the women's club movement, see Karen Blair, *The Clubwoman as Feminist: True Womanhood Redefined, 1868–1914* (New York: Holmes and Meier, 1980); Paula Giddings, "'To Be a Woman Sublime': The Ideas of the National Black Women's Club Movement (to 1917)," in *When and Where I Enter . . . The Impact of Black Women on Race and Sex in America,* by Giddings (New York: William Morrow, 1984), 95–118; Gerda Lerner, "Early Community Work of Black Clubwomen," *Journal of Negro History* 59 (Apr. 1974): 158–67; Scott, *Natural Allies*; and Anne Firor Scott, "Most Invisible of All: Black Women's Voluntary Associations," *Journal of Southern History* 56 (Feb. 1990): 3–22.

9. Matthews, *Rise of Public Woman*, 159.

10. "Women's Clubs and Suffrage," *Woman's Journal*, 18 Oct. 1913, 332.

11. Cott, *Grounding of Modern Feminism*, 30; and Ellen Carol DuBois, "Working Women, Class Relations, and Suffrage Militance: Harriot Stanton Blatch and the New York Woman Suffrage Movement, 1894–1909," *Journal of American History* 74 (1987): 35.

12. Kraditor, *Ideas of the Woman Suffrage Movement*, 7. In comparison, 13,150 women belonged in 1893. Ibid.

13. Beeton, *Women Vote in the West*, 110.

14. "Parade Protest Arouses Senate," *New York Times*, 5 Mar. 1912, 8.

15. Beeton, *Women Vote in the West*, 32. Mormon women employed the technique again (unsuccessfully) in 1886 to protest Congress' plans to repeal woman suffrage as part of its antipolygamy campaign. Ibid., 76.

16. Cynthia Neverdon-Morton, *Afro-American Women of the South and the*

Advancement of the Race, 1895–1925 (Knoxville: Univ. of Tennessee Press, 1989), 177.

17. Katzenstein, *Lifting the Curtain*, 83; "Votes for Women at the Home Stretch," Reel 58, NAWSA Papers; and "New York's Victory Convention," *Woman Citizen*, 1 Dec. 1917, 12.

18. Lerner, *Grimké Sisters*, 218, 222.

19. Flexner, *Century of Struggle*, 86.

20. Beeton, *Women Vote in the West*, 4.

21. "One Hundred Earnest Suffragets [sic] March Streets to Home of State Senator Walters," *Syracuse Journal*, n.d., n.p., Reel 1, microfilm edition, Papers of Harriot Stanton Blatch, Manuscript Division, Library of Congress (hereafter cited as HSB Papers).

22. Grimes, *Puritan Ethic*, 80.

23. Sterling, *We Are Your Sisters*, 412.

24. Anne Firor Scott and Andrew Scott, *One Half the People: the Fight for Woman Suffrage*, (Philadelphia: J. B. Lippincott, 1975), 97.

25. Ibid., 103, 105.

26. A. Elizabeth Taylor, *Citizens at Last: The Woman Suffrage Movement in Texas*, (Austin: Ellen C. Temple, 1987), 119.

27. "Two Speeches by Independent Women," Reel 1, HSB Papers.

28. "Women in Albany in Ballot Battle," *Progress*, 25 Feb. 1909, 1. The WPU later sent women to watch the polls, which involved considerable bravery because it could involve challenging the credentials of some of the city's "burliest citizens," as one newspaper put it. Several observers were arrested in Hell's Kitchen in 1910, but charges of obstructing the election were dropped. "College Girl Challenges Bowery Voters," unidentified newspaper clipping; and "Magistrates Uphold Women Watchers," *New York Evening Sun*, 14 Sept. 1910, n.p., both in Reel 1, HSB Papers.

29. "On to the Capitol, Suffragists Cry," unidentified newspaper clipping, Reel 64, NAWSA Papers; and "Pilgrimage to the Opening of the Maryland Legislature" *Suffragist*, 10 Jan. 1914, 7.

30. "Record Broken in Illinois," *Woman's Journal*, 25 Apr. 1909, 65.

31. Qtd. in "Broke All Records," *Woman's Journal*, 27 Jan. 1909, 34. Other newspapers also used war imagery to describe suffragist visits to legislatures. See "Suffrage Army Takes State Capitol in Silent Attack," *New York Evening Mail;* and "Women Storm Albany," *New York Daily Tribune*, both in Reel 1, HSB Papers.

32. "Woman Suffrage Demonstration in Boston," *Progress*, Mar. 1909, 4.

33. "The Great Boston Meeting," *Progress*, Apr. 1909, 1.

34. "Woman Suffragists Storm Congress with Petitions for Votes, Filling Galleries and Overwhelming Proceedings with Applause," *New York Herald*, 19 Apr. 1910, 4.

35. "Suffragists Storm National Capitol," *New York Times*, 19 Apr. 1910, 1.

36. Mabel Vernon, "Speaker for Suffrage and Petitioner for Peace," interview by Amelia Fry, Suffragists Oral History Collection, Univ. of California, Berkeley, microfiche edition (Sanford, N.C.: Microfilm Corp. of America, 1980) (hereafter cited as Vernon interview), 68–69; and Inez Haynes Irwin, *The Story of the Woman's Party,* (New York: Harcourt, Brace, 1921), 183–86.

37. Report of the Congressional Union, May 1913, Reel 87, National Woman's Party Papers: The Suffrage Years 1913–1920, microfilm edition, ed. Thomas Pardo. (Sanford, N.C.: Microfilm Corp. of America, 1979) (hereafter cited as NWP Papers: The Suffrage Years).

38. "President Refuses Aid to Deputation," *Suffragist,* 27 June 1914, 3.

39. "Heckling the President," *Suffragist,* 11 June 1914, 2.

40. Qtd. in Irwin, *Story of the Woman's Party,* 64.

41. "Polite to the President," *Woman's Journal,* 13 Dec. 1913, 396; and "President Will Favor Committee," *Woman's Journal,* 13 Dec. 1913, 393. The CU also sponsored mass meetings, lectures, receptions, tableaux, benefits, and teas. Irwin, *Story of the Woman's Party,* 46–47.

42. "Heckling the President," *Suffragist,* 22 May 1915, 4.

43. "President Will Favor Committee," *Woman's Journal,* 12 Dec. 1913, 393.

44. "Mrs. Catt Elected National President," *Woman's Journal,* 25 Dec. 1915, 407. Wilson's daughter Margaret supported suffrage. "Margaret Wilson Out for Woman Suffrage," *New York Tribune,* 29 Apr. 1913, n.p., Reel 3, HSB Papers.

45. "Speech of President Wilson at the 48th annual convention of the National American Woman Suffrage Association," 8 Sept. 1916, Reel 59, NAWSA Papers.

46. Freeman, *Social Movements of the Sixties and Seventies,* 8.

47. *Proceedings of the Eleventh National Woman's Rights Convention,* Church of the Puritans, New York City, 10 May 1866, 5, Reel 57, NAWSA Papers.

48. "Convention Gave Spirit of Union," *Woman's Journal,* 1 Jan. 1916, 2.

49. For discussions about women's progress in these sectors of the public sphere, see Susan Porter Benson, *Counter Cultures: Saleswomen, Managers, and Customers in American Department Stores, 1890–1940* (Urbana: Univ. of Illinois Press, 1986); Blair, *Clubwoman as Feminist;* Estelle Freedman, "Separatism as Strategy: Female Institution Building and American Feminism, 1870–1930," *Feminist Studies* 5 (Fall 1979): 512–49; Martin, *Sound of Our Own Voices;* Kathy Preiss, *Cheap Amusements: Working Women and Leisure in Turn-of-the-Century New York* (Philadelphia: Temple Univ. Press, 1986); Kathleen Kish Sklar, "Hull House in the 1890s: A Community of Women Reformers," *Signs* 10 (Summer 1985): 658–77; and Barbara Miller Solomon, *In the Company of Educated Women* (New Haven, Conn.: Yale Univ. Press, 1985).

50. "Convention Comes to a Successful Close," *Woman's Journal,* 28 Oct. 1911, 337.

51. "The National Convention," *Woman Voter,* Oct. 1916, 21.

52. "Not Used to Voting?" unidentified newspaper clipping, Ida Porter Boyer Scrapbooks, Reel 63, NAWSA Papers.

53. "The National Convention," *Woman's Journal,* 16 Sept. 1916, 300; and "Program of the National Convention," *Woman's Journal,* 26 Aug. 1916, 278.

54. Untitled, *New Republic* 7 (17 June 1916): 155.

55. "Convention Was Argument Itself," *Woman's Journal,* 23 Sept. 1916, 306.

56. "Suffragists in the Rose City," *Morning (Portland) Oregonian,* 28 June 1905, n.p., Ida Porter Boyer Scrapbooks, Reel 63, NAWSA Papers.

57. "Editors Grilled by Suffragists," unidentified newspaper clipping, 10 Feb. 1906, Reel 59, NAWSA Papers.

58. Wallace Irwin and Inez Milholland, "Two Million Women Vote," *McClure's Magazine,* Jan. 1913, 246–47. The authors repeated an exchange overheard at the convention to illustrate how the tenor of female conventions differed from male conventions: "The Chair: 'Do you mean to say the rule should apply to your State only?' The Delegate: 'My dear! I didn't say any such thing.'" Ibid., 251.

59. "Buffalo Convention," *Woman's Journal,* 24 Oct. 1908, 169.

60. "A Corner in Publicity," *Woman Citizen,* 2 Feb. 1918, 190.

61. See "The State Convention," *Woman Voter,* Nov. 1913, 17.

62. Program, Woman Voters' Convention, 14–16 Sept. 1915, Reel 140, National Woman's Party Papers, 1913–1974, microfilm edition (Glen Rock, N.J.: Microfilm Corp. of America, 1977–78) (hereafter cited as NWP Papers); and qtd. in "Assemble in Convention," *Suffragist,* 2 Oct. 1915, 6.

63. "Parties Greet State Meeting," *Woman's Journal,* 8 Nov. 1913, 358; and "The National Convention," *Woman's Journal,* 16 Feb. 1906, 25.

64. "What the 49th Annual Convention of the NAWSA Accomplished," *Woman Citizen,* 22 Dec. 1917, 68–69.

65. "A Boon in Suffrage Literature," *Woman Citizen,* 12 Apr. 1919, 961. The NWP Press Department also sent news stories, feature articles and photographs to hundreds of newspapers across the nation. "The Woman's Party and the Press," *Suffragist,* 13 Sept. 1919, 7.

66. See "Hold Convention in West Virginia," *Woman's Journal,* 8 Nov. 1913, 358; "Plan Convention for Wisconsin," *Woman's Journal,* 8 Nov. 1913, 358; "Hold Convention in Granite State," *Woman's Journal,* 20 Dec. 1913, 403; "Delegates Meet in Connecticut," *Woman's Journal,* 25 Oct. 1913, 342; "Twenty-three States Map Out Campaign," *Woman's Journal,* 13 Mar. 1915, 79; "Many States Hold Important Conventions," *Woman's Journal,* 20 Nov. 1915, 371; "Suffrage Work in the States," *Woman's Journal,* 16 Jan. 1915, 21; and "Across Country with Conventions," *Woman Citizen,* 1 Dec. 1917, 15.

67. "The National Convention," *Woman Voter,* Jan. 1913, 17.

68. "Will Petition Doubtful Congressmen," *Woman's Journal*, 18 Sept. 1915, 297.

69. "Convention Broadens Suffrage Policies," *Woman's Journal*, 20 Nov. 1912, 377.

70. "Conventions of the Woman's Party and Congressional Union," *Suffragist*, 10 Mar. 1917, 4–5.

71. "Delegates Pledged to Fill Money Chest," *Woman's Journal*, 13 Dec. 1913, 394; and "President Will Favor Committee," *Woman's Journal*, 13 Dec. 1913, 393.

72. "Conventions of the Woman's Party and Congressional Union," *Suffragist*, 10 Mar. 1917, 4–5.

73. A. Elizabeth Taylor, *The Woman Suffrage Movement in Tennessee* (New York: Bookman Associates, 1957), 59.

74. "New York Has Big Convention," *Woman's Journal*, 25 Oct. 1913, 342.

75. Minutes of the Meeting of the Executive Council of the National American Woman Suffrage Association at the Marlborough-Blenheim Hotel, Reel 59, NAWSA Papers. Catt's "winning plan" called for mobilizing committees in each of the states to lobby for a federal amendment; it also selected a few key states where it was feasible to win suffrage before Congress passed a federal amendment. Flexner, *Century of Struggle*, 280–81.

76. "Woman's Hour Strikes at Big National Convention," *Woman's Journal*, 16 Sept. 1916, 297.

77. "Platform Adopted at the Forty-eighth Annual Convention," Reel 59, NAWSA Papers; "The Crisis," manuscript, 16, Reel 59, NAWSA Papers; and "The Crisis," *Woman's Journal*, 16 Sept. 1916, 299, 303.

78. "Buffalo Convention," *Woman's Journal*, 24 Oct. 1908, 169; and "Across Country with the Conventions," *Woman Citizen*, 1 Dec. 1917, 15.

79. "Hold Convention in Granite State," *Woman's Journal*, 20 Dec. 1913, 403; and undated press release, Reel 49, NAWSA Papers.

80. "Suffragists Pick National Leaders," *Chicago Evening Post*, 18 Feb. 1907, n.p., in Ida Porter Boyer Scrapbooks, Reel 63, NAWSA Papers.

81. Carrie Chapman Catt and Nettie Rogers Shuler, *Woman Suffrage and Politics: The Inner Story of the Suffrage Movement* (New York: Charles Scribner's Sons, 1923), 381.

82. "Crowd at Suffrage Tea," *New York Times*, 10 Feb. 1915, 8; Doris Stevens, *Jailed for Freedom* (New York: Boni & Liveright, 1920), 72; "Special Convention Number," *Woman Citizen*, 14 Feb. 1920; and "Convention Issue," *Suffragist*, Jan.–Feb. 1920. After Congress approved the Nineteenth Amendment, the NWP raised funds to commission busts in the Capitol of Anthony, Stanton, and Lucretia Mott, who helped Stanton organize the Seneca Falls convention. "A Women's National Memorial," *Suffragist*, Dec. 1920, 303.

83. Beeton, *Women Vote in the West*, 133.

84. Paul Fuller, *Laura Clay and the Woman's Rights Movement* (Lexington: Univ. Press of Kentucky, 1975), 84.

85. "Convention News," *Progress,* Nov. 1908, 2; and "The National Convention," *Progress,* May 1910, 4.

86. Program of forty-third annual NAWSA convention, Louisville, Kentucky, Reel 58, NAWSA Papers.

87. "Convention Comes to a Successful Close," *Woman's Journal,* 28 Oct. 1911, 337.

88. Program of forty-third annual NAWSA convention, Louisville, Kentucky, 1911, Reel 58, NAWSA Papers.

89. Program of forty-fourth annual NAWSA convention, Philadelphia, 1912; and Taylor, *Woman Suffrage Movement in Tennessee,* 66.

90. Program of the forty-fifth annual NAWSA convention, Washington, D.C., 1913, Reel 58, NAWSA Papers; and "National Convention Strikes New Note," *Woman's Journal,* 6 Dec. 1913, 32.

91. "A Remarkable Evening," *Woman's Journal,* 16 Sept. 1916, 300.

92. "What the 49th Annual Convention of the NAWSA Accomplished," *Woman Citizen,* 22 Dec. 1917, 68–69.

93. Program of forty-fourth annual NAWSA convention, Philadelphia, 1912, Reel 59, NAWSA Papers; and "A Boon in Suffrage Literature," *Woman Citizen,* 12 Apr. 1919, 961.

94. "Parties Greet State Meeting," *Woman's Journal,* 8 Nov. 1913, 358.

95. Taylor, *Woman Suffrage Movement in Tennessee,* 58, 59.

96. Fuller, *Laura Clay,* 74.

97. Program of forty-third annual NAWSA convention, Louisville, Kentucky, 1911, Reel 58, NAWSA Papers; and "Rejoicing Suffragists Meet in National Convention," *Woman's Journal,* 21 Oct. 1911, 330.

98. "Conventions of the Woman's Party and Congressional Union," *Suffragist,* 10 Mar. 1917, 4–5.

99. Catt and Shuler, *Woman Suffrage and Politics,* 381; and "Pageant Closes Union Meeting," *Woman's Journal,* 18 Dec. 1915, 400.

100. Program of the forty-fourth annual NAWSA convention, Philadelphia, 1912, Reel 59, NAWSA Papers.

101. "Mrs. Catt Elected National President," *Woman's Journal,* 25 Dec. 1915, 408.

102. Program of forty-fourth annual NAWSA convention, Philadelphia, 1912, Reel 59, NAWSA Papers.

103. "After the Convention," *Woman's Journal,* 13 Dec. 1913, 397.

104. Kraditor, *Ideas of the Woman Suffrage Movement,* 254.

105. For a discussion of questions posed by the role privilege played in the suffrage movement, see Catherine Mitchell, "Historiography on the Woman's

Rights Press," in *Outsiders in 19th-Century Press History: Multicultural Perspectives,* ed. Frankie Hutton and Barbara Straus Reed (Bowling Green, Ohio: Bowling Green Univ. Popular Press, 1995), 159–68.

106. Kay Sloan, "Sexual Warfare in the Silent Cinema: Comedies and Melodramas of Woman Suffragism," *American Quarterly* 33 (1981): 429. A silent film produced by the Women's Political Union (successor to Blatch's Equality League of Self-Supporting Women), for instance, contained a scene in which a man asked, "My butler and my bootblack vote—why not my wife and daughter?" Ibid., 425.

107. *Suffragist* newspaper, for instance, championed African Americans after the race riots in East St. Louis and described blacks and suffragists as comrades in their quest for equal rights. "Negro Unrest," *Suffragist,* 25 Aug. 1917, 3.

108. Adele Logan Alexander, "How I Discovered My Grandmother . . . ," *Ms.* 12 (Nov. 1983): 34.

109. Giddings, *When and Where I Enter,* 162. For other discussions on racial discrimination in the suffrage movement, see also "Anti-Black Woman Suffrage Efforts," in Rosalyn Terborg-Penn, "Afro-Americans in the Struggle for Woman Suffrage" (Ph.D. diss., Howard Univ., 1977), 277–311; Rosalyn Terborg-Penn, "Discrimination Against Afro-American Women in the Woman's Movement, 1830–1920," in *The Afro-American Woman: Struggles and Images,* ed. Sharon Harley and Rosalyn Terborg-Penn (Port Washington, N.Y.: Kennikat Press, 1978), 17–27; Beverly Guy-Sheftall, "Books, Brooms, Bibles, and Ballots: Black Women and the Public Sphere," in Guy-Sheftall, *Daughters of Sorrow,* 91–158; Aileen Kraditor, "The 'Southern Question,'" in Kraditor, *Ideas of the Woman Suffrage Movement,* 162–218; and Marjorie Spruill Wheeler, "Southern Suffragists and 'the Negro Problem,'" in *New Women of the New South: The Leaders of the Woman Suffrage Movement in the Southern States,* by Wheeler (New York: Oxford Univ. Press, 1993), 100–132.

White suffragists also treated Native American women contradictorily. On the one hand, they held up the example of matriarchy in Indian culture as an alternative to American patriarchy, but they resented being classified with "savages" in their disfranchised state. See Gail Landsman, "The 'Other' as Political Symbol: Images of Indians in the Woman Suffrage Movement," *Ethnohistory* 39 (Summer 1992): 247–84.

110. Neverdon-Morton, *Afro-American Women of the South,* 203.

111. Wheeler, *New Women of the New South,* 111.

112. Southern suffragists maintained the white woman's vote would offset the large "undesirable" vote in the South. "Southern Suffragists Roused Over Slacker Vote," *Woman Citizen,* 12 Jan. 1918, 132. The National Woman's Party argued that poll taxes and literacy tests would continue to weed out undesirable voters of both races. "National Suffrage and the Race Problem," *Suffragist,* 14 Nov. 1914, 3.

113. Terborg-Penn, "Discrimination Against Afro-American Women," 27.

114. Giddings, *When and Where I Enter*, 161–63.

115. Mary Church Terrell, *A Colored Woman in a White World* (Washington, D.C.: Ransdell, 1940; reprint, Salem, N.H.: Ayer, 1992), 145–46; and "Programme, Anniversary Celebration of the 1848 Woman's Rights Convention," Reel 1, HSB Papers; Wilson Jeremiah Moses, "Domestic Female Conservatism, Sex Roles, and Black Women's Clubs 1893–1896," in *Black Women in American History: The Twentieth Century*, vol. 3, ed. Darlene Clark Hine, et al. (Brooklyn: Carlson Publishing, 1990), 968.

116. Guy-Sheftall, *Daughters of Sorrow*, 117. Du Bois dedicated several issues of the *Crisis* to woman suffrage. See issues for Sept. 1912, Aug. 1915, and Nov. 1917.

117. Alexander, "How I Discovered My Grandmother," 36.

118. Cott, *Grounding of Modern Feminism*, 31; and Terborg-Penn, "Afro-Americans in the Struggle," 287.

119. Terborg-Penn, "Afro-Americans in the Struggle," 109, 126; and Alexander, "How I Discovered My Grandmother," 30.

120. Terborg-Penn, "Afro-Americans in the Struggle," 184.

121. Giddings, *When and Where I Enter*, 129.

122. Alfreda Duster, ed., *Crusade for Justice: The Autobiography of Ida B. Wells* (Chicago: Univ. of Chicago Press, 1970), xxviii; and Rosalyn Terborg-Penn, "Discontented Black Feminists: Prelude and Postscript to the Passage of the Nineteenth Amendment," in *Black Women in American History: The Twentieth Century*, vol. 4, ed. Darlene Clark Hine (Brooklyn: Carlson Publishing, 1990), 1160.

123. *Woman Voter*, Mar. 1917, 24.

124. "Hopping for Suffrage," *Woman Voter and Suffrage News*, June 1915, 21.

125. "Society Mingles with Girl Toilers at Suffrage Ball," *New York American*, 12 Jan. 1913, n.p., Reel 2, HSB Papers.

126. "'Sunshade Race' and Other Novel Feats Attract Many Recruits at Shoreham," *New York American*, 20 July 1913, n.p.; and "Fair New York Girl Star of Suffrage Picnic," *New York Tribune*, 27 July 1913, n.p.; both in Reel 3, HSB Papers.

127. Harriot Stanton Blatch and Alma Lutz, *Challenging Years: The Memoirs of Harriot Stanton Blatch* (New York: G. P. Putnam's Sons, 1940), 192.

128. Taylor, *Woman Suffrage Movement in Tennessee*, 54, 55; and "Suffragist Baby Shows," *New York Times*, 16 Oct. 1913, 1.

129. "What Is Going On," *Woman Voter*, Apr. 1910, 6. See also the *Woman Voter* for Feb. 1901, 7; Mar. 1911, 3; Apr. 1912, 27; July 1913, 28; June 1914, 25; and Aug. 1915, 21.

130. "The Humors of Canvassing," *Woman Voter*, Aug. 1913, 12.

131. Taylor, *Woman Suffrage Movement in Tennessee*, 52.

132. Terborg-Penn, "Afro-Americans in the Struggle," 133.

133. "The Suffrage Store," *Woman's Journal*, 29 May 1909, 86.

134. "The Sunflower Lunch," *Woman Citizen*, 31 Aug. 1918, 272; and "An Impression of a Suffrage Tea Room," *Suffragist*, 21 Sept. 1918, 6.

135. Sherna Gluck, ed., *From Parlor to Prison: Five American Suffragists Talk About Their Lives, an Oral History* (New York: Vintage Books, 1976), 45.

136. "Parlor Meetings," Official Program, Woman Suffrage Procession, Washington, D.C., 3 Mar. 1913, Reel 49, NAWSA Papers; "Hospitality to Prevail in Old Cameron House," *Washington Star*, 27 Dec. 1916, n.p., in Reel 49, NAWSA Papers; and Invitation to Suffrage Ball, 21 Apr. 1914, Reel 149, NWP Papers.

137. Journalists so missed the ritual that they created the New York Newspaper Women's Club to fill the void in the 1920s. Ishbel Ross, *Ladies of the Press: The Story of Women in Journalism by an Insider* (New York: Harper & Brothers 1936), 126.

138. Alice Park, "Show Your Colors," Reel 49, NAWSA Papers.

139. "Trinkets and Songs of the Suffragists," *New York Times*, 28 June 1914, sec. 5, p. 8; and "The Suffrage Doll," *Woman's Journal*, 9 Sept. 1911, 286.

140. "Woman Suffrage Cook-Book," *Woman's Journal*, 24 July 1909, 1; "College Suffrage Calendar," *Woman's Journal*, 6 Nov. 1909, 177; "New Suffrage Post-Card," *Woman's Journal*, 9 Jan. 1909, 5; "Suffrage Game," *Suffragist*, 27 Dec. 1913, and "Trinkets and Songs of the Suffragists," *New York Times*, 28 June 1914, sec. 5, p. 8.

141. Reel 95, NWP Papers: The Suffrage Years.

142. "Suffrage Garden Grows Popular," *Woman's Journal*, 27 Mar. 1915, 102.

143. Untitled, *New Republic*, 17 June 1916, 155.

144. *New York Times*, 14 July 1916, 10.

145. See "The Election Policy of the Congressional Union for Woman Suffrage," Reel 149, NWP Papers; Anna Howard Shaw to Cora Lewis, 23 Sept. 1914, Reel 33, NAWSA Papers; and Mary Ware Dennett to Ruth McCormick, 6 Jan. 1914, Reel 33, NAWSA Papers.

146. "Novel Suffrage Stunts as Publicity Makers," *New York Sun*, 16 Feb. 1918, n.p., Reel 95, NWP Papers: The Suffrage Years.

147. "City Tie-Up Gets New Backing," *New York Times*, 19 Aug. 1915, 9; and "An Appalling Strike Is Threatened," *New York Times*, 20 Aug. 1915, 10.

148. For discussions of these state campaigns, see Beeton, *Women Vote in the West*; Eleanor Flexner, "First Victories in the West," in Flexner, *Century of Struggle*, 156–65; and Grimes, *Puritan Ethic*.

149. Sharon Hartman Strom, "Leadership and Tactics in the American Woman Suffrage Movement: A New Perspective from Massachusetts," *Journal of American History* 62 (1975): 302. Maud Wood Park then founded the College Equal Suffrage League and went on to head the NAWSA Congressional Committee from 1917 through 1920. Ibid. See also Park's memoir, *Front Door Lobby* (Boston: Beacon Press, 1960).

150. "The National Convention," *Woman's Journal*, 16 Feb. 1906, 25.

151. *Progress*, Mar. 1906, 1–2.

Chapter 2. The Open-Air Campaigns

1. Katzenstein, *Lifting the Curtain*, 51.

2. Abernathy, *Right of Assembly*, 55.

3. "The right of citizens of the United States to vote shall not be denied or abridged by the United States or by any State on account of sex." U.S. Constitution, amend. 19.

4. Beeton, *Women Vote in the West*, 107; and Ida Husted Harper, *The Life and Work of Susan B. Anthony* (Indianapolis: T. Bowen-Merrill, 1890), 1:490; and "Street-Suffrage Meeting in Lynn," *Woman's Journal*, 19 Sept. 1908, 150. One hint of the cool reception Anthony often received was that in the 1890s she recommended against women addressing men on suffrage. Beeton, *Women Vote in the West*, 126–27.

5. Detailed accounts of the British suffragettes' struggle can be found in E. Sylvia Pankhurst, *The Suffragette: The History of the Women's Militant Suffrage Movement, 1905–1910* (Boston: Woman's Journal, 1911); Christabel Pankhurst, *Unshackled: The Story of How We Won the Vote* (London: Hutchinson, 1959); Emmeline Pankhurst, *My Own Story* (New York: Hearst's International Library, 1914); Anita Raeburn, *The Militant Suffragettes* (London: Michael Joseph, 1973); Constance Rover, *Women's Suffrage and Party Politics in Britain, 1866–1914* (London: Routledge & Kegan Paul, 1967); and Ray Strachey, *The Cause: A Short History of the Women's Movement in Great Britain* (London: G. Bell & Sons, 1928).

6. Historian Michael McGerr suggested the all-encompassing British influence indicated the lack of an American women's political heritage. McGerr, "Popular Style," 881. The *Daily Mail* invented the name "suffragette" in 1906 to distinguish the militants from more conservative suffragists, who used conventional means to lobby for the vote. Anita Raeburn, *The Suffragette View* (New York: St. Martin's Press, 1976), 8.

7. Pankhurst, *Suffragette*, 17.

8. Ibid., 26.

9. Pankhurst, *Unshackled*, 49–52; and Midge MacKenzie, *Shoulder to Shoulder: A Documentary* (New York: Alfred A. Knopf, 1975), 332, x. Women property owners thirty years and older could vote in Britain in 1918; all women could vote in 1928. The latter richly illustrated book is the companion to the six-hour documentary film MacKenzie produced, *Shoulder to Shoulder* (Alexandria, Va.: PBS Video, 1988), videotape.

10. Emmeline Pankhurst, "Advancing," *Good Housekeeping*, Nov. 1913, 464.

11. Pankhurst, *Suffragette*, 79.

12. Raeburn, *Militant Suffragettes*, 199.

13. Ibid., 57, 118.

14. Emily Wilding Davison martyred herself for the cause when she hurled herself in front of the king's horse at the 1913 Derby Day race. Sylvia Pankhurst, *The*

Suffragette Movement: An Intimate Account of Persons and Ideals (London: Longmans, Green, 1932), 467–68.

15. Smith, "Development of the Right of Assembly," 361, 364.

16. Rheta Childe Dorr, *What Eight Million Women Want* (Boston: Small, Maynard, 1910), 297.

17. See, for example, "The Militant Women—and Women," *Century*, Nov. 1913, 13–15; "Feminist Intentions," *Atlantic Monthly*, Dec. 1913, 721–32; and "How to Repress the Suffragettes," *Literary Digest*, 19 Apr. 1913, 883.

18. Blatch's feminist influences also derived from her mother, Elizabeth Cady Stanton.

19. "A Suffrage Meeting in Mid Ocean," *Woman's Journal*, 13 Aug. 1910, 132.

20. Irwin, *Story of the Woman's Party*, 15.

21. Raeburn, *Militant Suffragettes*, 131.

22. Jacqueline Van Voris, *Carrie Chapman Catt: A Public Life* (New York: Feminist Press, 1987), 108–9. Catt was president of NAWSA from 1900 to 1904 and from 1916 to 1920. Dr. Anna Howard Shaw was president of NAWSA from 1905 to 1916.

23. Margaret Dreier, "Expansion Through Agitation and Education," *Life and Labor* 11 (1921): 164; and Nancy Schrom Dye, *As Equals and as Sisters: Feminism, the Labor Movement, and the Women's Trade Union League of New York* (Columbia: Univ. of Missouri Press, 1980), 47.

24. Philip Foner, *Women and the American Labor Movement*, vol. 1, *From Colonial Times to the Eve of World War I* (New York: Free Press, 1979), 396.

25. "Biographical Note," Reel 1, HSB Papers.

26. Blatch and Lutz, *Challenging Years*, 93.

27. Flexner, *Century of Struggle*, 248–49, 250 n.

28. Blatch and Lutz, *Challenging Years*, 92.

29. Women voted in Colorado, Idaho, Utah, and Wyoming. For discussions of these nineteenth-century campaigns, see Beeton, *Women Vote in the West*; Flexner, *Century of Struggle*, 156–63, 222; and Grimes, *Puritan Ethic*, 1967.

30. "English Suffragists," *Progress*, Jan. 1907, 3. *Progress*, the voice of NAWSA, merged into its successor, the *Woman's Journal*, in 1910.

31. "Hear Suffragettes' Appeal," *New York Sun*, 1 Jan. 1908, 4. Open-air speaking was just one aspect of the long, multifaceted suffrage campaign, which Carrie Chapman Catt once estimated involved 56 referenda campaigns, 480 campaigns to urge legislatures to submit suffrage amendments to voters; 47 campaigns to induce state constitutional conventions to write woman suffrage into state constitutions; 277 campaigns to persuade state party conventions to include woman suffrage planks; 30 campaigns to urge presidential party conventions to adopt woman suffrage planks in party platforms, and 19 campaigns with 19 successive Congresses.

Catt and Shuler, *Woman Suffrage and Politics*, 107. For other accounts of the suffrage movement, also see DuBois, *Feminism and Suffrage*; Flexner, *Century of Struggle*; Ford, *Iron-Jawed Angels*; Kraditor, *Ideas of the Woman Suffrage Movement*; Lunardini, *From Equal Suffrage to Equal Rights*; and O'Neill, *Everyone Was Brave*.

32. "Suffragettes Open Their Campaign Here," *New York Times*, 1 Jan. 1908, 16.

33. Female political reformers in New York City formed the league in 1905. DuBois, "Working Women, Class Relations, and Suffrage Militance," 45.

34. "Suffragists Here Divide," *New York Times*, 28 Dec. 1907, 5.

35. "The Hopes of the Suffragettes in America," *New York Times*, 13 Dec. 1908, sec. 6, p. 7.

36. "The Suffragettes," *New York Times*, 11 Dec. 1907, 10; and "Mrs. Sanderson Talks," *New York Times*, 13 Dec. 1907, 6.

37. John McKay, *Tramways and Trolleys: The Rise of Urban Mass Transportation in Europe* (Princeton, N.J.: Princeton Univ. Press, 1976), 51.

38. John Anderson Miller, *Fares, Please! A Popular History of Trolleys, Horsecars, Streetcars, Buses, Elevateds, and Subways* (New York: Dover Publications, 1960), 116; and "Report for Year 1908–1909," Reel 1, HSB Papers.

39. Irwin and Milholland, "Two Million Women Vote," 245.

40. Blatch and Lutz, *Challenging Years*, 107–8.

41. Gluck, *From Parlor to Prison*, 147. One suffragist described the platforms as boxes with heavy handles on one end so they could be easily carried. Laura Ellsworth Seiler, "From Tea Parties to Prison: On the Soapbox," interview by Sherna Gluck, Suffragists Oral History Collection, Univ. of California, Berkeley, microfiche edition (Sanford, N.C.: Microfilm Corporation of America, 1980) (hereafter cited as Seiler interview), 34. A photograph in the HSB Papers shows a brigade of women marching in the 1911 Fifth Avenue parade carrying their soapboxes at their sides. Reel 1, HSB Papers.

42. Gluck, *From Parlor to Prison*, 147.

43. "Items of Interest," *American Suffragette*, June 1909, 15; "Speakers Class," *American Suffragette*, Nov. 1909, 18.

44. "The Hopes of the Suffragettes in America," *New York Times*, 13 Dec. 1908, sec. 6, p. 7.

45. "Massachusetts Meetings," *Woman's Journal*, 28 Aug. 1909, 138; and *Progress*, July 1908, 2.

46. Blatch and Lutz, *Challenging Years*, 205, "Women Pitch Their Tent on the Court House Green," *Elmira Advertiser*, 21 July 1914, n.p., Reel 3, HSB Papers; and "Tired Hikers in Liberty," *New York Times*, 16 Apr. 1913, 5.

47. "A Suffrage Meeting in Mid Ocean," *Woman's Journal*, 13 Aug. 1910, 132.

48. Alice Sheppard, *Cartooning for Suffrage* (Albuquerque: Univ. of New Mexico Press, 1994), 107–8.

49. "Dock Meeting on July 27th," *American Suffragette*, Aug. 1909, 15; "New York Has Car Barn Day," *Woman's Journal*, 28 Aug. 1915, 278; "Preach Suffrage from Housetops," *New York Times*, 16 Apr. 1913, 5; and "Self Denial Week," *American Suffragette*, Aug. 1909, 12.

50. "Program for the Week," *Suffragist*, 22 Nov. 1913, 2.

51. "Not a Man Can Sleep Until Women Vote," *New York Times*, 4 Mar. 1911, n.p., Reel 1, HSB Papers. A sample lyric: "I long to vote / Pray won't you hear? / With my top note / I hail your ear." Ibid.

52. "Open Air Experiences," *Woman Voter*, Sept. 1910, 7; and "Suffrage Work in the States," *Woman's Journal*, 10 Apr. 1915, 116.

53. Anthony, *HWS* 5:421, 420.

54. Mabel Vernon, "A Suffragist Recounts the Hard-Won Victory," *AAUW Newsletter* (Apr. 1972): 27.

55. "Campaigning Through Nevada," *Suffragist*, 23 May 1914, 6–7.

56. Anne Howard, *The Long Campaign: A Biography of Anne Martin* (Reno: Univ. of Nevada Press, 1985), 94, 96.

57. "State Correspondence," *Woman's Journal*, 6 Nov. 1909, 180.

58. Qtd. in "CU Campaign in Nevada," *Suffragist*, 30 May 1914, 7.

59. McGerr, "Political Style," 873–74.

60. Ian Ward, *Motoring for the Millions* (New York: Dorset, Poole, 1981), 10; and James Flink, *America Adopts the Automobile, 1895–1910* (Cambridge, Mass: MIT Press, 1970), 50, 76.

61. Virginia Scharf, *Taking the Wheel: Women and the Coming of the Motor Age* (New York: Free Press, 1991), 15, 87.

62. Reda Davis, *California Women: A Guide to Their Politics, 1885–1911* (San Francisco: California Scene, 1967), 125.

63. "Connecticut Work," *Woman's Journal*, 26 Aug. 1911, 267; "State Correspondence," *Woman's Journal*, 13 Aug. 1910, 133; "Suffrage Women on Auto Tour," *Woman's Journal*, 16 Dec. 1911, 39; "State Correspondence," *Woman's Journal*, 10 Aug. 1910, 129; "Campaign States—Read!" *Woman's Journal*, 1 June 1912, 175; "Notes and News," *Woman's Journal*, 29 June 1912, 203; "To Tour Kansas," *Woman's Journal*, 31 Aug. 1912, 278; Flexner, *Century of Struggle*, 278; and Genevieve McBride, *On Wisconsin Women: Working for Their Rights from Settlement to Suffrage* (Madison: Univ. of Wisconsin Press, 1993), 210.

64. Scharf, *Taking the Wheel*, 86; McBride, *On Wisconsin Women*, 211; "Campaign in Wisconsin," *Woman's Journal*, 27 July 1912, 239; Scharf, *Taking the Wheel*, 85; and "Notes and News," *Woman's Journal*, 29 June 1912, 203.

65. Wheeler, *New Women of the New South*, xiii, 36.

66. "The Summer Campaign," *Suffragist*, 11 July 1914, 7; "Campaign States Hum with Suffrage Activity," *Woman's Journal*, 3 July 1915, 212; "North Carolina Now Has

State Organization," *Suffragist,* 5 Aug. 1916, 10; "Miss Vernon's Tour," *Suffragist,* 28 Mar. 1914, 2; "Suffrage Work in the States," *Woman's Journal,* 26 Feb. 1916, 69; "Street Meetings in Alabama," *Suffragist,* 7 Aug. 1915, 2; and "Arkansas Organizes for Federal Amendment," *Suffragist,* 5 Feb. 1916, 3.

67. Fuller, *Laura Clay,* 132.

68. Taylor, *Woman Suffrage Movement in Tennessee,* 40, 41.

69. "Brokers Held Up by Suffragettes," *New York Times,* 7 July 1909, 1.

70. "Miss Malone Quits the Suffragettes," *New York Times,* 27 Mar. 1908, 4.

71. The United States Supreme Court did not guarantee citizens the right to assemble peaceably until it ruled in a trio of landmark cases in the late 1930s. *DeJonge v. Oregon,* 288 U.S. 364 (1937) (right of assembly incorporated into the Bill of Rights by the Fourteenth Amendment); *Lovell v. City of Griffin,* 303 U.S. 444 (1938) (permit to license solicitors an unconstitutional prior restraint); and *Hague v. CIO,* 307 U.S. 496 (1939) (right to assemble a privilege inherent in U.S. citizenship).

72. Blanchard, *Revolutionary Sparks,* 63. These functions included banning films, preventing speeches and parades, picketing, or distributing leaflets. Ibid.

73. "Suffragists Here Divide," 5.

74. David Rabban, "The Free Speech League, the ACLU, and Changing Conceptions of Free Speech in American History," *Stanford Law Review* 45 (1992): 90.

75. Ibid., 82. A wealthy Tarrytown suffragist offered the Free Speech League the use of a private theater on her estate after it was barred from public halls. Ibid., 82 n.

76. Ibid., 96. The freethinkers were acquitted. Ibid.

77. Margaret Sanger, *My Fight for Birth Control* (New York: Farrar & Rinehart, 1931), 144–49.

78. Blanchard, *Revolutionary Sparks,* 64.

79. Whipple, *Story of Civil Liberty,* 276.

80. *Davis v. Massachusetts,* 167 U.S. 43 (1897). Despite the assembly clause in the First Amendment, the U.S. Supreme Court had ruled in *United States v. Cruikshank* in 1876 that citizens must rely on state constitutions to protect the right of assembly. 92 U.S. 542 (1875).

81. *Commonwealth v. Abrahams,* 156 Mass. 57, 30 N.E. 79 (1892).

82. *Love v. Phalen,* 128 Mich. 545, 87 N.W. 785 (1901).

83. *People v. Wallace,* 85 App. Div. N.Y.S. Ct. 170 (1903); *People v. Pierce,* 85 App. Div. N.Y.S. Ct. 125 (1903).

84. Jarrett and Mund, "Right of Assembly," 29.

85. Philip Foner, *History of the Labor Movement in the United States,* vol. 4, *The Industrial Workers of the World, 1905–1917* (New York: International Publishers, 1980), 147, 157, 172; and Joseph Conlin, *Bread and Roses Too: Studies of the Wobblies*

(Westport, Conn.: Greenwood Press, 1969), 5. The classic IWW free-speech fight lined up hundreds of volunteers at a designated corner to speak or read from documents such as the Constitution. Police predictably would arrest the speaker, who promptly would be replaced by the next volunteer, and so on until hundreds of protesters jammed the jails and courts. In Spokane, Washington, in 1909, for instance, more than twelve hundred arrests were made over five months before the Wobblies won most of their demands. Terry W. Cole, "The Right to Speak: The Free Speech Fights of the Industrial Workers of the World," *Free Speech Yearbook* 16 (1978): 113–14.

86. Kraditor, *Ideas of the Woman Suffrage Movement*, 252.

87. "Free Speech and Suffrage," *Woman Voter and Newsletter*, Aug. 1913, 8.

88. "The Right of Free Speech," *Woman's Journal*, 25 May 1912, 165. The U.S. Supreme Court finally agreed in 1969 that such speech is constitutionally protected unless it directly incites violence. *Brandenburg v. Ohio*, 395 U.S. 444 (1969).

89. "Anti-Suffrage Militancy," *Woman's Journal*, 15 Nov. 1913, 365; and "Anti-Suffrage Militancy," *Woman's Journal*, 8 Nov. 1913, 356.

90. "American Militancy," *Woman's Journal*, 23 Aug. 1913, 269.

91. "Attempt to Scare Suffrage Leader," *Woman's Journal*, 4 Mar. 1916, 75.

92. "Wall Street Derides the Suffragettes," *New York Times*, 28 Feb. 1908, 7.

93. "Editorial Notes," *Woman's Journal*, 7 Mar. 1908, 1.

94. "Police Bar Suffragettes," *New York Times*, 18 June 1908, 1.

95. "Street-Suffrage Meeting in Lynn," *Woman's Journal*, 19 Sept. 1908, 150.

96. "Novelties," *Woman's Journal*, 9 Sept. 1911, 287.

97. "State Correspondence," *Woman's Journal*, 7 Aug. 1909, 128.

98. "Salvationists and Suffragists," *New York Times*, 22 Jan. 1909, 8. The newspaper editorialized that the Free Speech League's fight for the right of labor organizers to speak on public streets would provoke riots. Rabban, "Free Speech League," 82.

99. "Brokers Held Up by Suffragettes," *New York Times*, 7 July 1909, 1.

100. "Suffrage Newsies Earn Eighteen Dollars," *American Suffragette*, Dec. 1909, 16–17.

101. The case against the woman was dismissed with a reprimand. "An Outrage," *Woman's Journal*, 4 Nov. 1911, 346.

102. "Suffragists in Auto Patrol," *New York Times*, 4 Sept. 1915, 7.

103. Abernathy, *Right of Assembly*, 49.

104. "Wall Street Our Enemy," *Woman's Journal*, 9 Dec. 1911, 385.

105. "Roughs Rout Meeting," *Woman's Journal*, 13 July 1912, 224.

106. "Suffragettes Protest," *New York Times*, 30 Apr. 1908, 16, and "Harlemites Hoot the Suffragettes," *New York Times*, 28 Apr. 1908, 2. Ibid.

107. Annual Report, Jan. 1911–Jan. 1912, 26–27, Reel 1, HSB Papers.

108. Blatch and Lutz, *Challenging Years*, 115–16.

109. "Suffrage Work in the States," *Woman's Journal*, 28 Aug. 1915, 275.

110. "Trolley Tour in New York," *Woman's Journal*, 13 June 1908, 95.

111. "Roughs Rout Meeting," *Woman's Journal*, 13 July 1912, 224.

112. "Boys Howl Down Suffrage Speakers," *New York Times*, 28 Nov. 1911, 9; "Take Up Women's Charges," *New York Times*, 29 Nov. 1911, 8; "Wall Street Subdued," *Woman's Journal*, 16 Dec. 1911, 394; and "Suffragists Get a Hearing," *New York Times*, 8 Dec. 1911, 13.

113. "Suffragettes Out Again," *New York Times*, 7 June 1908, pt. 2, p. 3.

114. "Broke Up Suffrage Rally," *New York Times*, 3 Nov. 1908, 5; and "Suffragists Attacked," *New York Times*, 6 Oct. 1908, 20.

115. Blatch and Lutz, *Challenging Years*, 150.

116. "Now the Voiceless Speech," *New York Times*, 19 Nov. 1912, 1.

117. The charge was dismissed with a reprimand. "Voiceless Speech Louder," *New York Times*, 3 Jan. 1913, 7; and Blatch and Lutz, *Challenging Years*, 192.

118. "Officer 979 is with 'Em," *New York Tribune*, 7 Jan. 1913, Reel 2, HSB Papers.

119. Katzenstein, *Lifting the Curtain*, 44–45.

120. "Mob Howls at Suffragettes," *New York Times*, 29 Oct. 1908, 1.

121. "Suffragettes Broadway," *New York Times*, 15 Sept. 1911, 4.

122. "Suffragists Adore 'Em All, So Will Boost Police Show," *New York Evening Sun*, 25 June 1914, n.p., HSB Papers.

123. "All States Will Be in Parade," *Woman's Journal*, 8 Feb. 1913, 46.

124. "The Police Are with Us," *Woman Voter and The Newsletter*, Sept. 1915, 12.

125. Arthur Ekirch Jr., *Progressivism in America: A Study of the Era from Theodore Roosevelt to Woodrow Wilson* (New York: New Viewpoints, 1974), 8–9, 32–33; Ronald Schaffer, "The New York City Woman Suffrage Party, 1909–1919," *New York History* 43 (1962): 284; Glenda Riley, *Inventing the American Woman*, vol. 2, *A Perspective on Women's History, 1865 to the Present* (Arlington Heights, Ill.: Harlan Davidson, 1986), 37. Alan Grimes has attributed the nineteenth-century suffrage victories in the West to Progressives' quest for a "purification" of the social order. See Grimes, *Puritan Ethic*.

126. David Danbom, *"The World of Hope": Progressives and the Struggle for a Regenerate America* (Philadelphia: Temple Univ. Press, 1987), 183.

127. Carl Schneider and Dorothy Schneider, *American Women in the Progressive Era, 1900–1920* (New York: Facts on File, 1993), 11.

128. *Fourteenth Census of the United States: Occupations* (Washington, D.C.: Government Printing Office, 1923), 4:33, table 1.

129. Ibid., 4:34, table 2. In 1910, 31.3 percent of female workers were employed as domestics, 22.5 percent in factories, 22.4 percent on farms, 9.1 percent in the professions, 7.3 percent as clerical workers, 5.8 percent in trades, 1.3 percent in transportation, and .2 percent in public service. Ibid.

130. Solomon, *In the Company of Educated Women*, 63, table 2; and *Fourteenth*

Census of the United States: Occupations 4:34, table 2. The percentage of women attending college rose from 2.8 percent in 1900 to 7.6 percent in 1920. Solomon, *In the Company of Educated Women,* 64, table 3.

131. Woloch, *Women and the American Experience,* 276, 282.

132. Cott, *Grounding of Modern Feminism,* 166; Schneider, *American Women in the Progressive Era,* 146; and Woloch, *Women and the American Experience,* 274.

133. For discussions about the "New Woman," see June Sochen, *The New Woman in Greenwich Village, 1910–1920* (New York Quadrangle Books, 1972); and Judith Schwarz, *Radical Feminists of Heterodoxy: Greenwich Village, 1912–1940* (Lebanon, N.H.: New Victoria Publishers, 1982).

134. "New York Aglow as 1908 Hailed with Revelry," *New York Herald,* 1 Jan. 1908, 1.

135. McGovern, "The American Woman's Pre-World War I Freedom in Manners and Morals," 320.

136. Ellen Chesler, *Woman of Valor: Margaret Sanger and the Birth Control Movement in America* (New York: Simon & Schuster, 1992), 99.

137. McGovern, "The American Woman's Pre-World War I Freedom in Manners and Morals," 331.

138. Peter Filene, *Him/Her/Self: Sex Roles in Modern America* (Baltimore: Johns Hopkins Univ. Press, 1986), 35.

139. "Suffragist and Suffragette, A Sure Cure for Anti-Suffragitis," *American Suffragette,* June 1909, 5. The newspaper further described the difference: "A Suffragette is one who not only BELIEVES in woman suffrage, but who DOES SOMETHING to aid the movement." "Who Is a Suffragette?" *American Suffragette,* Dec. 1911, 8–9.

140. "Suffragists at Oyster Bay," *Woman's Journal,* 29 Aug. 1908, 140.

141. *Woman's Journal,* 4 Jan. 1908, 4.

142. Annual Report, Jan. 1911–Jan. 1912, Reel 1, HSB Papers.

143. "The National President's Letter," *Progress,* Apr. 1910, 1.

144. "Convention Notes," *Progress,* Nov. 1908, 2.

145. "National Convention," *Woman's Journal,* 14 Aug. 1909, 130.

146. "The National President's Letter," *Progress,* Apr. 1910, 1. Dr. Shaw, who broke considerable ground for women herself as a minister and physician, was not averse to women speaking up for their rights. She spoke publicly for women's rights for forty years and was eulogized as the greatest orator of the movement. Karlyn Kohrs Campbell, *Women Public Speakers in the United States, 1800–1925: A Bio-Critical Sourcebook* (Westport, Conn.: Greenwood Press, 1993), 418.

147. "The National President's Letter," *Progress,* May 1910, 1. She addressed an open-air rally in the United States in 1912. "When Dr. Shaw Speaks," *Woman's Journal,* 14 Sept. 1912, 289.

148. Marjory Nelson, "Ladies in the Street: A Sociological Analysis of the National Woman's Party, 1910–1930" (Ph.D. diss., State Univ. of New York at Buffalo, 1976), 73.

149. "Suffragettes Open Their Campaign Here," *New York Times,* 1 Jan. 1908, 16.

150. Billington, "Ideology and Feminism," 666.

151. "Connecticut Work," *Woman's Journal,* 26 Aug. 1911, 267.

152. "Teachers to Enter Soapbox Campaign," *New York Times,* 2 June 1915, 13.

153. DuBois, "Working Women, Class Relations, and Suffrage Militance," 56.

154. Cott, *Grounding of Modern Feminism,* 27.

155. Sheppard, *Cartooning for Suffrage,* 179.

156. "Amusement Seekers Hear Suffrage Talk," *American Suffragette,* Sept.–Oct. 1909, 5.

157. "What Is Feminism?" pamphlet, Reel 95, NWP Papers: The Suffrage Years.

158. Cott, *Grounding of Modern Feminism,* 13–14.

159. "The Bogey of Feminism," *Woman's Journal,* 28 Oct. 1916; and "Mrs. Catt on Feminism," *Woman's Journal,* 9 Jan. 1915, 12.

160. "Suffragism Not Feminism," *American Suffragette,* Dec. 1909, 3.

161. "Novelties," *Woman's Journal,* 9 Sept. 1911, 287.

162. "Challenges Antis to Cook," *Woman's Journal,* 11 Sept. 1915, 292.

163. Wheeler, *New Women of the New South,* 76.

164. "Suffrage Fete for Cleveland," *Woman's Journal,* 16 Aug. 1913, 262.

165. "Suffragist Baby Show," *New York Times,* 16 Oct. 1913, 1; "$5 for Best Suffrage Baby," *New York Herald,* 9 May 1914, n.p., Reel 3, HSB Papers; and "Suffrage Work in the States," *Woman's Journal,* 3 Apr. 1915, 108.

166. "Suffragist Baby Shows," *New York Times,* 16 Oct. 1913, 1.

167. *Woman's Journal,* 20 Dec. 1913, 407.

168. "Suffragists Do Washing," *New York Times,* 21 Feb. 1913, 8.

169. *Woman Voter,* Jan. 1915, 1.

170. Sheppard, *Cartooning for Suffrage,* 187.

171. Cott, *Grounding of Modern Feminism,* 27.

172. For a discussion of the uneasy relationship between working-class women, Socialists, and suffragists, see chapter 7 in Tax, *Rising of the Women,* 164–200. Doris Daniels has argued that social workers, especially Lillian Wald of the Henry Street Settlement, served as the bridge between upper-class suffragists, working-class women, professional women, and immigrant women. See Doris Daniels, "Building a Winning Coalition: The Suffrage Fight in New York State," *New York History* 60 (1979): 59–80.

173. DuBois, "Working Women, Class Relations, and Suffrage Militance," 57.

174. "The Open-Air Meetings in Queens-Nassau County New York," *Progress,* Oct. 1908, 3.

175. "State Correspondence," *Woman's Journal*, 13 Aug. 1910, 133.

176. Anne Firor Scott, *The Southern Lady: From Pedestal to Politics, 1830–1930* (Chicago: Univ. of Chicago Press: 1991), 181.

177. "State Correspondence," *Woman's Journal*, 31 July 1909, 124. Altogether, those women addressed four thousand listeners at nineteen open-air meetings, including bathers at Nantasket beach, whom the suffragists addressed from the surf. Ibid.

178. "Suffragists Hold a Street Meeting," *New York Times*, 14 May 1909, 5.

179. "Miss Malone Quits the Suffragettes," *New York Times*, 27 Mar. 1908, 4.

180. "Mayor Wins City," *Woman's Journal*, 10 Aug. 1912, 254.

181. "Lone Suffragette Upsets Rally," *New York Times*, 9 Oct. 1909, 1; "Saffron Parade of One," *New York Times*, 13 Feb. 1909, 6; "Maud Malone Arrested," *New York Times*, 20 June 1909, pt. 2, p. 1; "Maud Malone on Her Rights," *New York Times*, 22 June 1909, 6; "Arrest Maud Malone Again," *New York Times*, 27 June 1909, 16; "Lone Suffragette Upsets Rally," *New York Times*, 9 Oct. 1909, 1; "Gaynor Won't Reply to Ivins," *New York Times*, 15 Oct. 1909, 1; and "Maud Malone Meets a Foe," *New York Times*, 18 Dec. 1909, 2. The *Woman's Journal* also reported that an unidentified Boston woman was kicked and manhandled by police when she interrupted a candidate's speech to ask if he supported suffrage. "Militant Methods," *Woman's Journal*, 7 Oct. 1911, 316.

182. "Militant Maud Malone," *Woman's Journal*, 4 Jan. 1913, 2. Little is known about Malone. Doris Stevens said Malone was a librarian and that her father was a physician. Stevens, *Jailed for Freedom*, 364; and "Maud Malone Comes of Fighting Stock," *Woman's Journal*, 11 May 1912, 151.

183. *People v. Malone*, 29 N.Y. Crim. Rts. 325, 326 (N.Y.S. Ct. 1913).

184. "Maud Malone Loses," *New York Times*, 29 Mar. 1913, 11. The judge wanted to suspend the sentence, but she refused. Ibid.

185. *People v. Malone*, 29 N.Y. Crim. Rts. 325 (N.Y.S. Ct. 1913). At least one law journal approved, lauding the "common-sense respect for others" embodied in the law. "Free Speech and Its Limits," *Case and Comment* 22 (1915): 455.

186. "Why Waste the Judges' Time?" *New York Times*, 29 Mar. 1913, sec. 3, p. 6. An earlier editorial also criticized Malone's interruption for using means "not tolerated" in the United States. "Just Resentment," *New York Times*, 21 Oct. 1912, 10.

187. "Militant Maud Malone," *Woman's Journal*, 2.

188. The women opted for the trolley after they were unable to borrow an automobile for the trip. "Wanted, An Automobile," *Woman's Journal*, 31 July 1909, 121.

189. "Mrs. Susan W. FitzGerald," *Woman's Journal*, 5 Feb. 1910, 21–22.

190. As reported in "Massachusetts Meetings," *Woman's Journal*, 28 Aug. 1909, 138.

191. See Welter, "Cult of True Womanhood," 21–41.

192. Billington, "Ideology and Feminism," 672.

193. "What's Doing in the Party," *Woman Voter*, Aug. 1912, 17.

194. "A Page of Suffrage Babies and Mothers," *Buffalo Sun Times*, n.d., n.p., Reel 60, NAWSA Papers.

195. "State Correspondence," *Woman's Journal*, 25 Dec. 1909, 213; and "Mrs. Susan W. FitzGerald," *Woman's Journal*, 5 Feb. 1910, 21–22.

196. *Woman's Journal*, 5 Feb. 1910, 21–22.

197. "Massachusetts Activity," *Progress*, Nov. 1909, 1; and "State Correspondence," *Woman's Journal*, 31 July 1909, 128.

198. "Hurrah for Ohio!" *Woman's Journal*, 8 June 1912, 178.

199. "State Correspondence," *Woman's Journal*, 4 Sept. 1909, 142.

200. "Blazing the Trail," *American Suffragette*, Sept. 1910, 16.

201. "Massachusetts Meetings," *Woman's Journal*, 28 Aug. 1909, 139.

202. "State Correspondence," *Woman's Journal*, 7 Aug. 1909, 128.

203. "Five Suffrage Posters," *Woman's Journal*, 18 Sept. 1909, 152.

204. "State Correspondence," *Woman's Journal*, 7 Aug. 1909, 128.

205. Ibid.

206. "Massachusetts Meetings," *Woman's Journal*, 28 Aug. 1909, 139.

207. "State Correspondence," *Woman's Journal*, 4 Sept. 1909, 142.

208. "Rules for Open Air Meetings," *Woman's Journal*, 30 Apr. 1910, 70.

209. *HWS* 5:286, and "The National Convention," *Progress*, 10 May 1910, 4.

210. "For Suffrage Oratory," *New York Tribune*, 21 Dec. 1912, 6.

211. Seiler interview, 17.

212. A *Woman's Journal* article in January, for instance, described various stages of legislative initiatives concerning woman suffrage in Nevada, Maine, New Hampshire, Texas, Connecticut, Minnesota, Missouri, Iowa, Alabama, and Wisconsin. "Suffrage Work in the States," *Woman's Journal*, 30 Jan. 1915, 35.

213. Arizona, California, Colorado, Idaho, Illinois, Kansas, Montana, Nevada, Oregon, Utah, Washington, and Wyoming.

214. "No Suffrage Street Talk," *New York Times*, 9 May 1917, 16. The suffragists' decision may have been influenced by the increasing repression of free speech that followed the United States' entrance into the war on 6 April 1917. A few months later, for instance, New York police announced they would break up disruptive street meetings at which radicals criticized World War I and the draft. "See End of Street Sedition," *New York Times*, 31 Aug. 1917, 18.

215. "To Cover City with Speakers," *Woman's Journal*, 18 Jan. 1913, 19.

216. Anna Howard Shaw to Alice Paul, 20 Feb. 1913, Reel 1, NWP Papers: The Suffrage Years.

217. "Ban Antis from Big Auditorium," *Woman's Journal*, 14 Aug. 1915, 262.

218. "The Summer Campaign," *Suffragist*, 25 July 1914, 7. The mayor also donated five dollars to the cause. Vernon interview, 29.

Chapter 3. Petitions

1. Catt and Shuler, *Woman Suffrage and Politics*, 108–9.

2. Carrie Chapman Catt to New York Legislature Judiciary Committee, 19 Feb. 1908, Reel 58, NAWSA Papers.

3. Norman Smith, "'Shall Make No Law Abridging . . .': An Analysis of the Neglected, But Nearly Absolute, Right of Petition," *University of Cincinnati Law Review* 54 (1986): 1153.

4. *Adderley v. Florida*, 385 U.S. 39, 49n (1966).

5. Jean Rydstrom, Annotation, "The Supreme Court and the First Amendment Right to Petition the Government for a Redress of Grievances," 30 L.Ed. 2d. 914, 922.

6. Anita Hodgkiss, "Petitioning and the Empowerment Theory of Practice," *Yale Law Journal* 96 (1987): 572. The U.S. Supreme Court in 1963, for instance, found that students marching to the state house with a petition were exercising the right of petition in its "most pristine and classic form." *Edwards v. South Carolina*, 372 U.S. 229, 235 (1963).

7. Smith, "Shall Make No Law," 1189.

8. Smith, "Development of the Right of Assembly," 361. The Magna Charta specifically provided for redress of grievances. After a wronged party stated his case to four of the twenty-five barons appointed as liaisons to King John, the barons would ask the king for redress. McKechnie, *Magna Charta*, 468.

9. Smith, "Shall Make No Law," 1169, 1180.

10. Smith, "Development of the Right of Assembly," 366; David Fellman, *Constitutional Rights of Association* (Chicago: Univ. of Chicago Press, 1963), 29; and 92 U.S. 542 (1875). The U.S. Supreme Court established the right of assembly as "cognate to those of free speech and free press" in 1937 in *DeJonge v. Oregon*, 288 U.S. 364–65 (1937).

11. Hodgkiss, "Petitioning," 571.

12. Stephen Higginson, "A Short History of the Right to Petition Government for the Redress of Grievances," *Yale Law Journal* 96 (1986): 155; and Hodgkiss, "Petitioning," 576. In contrast, Norman Smith argued that requiring a governmental response to petitions exceeds governmental capabilities. Smith, "Shall Make No Law," 1190–91.

13. "Report on the Committee of Libraries," *Woman's Journal*, 31 Oct. 1908, 176.

14. "Continuously Praying," *Woman Citizen*, 2 Feb. 1918, 192; and Lisa Tickner, *The Spectacle of Women: Imagery of the Suffrage Campaign, 1907–1914* (London: Chatto & Windus, 1987), 109.

15. Jill Liddington, *One Hand Tied Behind Us: The Rise of the Women's Suffrage Movement* (London: Virago, 1978), 145.

16. Raeburn, *Suffragette View*, 41.

17. R. C. Bailey, *Popular Influence upon Public Policy: Petitioning in Eighteenth Century Virginia* (Westport, Conn.: Greenwood Press, 1979), 43–44.

18. Lerner, *Female Experience*, 329. See also Baker, "Domestication of Politics," 623.

19. Higginson, "Short History of the Right to Petition," 153; and Kerber, *Women of the Republic*, 41.

20. Kerber, *Women of the Republic*, 52.

21. Angelina Grimké, "Appeal to the Christian Women of the South," in *The Public Years of Sarah and Angelina Grimké: Selected Writings, 1835–1839*, ed. Larry Ceplair (New York: Columbia Univ. Press, 1989), 66.

22. Yellin, *Women and Sisters*, 39.

23. Scott, *Natural Allies*, 50.

24. Flexner, *Century of Struggle*, 51. Flexner examined some of the countless file boxes containing the petitions at the National Archives that bear "witness to that anonymous and heartbreaking labor." She observed, "The petitions are yellowed and frail, glued together, page on page, covered with ink blots, signed with scratchy pens, with an occasional erasure by one who fearfully thought better of so bold an act." Ibid.

25. For a discussion of the gag rule controversy, see chapter 11 in Gilbert Barnes, *The Antislavery Impulse: 1830–44* (New York: D. Appleton-Century, 1933); and David C. Frederick, "John Quincy Adams, Slavery and the Disappearance of the Right of Petition," *Law and History Review* 9 (1991): 113–15.

26. Barnes, *The Antislavery Impulse*, 143.

27. Lerner, *Female Experience*, 335.

28. Flexner, *Century of Struggle*, 50–51.

29. Lerner, *Grimké Sisters*, 184.

30. "Continuously Praying," *Woman Citizen*, 2 Feb. 1918, 192.

31. *HWS* 1:856–57.

32. Flexner, *Century of Struggle*, 111.

33. *HWS* 2:324–25, 333.

34. "Continuously Praying," *Woman Citizen*, 2 Feb. 1918, 192.

35. *HWS* 3:59.

36. Wagner, *Time of Protest*, 77; and *HWS* 3:59.

37. Bordin, *Woman and Temperance*, 49. For accounts of other WCTU petitions, see also 55, 63, 111, 137, 192.

38. Ibid., 110–11.

39. *HWS* 3:78.

40. "Continuously Praying," *Woman Citizen,* 2 Feb. 1918, 192.

41. Terborg-Penn, "Afro-Americans in the Struggle," 166.

42. Ryan, *Women in Public,* 138.

43. Beeton, *Women Vote in the West,* 91, 110.

44. Fuller, *Laura Clay,* 98.

45. Terborg-Penn, "Afro-Americans in the Struggle," 144.

46. "Suffragettes Open Their Campaign Here," *New York Times,* 1 Jan. 1908, 16.

47. Van Voris, *Carrie Chapman Catt,* 212.

48. Catt and Shuler, *Woman Suffrage and Politics,* 234.

49. "President's New York Message," *Progress,* Jan. 1909, 1.

50. "Petition," *Progress,* Feb. 1909, 2.

51. Taylor, *Citizens at Last,* 122.

52. "State Correspondence," *Woman's Journal,* 31 July 1909, 124; and "Massachusetts Activity," *Progress,* Nov. 1909, 1.

53. "Massachusetts Activity," *Progress,* Nov. 1909, 2.

54. "State Correspondence," *Woman's Journal,* 9 Oct. 1909, 163.

55. "Petition," *Progress,* Feb. 1909, 2.

56. "State Correspondence," *Woman's Journal,* 4 Sept. 1909, 142.

57. "The Great Petition—Given a Werk [sic]," *Progress,* May 1909, 2.

58. *HWS* 5:275.

59. Suffragists adopted yellow as their color during the 1887 campaign for municipal suffrage in Kansas. Women began wearing yellow bows, representing the Kansas sunflower; eventually, suffragists said the color signified the golden dawn of the new era to begin when women voted. "Why the Yellow?" *Woman Citizen,* 16 June 1917, 47.

60. "The National Convention," *Progress,* May 1910, 4; and "Woman Suffragists Storm Congress with Petitions for Votes, Filling Galleries and Overwhelming Proceedings with Applause," *New York Herald,* 19 Apr. 1910, 4.

61. Catt and Shuler, *Woman Suffrage and Politics,* 236. If Congress had refused to accept the petition, Laura Clay of Kentucky had suggested NAWSA stage a protest meeting on the Capitol steps. Fuller, *Laura Clay,* 119.

62. "Woman Suffragists Storm Congress with Petitions for Votes, Filling Galleries and Overwhelming Proceedings with Applause," *New York Herald,* 19 Apr. 1910, 4; and *New York World,* 19 Apr. 1910, 2.

63. "The Petition," *Woman Voter,* May 1910, 4.

64. Terborg-Penn, "Afro-Americans in the Struggle," 144.

65. Tax, *Rising of the Women,* 175.

66. "Great Trolley Tour," *Woman's Journal,* 2 Mar. 1912, 71; "Nebraska Gets Petition Going," *Woman's Journal,* 19 July 1913, 225; "Petition Day in Alabama," *Woman's Journal,* 28 Aug. 1915, 271; "Suffrage Work in the States," *Woman's Journal,*

26 Feb. 1916, 69; and "Pilgrimage to the Opening of the Maryland Legislature," *Suffragist,* 10 Jan. 1914, 7.

67. "Pilgrims Troop to Albany," *Woman's Journal,* 21 Dec. 1912, 401.

68. "Suffragists Plan Albany Pilgrimage," *New York Times,* 10 Dec. 1912, 3.

69. "The Hike to Albany," *Woman Voter and the Newsletter,* Feb. 1913, 13.

70. "Doves to Disprove Tales of Militancy," *New York Times,* 14 Dec. 1912, 5; and "Christmas Suffrage 'Hike' for Spinsters Only," *New York Tribune,* 11 Dec. 1912, 9.

71. "On to Poughkeepsie! Suffragists Cry Today!" *New York Tribune,* 21 Dec. 1912, 6.

72. "Three Million Dollars Worth of Advertising," *Woman Voter and the Newsletter,* Feb. 1913, 20.

73. "Pilgrimages Weren't Like This," *New York Times,* 11 Dec. 1912, 12.

74. "Pilgrims March Bravely On," *Woman's Journal,* 28 Dec. 1912, 409; and Ross, *Ladies of the Press,* 124.

75. Ross, *Ladies of the Press,* 123.

76. Ibid., 124.

77. "Pilgrims March Bravely On," *Woman's Journal,* 28 Dec. 1912, 409. Yet suffragists helped set the lighthearted tone, because Stubbs supplied the press with much of the color in bulletins playfully dubbed "ammunition." "Peanuts to Sustain Albany Crusaders," *New York Times,* 12 Dec. 1912, 24. Press coverage benefited Stubbs in an unforeseen way when she was reunited with her father, who had abandoned her family when she was eight years old. "Hikers' Spirits Drop at Sulzer's Absence," *New York Tribune,* 31 Dec. 1912, 7.

78. "Sturdy Seven Stick to Suffrage Stride," *New York Times,* 17 Dec. 1912, 7; and "Hikers' Spirits Drop at Sulzer's Absence," *New York Tribune,* 31 Dec. 1912, 7. Hecklers also frustrated the pilgrims' assemblies, like the seventy-year-old anti who disrupted a Hughsonville open-air meeting. "'On to Poughkeepsie!' Suffragists' Cry Today," *New York Tribune,* 21 Dec. 1912, 6.

79. "Suffragists Reach Albany After 12 Days," *New York Tribune,* 29 Dec. 1912, 1. Fourteen national reporters and photographers and twenty Albany journalists recorded the arrival. Ibid. Other hikers who completed the entire trip were Jones, Ida Craft, and Lavinia Dock. "Details of Long March," *New York Tribune,* 29 Dec. 1912, 4; and Ross, *Ladies of the Press,* 124.

80. "Schedule of Votes for Women Pilgrimage to Washington, D.C.," Reel 1, NWP Papers: The Suffrage Years; and "Nation Rolls Up Huge Petition," *Woman's Journal,* 12 July 1913, 217.

81. "Boston Pilgrims Convert Crowds," *Woman's Journal,* 9 Aug. 1913, 256; and "Notes," *Woman's Journal,* 16 Aug. 1913, 264.

82. "A Unique Pilgrimage," *Woman's Journal,* 12 July 1913, 220.

83. "Boston Pilgrims Convert Crowds," *Woman's Journal,* 9 Aug. 1913, 256.

84. "Suffrage Work in the States," *Woman's Journal*, 1 Jan. 1916, 5.

85. "Suffrage Message in Sulzer's Hands," *New York Tribune*, 1 Jan. 1913, 9; and "Proved Their Ability to Get There," *New York Times*, 30 Dec. 1912, 6.

86. "Nation Rolls Up Huge Petition," *Woman's Journal*, 12 July 1913, 217.

87. "Storm Congress with Petitions," *Woman's Journal*, 9 Aug. 1913, 254.

88. *HWS* 5:626.

89. "Storm Congress with Petitions," *Woman's Journal*, 9 Aug. 1913, 249.

90. Irwin, *Story of the Woman's Party*, 39.

91. Carrie Chapman Catt, "How to Secure the Ratification of the Federal Suffrage Amendment by Petition," May 1918, 2, NAWSA Papers, Reel 60.

92. Statement of Miss Anne Martin, chairman of the Woman's Party, 17 July 1917, Reel 45, NWP Papers: The Suffrage Years. Vice Chair Martin briefly served as NWP chair while Alice Paul was hospitalized in Baltimore.

93. Irwin, *Story of the Woman's Party*, 237–38.

94. Ibid., 106–7.

95. "Carry Voters' Plea Across Continent," *New York Times*, 4 Aug. 1915, 5. The *Woman's Journal* reported the petition would be transported by scores of women on horseback and in automobiles. "To Go Overland with Petitions," *Woman's Journal*, 13 Aug. 1915, 256.

96. Ward, *Motoring for the Millions*, 203, 50.

97. Amelia Fry, "Along the Suffrage Trail," *The American West* 6 (Jan. 1969): 19.

98. "Eastern Journey of the Woman Voters' Envoy," *Suffragist*, 23 Oct. 1915, 5. That banner hangs today in the NWP headquarters at the Belmont-Sewell House in Washington, D.C.

99. "From San Francisco to Washington," *Suffragist*, 9 Oct. 1915, 5.

100. "Rousing Welcome Given Envoys of the Woman Voters," *Suffragist*, 6 Nov. 1915, 3.

101. "Illinois Greets Woman Voters' Envoy," *Suffragist*, 13 Nov. 1915, 13; and "Woman Voters' Envoys Reach the East," *Suffragist*, 20 Nov. 1915, 3.

102. "Woman Voters' Envoys Reach Unfree States," *Suffragist*, 30 Oct. 1915, 3; and Fry, "Along the Suffrage Trail," 20.

103. Fry, "Along the Suffrage Trail," 22; "The Woman Voters' Envoy in the Eastern States," *Suffragist*, 27 Nov. 1915, 3; Fry, "Along the Suffrage Trail," 20; and Irwin, *Story of the Woman's Party*, 113.

104. "The Woman Voters' Envoys Present Their Message to the President and Congress," *Suffragist*, 11 Dec. 1915, 4–5; and Howard, *Long Campaign*, 107.

105. Fry, "Along the Suffrage Trail," 23.

106. "Suffrage Envoys Win Adherent," *Woman's Journal*, 27 Nov. 1915, 382.

107. Irwin, *Story of the Woman's Party*, 116.

108. Fry, "Along the Suffrage Trail," 25.

109. "When Sara Comes, It's Always a Holiday!" *Bancroftiana* (Oct. 1980): 2.

110. "The Petition," *Woman Voter,* May 1910, 4.

111. *Adderley v. Florida,* 385 U.S. 39, 52 (1966).

112. "Continuously Praying," *Woman Citizen,* 2 Feb. 1918, 192.

113. *Woman Citizen,* 4 Sept. 1920, 364. When she was president of the Women's International League for Peace and Freedom in 1930, Catt scoffed when pacifists suggested they petition to protest the United States' plans to build the biggest battleship in the world. A petition "would probably have as much effect as a lone ladybug sitting on a cabbage rose while she longs for rain," Catt said. Van Voris, *Carrie Chapman Catt,* 212.

114. Catt and Shuler, *Woman Suffrage and Politics,* 295. Susan B. Anthony had organized a similar house-to-house canvass in New York in 1894. DuBois, "Working Women, Class Relations, and Suffrage Militance," 37.

115. Flexner, *Century of Struggle,* 289.

116. Van Voris, *Carrie Chapman Catt,* 146. See also Gertrude Foster Brown, "A Decisive Victory Won," in National American Woman Suffrage Association, *Victory! How Women Won It,* 119–20.

117. Sidney Bland, "Techniques of Persuasion: The National Woman's Party and Woman Suffrage, 1913–1919" (Ph.D. diss., George Washington Univ., 1972), 156, 160.

118. Carrie Chapman Catt, Bulletin No. 17, 21 June 1918, Reel 60, NAWSA Papers.

119. Carrie Chapman Catt, "How to Secure the Ratification of the Federal Suffrage Amendment by Petition," May 1918, 4, 8, Reel 60, NAWSA Papers.

120. Ibid., 13.

121. Carrie Chapman Catt, Bulletin No. 20, 6 July 1918, Reel 60, NAWSA Papers.

122. Catt, *Woman Suffrage and Politics,* 260.

123. "Walkless Parade," *Woman's Journal,* 6 May 1916, 145.

Chapter 4. Parades

1. "Suffragist Parade Despite the Police," *New York Times,* 17 Feb. 1908, 7.

2. "25,340 March in Suffrage Parade to the Applause of 250,000 Admirers; Spectacle Runs on In the Moonlight," *New York Times,* 24 Oct. 1915, 1, 2. The tally included about twenty-five hundred men. Ibid.

3. "First Southern Parade," *Woman's Journal,* 18 Oct. 1913, 334.

4. Ryan, *Women in Public,* 23.

5. Ulrich, *Midwife's Tale,* 32.

6. Ryan, *Women in Public,* 52, 45–47, 177.

7. *In re Frazee,* 30 N.W. 72, 75 (Mich. Sup. Ct. 1886).

8. *Shuttlesworth v. Birmingham,* 394 U.S. 147 (1969) (city parade permit system lacking well-defined, objective criteria unconstitutional). The Court described marches as "pristine and classic" examples of the exercise of democracy in *Edwards v. South Carolina,* 372 U.S. 229, 235 (1963).

9. *In re Frazee,* 30 N.W. 74.

10. *Anderson v. City of Wellington,* 19 P. 719 (1888).

11. *Rich v. City of Naperville,* 42 Ill. App. 222, 223 (1891).

12. Abernathy, *Right of Assembly,* 91.

13. Ibid., 84, 90.

14. Blackstone wrote, "The liberty of the press . . . consists in laying no *previous* restraints upon publications, and not in freedom from censure for criminal matter when published." William Blackstone, *Commentaries on the Laws of England* (Boston: T. B. Wait and Sons, 1818), 4:151–52. Legal scholars' first challenges to the view that freedom of expression extended no further than prohibiting prior restraints coincided with the final decade of vigorous suffrage protests. See Theodore Schroeder, "The Historical Interpretation of 'Freedom of Speech and of the Press,'" in *"Obscene" Literature and Constitutional Law,* by Schroeder (New York: private printing for forensic use, 1911), 206–39; and Zechariah Chafee Jr., "Freedom of Speech in War Time," *Harvard Law Review* 32 (June 1919): 939–40.

15. *In re Flaherty,* 38 P. 981 (Cal. Sup. Ct. 1895); and *Mashburn v. Bloomington,* 32 Ill. App. 245 (1889).

16. "IWW Protestor Arrested After March," *New York Times,* 7 Mar. 1914, 1.

17. *People v. Burman,* 117 N.W. 589, 592 (Mich. Sup. Ct. 1908).

18. *Commonwealth v. Karvonen,* 106 N.E. 556 (Mass. Sup. Ct. 1914). A 1931 U.S. Supreme Court landmark case expanded protections for symbolic expression when it reversed a conviction under a state statute prohibiting the display of red flags as emblems of opposition to organized government. *Stromberg v. California,* 283 U.S. 359 (1931).

19. Philip Foner, *Women and the American Labor Movement,* vol. 2, *From the First Trade Unions to the Present* (New York: Free Press, 1982), 47.

20. Three other suffrage parades occurred later in 1908. In Oakland, California, three hundred women marched into the state Democratic convention in pairs, hoisting a silk suffrage banner and streamers, before requesting a party plank calling for a suffrage referendum. "The Republican Hearing," *Woman's Journal,* 19 Sept. 1908, 151; and Davis, *California Women,* 121. That April, bejeweled suffragists sped across New York City in a small auto parade, stopping to make speeches from the rear seats in what was then their "most conspicuous appearance" in the city. "Suffragists in Autos," *New York Times,* 23 Apr. 1908, 16. In Boone, Iowa, that autumn two English suffragettes led one hundred women behind a yellow banner reading "Taxation Without Representation Is Tyranny" to welcome Dr. Anna

Howard Shaw to their state convention. "Boone, Iowa, Convention," *Progress*, Nov. 1908, 4.

21. Raeburn, *Militant Suffragettes*, 60.

22. "May Ignore Bingham," *New York Times*, 14 Feb. 1908, 2; and "The Suffrage Parade," *Woman's Journal*, 22 Feb. 1908, 30.

23. "Suffragist Parade Despite the Police," *New York Times*, 17 Feb. 1908, 7.

24. "Editorial Notes," *Woman's Journal*, 22 Feb. 1908, 1.

25. Tickner, *Spectacle of Women*, 56.

26. Strachey, *Cause*, 316.

27. *Woman's Standard*, 1909, qtd. in Louise R. Noun, *Strong-Minded Women: The Emergence of the Woman-Suffrage Movement in Iowa* (Ames: Iowa State Univ. Press, 1969), 250.

28. Blatch and Lutz, *Challenging Years*, 129.

29. "Suffrage Parade Has Police Guard," *New York Times*, 22 May 1910, 11. Dr. Shaw became an enthusiastic convert to parades; that summer she led the American contingent among a half million marchers in London and when it ended addressed the mammoth rally in Trafalgar Square. *Woman's Journal*, 30 July 1910, 121; and "Letter from Rev. Anna Howard Shaw," *Woman's Journal*, 27 Aug. 1910, 142.

30. "From New York," *Woman's Journal*, 4 June 1910, 92.

31. "Suffragists in Auto Parade," *New York Times*, 14 May 1910, 3.

32. Catt and Shuler, *Woman Suffrage and Politics*, 285.

33. Van Voris, *Carrie Chapman Catt*, 77. In retrospect, however, Catt believed parades alienated more men than they persuaded because the sight of marching women offended them. She may have said this because the 1915 New York suffrage referendum failed just weeks after the biggest suffrage parade of more than twenty-five thousand women. Catt and Shuler, *Woman Suffrage and Politics*, 290–91.

34. "The March of 3,000 Women," *Harper's Weekly*, 20 May 1911, 8; "Suffrage Army on Parade," *New York Times*, 5 May 1912, 1; "10,000 Marchers in Suffrage Line," *New York Times*, 4 May 1913, 1; "25,340 March in Suffrage Parade to the Applause of 250,000 Admirers; Spectacle Runs on In the Moonlight," *New York Times*, 24 Oct. 1915, 1; and "20,000 March in Suffrage Line," *New York Times*, 28 Oct. 1917, sec. 1, 1.

35. "Saturday's Parade Reviewed," *New York Times*, 10 May 1911, 10.

36. See "Oklahoma Women in First Parade," *Woman's Journal*, 13 Sept. 1913, 296; "Utica Welcomes Suffrage Parade," *Woman's Journal*, 14 June 1913, 192; "Doves to Disprove Tales of Militancy," *New York Times*, 14 Dec. 1912, 5; "Splendid Parade in Baltimore," *Woman's Journal*, 24 May 1913, 168; "Brooklyn Holds Splendid Parade," *Woman's Journal*, 8 Nov. 1913, 353; "Woman Voters Celebrate Victory," *Woman's Journal*, 11 Nov. 1911, 353; "Dakota Women Have Parade," *Woman's Journal*, 19 July 1913, 232; "Indiana Suffragists Hold Conventions," *Woman's Journal*, 20 July 1912, 226; and Taylor, *Citizens at Last*, 166.

37. "First Suffrage Parade," *Woman's Journal,* 18 Oct. 1913, 334. Suffragists also marched for the cause as a part of other community festivities in Boston, Massachusetts; Reno, Nevada; Atlanta, Georgia; Fayetteville, North Carolina; Erie and Scranton, Pennsylvania; and elsewhere. "Report of the Float Committee," Reel 49, NAWSA Papers; "Campaign in Nevada," *Suffragist,* 27 June 1914, 6; "Georgia Women Initiate Parade," *Woman's Journal,* 6 Dec. 1913, 387; Taylor, *Woman Suffrage Movement in Tennessee,* 53; "Crowds Applaud Suffrage Line," *Woman's Journal,* 19 July 1913, 225; and "Scranton Women in Labor Parade," *Woman's Journal,* 13 Sept. 1913, 290.

38. Fuller, *Laura Clay,* 132–33, 147; and Taylor, *Woman Suffrage Movement in Tennessee,* 53.

39. Blatch and Lutz, *Challenging Years,* 132.

40. "Suffrage Parade Has Police Guard," *New York Times,* 22 May 1910, 11.

41. "Suffragists March in Procession To-Day," *New York Times,* 6 May 1911, 13.

42. Blatch and Lutz, *Challenging Years,* 132.

43. "Parades as Persuaders," unidentified newspaper clipping, Reel 49, NAWSA Papers.

44. Edwin Emery and Michael Emery, *The Press and America: An Interpretive History of the Mass Media,* 5th ed. (Englewood Cliffs, N.J.: Prentice-Hall, 1984), 399.

45. "Pilgrimages Were Not Like This," *New York Times,* 11 Dec. 1912, 12. Women newspaper reporters complained that they were replaced by men to cover suffrage parades because parades were front-page news. Ross, *Ladies of the Press,* 123.

46. "The Parade of Protest," *Woman Voter,* June 1911, 7.

47. "The Party and the Parade," *Woman Voter and the Newsletter,* June 1913, 10.

48. "Novel Suffrage Stunts as Publicity Makers," *New York Sun,* 16 Feb. 1918, n.p., Reel 95, NWP Papers: The Suffrage Years.

49. "Suffrage Parade Has Police Guard," *New York Times,* 22 May 1910, 11; and "From New York," *Woman's Journal,* 4 June 1910, 92.

50. "Press Comment on the Procession," *Woman's Journal,* 11 June 1910, 96.

51. Stevens, *Jailed for Freedom,* 21.

52. Official Program of the Woman's Suffrage Procession, Reel 49, NAWSA Papers.

53. Elsie Hill, Chair of the College Section, to "Fellow Suffragist," 8 Jan. 1913, Reel 1, NWP Papers: The Suffrage Years.

54. "5,000 Women March, Beset By Crowds," *New York Times,* 4 Mar. 1913, 4. Inez Haynes Irwin estimated the number of women at eight thousand, and Doris Stevens estimated ten thousand. Irwin, *Story of the Woman's Party,* 21.

55. "Woman's Beauty, Grace, and Art Bewilder the Capital," *Washington Post,* 4 Mar. 1913, 1. NAWSA apparently found the hikers too quaint to meet with President Wilson, and Alice Paul took from Jones a message she had carried from NAWSA to

Wilson, a rebuff that stung Jones. Anna Howard Shaw to Alice Paul, 5 Mar. 1913, Reel 2, NWP Papers: The Suffrage Years.

56. Alice Paul, "Conversations with Alice Paul: Woman Suffrage and the Equal Rights Amendment." interview by Amelia Fry, Suffragists Oral History Collection, Univ. of California, Berkeley, microfiche edition (Sanford, N.C.: Microfilm Corporation of America, 1980) (hereafter cited as Paul interview), 73.

57. Alice Paul to Mary Ware Dennett, 6 Jan. 1913, Reel 1, NWP: The Suffrage Years; and "Interest Grows in Big Parade," Woman's Journal, 18 Jan. 1913, 23.

58. Blanchard, Revolutionary Sparks, 12. Later the trio was convicted of carrying banners, which carried a twenty-day sentence, and Coxey and one of the men were fined five dollars for walking on the grass. Ibid.

59. Paul interview, 74.

60. "Suffrage Invasion Is On for Earnest," New York Times, 3 Mar. 1913, 15; and "5,000 of Fair Sex Ready to Parade," Washington Post, 3 Mar. 1913, 2.

61. "5,000 Women March, Beset By Crowds," New York Times, 4 Mar. 1913, 4.

62. "Woman's Beauty, Grace, and Art Bewilder the Capital," Washington Post, 4 Mar. 1913, 1.

63. Unidentified newspaper clipping, Reel 59, NAWSA Papers; and "Parade Struggles to Victory Despite Disgraceful Scenes," Woman's Journal, 8 Mar. 1913, 73.

64. Rossi, Feminist Papers, 539. The speaker was Suzanne LaFollette, daughter of a congressman and second cousin of Senator Robert LaFollette. Suzanne wrote an influential feminist tract, Concerning Women, in 1926.

65. "Boston Women to Protest Treatment at Mass Meeting," unidentified newspaper clipping, Reel 49, NAWSA Papers; and "100 Are in Hospital," Washington Post, 4 Mar. 1913, 10. The New York Times said the hospital treated two hundred persons. "Parade Protest Arouses Senate," New York Times, 5 Mar. 1912, 8.

66. "Newspaper Comment," Woman's Journal, 8 Mar. 1913, 77; and "Parade Struggles to Victory Despite Disgraceful Scenes," Woman's Journal, 8 Mar. 1913, 73.

67. Blatch and Lutz, Challenging Years, 196.

68. "Parade Protest Arouses Senate," New York Times, 5 Mar. 1912, 8.

69. A similar incident on a smaller scale occurred in New York the previous May. Suffragists charged that police lines were inadequate to contain the packed throng so that marchers had to fight their way through the crowd. Women claimed many of the officers on duty seemed amused by the catcalls and hisses that rang in the marchers' ears. The police apologized. "Suffragists Tell Waldo Their Woes," New York Times, 11 May 1912, 22; "Glimpses of the Parade," Woman's Journal, 11 May 1912, 148; and "Suffrage Army on Parade," New York Times, 5 May 1912, 1.

70. "Begin Police Grill," Washington Post, 5 Mar. 1913, 5, 12. See also Annual Report for 1913, Reel 87, NWP Papers: The Suffrage Years. Paul had mellowed sixty years later and recalled, "My impression is of the police doing the best they could, having their leaders not providing enough policemen." Paul interview, 79.

71. "Says Police Sided with Mob," *New York Times,* 11 Mar. 1913, 18.

72. Lunardini, *From Equal Suffrage to Equal Rights,* 30.

73. Blatch and Lutz, *Challenging Years,* 197. Blatch was among many who telegrammed Wilson in protest. Ibid. For a radical feminist critique of American government, see, for example, Catharine MacKinnon, *Toward a Feminist Theory of the State* (Cambridge: Harvard Univ. Press, 1989).

74. "Newspaper Comment," *Woman's Journal,* 8 Mar. 1913, 77. Reel 2 of the NWP Papers: The Suffrage Years contains numerous letters and telegrams deploring the parade chaos.

75. "Anti-Suffragism Gets a Hard Blow," *New York Times,* 5 Mar. 1913, 16.

76. "'Antis' See Reaction," *Washington Post,* 3 Mar. 1913, 2; and "The Suffragette Parade," *Washington Post,* 3 Mar. 1913, 6.

77. Wheeler, *New Women of the New South,* 23.

78. "Washington," *Woman's Protest,* Apr. 1913, 5.

79. Anna Howard Shaw to Alice Paul, 22 Jan. 1913, Reel 1, NWP Papers: The Suffrage Years; and Anna Howard Shaw to Alice Paul and Lucy Burns, 7 Mar. 1913, Reel 2, NWP Papers: The Suffrage Years. Shaw threatened to bow out of the parade because she feared the official parade colors of white, purple, and green would be assumed to endorse British violence, because those were the colors of the militant Women's Social and Political Union. Anna Howard Shaw to Alice Paul, 24 Feb. 1913, Reel 1, NWP Papers: The Suffrage Years.

80. Catt and Shuler, *Woman Suffrage and Politics,* 241. Catt, as head of the International Woman Suffrage Alliance, led the inaugural parade's first section, depicting woman suffrage in other countries. Van Voris, *Carrie Chapman Catt,* 107.

81. Irwin, *Story of the Woman's Party,* 31.

82. "20,000 March in Suffrage Line," *New York Times,* 28 Oct. 1917, sec. 1, pp. 1, 18; and "Souvenir Program," Woman Suffrage Parade, 27 Oct. 1917, Reel 95, NWP Papers: The Suffrage Years.

83. Harriot Stanton Blatch, "The Value of a Woman Suffrage Parade," *Woman's Journal,* 4 May 1912, 137.

84. Bertha D. Knoble, "The March of 3,000 Women," *Harper's Weekly,* 20 May 1911, 8.

85. "The Value of a Woman Suffrage Parade," *Woman's Journal,* 4 May 1912, 137.

86. "To the Men and Women in the Street," *Woman Voter,* May 1912, 2.

87. "Suffrage Army Out on Parade," *New York Times,* 5 May 1912, 1.

88. "Nothing Dreadful Happened," *New York Times,* 12 Nov. 1912, 12.

89. McGerr, "Popular Style," 876.

90. "Parade to Glow Like Rainbow," *Woman's Journal,* 22 Feb. 1913, 57.

91. "Vast Suffrage Host Is On Parade To-Day," *New York Times,* 4 May 1912, 22; and "Suffrage Army Out On Parade," *New York Times,* 5 May 1912, 1.

92. "10,000 March in Suffrage Line," *New York Times,* 4 May 1913, sec. 2, p. 1.

93. "20,000 March in Suffrage Line," *New York Times*, 28 Oct. 1917, sec. 1, p. 1.

94. Van Voris, *Carrie Chapman Catt*, 146.

95. Fifty thousand feminists marched on Fifth Avenue on 26 August 1970 to celebrate the golden anniversary of the ratification of the suffrage amendment. Woloch, *Women and the American Experience*, 354.

96. "Vast Suffrage Host Is on Parade To-Day," *New York Times*, 4 May 1912, 22.

97. Nelson, "Ladies in the Street," 240–41.

98. "10,000 Marchers in Suffrage Line," *New York Times*, 4 May 1913, 1; and unidentified newspaper clipping, Reel 59, NAWSA Papers. See also "Women Parade and Rejoice at the End," *New York Times*, 7 May 1911, 1; and "Suffragists Big Night," *New York Times*, 23 Apr. 1913, 20. In the 1911 parade, Milholland and two other women carried the "Forward Into Light" banner that became the rallying cry of the yet-to-be-created National Woman's Party. The banner read "Forward out of error, / Leave behind the night: / Forward through the darkness, Forward into light" ("Women Parade and Rejoice at the End," *New York Times*, 7 May 1911, 1).

99. "Vote as Aid to Beauty," *Washington Post*, 3 Mar. 1913, 10. See also Paul Boyer, "Inez Milholland Boissevain," in *Notable American Women, 1607–1950*, ed. Edward James, Janet Wilson James, and Paul Boyer (Cambridge: Belknap Press, Harvard Univ. Press, 1971), 1:188–90.

100. "25,340 March in Suffrage Parade to the Applause of 250,000 Admirers; Spectacle Runs on In the Moonlight," *New York Times*, 24 Oct. 1915, 1.

101. "The Suffrage Parade," *New York Times*, 24 Oct. 1915, sec. 2, p. 16.

102. "Glimpses of the Parade," *Woman's Journal*, 11 May 1912, 148.

103. Harriot Stanton Blatch, "The Value of a Woman Suffrage Parade," *Woman's Journal*, 4 May 1912, 137.

104. Blatch and Lutz, *Challenging Years*, 180.

105. "Vast Suffrage Host is on Parade To-Day," *New York Times*, 4 May 1912, 22; and "The Press and the Parade," *Woman Voter*, June 1912, 1.

106. "Parade Will Be Mass of Color," *Woman's Journal*, 1 Feb. 1913, 38.

107. "25,340 March in Suffrage Parade to the Applause of 250,000 Admirers; Spectacle Runs on In the Moonlight," *New York Times*, 24 Oct. 1915, 2.

108. "Great Spring Parade May 3," *Woman Voter and Newsletter*, Apr. 1913, 7.

109. "Plan Big Demonstration for Chicago Convention," *Woman's Journal*, 13 May 1916, 160.

110. "The March in the Rain," *Woman's Journal*, 17 June 1916, 196.

111. Catt and Shuler, *Woman Suffrage and Politics*, 252.

112. "Closing Sessions of the Woman Party's Convention," *Suffragist*, 17 June 1916, 7; and *HWS* 5:710.

113. "5,500 Women March to Meeting Through Downpour," *Woman's Journal*, 17 June 1916, 193. Suffragists credited the success to their presence on Chicago streets, both in the parade and at nightly street meetings.

114. "4,000 Suffragists in Silent Appeal," *New York Times,* 16 June 1916, 3; "In St. Louis," *Woman Voter,* July 1916, 7–8; and "Big Demonstration Staged in St. Louis Despite Heat," *Woman's Journal,* 24 June 1916, 208.

115. "Suffrage Parade Plans," *New York Times,* 18 May 1910, 6; "Suffrage Parade Has Police Guard," *New York Times,* 22 May 1910, 11; and "The Woman Suffrage Parade," *Progress,* June 1910, 4.

116. "The Foot Parade," *Woman Voter,* Sept. 1910, 6.

117. "Women Parade and Rejoice at the End," *New York Times,* 7 May 1911, 1.

118. "The Parade of Protest," *Woman Voter,* June 1911, 6.

119. "Vast Suffrage Host is on Parade To-Day," *New York Times,* 4 May 1912, 22.

120. "New States to Lead in Suffrage Parade," *New York Times,* 9 Nov. 1912, 22.

121. *New York Tribune,* qtd. in "The Parade," *Woman Voter,* Dec. 1912, 1.

122. Blanche Arms to Mrs. Lewis Johnston, 14 Oct. 1915, Reel 49, NAWSA Papers.

123. "To the Men and Women in the Street," *Woman Voter,* May 1912, 2.

124. "The Women's March," *Woman's Journal,* 4 May 1912, 141.

125. Bettina Borrmann Wells, "The Militant Movement for Woman Suffrage," *Independent* 64 (Apr. 1908): 902.

126. "Suffragists in Auto Parade," *New York Times,* 14 May 1910, 13.

127. Pledge to March, Reel 2, HSB Papers.

128. Gluck, *From Parlor to Prison,* 140. This contradicts an account in the Woman Suffrage Party newsletter that contended not a single insult was flung at the marchers. "The Protest Meeting," *Woman Voter,* June 1910, 5.

129. "As to Processions," *Woman's Journal,* 21 Mar. 1908, 48.

130. "Suffragists March in Procession To-Day," *New York Times,* 6 May 1911, 13; "Women Parade and Rejoice at the End," *New York Times,* 7 May 1911, 1; and "Suffrage Parader Loses Teaching Job," *New York Times,* 22 May 1912, 1.

131. "Unable to March Women Use Wits," *Woman's Journal,* 21 June 1913, 198.

132. "20,000 March in Suffrage Line," *New York Times,* 28 Oct. 1917, sec. 1, pp. 1, 18; and "Souvenir Program," Woman Suffrage Parade, 27 Oct. 1917, Reel 95, NWP Papers: The Suffrage Years.

133. "Suffragists Block Anti-Parade Bill," *New York Telegraph,* 19 Nov. 1913, n.p., Reel 3, HSB Papers.

134. Taylor, *Woman Suffrage Movement in Tennessee,* 28.

135. Knobe, "The March of 3,000 Women," 8.

136. "The Parade," *Woman Voter and the Newsletter,* May 1913, 15.

137. "Saturday's Parade Reviewed," *New York Times,* 10 May 1911, 10.

138. Qtd. in "Kellogg Durand on the Parade," *Woman's Journal,* 20 May 1911, 155.

139. "400,000 Cheer Suffrage March," *New York Times,* 10 Nov. 1912, 1, 8.

140. Ibid.

141. "Half Million Cheer Parade," *Woman's Journal*, 16 Nov. 1912, 361.

142. Qtd. in "The Republican Hearing," *Woman's Journal*, 19 Sept. 1908, 151.

143. "Vote as Aid to Beauty," *Washington Post*, 3 Mar. 1913, 10.

144. "400,000 Cheer Suffrage March," *New York Times*, 10 Nov. 1912, 1.

145. "The Suffragette Parade," *Washington Post*, 3 Mar. 1913, 6.

146. "The Limitations and Possibilities of Pageantry," *Woman's Protest*, June 1913, 7.

147. "Antis Condemn Paraders," *New York Times*, 6 May 1913, 16.

148. "10,000 Marchers in Suffrage Line," *New York Times*, 4 May 1913, 1.

149. See Jacquelyn Dowd Hall, "Disorderly Women: Gender and Labor Militancy in the Appalachian South," *Journal of American History* 73 (Sept. 1976): 354–82.

150. McGovern, "The American Woman's Pre–World War I Freedom in Manners and Morals," 326–27.

151. "Can Militant Methods Gain a Hold Here?" unidentified newspaper clipping, Reel 3, HSB Papers; and "Suffrage and Women's Ideals," *New York Times*, 13 May 1913, 10.

152. For discussions on the feminist movement in the 1910s, see Nancy Cott, "The Birth of Feminism," in Cott, *Grounding of Modern Feminism*, 11–50; Sara Evans, "Women and Modernity, 1890–1920," in Evans, *Born for Liberty*, 145–73; Sochen, *New Woman in Greenwich Village*; and Woloch, *Women and the American Experience*, 343–48.

153. The dissemination of birth-control information also raised First Amendment questions, most significantly when the United States Post Office banned the *Woman Rebel* newspaper and charged publisher Sanger with two counts of obscenity. Linda Gordon, *Woman's Body, Woman's Right: Birth Control in America*, rev. ed. (New York: Penguin Books: 1990), 218. For detailed discussions of the birth control movement in the 1910s, see Chesler, *Woman of Valor*; Linda Gordon, "Birth Control and Social Revolution," in Gordon, *Woman's Body, Woman's Right*, 183–242; David Kennedy, *Birth Control in America: The Career of Margaret Sanger* (New Haven, Conn.: Yale Univ. Press, 1970); and Sanger, *My Fight for Birth Control*.

154. Manuela Thurner, "'Better Citizens Without the Ballot': American Antisuffrage Women and Their Rationale During the Progressive Era," *Journal of Women's History* 5 (Spring 1993): 48. For other discussions of antisuffrage views, see Jane Jerome Camhi, "Women Against Women: American Anti-Suffragism, 1880–1920" (Ph.D. diss., Tufts Univ., 1973); "Who Opposed Woman Suffrage?" in Flexner, *Century of Struggle*, 294–405; Kraditor, *Ideas of the Woman Suffrage Movement*, 14–42; Catherine Cole Mambretti, "'The Burden of the Ballot': The Woman's Anti-Suffrage Movement," *American Heritage* 30 (Dec. 1978): 24–25; Susan Marshall, "In Defense of Separate Spheres: Class and Status Politics in the Antisuffrage Move-

ment," *Social Forces* 65 (Dec. 1986): 327–51; Anastasia Sims, "Beyond the Ballot: The Radical Vision of the Antisuffragists," in *Votes for Women!* ed. Marjorie Spruill Wheeler (Knoxville: Univ. of Tennessee Press, 1995); and Louise Stevenson, "Women Antisuffragists in the 1915 Massachusetts Campaign," *New England Quarterly* 52 (Mar. 1979): 80–93.

155. "Missing Their Opportunities," *Woman's Protest*, Sept. 1912, 4.

156. On antisuffrage campaign tactics, see Susan Marshall, "Ladies Against Women: Mobilization Dilemmas of the Antifeminist Movement," *Social Problems* 32 (Apr. 1985): 348–62. In addition to the NAOWS, some twenty state antisuffrage organizations existed in the 1910s. Schneider, *American Women in the Progressive Era*, 166.

157. NAWSA president Shaw was among those who taunted the antisuffragists for adopting the color of "anarchy." "Brooklyn Holds Splendid Parade," *Woman's Journal*, 8 Nov. 1913, 353.

158. "Hester Prynne Gives Smiles to Washington," *New York Telegraph*, 6 Mar. 1913, n.p., Reel 2, HSB Papers.

159. "Antis Now Face Parade Dilemma," *Woman's Journal*, 13 May 1916, 155. Antisuffragists solved the dilemma by staffing a first-aid station at which they dispensed to marchers some fifteen thousand drinks and sandwiches. "Anti-Suffragists—For Patriotism and Preparedness," *Woman's Protest*, June 1916, 5.

160. "Imitating Men," *Woman's Journal*, 3 June 1916, 180.

161. See *Woman Voter*, Feb. 1915, 19.

162. Ellen Carol DuBois, for instance, overemphasized working women's influence in "Working Women, Class Relations, and Suffrage Militance," 34–58. Although Blatch was impressed with the example of independent working women and their demonstrations, my research indicated that virtually all of the features of public demonstrations by American suffragists originated with British suffragettes. Further, Blatch and other wealthy reformers served as generals and working women as soldiers in their partnership. On the other hand, suffrage historian Aileen Kraditor may have gone too far in the other direction when she contended working-class women never comprised more than a small minority of suffragists. Kraditor, *Ideas of the Woman Suffrage Movement*, 261. Labor historian Philip Foner omitted any evidence of some collaboration between suffragists and wage-earning women, mentioning neither Blatch nor the Equality League of Self-Supporting Women in his two-volume history of the American women's labor movement. He said radicals disliked the upper- and middle-class suffragists' paternalistic attitude but failed to mention their cooperation in a number of demonstrations. Foner, *Women and the American Labor Movement* 1:483. Although working women were not active in suffrage leadership, they supported the suffrage movement, most visibly by marching in the parades.

163. Cott, *Grounding of Modern Feminism*, 23.

164. "The Strike of the 40,000," *Woman's Journal*, 22 Jan. 1910, 14. Suffragists supported women out on strike. For example, supporting the arrested pickets was Inez Milholland, star of the suffrage parades, and millionaire suffragist Alva Belmont sponsored a huge suffrage demonstration at the Hippodrome in sympathy with the striking workers. Ibid. During a garment workers strike, the *Woman's Journal* pledged to stand behind arrested pickets. "Pickets and Suffrage," *Woman's Journal*, 8 Feb. 1913, 45.

165. Philip Foner, *May Day: A Short History of the International Workers' Holiday, 1886–1986* (New York: International Press, 1986), 78–79. May Day parades originated in 1890 in cities around the world as part of the call for an eight-hour day. Ibid., 44.

166. "Great Parade," *Woman's Journal*, 13 May 1911, 146; and "Women Parade and Rejoice at the End," *New York Times*, 7 May 1911, 4.

167. "Vast Suffrage Host is on Parade To-Day," *New York Times*, 4 May 1912, 22; and "Crowds Cheer Suffrage Host in Big Parade," *New York Evening Mail*, 3 May 1913, n.p., Reel 3, HSB Papers.

168. "Suffragists Tell Waldo Their Woes," *New York Times*, 11 May 1912, 22.

169. Terborg-Penn, "Afro-Americans in the Struggle for Woman Suffrage," 180–81.

170. Unsigned letter to Alice Stone Blackwell, 14 Jan. 1913, Reel 1, NWP Papers: The Suffrage Years; and Alice Stone Blackwell to Alice Paul, 23 Jan. 1913, Reel 1, NWP Papers: The Suffrage Years.

171. Lucy Daniels to Emma Gillett, committee treasurer, 5 Feb. 1913, Reel 1, NWP Papers: The Suffrage Papers; and Emma Gillett to Lucy Daniels, 6 Feb. 1913, Reel 1, NWP Papers: The Suffrage Years. Daniels, a white woman who later served time for picketing the White House for suffrage, also suggested a float depicting how the woman's rights movement was rooted in the abolition movement. Ibid.

172. Alice Paul to Alice Stone Blackwell, 15 Jan. 1913, Reel 1, NWP Papers: The Suffrage Years.

173. Mary Ware Dennett to Alice Paul, 14 Jan. 1913, Reel 1, NWP Papers: The Suffrage Years.

174. Unsigned NAWSA telegram to Alice Paul, 28 Feb. 1913, Reel 1, NWP Papers: The Suffrage Years; and Anna Howard Shaw to Alice Paul, 5 Mar. 1913, Reel 2, NWP Papers: The Suffrage Years. The NAWSA telegram said: "Am informed that Parade committee has so strongly urged Colored women not to march that it amounts to official discrimination which is distinctly contrary to instruction from National Headquarters. Please instruct all marshalls to see that all colored women who wish to march shall be accorded every service given to other marchers." Ibid.

175. Alice Paul to Mary Ware Dennett, 15 Jan. 1913; Nellie Quander to Alice Paul,

15 Feb. 1913; Nellie Quander to Alice Paul, 17 Feb. 1913; and Alice Paul to Nellie Quander, 23 Feb. 1913, all in Reel 1, NWP Papers: The Suffrage Years.

176. "Politics," *Crisis*, Apr. 1913, 267; and Alice Paul to Mary Beard, Apr. 18, 1913, Reel 2, NWP Papers, The Suffrage Years.

177. "Illinois Women Feature Parade," *Chicago Tribune*, 4 Mar. 1914, 3. Barnett did not mention the incident in her posthumously published autobiography, edited by her daughter. Duster, *Crusade for Justice*.

178. "Suffrage Paraders," *Crisis*, Apr. 1913, 296. Racism appeared to be at least one thing suffragists and antisuffragists had in common; the president of the NAOWS derided the inaugural parade as "motley" because it included African American women. "Motley Array of Women," *Washington Post*, 4 Mar. 1913, 10.

179. "Illinois Women Feature Parade," *Chicago Tribune*, 4 Mar. 1914, 1919, 3.

180. "Woman's Beauty, Grace, and Art Bewilder the Capital," *Washington Post*, 4 Mar. 1913, 1.

Historical confusion reigns over how the African American women marched. At least two scholars wrote that black civil rights activist Mary Church Terrell led the Howard chapter of the Delta Sigma Theta sorority and that Ida Wells-Barnett led a contingent of African American women from Chicago, but no papers uncovered in this research corroborated those statements. Terborg-Penn, "Afro-Americans in the Struggle for Woman Suffrage," 180; and Giddings, *When and Where I Enter . . .* , 127. Terrell did not mention the parade in her memoirs. Terrell, *Colored Woman in a White World*. In a 1972 interview, Paul made the self-serving and untrue claim that she placed the African American women in the men's division to protect them. Paul interview, 132–33. Paul's statement is repeated in Lunardini, *From Equal Suffrage to Equal Rights*, 26–27.

Ford wrote that Wells-Barnett led a delegation of the National Association for Colored Women, but no evidence was found supporting that statement, either. Ford, *Iron-Jawed Angels*, 110. On 26 August 1995, some five hundred members of Delta Sigma Theta joined a march down the 1913 parade route celebrating the seventy-fifth anniversary of the Nineteenth Amendment. "They've Come a Long Way," *Washington Post*, 27 Aug. 1995, B1, B8.

181. "Suffragists Ask Congress for a Vote," *New York Times*, 10 May 1914, sec. 4, p. 7.

182. "20,000 March in Suffrage Line," *New York Times*, 28 Oct. 1917, sec. 1, pp. 1, 18.

183. "Marching for Suffrage," *Harper's Weekly*, 11 May 1912, sec. 2, p. 27; and "10,000 Marchers in Suffrage Line," *New York Times*, 4 May 1913, 1.

184. Brown, "Decisive Victory Won," 110.

185. "Suffragists Sing New Marching Song," *New York Times*, 1 May 1911, 5.

186. "Mrs. Reynolds on the Parade," *Woman's Journal*, 13 May 1911, 150.

187. "Host of Proud Men March for Women," *New York Tribune*, 5 May 1912, n.p., Reel 64, NAWSA Papers.

188. "25,340 March in Suffrage Parade to the Applause of 250,000 Admirers; Spectacle Runs on In the Moonlight," *New York Times*, 24 Oct. 1915, 2.

189. See "Host of Proud Men March for Women," *New York Tribune*, 5 May 1912, n.p., Reel 1, HSB Papers; and "89 Gallant Men March in the Line Defiant of Jeers," unidentified newspaper clipping, Reel 1, HSB Papers. "Men Make Brave Showing" was a subhead of "20,000 Women in Suffrage March; 500,000 Look On," *New York Tribune*, 5 May 1912, 1.

190. "25,340 March in Suffrage Parade to the Applause of 250,000 Admirers; Spectacle Runs on In the Moonlight," *New York Times*, 24 Oct. 1915, 1, 2.

191. "16,000 March in Boston Parade," *Woman's Journal*, 16 Oct. 1915, 382; "Springfield Has Mile-Long Line," *Woman's Journal*, 30 Oct. 1915, 348; "8,000 March in Philadelphia," *New York Times*, 23 Oct. 1915, 5; and "Parades and Rallies Mark Closing Days," *Woman's Journal*, 23 Oct. 1915, 337.

192. "Million Votes Cast for Women in First Eastern Campaign," *Woman's Journal*, 6 Nov. 1915, 351.

193. "Nothing Dreadful Happened," *New York Times*, 12 Nov. 1912, 12.

194. "The Protest Meeting," *Woman Voter*, June 1910, 5.

Chapter 5. Pageants

1. Bettina Friedl, *On to Victory: Propaganda Plays of the Woman Suffrage Movement* (Boston: Northeastern Univ. Press, 1987), 196.

2. Mary Porter Beegle and Jack Randall Crawford, *Community Drama and Pageantry* (New Haven, Conn.: Yale Univ. Press, 1916), 13.

3. Hazel MacKaye, "Pioneering in Pageantry," MacKaye Family Papers, Special Collections, Dartmouth College Library, Hanover, N.H. (hereafter cited as MacKaye Family Papers).

4. Beegle and Crawford, *Community Drama and Pageantry*, 43.

5. *Tableaux vivants* began as popular parlor entertainments in which costumed figures frozen in place imitated famous scenes or allegorical virtues. Guidebooks in the 1870s and 1880s explained how to present historical scenes staged by elite citizens seeking safer ways for communities to celebrate July Fourth and other holidays, which in many cities had degenerated into dangerous bacchanals. David Glassberg, *American Historical Pageantry* (Chapel Hill: Univ. of North Carolina Press, 1990), 16, 18, 30.

6. Hazel MacKaye, untitled lecture, 1914, in MacKaye Family Papers.

7. William Langdon, "America, Like England, Has Become Pageant Mad," *New York Times*, 15 June 1913, 5.

8. Ibid.

9. Irwin, *Story of the Woman's Party*, 67, 100.

10. Glassberg, *American Historical Pageantry*, 39.

11. "Women in Historical Poses for Suffrage," *New York Times*, 18 Jan. 1911, 9.

12. WPU Annual Report Jan. 1911–Jan. 1912, Reel 1, HSB Papers.

13. "Women in Historical Poses for Suffrage," *New York Times*, 18 Jan. 1911, 9.

14. "Pageant of Protest Given for Suffrage," *New York Times*, 29 Mar. 1911, 13.

15. Friedl, *On to Victory*, 9.

16. "'Everywoman's Road' a Success," *Woman's Journal*, 29 Mar. 1913, 104.

17. Taylor, *Woman Suffrage Movement in Tennessee*, 44.

18. "Suffragists Big Night," *New York Times*, 23 Apr. 1913, 20.

19. "Roosevelt Center of Suffrage Host," *New York Times*, 3 May 1913, 1.

20. Karen Blair, "Pageantry for Women's Rights: The Career of Hazel MacKaye 1913–1923," *Theatre Survey* 31 (1990): 23.

21. "Pageants as a Means of Suffrage Propaganda," *Suffragist*, 28 Nov. 1914, 6.

22. Undated lecture, MacKaye Family Papers.

23. "Pioneering for Pageantry," 8, MacKaye Family Papers.

24. Ibid., 6.

25. "Told the Story of the Ages," *New York Times*, 4 Mar. 1913, 4. Like every other American suffrage innovation, the inaugural-eve pageant had a British precedent. The Women's Coronation Procession on 17 June 1911, which began a week of national festivities leading up to the coronation of the king, consisted of a Prisoners' Pageant, Historical Pageant, and Pageant of Empire. The women called these processions pageants because their many floats and costumes depicted historical and allegorical scenes. Tickner, *Spectacle of Women*, 124–26.

26. "Pageant Will Be Wonderful Scene," *Woman's Journal*, 15 Feb. 1913, 49.

27. "Why the Pageant?" *Woman's Journal*, 15 Feb. 1913, 50. Alice Paul, however, wrote privately that she planned the pageant because she lacked enough marchers to make a suitable impression. Alice Paul to Agnes Ryan, 13 Jan. 1913, Reel 1, NWP Papers: The Suffrage Years.

28. "Moon Helps Her Write Pageants," *Washington Herald*, 1 Nov. 1915, n.p., MacKaye Family Papers.

29. "Pioneering for Pageantry," 6, MacKaye Family Papers.

30. "Told the Story of the Ages," *New York Times*, 4 Mar. 1913, 4.

31. "Pioneering for Pageantry," 7–8, MacKaye Family Papers; "Suffrage Procession," flier, MacKaye Family Papers; and "Barefoot Women in Gauze, Despite Cold, Pose in Tableau on the Treasury Plaza," *Washington Post*, 3 Mar. 1913, 10.

32. "Pageant Wins Throng," *Woman's Journal*, 8 Mar. 1913, 80.

33. "Washington," *Woman's Protest*, Apr. 1913, 4.

34. "The Limitations and Possibilities of Pageantry," *Woman's Protest*, June 1913, 7.

35. Percy MacKaye, "Art and the Woman's Movement," *Forum* 49 (1913): 684.

36. Secretary of the Treasury Franklin MacVeagh to Elizabeth Kent, 2 Jan. 1913, Reel 1, NWP Papers: The Suffrage Years.

37. Paul interview, 73.

38. MacKaye, "Art and the Woman's Movement," 681.

39. "Woman's Beauty, Grace, and Art Bewilder the Capital," *Washington Post,* 4 Mar. 1913, 1; and "The Suffragette Parade," *Washington Post,* 3 Mar. 1913, 6.

40. "Adonises Aplenty for Suffrage Show," *New York Times,* 29 Apr. 1913, 8.

41. "'Adonis' Story Flagrant Myth," *Woman's Journal,* 10 May 1913, 146.

42. "Why the Pageant?" *Woman's Journal,* 15 Feb. 1913, 50.

43. See Claudia Johnson, "Enter the Harlot," in Chinoy and Jenkins, *Women in American Theatre,* 66–74.

44. Qtd. in Rabban, "Free Speech League," 80.

45. "The Drama and Suffrage," *Woman Voter,* Feb. 1914, 7.

46. Sheila Stowell, *A Stage of Their Own: Feminist Playwrights of the Suffrage Era* (Ann Arbor: Univ. of Michigan Press, 1992), 44–45.

47. "Pledge Actresses to Suffrage Parade," *New York Times,* 22 Apr. 1912, n.p., Reel 2, HSB Papers.

48. "Pageant of Protest," *Woman Voter,* Apr. 1911, 1.

49. "The Drama and Suffrage," *Woman Voter,* Feb. 1914, 7.

50. Flier, Reel 95, NWP Papers: The Suffrage Years.

51. Flier; and "First Suffragists Seen in Greek Play," *New York Times,* 18 Feb. 1913, n.p., both in Reel 2, HSB Papers. The play's content continued to threaten twentieth-century men, judging by newspaper headlines: "Suffrage Play Frightens Husbands," *New York American,* 18 Feb. 1913, n.p.; "Suffrage Play Was No Place at All for Mere Man," *New York World,* n.d., n.p.; and "Men Who See 'Lysistrata' Are Glad It Is Only Play Acting," *New York Tribune,* 18 Feb. 1913, n.p., all in Reel 2, HSB Papers.

52. Staging suffrage plays was another imported British suffrage technique. Upper-class suffragists also staged balls, carnivals, and other socially oriented assemblies in the 1910s to raise money and support suffrage. Friedl, *On to Victory,* 12.

53. "Suffrage Opera Scores Immediate Success," *Suffragist,* 26 Feb. 1916, 6. Staged at the Waldorf Astoria Hotel, "Melinda" sold out its $150 boxes and raised $8,000 for the Congressional Union. Ibid.

54. Friedl, *On to Victory,* 230.

55. "State Correspondence," *Woman's Journal,* 27 Mar. 1909, 51.

56. Sloan, "Sexual Warfare in the Silent Cinema," 422. Copies survive of the WPU film "80 Million Women Want—?" and the NAWSA film "Votes for Women." Thomas Edison filmed antisuffrage comedies such as "A Suffragette in Spite of Himself," and Charlie Chaplin starred in drag as a disruptive, dominating suffragist in "A Busy Day." Ibid., 422, 417, 414.

57. "Six Periods of American Life," manuscript, MacKaye Family Papers.

58. Blair, "Pageantry for Women's Rights," 40.

59. Ibid., 25. See "Real Beauty Shown in League Pageant," *New York Times*, 18 Apr. 1914, 11; and "Woman's Advance Told By Pageant," *New York Tribune*, 18 Apr. 1914, 7.

60. Two months after the debut of "Six Episodes," socialist John Reed wrote and directed the "Pageant of the Paterson Mill Strike" in which one thousand strikers reenacted the Industrial Workers of the World's version of the confrontation amid a flaming red stage set. A standing-room-only crowd of fifteen thousand persons at Madison Square Garden burst into revolutionary songs and chants as they watched the gritty depiction of women being clubbed and babies being torn from the arms of their picketing mothers. Foner, *Women and the American Labor Movement* 1:451; Chesler, *Woman of Valor*, 79; and Glassberg, *American Historical Pageantry*, 128, 132. That October, W. E. B. Du Bois staged "The Star of Ethiopia," his three-hour pageant featuring a thousand players expounding his ideology of black supremacy through an unflinching panorama of African American history. Du Bois, an enthusiastic convert to pageantry, believed it offered the ideal form to teach both blacks and whites about black contributions to civilization. David Levering Lewis, *W. E. B. Du Bois, Biography of a Race, 1868–1919* (New York: Henry Holt, 1993), 459–61.

61. "Pageant Closes Union Meeting," *Woman's Journal*, 18 Dec. 1915, 400.

62. MacKaye, "Pioneering in Pageantry," 10, MacKaye Family Papers.

63. "Anthony Pageant to Go On Road," *Washington, D.C. Sunday Star*, 12 Dec. 1915, n.p., MacKaye Family Papers.

64. Unidentified newspaper clipping and "Susan B. Anthony," original manuscript, MacKaye Family Papers.

65. Ford, *Iron-Jawed Angels*, 68.

66. "'Antis' Refuse Honor Box at a Suffrage Pageant," *Washington Herald*, 14 Dec. 1915, 1.

67. "Suffragists 'Golden Lane,'" *New York Times*, 12 June 1916, 3; "4,000 Suffragists in a Silent Appeal," *New York Times*, 16 June 1916, 3; and "Big Demonstration Staged in St. Louis Despite Heat," *Woman's Journal*, 24 June 1916, 208. Women from the enfranchised states also relied upon another aspect of the right of assembly when they conducted nightly open-air meetings during the convention. "Big Demonstration Staged in St. Louis Despite Heat," *Woman's Journal*, 24 June 1916, 208.

68. Flexner, *Century of Struggle*, 278. It was a rather weak plank that called for the state-by-state route to suffrage. Ibid.

69. "Suffragists Forced to Alter Park Plan," *New York Times*, 21 Sept. 1916, 6.

70. "No Place for Propaganda," *New York Times*, 22 Sept. 1916, 6.

71. "Suffragist Songs But No Talk in Park," *New York Times,* 23 Sept. 1916, 18.

72. "Suffragists Silent in Park Gathering," *New York Times,* 24 Sept. 1916, 1.

73. Catt and Shuler, *Woman Suffrage and Politics,* 381.

74. "A Pageant—The Victory Goal," *Suffragist,* Oct. 1920, 248. In it, Columbia again held center stage followed by the Fourteenth to the Nineteenth Amendments with the thirty-six ratifying states bringing up the rear. Once onstage, all would sing Sara Bard Field's "Song of the Women" and unfurl a big banner listing the ratifying states. Ibid.

75. "Equality of rights under the law shall not be denied or abridged by the United States or by any state on account of sex." Cott, *Grounding of Modern Feminism,* 324–25 n.

76. "Women Adopt Form for Equal Rights," *New York Times,* 22 July 1923, 1; "Women Open Campaign for Equal Rights," *New York Tribune,* 22 July 1923, 1; and "Women's Great Memorial Celebration of the Seventy-fifth Anniversary of the First Equal Rights Meeting in the United States," Reel 149, NWP Papers.

77. "All Roads Lead to Pageant in Garden Today," *Colorado Springs Gazette and Telegraph,* 23 Sept. 1923, sec. 2, p. 1, in MacKaye Family Papers. The pageant's final incarnation under the title "Forward Into Light" occurred at the NWP's 1924 convention in Essex County, New York, as a tribute to the late Inez Milholland, who was buried at her family's estate there. Program, "Forward Into Light," 17 Aug. 1924, Reel 149, NWP Papers.

78. Gerald Mast, *A Short History of the Movies* (New York: Pegasus, 1971), 80–81.

79. Emery and Emery, *Press and America,* 371, 376, 378.

80. Shari Benstock, *Women of the Left Bank: Paris, 1900–1940* (New York: Austin: Univ. of Texas Press, 1986), 26.

81. For a discussion of mass assemblies in Nazi Germany, see George Mosse, *The Nationalization of the Masses: Political Symbolism and Mass Movements in Germany from the Napoleonic Wars Through the Third Reich* (New York: New American Library, 1977).

82. In 1996, ninety-five outdoor theaters in three categories (historical dramas, religious dramas, and Shakespearean productions) operated in thirty-three states and the District of Columbia. Telephone interview, Institute for Outdoor Drama, Univ. of North Carolina at Chapel Hill, 25 May 1996.

83. Evans, *Born for Liberty,* 178.

84. This irony is pointed out in Cynthia Patterson and Bari Watkins, "Rites and Rights," in Chinoy and Jenkins, *Women in American Theatre,* 29–32. Perhaps the most infamous "Miss America" protest occurred when women crowned a sheep on the Atlantic City boardwalk to protest the 1968 pageant. Robin Morgan, *Going Too Far, The Personal Chronicle of a Feminist* (New York: Vintage Books, 1978), 64.

85. "Hazel MacKaye, Writer and Pageantry Adviser," *New York Herald Tribune,* 12 Aug. 1944, n.p., MacKaye Family Papers.

Chapter 6. Picketing

1. Stevens, *Jailed for Freedom,* 177.

2. Flexner, *Century of Struggle,* 283.

3. Stevens, *Jailed for Freedom,* 354; and Irwin, *Story of the Woman's Party,* 197.

4. "Veils for Suffrage Sentinels Today," *Washington Herald,* 29 Jan. 1917, n.p., Reel 33, NAWSA Papers.

5. "The Woman's Party and Pageantry," *Suffragist,* 11 Jan. 1919, 7.

6. Bordin, *Woman and Temperance,* 31. See also Taylor, *Citizens at Last,* 80.

7. *Thornhill v. Alabama,* 310 U.S. 88 (1940). Although the expression of opinions exhibited in picketing is fully protected by the First Amendment, the conduct aspects of picketing may be regulated. See Ibid., 105; *Edwards v. South Carolina,* 372 U.S. 229, 236 (1963); *Cox v. Louisiana I,* 379 U.S. 536, 555 (1965); and Krout, "Symbolic Conduct," 120.

8. Fortas, "Concerning Dissent and Civil Disobedience," 16.

9. A Missouri court, for instance, removed a St. Louis ban on all picketing as an invasion of personal liberty in 1908. *St. Louis v. Gloner,* 210 Mo. 502, 109 S.W. 30 (1908). See also Joseph Tanenhaus, "Picketing as Free Speech: Early Stages in the Growth of the New Law of Picketing," *University of Pittsburgh Law Review* 14 (1953): 402. For discussions of court treatment of picketing after 1920, see William Sherwood, "The Picketing Cases and How They Grew," *George Washington Law Review* 10 (May 1942): 763–98; and Paul Dembling, "Picketing as Constitutionally Protected Freedom of Speech," *George Washington Law Review* 19 (1951): 287–312.

10. *Atchison, T. & S.F. Ry. v. Gee Co.,* 139 F. 582, 584 (C.C.S.D. Iowa 1905).

11. Foner, *Women and the American Labor Movement* 1:209.

12. Philip Foner, *History of the Labor Movement in the United States,* vol. 4, *The Industrial Workers of the World: 1905–1917* (New York: International Publishers, 1980), 223, 508.

13. The American Federation of Labor believed Section 20 of the Clayton Act forbade injunctions against labor pickets, boycotts, and strikes; however, the act was so vaguely written that the Supreme Court ruled in 1921 it offered unions no special protection. Philip Foner, *History of the Labor Movement in the United States,* vol. 5, *The AFL in the Progressive Era, 1910–1915* (New York: International Publishers, 1980), 140–41; Charles Gregory, *Labor and the Law* (New York: W. W. Norton, 1949), 164; Betty Justice, *Unions, Workers and the Law* (Washington, D.C.: Bureau of National Affairs, 1983), 11. See also *Duplex Printing Co. v. Deering,* 254 U.S. 443 (1921).

14. "Picketing Facts," press release, Reel 91, NWP Papers: The Suffrage Years.

15. Blanchard, *Revolutionary Sparks,* 76; Act of 15 June 1917, chap. 30, tit. 1, Sec. 3, 40 Stat. 217, 219 (current version at 18 U.S.C. Sec. 2388(a) (1976); amended by Act of 16 May 1918, c. 75, Sec. 1, 40 Stat. 219 (1917). Punishment for a conviction under the espionage or sedition acts included a fine of up to ten thousand dollars, imprisonment for as long as twenty years, or both. Ibid.

16. "Dear Subscribers" from Merrill Rogers, *Masses* business manager, 17 July 1917, Reel 45, NWP Papers: The Suffrage Years; *Goldman v. United States,* 245 U.S. 474 (1918); and *Debs v. United States,* 249 U.S 211, 212 (1919).

17. Sochen, *New Woman in Greenwich Village,* 112–13.

18. According to scholar David Rabban, some of the most important of these writings included sections on free speech in Cooley, *Treatise on the Constitutional Limitations;* Ernest Freund, *The Police Power: Public Power and Constitutional Rights* (Chicago: Callahan, 1904); Roscoe Pound, "Interests of Personality," *Harvard Law Review* 28 (1915): 343–65; and Theodore Schroeder, *Free Speech for Radicals,* enl. ed. (New York, 1916; reprint, New York: Burt Franklin, 1969). Rabban, "Free Speech League," 56–61. See also Chafee, "Freedom of Speech in Wartime."

19. "Silent, Silly, and Offensive," *New York Times,* 11 Jan. 1917, 14.

20. Flexner, *Century of Struggle,* 284–85.

21. O'Neill, *Everyone Was Brave,* 202.

22. Exceptions are Blanchard, *Revolutionary Sparks,* 90–91; Haig Bosmajian, "The Abrogation of the Suffragists' First Amendment Rights," *Western Speech* 38 (1974): 218–32, and Whipple, *Story of Civil Liberty,* 312–17.

23. Ford, *Iron-Jawed Angels;* and Lunardini, *From Equal Suffrage to Equal Rights.*

24. "Facts of Women's Fight for Freedom Including History of the National Woman's Party," Reel 91, NWP Papers: The Suffrage Years.

25. Itinerary of the "Suffrage Special," 9 Apr.–16 May 1916, Reel 149, NWP Papers. The twelve states where women voted in 1916 included Arizona, California, Colorado, Idaho, Illinois, Iowa, Kansas, Nevada, Oregon, Utah, Washington, and Wyoming.

26. Stevens, *Jailed for Freedom,* 48; and Lunardini, *From Equal Suffrage to Equal Rights,* 99.

27. Paul staged a resplendent memorial on Christmas Day of 1916 in Statuary Hall under the Capitol dome, the first service for a woman in the building. "The National Memorial Service in Memory of Inez Milholland," *Suffragist,* 30 Dec. 1916, 7.

28. "Suffragists Will Picket White House," *New York Times,* 10 Jan. 1917, 1; and press release, 9 Jan. 1917, Reel 91, NWP Papers: The Suffrage Years.

29. Minutes of the National Executive Committee of the Congressional Union Held January 5, 1917, Washington, D.C., Reel 87, NWP Papers: The Suffrage Years.

30. Irwin, *Story of the Woman's Party,* 195.

31. Stevens, *Jailed for Freedom*, 122–24.

32. Blatch shut down the Women's Political Union to work with the Woman's Party. Blatch and Lutz, *Challenging Years*, 240.

33. "The Silent Siege," *Woman's Journal*, 14 Aug. 1909, 130. Dutch women also had picketed the government for the vote. Press release, 10 Aug. 1918, Reel 91, NWP Papers: The Suffrage Years.

34. Annual Report of the Women's Political Union, Jan. 1912–Jan. 1913, Reel 2, HSB Papers.

35. Marshall, "Ladies Against Women," 352.

36. Brown, "Decisive Victory Won," 111. Radical Upton Sinclair also used the technique when he stationed "peaceable mourners" outside of John D. Rockefeller's Bible class to protest the shooting of strikers at one of the oil baron's Colorado work camps. "Pickets Await Bible Class," *New York Times*, 2 May 1914, 3.

37. "The Horrors of Picketing," *Woman Voter*, Jan. 1916, 21.

38. "The Original Pickets," *Suffragist*, 25 May 1918, 11; and James Louis, "Sue Shelton White and the Woman Suffrage Movement in Tennessee," *Tennessee Historical Quarterly* 22 (1963): 176. White was convinced the protest by the Nashville Equal Suffrage League and the Business and Professional Women's chapter inspired the White House protest. Ibid.

39. NWP colors were carefully chosen to optimize their symbolism: Purple stood for power, white for purity, and gold for spirituality. *Suffragist* said the colors suggested an early morning, indicative of the new dawn they believed would arrive when women voted. "The Meaning of Our Colors," *Suffragist*, 5 Feb. 1916, 8.

40. The *New York Times* reported the White House had been picketed before, but my research has turned up no evidence of previous picketing at the White House. "President Ignores Suffrage Pickets" *New York Times*, 11 Jan. 1917, 3; Irwin, *Story of the Woman's Party*, 196; "Heard on the Firing Line," *Suffragist*, 12 May 1917, 4; and "Suffragists Wait at the White House for Action," *Suffragist*, 17 Jan. 1917, 7.

41. Irwin, *Story of the Woman's Party*, 196; "Silent, Silly, and Offensive," *New York Times*, 11 Jan. 1917, 14; Stevens, *Jailed for Freedom*, 64; and "Charge Suffragists Menace Wilson's Life," *New York Times*, 17 Jan. 1917, 7.

42. Stevens, *Jailed for Freedom*, 67–68; and "Suffrage Sentinels Still Wait at the White House," *Suffragist*, 23 Jan. 1917, 4.

43. "Suffragists Wait at the White House for Action," *Suffragist*, 17 Jan. 1917, 7. So many passersby asked the pickets about their case that they broke their silence to answer questions. Stevens, *Jailed for Freedom*, 214.

44. "State Delegations Join the Picket Line at the White House," *Suffragist*, 31 Jan. 1917, 4; and "Labor Day on the Picket Line," *Suffragist*, 24 Feb. 1917, 3.

45. "At the Home of the President," *Suffragist*, 26 May 1917, 4.

46. Terrell, *Colored Woman in a White World*, 316. Other African Americans also

NOTES TO PAGES 119–22

may have picketed. A black woman named Mrs. M. M. Young from New York City offered to picket. "Talk of Dropping Capital Pickets," *New York Times,* 9 Nov. 1917, 13.

47. Irwin, *Story of the Woman's Party,* 197, and "Arrest 41 Pickets for Suffrage at the White House," *New York Times,* 11 Nov. 1917, 1.

48. "At the Home of the President," *Suffragist,* 19 May 1917, 4.

49. "The Seventh Week of the Suffrage Picket," *Suffragist,* 3 Mar. 1917, 5.

50. "'Silent Sentinels' at White House for Suffrage Cause Are Actually Silent," *New York Herald,* 11 Jan. 1917, n.p., in NAWSA Papers, Reel 33; "Silent Picketing of White House Begun," *New York Evening Mail,* 10 Jan. 1917, n.p., in Reel 33, NAWSA Papers.

51. "Suffragists Girdle White House in Rain," *New York Times,* 5 Mar. 1917, 3. The demonstration failed to meet CU expectations, perhaps because of the rain. The CU had predicted ten thousand women would circle the White House seven times. "Suffragists Will Parade March 4," *Washington Herald,* 28 Dec. 1916, n.p., in Reel 33, NAWSA Papers. Antisuffragists labeled the march a flop. "The Suffrage Siege of the White House," *Woman's Protest,* Apr. 1913, 5.

52. "The Suffrage Pickets," *Suffragist,* 16 June 1917, 5.

53. Paul interview, 214.

54. "Suffrage Riot Staged for Russians," *San Francisco Chronicle,* 21 June 1917, 1; "Women's Banner Torn to Pieces at White House," *Chicago Tribune,* 21 June 1917, 2; and "The Woman Party's Appeals to the Russian Missions," *Suffragist,* 23 June 1917, 7.

55. Irwin, *Story of the Woman's Party,* 208.

56. Ryan, *Women in Public,* 36, 139.

57. "Banners," *Woman's Journal,* 29 Apr. 1911, 130.

58. "Suffragists to Parade," *New York Times,* 28 Jan. 1908, 7.

59. For a discussion of the role of banners in the British suffrage campaign, see Tickner, *Spectacle of Women,* 60–73.

60. "London Procession," *Woman's Journal,* 4 July 1908, 106.

61. Bland, "Techniques of Persuasion," 119, 120.

62. "Arrest Capital Women Pickets," *Chicago Tribune,* 23 June 1917, 4; "Pickets Dealt with Ungently by the Police," *San Francisco Chronicle,* 23 June 1917, 3; "Arrest Capital Women Pickets," *Chicago Tribune,* 23 June 1917, 4; and telegram, Alice Paul to Agnes Morey, 22 June 1917, Reel 44, NWP Papers: The Suffrage Years.

63. Henry David Thoreau, "Civil Disobedience," in *On Civil Disobedience: Essays Old and New,* ed. Robert Goldwin (Chicago: Rand McNally, 1969), 20.

64. David Daube, *Civil Disobedience in Antiquity* (Edinburgh: Edinburgh Univ. Press, 1972), 5–6.

65. William Taylor, "Civil Disobedience: Observations on the Strategies of

Protest," in *Dissent, Symbolic Behavior and Rhetorical Strategies,* ed. Haig Bosmajian (Westport, Conn.: Greenwood Press, 1980), 86, 87, 89.

66. Paul Harris, ed., *Civil Disobedience* (Lanham, Md.: Univ. Press of America, 1989), 3.

67. Dora Lewis to Lucy Burns, telegram, 18 July 1917, Reel 45, NWP Papers: The Suffrage Years. For a discussion on how suffragists used nonviolent protest, see George Lakey, "Technique and Ethos in Nonviolent Action: The Woman Suffrage Case," in *Dissent, Symbolic Behavior and Rhetorical Strategies,* ed. Haig Bosmajian (Westport, Conn.: Greenwood Press, 1980), 14–23.

68. See, for example, Stevens, *Jailed for Freedom,* 103, 212, 273, 308, 310.

69. Lucy Burns to L. Daniels, 6 Nov. 1917, Reel 52, NWP Papers. This was the same Lucy Daniels who offered to pay NAWSA's Congressional Committee fifty dollars if it organized a contingent of African American women in the 1913 parade. She did picket and served jail time. See also Lucy Burns to Dorothy Day, 7 Nov. 1917, Reel 52, NWP Papers. The NWP also refused to let men picket, although at least one man offered. Lucy Burns to Elizabeth Hara, 6 Nov. 1917, Reel 52, NWP Papers; and "Err in Naming Men as Pickets," newspaper clipping, 29 Jan. 1917, Reel 33, NAWSA Papers. Two men were reported to have participated in the March 4 march around the White House; one carried a banner for a group of women unable to attend and the other held an umbrella for his wife. "Suffragists No Match for White House Jericho," *World,* 5 Mar. 1917, n.p., Reel 33, NAWSA Papers.

70. Alice K. Wiley, "Why We Picketed the White House," *Suffragist,* 2 Feb. 1918, 2.

71. Stevens, *Jailed for Freedom,* 94–95, 102; and Irwin, *Story of the Woman's Party,* 220.

72. Appendix 4 in *Jailed for Freedom* names all of the imprisoned pickets, and another section contains photographs of many of them.

73. Press release, Anne Martin, 11 July 1917, Reel 91, NWP Papers: The Suffrage Years. Martin filled in as chair while Paul was hospitalized for exhaustion.

74. "Our History Books," *Suffragist,* 22 Feb. 1919, 7.

75. "Mrs. Brannan Tells of Jail Treatment," *New York Times,* 29 Nov. 1917, 11.

76. Stevens, *Jailed for Freedom,* 103.

77. Irwin, *Story of the Woman's Party,* 252.

78. See Loretta Zimmerman, "Alice Paul and the National Woman's Party 1912–1920" (Ph.D. diss., Tulane Univ., 1964), 238; Bland, "Techniques of Persuasion," 134; and Ford, *Iron-Jawed Angels,* 151–52.

79. Kraditor, *Ideas of the Woman Suffrage Movement,* 239 n.

80. "Editorial Notes," *New Republic,* 28 July 1917, 344.

81. Qtd. in "The Picket Temperament," *Suffragist,* 30 Mar. 1918, 14.

82. Column by John Reed qtd. in "An Arraignment of the Police," *Suffragist,* 20

June 1917, 5; "The Picket Temperament," *Suffragist,* 22 Dec. 1917, 7; 11 Aug. 1917, qtd. in "Comments of the Press, *Suffragist,* 8 Sept. 1917, 10; and 14 Nov. 1917, qtd. in "Comments of the Press, *Suffragist,* 24 Nov. 1917, 13. See also *New York Call,* 25 June 1917, qtd. in "Comments of the Press," *Suffragist,* 22 June 1917, 10; *Detroit Times,* qtd. in "Comments of the Press," *Suffragist,* 28 July 1917, 10; *Baltimore Evening Post,* qtd. in "Comments of the Press," *Suffragist,* 4 Aug. 1917, 8; *St. Paul Pioneer Daily News,* 28 July 1917, qtd. in "Comments of the Press," *Suffragist,* 11 Aug. 1917, 9; *Hartford Globe,* 15 July 1917, qtd. in "Comments of the Press," *Suffragist,* 4 Aug. 1917, 10; *St. Paul Daily News,* 28 July 1917, qtd. in "Comments of the Press," *Suffragist,* 11 Aug. 1917, 9; and *Rocky Mountain News,* 2 Aug. 1917, qtd. in "Comments of the Press," *Suffragist,* 18 Aug. 1917, 9.

83. 15 Sept. 1917, qtd. in "Comments of the Press," *Suffragist,* 30 Mar. 1918, 14; 19 June 1917, qtd. in "Comments of the Press," *Suffragist,* 7 July 1917, 10; 23 Aug. 1917, qtd. in "Comments of the Press," *Suffragist,* 15 Sept. 1917, 10; and *Washington Post,* 10 Nov. 1917, 6.

84. "Silent, Silly, and Offensive," *New York Times,* 11 Jan. 1917, 14; and "The Martyrs," *New York Times,* 19 July 1917, 10.

85. "Militant Tactics a Failure," *Washington Post,* 12 Nov. 1917, 6.

86. See, for example, "Arrest 41 Pickets for Suffrage at the White House," *New York Times,* 11 Nov. 1917, 1; and "Mrs. Brannan Tells of Jail Treatment," *New York Times,* 29 Nov. 1917, 11.

87. Alva Belmont to Lucy Burns, 19 July 1917, Reel 45, NWP Papers: The Suffrage Years.

88. "Why We Keep on Picketing," *Suffragist,* 1 Sept. 1917, 6.

89. Letter to "Friendly Editors" from NWP, 8 Aug. 1917, and telegram from Press Department, 22 Aug. 1918 (?), both in Reel 91, NWP Papers: The Suffrage Years.

90. Bland, "Techniques of Persuasion," 144 n. The bill never made it out of committee. Stevens, *Jailed for Freedom,* 131.

91. "Ask Special Law to Stop Picketing," *New York Times,* 19 Aug. 1917, 1. The defeated bill also banned flags or other devices that referred to the president or vice president, the Constitution, suffrage, citizenship, the duties of federal officials, or any proposed law calculated to bring the president or government into contempt. Punishment would have been a fine of up to one thousand dollars or imprisonment for as long as a year or both. Ibid.

92. "White House 'Riot' Broken Up by Police," *New York Times,* 5 July 1917, 9; "13 Suffragists Jail in Riots at White House," *Washington Post,* 5 July 1917, 2; and "12 Suffragists are Arrested by Capital Police," *San Francisco Chronicle,* 5 July 1917, 1.

93. "Kaiser Wilson," *Suffragist,* 18 Aug. 1917, 6.

94. Kenneth MacKenzie, *America Challenged 1916–1945* (Wellesley Hills, Mass: Independent School Press, 1983), 43.

NOTES TO PAGES 125–27

95. "Washington Crowd Eggs Suffragettes," *New York Times,* 15 Aug. 1917, 3; "President Onlooker at Mob Attack on Suffragists," *Suffragist,* 18 Aug. 1917, 6; "Report of the Demonstration Department," Aug. 1917, Reel 87, NWP Papers: The Suffrage Years; and Irwin, *Story of the Woman's Party,* 232. The "Kaiser" banner offended many Americans, including Mabel Vernon, one of the first jailed pickets. Vernon interview, 74.

96. "The Administration Versus the Woman's Party," *Suffragist,* 25 Aug. 1917, 6–7; and Irwin, *Story of the Woman's Party,* 232.

97. Ernestine Hara Kettler interview, "From Tea Parties to Prison: Behind Bars," interview by Sherna Gluck, Suffragists Oral History Collection, Univ. of California, Berkeley, microfiche edition (Sanford, N.C.: Microfilm Corporation of America, 1980) (hereafter cited as Kettler interview), 18.

98. Ford, *Iron-Jawed Angels,* 146.

99. McBride, *On Wisconsin Women,* 280. Brown campaigned anyway. Ibid., 281.

100. "Patriotic Suffragists," *Woman Citizen,* 7 July 1917, 107; and Wheeler, *New Women of the New South,* 77.

101. Blatch also may have resented her subordinate role in the NWP. Ford, *Iron-Jawed Angels,* 131.

102. Sarah Colvin to Anne Martin, 27 June 1917. See also Alison Hopkins to Anne Martin, 27 June 1917; and Beatrice Castleton to Anne Martin, 28 June 1917, Reel 44, NWP Papers: The Suffrage Years.

103. Lucy Burns to NWP members, Nov. 1917, Reel 52, NWP Papers.

104. Paul interview, 225.

105. Catt was elected to her second term as NAWSA president in December 1915. Previously, she served as NAWSA president from 1900–1904, when she retired to care for her terminally ill husband. Between NAWSA terms she headed the New York State referenda campaigns and the International Woman Suffrage Alliance. Catt spoke frequently and forcefully for suffrage and once warned that the delay was making women "rebellious." "Carrie Chapman Catt Speech in Columbus, Ohio," 13 May 1917, Reel 60, NAWSA Papers.

106. See "Two Million Women Offer to Serve U.S.," *Washington Times,* 25 Feb. 1917, n.p., in Reel 33, NAWSA Papers; "Constructive Patriotism," *Woman Voter,* Mar. 1917, 7; "The Clearing House for Women's War Service," *Woman Citizen,* 30 June 1917, 87; "National Woman Suffrage and Congress," *Woman Citizen,* 15 Sept. 1917, 292; "An Appeal to All Suffragists," *Woman Citizen,* 19 Oct. 1918, 409; and Blatch and Lutz, *Challenging Years,* 278. NAWSA's war service also broke gender barriers, like the all-woman hospital unit it sent to France. The United States had rejected NAWSA's offer of the unit because the Red Cross did not accept women's units. Minutes of New York Section of the National American Woman Suffrage Board, 5 July 1918, Reel 60, NAWSA Papers.

107. Carrie Chapman Catt, "Why Woman Suffrage Is a War Measure," n.d., Reel 60; and statement by Dr. Anna Howard Shaw, 20 June 1917; both in Reel 60, NAWSA Papers.

108. "The Pickets and the Public," *Woman Citizen*, 30 June 1917, 79. See also "Pickets Are Behind the Times," *Woman Citizen*, 17 Nov. 1917, 470–71. The *Citizen*, founded in June 1917 with part of a $1-million bequest to Catt by a wealthy suffragist, replaced the *Woman's Journal* as well as the Woman Suffrage Party's *Woman Voter* and the *NAWSA Headquarters Newsletter*.

109. Carrie Chapman Catt to Alice Paul, 24 May 1917, Reel 33, NAWSA Papers.

110. Statement by Dr. Anna Howard Shaw, 20 June 1917, Reel 60, NAWSA Papers.

111. Undated letter from Carrie Chapman Catt to press correspondents, Reel 33, NAWSA Papers; and Carrie Chapman Catt, "An Open Letter to the Public," 13 July 1917, Reel 60, NAWSA Papers.

112. Minutes of the Meeting of the Executive Committee of the National Woman's Party, 10 Aug. 1917, Reel 87, NWP Papers: The Suffrage Years.

113. Bland, "Techniques of Persuasion," 136, quoting Wilson correspondence.

114. "Report on Press Situation," 5 July 1917, Reel 60, NAWSA Papers.

115. Kraditor, *Ideas of the Woman Suffrage Movement*, 240; and "Talk of Dropping Capital Pickets," *New York Times*, 9 Nov. 1917, 13.

116. Susan Frost to Marion May, 29 June 1917, Reel 44, NWP Papers: The Suffrage Years.

117. Edward Rumely to Mabel Vernon, 18 July 1917, Reel 45, NWP Papers: The Suffrage Years.

118. "Treasurer's Annual Report," *Suffragist*, 13 Apr. 1918, 12. Donations for the year totaled $106,734.36. Ibid. The CU and NWP raised three-quarters of a million dollars from 1913 to 1920. Irwin, *Story of the Woman's Party*, 4.

119. Janice Law Trecker, "The Suffrage Prisoners," *American Scholar* 21 (Summer 1972): 421.

120. Kettler interview, 32.

121. Irwin, *Story of the Woman's Party*, 263; and Eleanor Calnan affidavit, 5 Nov. 1917, Reel 51, NWP: The Suffrage Years.

122. Irwin, *Story of the Woman's Party*, 261–62. Fasting inmates in 1918 came up with a ditty to the tune of "I've Been Working on the Railroad": "We've been starving in the workhouse / All the live-long day / We've been starving in the workhouse / Just to pass the S.B.A." "A New Prison Song," *Suffragist*, 31 Aug. 1918, 9.

123. Katherine B. Heffelfinger to Beulah Amidon, 8 Nov. 1917, Reel 52, NWP Papers: The Suffrage Years.

124. Virginia Arnold to Maud Younger, 28 June 1917, Reel 44, NWP Papers: The Suffrage Years; Stevens, *Jailed for Freedom*, 155; and Irwin, *Story of the Woman's Party*, 293.

125. Irwin, *Story of the Woman's Party*, 264.

126. Kettler interview, 25; and Stevens, *Jailed for Freedom*, 155.

127. Presidential Pardon, 19 July 1917, Reel 45, NWP Papers: The Suffrage Years.

128. Wilson's campaign manager Dudley Field Malone and J. A. H. Hopkins, a Progressive Party leader and Wilson supporter, met with the president to protest the women's treatment in July. Ford, *Iron-Jawed Angels*, 155.

129. Report of the Demonstration Department, Nov. 1917, Reel 87, NWP Papers: The Suffrage Years.

130. "Political Prisoners," *Suffragist*, 27 Oct. 1917, 8; "That Night of Terror," *Suffragist*, 1 Dec. 1917, 7; and "The Rights of Political Prisoners," *Suffragist*, 8 Feb. 1919, 10; and "Give Jail Experiences," *Washington Post*, 5 Nov. 1917, 4.

131. Stevens, *Jailed for Freedom*, 177, 178, 356, 364.

132. Irwin, *Story of the Woman's Party*, 271–75; and "A Week of the Women's Revolt," *Suffragist*, 23 Nov. 1917, 4. A fellow prisoner stood in the same position until Burns was freed in the morning. Ibid.

133. Painter Marion Wallace Dunlop began the first British suffrage hunger strike on 27 June 1909, three days after she received a one-month sentence for stenciling a section of the 1689 Bill of Rights on a wall of the House of Commons. She refused food for ninety-one hours before she was released. Tickner, *Spectacle of Women*, 104.

134. Stevens, *Jailed for Freedom*, 185–86; and Edna Kenton, "The Militant Women—and Women," *Century*, Nov. 1913, 14.

135. Stevens, *Jailed for Freedom*, 191; and "Miss Alice Paul on Hunger Strike," *New York Times*, 7 Nov. 1917, 13.

136. Chesler, *Woman of Valor*, 100. Her "splendid stand for Free Speech" failed to deter the court from sentencing Edelsohn to ninety days. "The History of the Hunger Strike," *The Woman Rebel*, Aug. 1914, 46.

137. In January 1917, New York City prison officials had thrust tubes down Ethel Byrne's throat on the fourth day of her strike protesting her one-month sentence for handing out birth-control information at a clinic operated by her sister, Margaret Sanger. Chesler, *Woman of Valor*, 153. The governor pardoned Byrne. Whipple, *Story of Civil Liberty*, 278.

138. Susan Brown to the *Suffragist*, 24 Oct. 1917, Reel 51, NWP Papers: The Suffrage Years.

139. Although NWP historian Inez Haynes Irwin said Burns's group at Occoquan was the first to hunger strike beginning 16 November, Paul began to fast 5 November. "Miss Paul on Hunger Strike, *New York Times*, 7 Nov. 1917, 13; "Miss Paul, Picket, Declines to Feast," *Washington Post*, 7 Nov. 1917, 7; Lucy Burns to NWP members, telegram, 9 Nov. 1917, Reel 52, NWP Papers: The Suffrage Years; Irwin, *Story of the Woman's Party*, 271; and "Joins Hunger Strike," *New York Times*, 8 Nov. 1917, 4. Paul received a one-month sentence on top of a six-month sentence after leading pickets

on 6 October and again on the twentieth. "Alice Paul Sentenced," *New York Times,* 23 Oct. 1917, 12. In all, Paul served three prison sentences in the United States and one in England. Stevens, *Jailed for Freedom,* 366.

140. O'Neill, *Everyone Was Brave,* 126.

141. "The Making of a Militant," *Suffragist,* 13 Apr. 1918, 6.

142. Trecker, "Suffrage Prisoners," 409; Irwin, *Story of the Woman's Party,* 24; and Stevens, *Jailed for Freedom,* 110.

143. "The East Hears of the Western Campaign," *Suffragist,* 2 Dec. 1916, 9; and "An Impression of the Last War Congress Picket Line," *Suffragist,* 13 Oct. 1917, 4.

144. Press release, 20 Oct. 1917, Reel 91, NWP Papers: The Suffrage Years.

145. Ruth McCormick to Harriet Vittum, 31 July 1914, Reel 33, NAWSA Papers.

146. Mary O'Neill to Lucy Burns, 22 Oct. 1917, Reel 51, NWP Papers: The Suffrage Years.

147. Caroline Katzenstein to Dora Lewis, 22 Oct. 1917, Reel 51, NWP Papers: The Suffrage Years.

148. "Miss Paul Describes Feeding by Force," *New York Times,* 10 Dec. 1909, 1.

149. Accounts differ as to whether Paul was moved to a psychiatric ward at the district jail or to St. Elizabeth Insane Asylum. See, for example, "Picket Exposes Officials' Tortures," *New York Evening Call,* 19 Nov. 1917, n.p., Reel 95, NWP Papers: The Suffrage Years; and Agnes Morey to Mrs. Thomas Grey Jr., telegram, 10 Nov. 1917, Reel 52, NWP: The Suffrage Years.

150. Alice Paul to Dora Lewis, Nov. 1917 (?), Reel 53, NWP Papers: The Suffrage Years.

151. "Woman Suffrage Wins Probably by 80,000," *New York Times,* 7 Nov. 1917, 1.

152. "New York for Suffrage," *Washington Post,* 8 Nov. 1917, 6.

153. "Miss Paul on Hunger Strike, *New York Times,* 7 Nov. 1917, 13; and "Wilson Unshaken in Suffrage view," *New York Times,* 10 Nov. 1917, 1.

154. "Hunger Striker is Forcibly Fed," *New York Times,* 9 Nov. 1917, 13. She once described the forced feedings she received in London as "something like vivisection." Paul interview, 290; and "Miss Alice Paul Returns," *Woman's Journal,* 29 Jan. 1910, 19. In later years, she refused to discuss her forced feeding. Robert Gallagher, "I Was Arrested, Of Course . . ." *American Heritage,* Feb. 1974, 18.

155. "A Note from Alice Paul," *Suffragist,* 23 Nov. 1917, 5.

156. Stevens, *Jailed for Freedom,* 222.

157. "Pickets Charge Insanity Plot," *Washington Post,* 10 Nov. 1917, 3; Agnes Morey to Olive Belches, telegram, 10 Nov. 1917, Reel 52, NWP Papers: The Suffrage Years. See also Agnes Morey to Mrs. Thomas Grey Jr., 10 Nov. 1917; unsigned telegram to Matilda Gardner, 9 Nov. 1917; and Vivian Pierce to Beulah Amidon, 11 Nov. 1917, all in Reel 52, NWP Papers: The Suffrage Years.

158. See Paul interview, 234; Irwin, *Story of the Woman's Party,* 285–87; and Stevens, *Jailed for Freedom,* 223–25.

159. Lucy Burns to NWP members, 9 Nov. 1917, Reel 52, NWP Papers: The Suffrage Years.

160. See Lucy Burns to Mrs. R. B. Walker, 5 Nov. 1917, Reel 51, NWP Papers: The Suffrage Years; Virginia Arnold to Hazel Hunkins, undated; Dora Lewis to Lavinia Dock, 1 Nov. 1917; and Lucy Burns to Ella Abeel, telegram, 6 Nov. 1917, all in Reel 51, NWP Papers: The Suffrage Years.

161. "Arrest 41 Pickets for Suffrage at the White House," *New York Times*, 11 Nov. 1917, 1; "Police Net 40 Pickets," *Washington Post*, 11 Nov. 1917, 2; and "Forty-one Suffrage Pickets Answer the Attempt of the Democratic Administration to Crush Suffrage," *Suffragist*, 17 Nov. 1917, 6–7.

162. Irwin, *Story of the Woman's Party*, 276.

163. "Suffrage Picket Weds After Hunger Strike," *New York Tribune*, n.d., Reel 95, NWP Papers: The Suffrage Years.

164. Samuel Merwin, "The Measure of the Militants," *Good Housekeeping*, Oct. 1913, 454.

165. "A Week of the Women's Revolt," *Suffragist*, 23 Nov. 1917, 5.

166. For a discussion of the newspaper's role in the NWP campaign, see Linda Lumsden, "*Suffragist*: The Making of a Militant," *Journalism Quarterly* 72 (1995): 525–38.

167. Alice Paul to Dora Lewis, Nov. 1917 (?), Reel 53, NWP Papers: The Suffrage Years.

168. "Notes from the Prisoners," *Suffragist*, 24 Aug. 1918, 8.

169. "The Woman's Party and the Press," *Suffragist*, 13 Sept. 1919, 7.

170. "Government Forced to Release Suffrage Prisoners from Occoquan," *Suffragist*, 30 Nov. 1917, 4–5.

171. "Suffrage Pickets Freed from Prison," *New York Times*, 28 Nov. 1917, 13.

172. *Hunter v. District of Columbia*, 47 App. D.C. 406, 408, 409 (1918).

173. Ibid.; and "Ten Picket Cases Heard in D.C. Court of Appeals," *Suffragist*, 12 Jan. 1918, 9.

174. "President Wilson Comes Out for Federal Amendment," *Suffragist*, 12 Jan. 1918, 8; and "Susan B. Anthony Amendment Passes House," *Suffragist*, 12 Jan. 1918, 5.

175. "Suffragists Again Attack the President," *New York Times*, 7 Aug. 1918, 1; "Postpone Hearing on Suffragists," *New York Times*, 8 Aug. 1918, 7; and "Suffrage Disorders Again," *New York Times*, 8 Aug. 1918, 10.

176. "Suffrage Fanaticism," *Woman's Protest*, July–Aug. 1917, 7.

177. "Woman's Party Protests Against Wilful Senators," *Suffragist*, 19 Oct. 1918, 6–7; and "Capitol Police Forced to Return Suffrage Banners," *Suffragist*, 16 Nov. 1918, 5.

178. See "Women's Protests Against Disfranchisement Broken Up by Federal Police," *Suffragist*, 17 Aug. 1918, 5; "Summation of Facts About the Demonstra-

tions," *Suffragist*, 31 Aug. 1918, 9; and "President's Words Burn at Suffrage Protest in Front of White House," *Suffragist*, 28 Sept. 1918, 6–7.

179. "American Women Burn President Wilson's Meaningless Words on Democracy," *Suffragist*, 21 Dec. 1918, 6–7.

180. Krout, "Symbolic Conduct," 118.

181. "While Women Go to Jail," *Suffragist*, 18 Jan. 1918, 4; "Welcoming Suffrage Prisoners Home," *Suffragist*, 25 Jan. 1919, 5; and "The Watchfire Goes On," *Suffragist*, 8 Feb. 1919, 8–9.

182. Accounts differ about what constituted the effigy. *Suffragist* said White merely burned a cartoon of Wilson, while the *New York Times* said the effigy was a two-foot doll stuffed with straw. The *Washington Post* reported the women carried the effigy on a stretcher. "The Demonstration of February 9," *Suffragist*, 22 Feb. 1919, 10–12; "Suffragists Burn Wilson in Effigy; Many Locked Up," *New York Times*, 10 Feb. 1919, 1; and "Save Wilson Effigy," *Washington Post*, 10 Feb. 1919, 3.

183. Bland, "Techniques of Persuasion," 168. NAWSA also was appalled and "shamed" by the incident. "Suffragists Burn Wilson in Effigy; Many Locked Up," *New York Times*, 10 Feb. 1919, 1. Twenty-five of thirty-nine women charged with setting fires in connection with the effigy burning were sentenced five to ten days; an apparently tired judge dismissed the remainder of cases. "The Suffrage Trial," *Suffragist*, 22 Feb. 1913, 13.

184. "Vote of Senate Defeats Suffrage," *Christian Science Monitor*, 11 Feb. 1919, 1, 6. On the other hand, the *New York Times* attributed the defeat to southern Democrats who "feared giving negro women the vote." "Senate Again Beats Suffrage," *New York Times*, 11 Feb. 1919, 1.

185. Louis, "Sue Shelton White," 181.

186. "Women Jailed in Boston," *Suffragist*, 8 Mar. 1919, 4.

187. "Suffrage Protest at Presidents' Meeting in New York," *Suffragist*, 15 Mar. 1919, 4.

188. "Summer Organization Activities," *Suffragist*, 4 Aug. 1917, 5; and Irwin, *Story of the Woman's Party*, 293.

189. On the other hand, some cities seemed less than overwhelmed by the arrival of the prison special. Unidentified newspaper clipping, "21 Militant Suffragettes Arrive on Prison Special with None at Depot to Greet Them," Reel 95, NWP Papers: The Suffrage Years; Irwin, *Story of the Woman's Party*, 407; Taylor, *Woman Suffrage Movement in Tennessee*, 57; and "Singing Prison Songs, Militants Invade," *Los Angeles Evening Herald*, 27 Feb. 1919, 1. See also "Police Needed to Hold Crowd Which Greets Prison Special," *Milwaukee Leader*, 6 Mar. 1919, n.p., Reel 95, NWP Papers: The Suffrage Years; "Prison Special Arouses South," *Suffragist*, 8 Mar. 1919, 4; "The Prison Special," *Suffragist*, 15 Mar. 1919, 8–9; and "The Prison Special through the West," *Suffragist*, 27 Mar. 1919, 7–9.

190. Ford, *Iron-Jawed Angels*, 185; and "Singing Prison Songs, Militants Invade,"

Los Angeles Evening Herald, 27 Feb. 1919, 1. The Department of Justice investigated the NWP because some of its members were avowed pacifists. "Pacifism and Picketing Are Now Linked," *New York Tribune,* 22 Nov. 1917, n.p., Reel 95, NWP Papers: The Suffrage Years.

191. Irwin, *Story of the Woman's Party,* 293–94.

192. Sociologist Marjory Nelson recalled a poignant moment that occurred as she researched her dissertation on the NWP in 1971. When she drove Paul and Vernon to the funeral of a fellow White House picket, the only other people there were an Episcopal minister and the funeral director. Paul, eighty-four, looked up from the grave to the two men. "We were all in jail together, you know," she said. Nelson, "Ladies in the Street," 255.

193. "The Garnet Philosopher," *Illustrated Buffalo Express,* 25 Nov. 1917, 55, Reel 5, NWP Papers: The Suffrage Years.

194. "Impressions from the District Jail," *Suffragist,* 25 Jan. 1919, 12.

195. Mary Winsor, "The Punishment of the Pickets—A Letter from Jail," Reel 149, NWP Papers.

196. "Impressions from the District Jail," *Suffragist,* 25 Jan. 1919, 13.

197. One of those pins is among the suffrage memorabilia on display in "From Parlor to Politics: Women and Reform in America, 1890–1925," an exhibit at the National Museum of American History at the Smithsonian Institution in Washington, D.C. See Minna Morse, "The Object at Hand," *Smithsonian* 23 (Mar. 1993): 28–32.

198. Belle Case LaFollette, *LaFollette's Magazine,* Sept. 1917, qtd. in "Justice for Pickets," *Suffragist,* 6 Oct. 1917, 9.

199. "Why Picket the President?" Reel 91, NWP Papers: The Suffrage Years.

200. Carrie Chapman Catt, "An Open Letter to the Public," 13 July 1917, Reel 60, NAWSA Papers; and "Annual Report of the Membership Department, Year of 1916–1917," Reel 87, NWP Papers: The Suffrage Years. NWP membership was 26,292 women in January 1917 and 47,812 women in April 1918, including some 15,000 members of state suffrage organizations who were affiliated with the NWP. Ibid. For a first-person account of NAWSA's legislative work during World War I, see the memoirs of the chair of its Congressional Committee from 1917 through 1920. Park, *Front Door Lobby,* 1960.

201. Flexner, *Century of Struggle,* 314.

202. Stevens, *Jailed for Freedom,* 348.

203. Flexner, *Century of Struggle,* 324.

204. J. Stanley Lemons, *The Woman Citizen: Social Feminism in the 1920s* (Urbana: Univ. of Illinois Press, 1973), 10. See also Ford, *Iron-Jawed Angels,* 253; Evans, *Born for Liberty,* 166–67; Lunardini, *From Equal Suffrage to Equal Rights,* 141, 149; MacKenzie, *America Challenged,* 45; and Scott, *Natural Allies,* 171. Flexner

concluded the picketing and watch fires alienated as many supporters as they gained. Flexner, *Century of Struggle*, 284–87. William O'Neill dismissed the wartime picketing as "destructive, hostile posturing." O'Neill, *Everyone Was Brave*, 203–4. Historian Sidney Bland termed their protests "nearly pathological." Bland, "Techniques of Persuasion," 173.

205. Catt and Shuler, *Woman Suffrage and Politics*, 260. Catt also declined to contribute a chapter about NAWSA to Irwin's history of the NWP. Carrie Chapman Catt to Inez Haynes Irwin, 29 Mar. 1933, Reel 33, NAWSA Papers.

206. Wheeler, *New Women of the New South*, 166.

207. Seiler interview, 25; Jessie Haver Butler, "From Tea Parties to Prison: On the Platform," interview by Sherna Gluck, Suffragists Oral History Collection, Univ. of California, Berkeley, microfiche edition (Sanford, N.C.: Microfilm Corporation of America, 1980), 48; and Walter Clark, chief justice of the North Carolina Supreme Court, qtd. in Stevens, *Jailed for Freedom*, 17–18.

208. "Treasurer's Report," *Suffragist*, 5 Jan. 1918, 15.

209. See, for example, "Arrest 41 Pickets for Suffrage at the White House," *New York Times*, 11 Nov. 1917, 1; and "Suffragists Burn Wilson in Effigy; Many Locked Up," *New York Times*, 10 Feb. 1919, 1.

210. Flexner, *Century of Struggle*, 287.

211. Ibid., 291.

212. 18 Aug. 1917, qtd. in *Suffragist*, 1 Sept. 1917, 11.

213. Bosmajian, "Abrogation of the Suffragists' First Amendment Rights," 230.

214. "Notes and Comments," *Woman's Protest*, May 1913, 15.

215. Press release, 14 Sept. 1917, Reel 91, NWP Papers: The Suffrage Years.

216. Stevens, *Jailed for Freedom*, 322.

217. 23 June 1917, qtd. in "Comments of the Press," *Suffragist*, 7 July 1917, 10; See also "Editorial Notes," *New Republic*, 28 July 1917, 344; *Pittsburgh Press*, qtd. in "Comments of the Press," *Suffragist*, 30 Mar. 1918, 14; *New York Call*, 25 June 1917, qtd. in "Comments of the Press," *Suffragist*, 22 June 1917, 10; *Detroit Times*, qtd. in "Comments of the Press," *Suffragist*, 28 July 1917, 10; *Baltimore Evening Post*, qtd. in "Comments of the Press," *Suffragist*, 4 Aug. 1917, 8; and *St. Paul Pioneer Daily News*, 28 July 1917, qtd. in "Comments of the Press," *Suffragist*, 11 Aug. 1917, 9.

218. "Protected," *Suffragist*, 17 May 1919, 4.

219. Bland, "Techniques of Persuasion," 114, 113.

220. "Noted Feminist, Grandmother, Here After Trip Around World," *Boston Globe*, 1 Sept. 1926, n.p., in Reel 49, NAWSA Papers; and James Hunt, *Gandhi in London* (New Delhi: Promilla, 1978), 101. Gandhi, however, disapproved of suffragette violence. Ibid.

221. See David Garrow, *Bearing the Cross: Martin Luther King Jr. and the Southern Christian Leadership Conference* (New York: William Morrow, 1986), 32,

43, 72, 75, 113–14; James Hanigan, *Martin Luther King Jr. and the Foundations of Nonviolence* (Lanham, Md.: Univ. Press of America, 1984), 1; and Stephen Oates, *Let the Trumpet Sound: The Life of Martin Luther King Jr.* (New York: Harper & Row, 1982), 31–33, 142, 144.

222. Lemons, *Woman Citizen*, 5.

223. Martin Luther King Jr., "Letter from Birmingham Jail," in Harris, *Civil Disobedience*, 63.

224. Fortas, "Concerning Dissent and Civil Disobedience," 22.

Conclusion

1. Jarrett and Mund, "The Right of Assembly," 1–38.

2. See Flexner, *Century of Struggle*; Kraditor, *Ideas of the Woman Suffrage Movement*; and O'Neill, *Everyone Was Brave*.

3. Bosmajian, "Abrogation of the Suffragists' First Amendment Rights," 218–32; Ford, *Iron-Jawed Angels*; and Lunardini, *From Equal Suffrage to Equal Rights*, 1986).

4. DuBois, "Working Women, Class Relations, and Suffrage Militance," 34–58; Schaffer, "New York City Woman Suffrage Party," 269–87; and Strom, "Leadership and Tactics," 296–315.

5. "Suffragettes Protest," *New York Times*, 30 Apr. 1908, 16.

6. Irwin, *Story of the Woman's Party* , 179.

7. "Hear Suffragettes' Appeal," *New York Sun*, 1 Jan. 1908, 4.

8. Eckhardt, *Fanny Wright*, 247–50.

9. See "Teachers to Enter Soapbox Campaign," *New York Times*, 2 June 1915, 13; and "Miss Malone Quits the Suffragettes," *New York Times*, 27 Mar. 1908, 4.

10. Catt and Shuler, *Woman Suffrage and Politics*, 290.

11. Manuscript, MacKaye Family Papers.

12. Lynne Cheney, "How Alice Paul Became the Most Militant Feminist of Them All," *Smithsonian* 3 (1972): 97.

13. Kerber, *Women of the Republic*, 52.

14. Barnes, *The Antislavery Impulse*, 143.

15. "The Woman Voters Present Their Message to the President and Congress," *Suffragist*, 11 Dec. 1915, 4–5; and Carrie Chapman Catt, "Bringing the Victors Home," *Woman Citizen*, 4 Sept. 1920, 374.

16. Irwin, *Story of the Woman's Party*, 252.

17. *Hunter v. District of Columbia*, 47 App. D.C. 406–9 (1918).

18. Wagner, *Time of Protest*, 49–50.

19. "Police Bar Suffragettes," *New York Times*, 18 June 1908, 1.

20. "Boys Howl Down Suffrage Speakers," *New York Times*, 28 Nov. 1911, 9; and "Take Up Women's Charges," *New York Times*, 29 Nov. 1911, 8.

21. "5,000 Women March, Beset By Crowds," *New York Times,* 4 Mar. 1913, 4.

22. "Suffragist Songs But No Talk in Park," *New York Times,* 23 Sept. 1916, 18.

23. *HWS* 1:557.

24. American working-class women at least were no strangers to mob violence. Just days before suffragists staged their first Fifth Avenue parade, mobs of East Side women shot milk bottles filled with kerosene into hundreds of kosher shops to protest high meat prices, and "Amazons in gray wigs and shawls" assaulted butchers with horsewhips and hoses. "Women in Meat Riots," *Woman's Journal,* 30 Apr. 1910, 70.

25. "Women to Mrs. Pankhurst's Aid," *New Jersey Journal,* 20 Oct. 1913, 1; and "Mrs. Sanderson Talks," *New York Times,* 13 Dec. 1907, 6.

26. See W. L. George, "Feminist Intentions," *Atlantic Monthly,* Dec. 1913, 9–12; Wells, "Militant Movement for Woman Suffrage," 902; "Setback to British Suffragettes," *Literary Digest,* 13 Aug. 1910, 229–30; "What to Do with the Raging Suffragettes," *Literary Digest,* 19 Apr. 1913, 883; "How to Repress the Suffragettes," *Literary Digest,* 18 July 1914, 96–98; and "What Should Be Done with the Wild Women," *Outlook,* 4 July 1914, 519–20.

27. "She's a Window Smasher," *New York Times,* 18 Dec. 1911, 1.

28. "A Militant Invasion," *Woman's Journal,* 3 May 1913, 140.

29. See illustration of a picket entitled "The Militant" on the cover of the NWP newspaper, *Suffragist,* 15 Dec. 1917, 1.

30. "Hurrah for the Suffrage Parade," *Woman's Journal,* 13 May 1911, 148.

31. "Four Militant Bible Women," Reel 64, NAWSA Papers.

32. "Excuse for White House Picketing," *New York Times,* 9 July 1917, 8.

33. "Suffragettes Explain," *Troy (N.Y.) Standard Times,* 29 Mar. 1912, n.p., Reel 1, HSB Papers.

34. See "Suffrage Fete for Cleveland," *Woman's Journal,* 16 Aug. 1913, 262; "Amusement Seekers Hear Suffrage Talk," *American Suffragette,* Sept.–Oct. 1909, 5; and "Suffragist Baby Show," *New York Times,* 16 Oct. 1913, 1.

35. "Resolutions Passed by Convention," *Woman's Journal,* 25 Dec. 1915, 412.

36. "A Bourgeois Movement," *Woman Citizen,* 7 July 1917, 99.

37. Flexner, *Century of Struggle,* 283.

38. "Militant Methods," *Woman's Journal,* 30 Oct. 1909, 174. See also "As to Militant Methods," *Woman's Journal,* 25 July 1908, 118.

39. "Can Militant Methods Gain a Hold Here?" unidentified newspaper clipping, Reel 3, HSB Papers.

40. "Storm Congress with Petitions," *Woman's Journal,* 9 Aug. 1913, 254; and Irwin, *Story of the Woman's Party,* 39.

41. See "Mob Howls at Suffragettes," *New York Times,* 29 Oct. 1908, 1; "Suffragettes Broadway," *New York Times,* 15 Sept. 1911, 4; "All States Will Be in Parade," *Woman's Journal,* 8 Feb. 1913, 46.

42. "10,000 Marchers in Suffrage Line," *New York Times*, 4 May 1913, 1.

43. *Hunter v. District of Columbia*, 47 App. D.C. 406 (1918).

44. Stevens, *Jailed for Freedom*, 31.

45. Editorial, *Woman Voter*, Apr. 1912, 20.

46. See Appendix 4.

47. "Militancy and America," *Woman Voter*, June 1913, 21.

48. Raeburn, *Militant Suffragettes*, 131.

49. See, for example, "Forward by Alice Paul," *Suffragist*, 15 Nov. 1913, 1.

50. "Newspaper Comment," *Woman's Journal*, 8 Mar. 1913, 77; "The Suffragette Parade," *Washington Post*, 3 Mar. 1913, 6; and "Parade Protest Arouses Senate," *New York Times*, 5 Mar. 1913, 8.

51. "Advertising Suffrage," *Woman's Journal*, 4 Jan. 1913, 54. The *Journal* claimed the disapproving British press conducted a blackout of similar events in Britain. Ibid.

52. Seiler interview, 29.

53. See Dreier, "Expansion through Agitation and Education," 164; Foner, *Women and the American Labor Movement* 1:47 and 2:209.

54. *Suffragist*, 15 Sept. 1917, 1.

55. Giddings, *When and Where I Enter*, 161–62.

56. "Mayor Wins City," *Woman's Journal*, 10 Aug. 1912, 254; "Petition," *Progress*, Feb. 1909, 2; "Great Parade," *Woman's Journal*, 13 May 1911, 146; Terrell, *Colored Woman in a White World*, 316.

57. See "Ban Antis from Big Auditorium," *Woman's Journal*, 14 Aug. 1915, 262; and Anna Howard Shaw to Alice Paul, 20 Feb. 1913, Reel 1, NWP Papers: The Suffrage Years.

58. Tax, *Rising of the Women*, 18.

59. Kettler interview, 34–35.

60. Eric Goldman, *Rendezvous with Destiny* (New York: Alfred A. Knopf, 1963), 292, 440; and William Chafe, *The American Woman: Her Changing Social, Economic, and Political Roles, 1920–1970* (New York: Oxford Univ. Press, 1972), 29.

61. Charles Selden, "The Most Powerful Lobby in Washington," *Ladies Home Journal*, Apr. 1922, 5.

62. Cott, *Grounding of Modern Feminism*, 98; and Lemons, *Woman Citizen*, 147, 176, 228. See also William Chafe, "Women's History and Political History: Some Thoughts on Progressivism and the New Deal," in *Visible Women: New Essays on American Activism*, ed. Nancy Hewitt and Suzanne Lebsock (Urbana: Univ. of Illinois Press, 1993), 101–18.

63. Freedman, "Separatism as Strategy," 524.

64. Cott, *Grounding of Modern Feminism*, 283. For other discussions on how the woman's movement changed in the 1920s, see "Beyond Suffrage: The Struggle for Reform," in Dorothy Brown, *Setting a Course: American Women in the 1920s*

(Boston: Twayne, 1987), 49–76; William Chafe, "Politics and Ideology, 1848–1940," in *The Paradox of Change: American Women in the 20th Century* (New York: Oxford Univ. Press, 1991), 3–60; Lemons, *Woman Citizen*; and Rosalind Rosenberg, "Claiming the Rights of Men, 1912–29," in *Divided Lives: American Women in the Twentieth Century*, by Rosenberg (New York: Hill and Wang, 1992), 63–101.

65. Leila Rupp and Vera Taylor, *Survival in the Doldrums: The American Women's Movement, 1945 to the 1960s* (New York: Oxford Univ. Press, 1987), 39.

66. *New York Times*, 14 July 1916, 10.

67. "A National Union of Woman Citizens," *Woman Citizen*, 15 Mar. 1919, 857; and "The League of Women Voters," *Woman Citizen*, 5 Apr. 1919, 957.

68. "Slogan 'Ballots for Both' Wins," *Woman's Journal*, 25 Nov. 1916, 377.

69. "The League of Women Voters," *Woman Citizen*, 12 Apr. 1919, 957.

70. Lemons, *Woman Citizen*, 228. The infamous Spider Web Chart concocted by the federal Chemical Warfare Department, for instance, connected many women leaders and organizations to an international communist conspiracy. Ibid., 216.

71. By the end of the tumultuous 1920s, however, Americans began to grasp a "greater understanding of the right to be different and to express dissident ideas," according to Margaret Blanchard. Blanchard, *Revolutionary Sparks*, 125.

72. Walter Lippmann, *A Preface to Morals* (New York: Macmillan, 1929), 6.

73. Woloch, *Women and the American Experience*, 381–82.

74. Brown, *Setting a Course*, 73–74.

75. Evans, *Born for Liberty*, 195.

76. "No Loafing," *Woman Citizen*, 14 June 1919, 39.

77. Charles Van Doren, ed., *Webster's American Biographies* (Springfield, Mass.: Merriam-Webster, 1984), 804; and Neverdon-Morton, *Afro-American Women of the South*, 205. For more on ERA campaigns, see Susan Becker, *The Origins of the Equal Rights Amendment: American Feminism Between the Wars* (Westport, Conn.: Greenwood Press, 1981); Cott, *Grounding of Modern Feminism*, 117–42; and Donald Mathews and Jane Sherron DeHart, *Sex, Gender, and the Politics of ERA: A State and the Nation* (New York: Oxford Univ. Press, 1990).

78. "The New Headquarters of the Woman's Party," Reel 149, NWP Papers; and telephone interview with Sewell-Belmont House spokeswoman, Washington, D.C., 15 June 1994.

79. Eleanor Flexner, "Carrie Chapman Catt," in James, James, and Boyer, *Notable American Women* 3:312.

80. Eleanor Flexner, "Harriot Stanton Blatch," in James, James, and Boyer, *Notable American Women* 1:173.

81. Blair, "Pageantry for Women's Rights," 39, 45.

82. Sidney Bland, "'Never Quite as Committed as We'd Like': The Suffrage Militancy of Lucy Burns," *Journal of Long Island History* (Summer/Fall 1981): 19.

83. Nelson, "Ladies in the Street," 182.

84. "Suffragettes Open Their Campaign Here, *New York Times*, 1 Jan. 1908, 16; "Suffragist Parade Despite the Police," *New York Times*, 17 Feb. 1908, 7; *The People v. Maud Malone*, 156 [New York] App. Div. 10, 325 (1913); and Stevens, *Jailed for Freedom*, 364.

85. Anne Standley, "The Role of Black Women in the Civil Rights Movement," in *Women in the Civil Rights Movement: Trailblazers and Torchbearers, 1941–1965*, ed. Vicki Crawford, Jacqueline Anne Rouse, and Barbara Woods (Brooklyn: Carlson Publishing, 1990), 184.

86. Mary Fair Burks, "Trailblazers: Women in the Montgomery Bus Boycott," in Crawford, Rouse, and Woods, *Women in the Civil Rights Movement*, 76.

87. Sara Evans, *Personal Politics: The Roots of Women's Liberation in the Civil Rights Movement and the New Left* (New York: Vintage Books, 1980), 39–40.

88. Standley, "Role of Women in the Civil Rights Movement," 185–86.

89. Evans, *Personal Politics*, 52. Evans traces the roots of the women's liberation movement in the civil rights movement.

90. Ethel Klein, *Gender Politics: From Consciousness to Mass Politics* (Cambridge: Harvard Univ. Press, 1984), 1.

91. Amy Swerdlow, *Women Strike for Peace: Traditional Motherhood and Radical Politics in the 1960s* (Chicago: Univ. of Chicago Press, 1993), xi, 1, 22.

92. "They've Come a Long Way," *Washington Post*, 27 Aug. 1995, B1; "A Celebration of Women's Right to Vote," *New York Times*, 27 Aug. 1995, sec. 1, p. 9N; and Kathy Kiely, "A Capital Commotion—75 Years Late," *Working Woman*, Aug. 1995, 11.

93. Echols, *Daring to Be Bad*, 93–94. This incident spawned the women's liberation movement's "bra burning" image, although the protesters decided against burning the can's contents because they feared arrests. Ibid.

94. Ibid., 12.

95. See *DeJonge v. Oregon*, 288 U.S. 364 (1937) (right of assembly incorporated into the Bill of Rights by the Fourteenth Amendment); *Lovell v. City of Griffin*, 303 U.S. 444 (1938) (permit to license solicitors an unconstitutional prior restraint); *Hague v. CIO*, 37 U.S. 496 (1939) (right to assemble a privilege inherent in U.S. citizenship); *Thornhill v. Alabama*, 310 U.S. 88 (1940) (peaceful picketing is protected expression); *Edwards v. South Carolina*, 372 U.S. 229 (1963) (peaceful protests protected by rights of free speech, assembly, and petition); and *Shuttlesworth v. Birmingham*, 394 U.S. 147 (1969) (parading is protected expression and discriminatory parade permit system unconstitutional).

BIBLIOGRAPHY

Archival Sources

Annals of Congress. Microfiche edition. Library of Congress, Washington, D.C.

The Papers of Harriot Stanton Blatch. Manuscripts Division, Library of Congress, Washington, D.C.

The MacKaye Family Papers. Special Collections, Dartmouth College Library, Hanover, New Hampshire.

National American Woman Suffrage Association Papers. Microfilm edition. Sanford, N.C.: Microfilm Corp. of America, 1979.

National Woman's Party Papers, 1913–1974. Microfilm edition. Glen Rock, N.J.: Microfilm Corp. of America, 1977–78.

National Woman's Party Papers: The Suffrage Years, 1913–1920. Microfilm edition, Thomas Pardo, ed. Sanford, N.C.: Microfilm Corp. of America, 1979.

Primary Published Sources

BOOKS BY CONTEMPORARY AUTHORS

Anthony, Susan, Matilda Gage, and Elizabeth Cady Stanton, eds. *History of Woman Suffrage.* 6 vols. Reprint. New York: Source Book Press, 1970.

Beegle, Mary Porter, and Jack Randall Crawford. *Community Drama and Pageantry.* New Haven, Conn.: Yale Univ. Press, 1916.

Blatch, Harriot Stanton, and Alma Lutz. *Challenging Years: The Memoirs of Harriot Stanton Blatch.* New York: G. P. Putnam's Sons, 1940.

Catt, Carrie Chapman, and Nettie Rogers Shuler. *Woman Suffrage and Politics: The Inner Story of the Suffrage Movement.* New York: Charles Scribner's Sons, 1923.

Dorr, Rheta Childe. *What Eight Million Women Want.* Boston: Small, Maynard, 1910.

Duster, Alfreda, ed. *Crusade for Justice: The Autobiography of Ida B. Wells.* Chicago: Univ. of Chicago Press, 1970.

Harper, Ida Husted. *The Life and Work of Susan B. Anthony.* Indianapolis: T. Bowen-Merrill, 1890.

Irwin, Inez Haynes. *Angels and Amazons: A Hundred Years of American Women.* Garden City, N.Y.: Doubleday, Doran, 1933.

——. *The Story of the Woman's Party.* New York: Harcourt, Brace, 1921.

Katzenstein, Caroline. *Lifting the Curtain: The State and National Woman Suffrage Campaigns in Pennsylvania as I Saw Them.* Philadelphia: Dorrance, 1955.

Lippmann, Walter. *A Preface to Morals.* New York: Macmillan, 1929.

National American Woman Suffrage Association, ed. *Victory! How Women Won It: A Centennial Symposium, 1840–1940.* New York: H. W. Wilson, 1940.

Pankhurst, Christabel. *Unshackled: The Story of How We Won the Vote.* London: Hutchinson, 1959.

Pankhurst, E. Sylvia. *The Suffragette: The History of the Women's Militant Suffrage Movement, 1905–1910.* Boston: Woman's Journal, 1911.

Pankhurst, Sylvia. *The Suffragette Movement: An Intimate Account of Persons and Ideals.* London: Longmans, Green, 1932.

Park, Maud Wood. *Front Door Lobby.* Boston: Beacon Press, 1960.

Ross, Ishbel. *Ladies of the Press: The Story of Women in Journalism by an Insider.* New York: Harper & Brothers, 1936.

Sanger, Margaret. *My Fight for Birth Control.* New York: Farrar & Rinehart, 1931.

Stevens, Doris. *Jailed for Freedom.* New York: Boni & Liveright, 1920.

Strachey, Ray. *The Cause: A Short History of the Women's Movement in Great Britain.* London: G. Bell & Sons, 1928.

Terrell, Mary Church. *A Colored Woman in a White World.* Washington, D.C.: Ransdell, 1940. Reprint. Salem, N.H.: Ayers, 1992.

CONTEMPORARY MAGAZINE ARTICLES

Adams, Henry. "Shall We Muzzle the Anarchists." *Forum* 1 (1886): 448–49.

Dreier, Mary. "Expansion Through Agitation and Education." *Life and Labor,* June 1921, 163–65, 192.

"Editorial Notes." *New Republic,* 28 July 1917, 344.

Irwin, Wallace, and Inez Milholland. "Two Million Women Vote." *McClure's Magazine,* Jan. 1913, 245–48.

Kenton, Edna. "The Militant Women—and Women." *Century,* Nov. 1913, 13–20.

Knobe, Bertha. "The March of 3,000 Women." *Harper's Weekly,* 20 May 1911, 8.

Laski, Harold. "The Militant Wing and the Federal Suffrage Amendment." *Dial,* 31 May 1919, 541–43.

MacKaye, Percy. "Art and the Woman's Movement." *Forum* 49 (1913): 680–84.

"Marching for Suffrage." *Harper's Weekly,* 11 May 1912, sec. 2, p. 27.

Vernon, Mabel. "A Suffragist Recounts the Hard-Won Victory." *AAUW Newsletter,* Apr. 1972, 27.

Wells, Bettina Borrmann. "The Militant Movement for Woman Suffrage." *Independent*, Apr. 1908, 902.

ORAL HISTORIES

Butler, Jessie Haver. "From Tea Parties to Prison: On the Platform." Interview by Sherna Gluck. Suffragists Oral History Collection, Univ. of California, Berkeley. Microfiche edition, Sanford, N.C.: Microfilming Corp. of America, 1980.

DeFord, Miriam. "From Tea Parties to Prison: In the Streets." Interview by Sherna Gluck. Suffragists Oral History Collection. Univ. of California, Berkeley. Microfiche edition, Sanford, N.C.: Microfilming Corp. of America, 1980.

Gluck, Sherna, ed. *From Parlor to Prison: Five American Suffragists Talk about Their Lives, an Oral History.* New York: Vintage Books, 1976.

Kettler, Ernestine Hara. "From Tea Parties to Prison: Behind Bars." Interview by Sherna Gluck. Suffragists Oral History Collection. Univ. of California, Berkeley. Microfiche edition, Sanford, N.C.: Microfilming Corp. of America, 1980.

Paul, Alice. "Conversations with Alice Paul: Woman Suffrage and the Equal Rights Amendment." Interview by Amelia Fry. Suffragists Oral History Collection. Univ. of California, Berkeley. Microfiche edition, Sanford, N.C.: Microfilming Corp. of America, 1980.

Seiler, Laura Ellsworth. "From Tea Parties to Prison: On the Soapbox." Interview by Sherna Gluck. Suffragists Oral History Collection. Univ. of California, Berkeley. Microfiche edition, Sanford, N.C.: Microfilming Corp. of America, 1980.

Vernon, Mabel. "The Suffrage Campaign, Peace and International Relations." Interview by Amelia Fry. Suffragists Oral History Collection. Univ. of California, Berkeley. Microfiche edition, Sanford, N.C.: Microfilming Corp. of America, 1980.

PERIODICALS

American Suffragette (New York). 1909–11.
New York Times. 1908–19.
Progress (Ohio). 1907–10.
Suffragist (Washington, D.C.). 1913–20.
Washington Post. 1913–19.
Woman Citizen (New York). 1917–20.
Woman's Journal (Boston). 1907–17.
Woman's Protest (New York). 1912–18.
Woman Voter (New York). 1913–17.

Legal Sources

BOOKS

Abernathy, M. Glenn. *The Right of Assembly and Association.* Columbia: Univ. of South Carolina Press, 1961.

Bailey, R. C. *Popular Influence Upon Public Policy: Petitioning in Eighteenth Century Virginia.* Westport, Conn.: Greenwood Press, 1979.

Blackstone, William. *Commentaries on the Laws of England,* vol. 4. Boston: T. B. Wait and Sons, 1818.

Cooley, Thomas. *A Treatise on the Constitutional Limitations Which Rests Upon the Legislative Power of the States of the American Union.* 7th ed. Boston: Little, Brown, 1903.

Fellman, David. *Constitutional Rights of Association.* Chicago: Univ. of Chicago Press, 1975.

McKechnie, William Sharp. *The Magna Charta.* Rev. ed. New York: Burt Franklin, 1958.

Stimson, Frederic Jesup. *The Law of the Federal and State Constitutions of the United States.* Boston: Boston Book, 1908.

ARTICLES

Ackerly, Will. "Constitutional Freedom of Speech and of the Press." *Case and Comment* 22 (Nov. 1915): 456–60.

Anderson, Alexis. "The Formative Period of First Amendment Theory, 1870–1915." *American Journal of Legal History* 24 (1980): 56–75.

Blanchard, Margaret. "Filling in the Void: Speech and Press in State Courts Prior to *Gitlow.*" In *The First Amendment Reconsidered,* ed. Bill F. Chamberlin and Charlene Brown. New York: Longman, 1982, 14–59.

Byrd, Richard. "The Decay of Personal Rights and Guarantees." *Yale Law Journal* 18 (1907): 252–54.

Chafee, Zechariah, Jr. "Freedom of Speech in War Time." *Harvard Law Review* 32 (June 1919): 932–73.

Chamberlain, John. "Freedom of Speech in Public Streets, Parks and Commons." *Case and Comment* 22 (Nov. 1915): 461–65.

D'Arcy, Edward. "Some Observations on State Laws and Municipal Ordinances in Contravention of Common Rights." *Central Law Journal* 64 (1907): 212–20.

Frederick, David. "John Quincy Adams, Slavery and the Disappearance of the Right of Petition." *Law and History Review* 9 (1991): 113–15.

"Free Speech and Its Limits." *Case and Comment* 22 (Nov. 1915): 455.

Gibson, Michael. "The Supreme Court and Freedom of Expression from 1791 to 1917." *Fordham Law Review* 55 (1986): 263–333.

Higginson, Stephen. "A Short History of the Right to Petition Government for the Redress of Grievances." *Yale Law Journal* 96 (1986): 142–66.

Hodgkiss, Anita. "Petitioning and the Empowerment Theory of Practice." *Yale Law Journal* 96 (1987): 569–92.

Jarrett, James, and Vernon Mund. "The Right of Assembly." *New York University Law Quarterly Review* 9 (1931): 1–38.

Morton, James, Jr. "Free Speech and Its Enemies." *Case and Comment* 22 (1915): 471.

"Public Order and the Right of Assembly in England and the United States: A Comparative Study." *Yale Law Journal* 47 (1938): 404–32.

Rabban, David. "The First Amendment in Its Formative Period." *Yale Law Journal* 90 (1980–81): 514–95.

———. "The Free Speech League, the ACLU, and Changing Conceptions of Free Speech in American History." *Stanford Law Review* 45 (1992): 47–114.

Rishe, Melvin. Note. "Freedom of Assembly." *DePaul Law Review* 15 (1966): 317–39.

Rydstrom, Jean. Annotation. "The Supreme Court and the First Amendment Right to Petition the Government for a Redress of Grievances." *L.Ed.* 30 2d ser. (1971): 914–25.

Schroeder, Theodore. "The Historical Interpretation of 'Freedom of Speech and of the Press.'" In *"Obscene" Literature and Constitutional Law,* by Schroeder. New York: Private printing for forensic use, 1911: 206–39.

Smith, George, II. "The Development of the Right of Assembly—A Current Socio-Legal Investigation." *William and Mary Law Review* 9 (1967–68): 359–76.

Smith, Norman. "'Shall Make No Law Abridging . . .': An Analysis of the Neglected, but Nearly Absolute, Right of Petition." *University of Cincinnati Law Review* 54 (1986): 1153–97.

Tanenhaus, Joseph. "Picketing as Free Speech: Early Stages in the Growth of the New Law of Picketing." *University of Pittsburgh Law Review* 14 (1953): 397–418.

CASES

Adderley v. Florida, 385 U.S. 39 (1966).

Anderson v. City of Wellington, 40 Kan. 173 (1888).

Atchison, T. & S.F. Ry. v. Gee Co., 139 F. 582 (C.C.S.D. Iowa 1905).

Brandenburg v. Ohio, 395 U.S. 444 (1969).

Bryant v. Zimmerman, 278 U.S. 63 (1928).

Commonwealth v. Abrahams, 156 Mass. 57, 30 N.E. 79 (1892).

Commonwealth v. Karvonen, 219 Mass. 30, 106 N.E. 556 (1914).

Cox v. Louisiana I, 379 U.S. 536 (1965).

Davis v. Massachusetts, 167 U.S. 43 (1897).

Debs v. United States, 249 U.S. 211 (1919).

DeJonge v. Oregon, 288 U.S. 364 (1937).

Edwards v. South Carolina, 372 U.S. 229 (1963).

Fitts v. City of Atlanta, 121 Ga. 567 (1905).

Gitlow v. New York, 268 U.S. 652 (1925).

Goldman v. Reyburn, 18 Pa. Dist. R. 883 (1909).

Goldman v. United States, 245 U.S. 474 (1918).

Hague v. CIO, 307 U.S. 496 (1939).

Hunter v. District of Columbia, 47 App. D.C. 406 (1918).

In re Flaherty, 38 P. 981 (Cal. St. Ct. 1895).

In re Frazee, 63 Mich. 396 (1886).

Love v. Phalen, 128 Mich. 545, 87 N.W. 785 (1901).

Lovell v. City of Griffin, 303 U.S. 444 (1938).

Mashburn v. Bloomington, 32 Ill. App. 245 (1889).

NAACP v. Alabama, 357 U.S. 449 (1958).

People v. Burman, 154 Mich. 150 (1908).

People v. Malone, 29 N.Y. Crim. Rpts. 325 (N.Y.S. Ct. 1913).

People v. Pierce, 85 App. Div. 125 (N.Y.S. Ct. 1903).

People v. Wallace, 85 App. Div. 170 (N.Y.S. Ct. 1903).

Rich v. City of Naperville, 42 Ill. App. 222 (1891).

St. Louis v. Gloner, 210 Mo. 502, 109 S.W. 30 (1908).

Shuttlesworth v. Birmingham, 394 U.S. 147 (1969).

Spies v. Illinois, 122 Ill. 1 (1887).

State v. Derring, 84 Wis. 585 (1893).

Stromberg v. California, 283 U.S. 359 (1931).

Sweezy v. New Hampshire, 354 U.S. 237 (1957).

Thornhill v. Alabama, 310 U.S. 88 (1940).

U.S. v. Cruikshank, 92 U.S. 542 (1875).

Secondary Sources

BOOKS

Arendt, Hannah. *The Human Condition.* Chicago: Univ. of Chicago Press, 1958.

Barnes, Gilbert. *The Antislavery Impulse: 1830–44.* New York: D. Appleton-Century, 1933.

Beeton, Beverly. *Women Vote in the West: The Woman Suffrage Movement, 1869–1896.* New York: Garland Publishing, 1986.

Benstock, Shari. *Women of the Left Bank: Paris, 1900–1940.* Austin: Univ. of Texas Press, 1986.

Blanchard, Margaret. *Revolutionary Sparks: Freedom of Expression in Modern America.* New York: Oxford Univ. Press, 1992.

Bordin, Ruth. *Woman and Temperance: The Quest for Power and Liberty, 1873–1900.* Philadelphia: Temple Univ. Press, 1981.

Brown, Dorothy. *Setting a Course: American Women in the 1920s.* Boston: Twayne, 1987.

Campbell, Karlyn Kohrs. *Women Public Speakers in the United States, 1800–1925: A Bio-Critical Sourcebook.* Westport, Conn.: Greenwood Press, 1993.

Cary, Eve. *Woman and the Law.* Skokie, Ill.: National Textbook. 1978.

Ceplair, Larry, ed. *The Public Years of Sarah and Angelina Grimké: Selected Writings, 1835–1839.* New York: Columbia Univ. Press, 1989.

Chafe, William. *The American Woman: Her Changing Social, Economic, and Political Roles, 1920–1970.* New York: Oxford Univ. Press, 1972.

Chafee, Zechariah. *Freedom of Speech.* New York: Harcourt, Brace and Howe, 1920.

Chesler, Ellen. *Woman of Valor: Margaret Sanger and the Birth Control Movement in America.* New York: Simon & Schuster, 1992.

Chinoy, Helen Krich, and Linda Walsh Jenkins, eds. *Women in American Theatre.* New York: Theatre Communications Group, 1987.

Conlin, Joseph. *Bread and Roses Too: Studies of the Wobblies.* Westport, Conn.: Greenwood Press, 1969.

Cott, Nancy. *The Grounding of Modern Feminism.* New Haven, Conn.: Yale Univ. Press, 1987.

Crawford, Vicki, Jacqueline Anne Rouse, and Barbara Woods, eds. *Women in the Civil Rights Movement: Trailblazers and Torchbearers, 1941–1965.* Brooklyn, N.Y.: Carlson Publishing, 1990.

Danbom, David. *"The World of Hope": Progressivism and the Struggle for a Regenerate America.* Philadelphia: Temple Univ. Press, 1987.

Daube, David. *Civil Disobedience in Antiquity.* Edinburgh: Edinburgh Univ. Press, 1972.

Davis, Reda. *California Women: A Guide to Their Politics, 1885–1911.* San Francisco: Scene, 1967.

De Tocqueville, Alexis. *Democracy in America.* 4th ed. New York: Henry G. Langley, 1845.

DuBois, Ellen Carol. *Feminism and Suffrage: The Emergence of an Independent Women's Movement in America, 1848–1869.* Ithaca, N.Y.: Cornell Univ. Press, 1978.

Dye, Nancy Schrom. *As Equals and as Sisters: Feminism, the Labor Movement, and the Women's Trade Union League of New York.* Columbia: Univ. of Missouri Press, 1980.

Echols, Alice. *Daring to Be Bad: Radical Feminism in America, 1967–1975.* Minneapolis: Univ. of Minnesota Press, 1989.

Eckhardt, Celia Morris. *Fanny Wright: Rebel in America.* Cambridge: Harvard Univ. Press, 1984.

Ekirch, Arthur, Jr. *Progressivism in America: A Study of the Era from Theodore Roosevelt to Woodrow Wilson*. New York: New Viewpoints, 1974.

Elshtain, Jean Bethke, ed. *The Family in Political Thought*. Amherst: Univ. of Massachusetts Press, 1982.

Emery, Edwin, and Michael Emery. *The Press and America: An Interpretive History of the Mass Media*. 5th ed. Englewood Cliffs, N.J.: Prentice-Hall, 1984.

Evans, Sara. *Born for Liberty: A History of Women in America*. New York: Free Press, 1989.

————. *Personal Politics: The Roots of Women's Liberation in the Civil Rights Movement and the New Left*. New York: Vintage Books, 1980.

Filene, Peter. *Him/Her/Self: Sex Roles in Modern America*. Baltimore: Johns Hopkins Univ. Press, 1986.

Flexner, Eleanor. *Century of Struggle: The Woman's Rights Movement in the United States*. Cambridge: Belknap Press, Harvard Univ. Press, 1959. Rev. ed. New York: Atheneum, 1971.

Flink, James. *America Adopts the Automobile, 1895–1910*. Cambridge, Mass.: MIT Press, 1970.

Foner, Philip. *History of the Labor Movement in the United States*. Vol. 4, *The Industrial Workers of the World: 1905–1917*. New York: International Publishers, 1980.

————. *History of the Labor Movement in the United States*. Vol. 5, *The AFL in the Progressive Era, 1910–1915*. New York: International Publishers, 1980.

————. *May Day: A Short History of the International Workers' Holiday, 1886–1986*. New York: International Press, 1986.

————. *Women and the American Labor Movement*. Vol. 1, *From Colonial Times to the Eve of World War I*. New York: Free Press, 1979.

————. *Women and the American Labor Movement*. Vol. 2, *From the First Trade Unions to the Present*. New York: Free Press, 1979.

Ford, Linda. *Iron-Jawed Angels: The Suffrage Militancy of the National Woman's Party, 1912–1920*. Lanham, Md.: Univ. Press of America, 1991.

Fourteenth Census of the United States: Occupations. Washington, D.C.: Government Printing Office, 1923.

Freeman, Jo., ed. *Social Movements of the Sixties and Seventies*. New York: Longman, 1983.

Friedl, Bettina. *On to Victory: Propaganda Plays of the Woman Suffrage Movement*. Boston: Northeastern Univ. Press, 1987.

Fuller, Paul. *Laura Clay and the Woman's Rights Movement*. Lexington: Univ. Press of Kentucky, 1975.

Garrow, David. *Bearing the Cross: Martin Luther King Jr. and the Southern Christian Leadership Conference*. New York: William Morrow, 1986.

Giddings, Paula. *When and Where I Enter . . . The Impact of Black Women on Race and Sex in America*. New York: William Morrow, 1984.

Glassberg, David. *American Historical Pageantry.* Chapel Hill: Univ. of North Carolina Press, 1990.

Goldman, Eric. *Rendezvous with Destiny.* New York: Alfred A. Knopf, 1963.

Goldwin, Robert, ed. *On Civil Disobedience: Essays Old and New.* Chicago: Rand McNally, 1969.

Gordon, Linda. *Woman's Body, Woman's Right: Birth Control in America.* Rev. ed. New York: Viking Penguin, 1990.

Gregory, Charles. *Labor and the Law.* New York: W. W. Norton, 1949.

Grimes, Alan. *The Puritan Ethic and Woman Suffrage.* New York: Oxford Univ. Press, 1967.

Guy-Sheftall, Beverly. *Daughters of Sorrow: Attitudes Toward Black Women, 1880–1920.* Brooklyn: Carlson Publishing, 1990.

Hanigan, James. *Martin Luther King Jr. and the Foundations of Nonviolence.* Lanham, Md.: Univ. Press of America, 1984.

Harley, Sharon, and Rosalyn Terborg-Penn. *The Afro-American Woman: Struggles and Images.* Port Washington, N.Y.: Kennikat Press, National Univ. Publications, 1978.

Harris, Paul, ed. *Civil Disobedience.* Lanham, Md.: Univ. Press of America, 1989.

Hewitt, Nancy, and Suzanne Lebsock, eds. *Visible Women: New Essays on American Activism.* Urbana: Univ. of Illinois Press, 1993.

Hine, Darlene Clark, ed. *Black Women in American History: The Twentieth Century.* 4 vols. Brooklyn: Carlson Publishing, 1990.

Howard, Anne. *The Long Campaign: A Biography of Anne Martin.* Reno: Univ. of Nevada Press, 1985.

Hunt, James. *Gandhi in London.* New Delhi: Promilla, 1978.

James, Edward, Janet Wilson James, and Paul Boyer, eds., *Notable American Women, 1607–1950.* 3 vols. Cambridge: Belknap Press, Harvard Univ. Press, 1971.

Justice, Betty. *Unions, Workers and the Law.* Washington, D.C.: Bureau of National Affairs, 1983.

Kerber, Linda. *Women of the Republic: Intellect and Ideology in Revolutionary America.* Chapel Hill: Univ. of North Carolina Press, 1980.

Kerr, Andrea Moore. *Lucy Stone: Speaking Out for Equality.* New Brunswick, N.J.: Rutgers Univ. Press, 1992.

Klein, Ethel. *Gender Politics: From Consciousness to Mass Politics.* Cambridge: Harvard Univ. Press, 1984.

Kraditor, Aileen. *The Ideas of the Woman Suffrage Movement, 1890–1920.* New York: Columbia Univ. Press, 1965.

Lemons, J. Stanley. *The Woman Citizen: Social Feminism in the 1920s.* Urbana: Univ. of Illinois Press, 1973.

Lerner, Gerda. *The Female Experience: An American Documentary.* Indianapolis: Bobbs-Merrill, 1977.

———. *The Grimké Sisters from South Carolina: Pioneers for Women's Rights and Abolition.* Boston: Houghton Mifflin, 1967. Reprint. New York: Schocken, 1971.

Lewis, David Levering. *W. E. B. Du Bois, Biography of a Race, 1868–1919.* New York: Henry Holt, 1993.

Liddington, Jill. *One Hand Tied Behind Us: The Rise of the Women's Suffrage Movement.* London: Virago, 1978.

Lunardini, Christine. *From Equal Suffrage to Equal Rights: Alice Paul and the National Woman's Party, 1910–1928.* New York: New York Univ. Press, 1986.

MacKenzie, Kenneth. *America Challenged 1916–1945.* Wellesley Hills, Mass.: Independent School Press, 1983.

MacKenzie, Midge. *Shoulder to Shoulder: A Documentary.* New York: Alfred A. Knopf, 1975.

Maier, Pauline. "Popular Uprising and Civil Authority in Eighteenth-Century America." In *Interpreting Colonial America: Selected Readings,* ed. James Kirby Martin. New York: Harper & Row, 1978.

Martin, Theodora Penny. *The Sound of Our Own Voices: Women's Study Clubs, 1860–1910.* Boston: Beacon Press, 1987.

Mast, Gerald. *A Short History of the Movies.* New York: Pegasus, 1971.

Matthews, Glenna. *The Rise of Public Woman: Woman's Power and Woman's Place in the United States, 1630–1970.* New York: Oxford Univ. Press, 1992.

McBride, Genevieve. *On Wisconsin Women: Working for Their Rights from Settlement to Suffrage.* Madison: Univ. of Wisconsin Press, 1993.

McKay, John. *Tramways and Trolleys: The Rise of Urban Mass Transportation in Europe.* Princeton, N.J.: Princeton Univ. Press, 1976.

Mill, John Stuart. *The Subjection of Women.* New York: D. Appleton, 1870.

Miller, John Anderson. *Fares, Please! A Popular History of Trolleys, Horsecars, Streetcars, Buses, Elevateds, and Subways.* New York: Dover Publications, 1960.

Morgan, Robin. *Going Too Far: The Personal Chronicle of a Feminist.* New York: Vintage Books, 1978.

Neverdon-Morton, Cynthia. *Afro-American Women of the South and the Advancement of the Race, 1895–1925.* Knoxville: Univ. of Tennessee Press, 1989.

Norton, Mary Beth. *Liberty's Daughters: The Revolutionary Experience of American Women, 1750–1800.* Boston: Little, Brown, 1980.

Noun, Louise. *Strong-Minded Women: The Emergence of the Woman-Suffrage Movement in Iowa.* Ames: Iowa State Univ. Press, 1969.

Oates, Stephen. *Let the Trumpet Sound: The Life of Martin Luther King Jr.* New York: Harper & Row, 1982.

Okin, Susan Moller. *Women in Western Political Thought.* Princeton, N.J.: Princeton Univ. Press, 1979.

O'Neill, William. *Everyone Was Brave: The Rise and Fall of Feminism in America.* Chicago: Quadrangle Books, 1969.

Raeburn, Anita. *The Militant Suffragettes.* London: Michael Joseph, 1973.

———. *The Suffragette View.* New York: St. Martin's Press, 1976.

Riley, Glenda. *Inventing the American Woman.* Vol. 2, *A Perspective on Women's History, 1865 to the Present.* Arlington Heights, Ill.: Harlan Davidson, 1986.

Rosaldo, Michelle Zimbalist, and Louise Lamphere, eds. *Woman, Culture and Society.* Stanford, Calif.: Stanford Univ. Press, 1974.

Rosenberg, Rosalind. *Divided Lives: American Women in the Twentieth Century.* New York: Hill and Wang, 1992.

Rossi, Alice, ed. *The Feminist Papers: From Adams to de Beauvoir.* New York: Columbia Univ. Press, 1973. Reprint. Boston: Northeastern Univ. Press, 1988.

Rupp, Leila, and Vera Taylor. *Survival in the Doldrums: The American Women's Movement, 1945 to the 1960s.* New York: Oxford Univ. Press, 1987.

Ryan, Mary. *Women in Public: Between Banners and Ballots, 1825–1880.* Baltimore: Johns Hopkins Univ. Press, 1990.

Scharf, Virginia. *Taking the Wheel: Women and the Coming of the Motor Age.* New York: Free Press, 1991.

Schwarz, Judith. *Radical Feminists of Heterodoxy: Greenwich Village, 1912–1940.* Lebanon, N.H.: New Victoria Publishers, 1982.

Schneider, Dorothy, and Carl Schneider. *American Women in the Progressive Era, 1900–1920.* New York: Facts on File, 1993.

Scott, Anne Firor. *Natural Allies: Women's Associations in American History.* Urbana: Univ. of Illinois Press, 1991.

———. *The Southern Lady: From Pedestal to Politics, 1830–1930.* Chicago: Univ. of Chicago Press, 1970.

Scott, Anne Firor, and Andrew Scott. *One Half the People: The Fight for Woman Suffrage.* Philadelphia: J. B. Lippincott, 1975.

Sheppard, Alice. *Cartooning for Suffrage.* Albuquerque: Univ. of New Mexico Press, 1994.

Sochen, June. *The New Woman in Greenwich Village, 1910–1920.* New York: Quadrangle Books, 1972.

Solomon, Barbara Miller. *In the Company of Educated Women.* New Haven, Conn.: Yale Univ. Press, 1985.

Stansell, Christine. *City of Women: Sex and Class in New York, 1789–1860.* Urbana: Univ. of Illinois Press, 1987.

Sterling, Dorothy. *Ahead of Her Time: Abby Kelley and the Politics of Antislavery.* New York: W. W. Norton, 1991.

———. *We Are Your Sisters: Black Women in the Nineteenth Century.* New York: W. W. Norton, 1984.

Swerdlow, Amy. *Women Strike for Peace: Traditional Motherhood and Radical Politics in the 1960s.* Chicago: Univ. of Chicago Press, 1993.

Tax, Meredith. *The Rising of the Women: Feminist Solidarity and Class Conflict, 1880–1917.* New York: Monthly Review Press, 1980.

Taylor, A. Elizabeth. *Citizens at Last: The Woman Suffrage Movement in Texas.* Austin: Ellen C. Temple, 1987.

———. *The Woman Suffrage Movement in Tennessee.* New York: Bookman Associates, 1957.

Tedford, Thomas. *Freedom of Speech in the United States.* New York: McGraw-Hill, 1993.

Tickner, Lisa. *The Spectacle of Women: Imagery of the Suffrage Campaign, 1907–1914.* London: Chatto & Windus, 1987.

Ulrich, Laurel Thatcher. *A Midwife's Tale: The Life of Martha Ballard, Based on Her Diary, 1785–1812.* New York: Vintage Books, 1991.

Van Doren, Charles, ed. *Webster's American Biographies.* Springfield, Mass.: Merriam-Webster, 1984.

Van Voris, Jacqueline. *Carrie Chapman Catt: A Public Life.* New York: Feminist Press, 1987.

Wagner, Sally Roesch. *A Time of Protest: Suffragists Challenge the Republic, 1870–1877.* Carmichael, Calif.: Sky Carrier Press, 1988.

Ward, Ian. *Motoring for the Millions.* New York: Dorset Press, 1981.

Wheeler, Marjorie Spruill. *New Women of the New South: The Leaders of the Woman Suffrage Movement in the Southern States.* New York: Oxford Univ. Press, 1993.

———, ed. *Votes for Women!* Knoxville: Univ. of Tennessee Press.

Whipple, Leon. *The Story of Civil Liberty in the United States.* New York: Vanguard Press, 1927.

Woloch, Nancy. *Women and the American Experience.* New York: Alfred A. Knopf, 1984.

Yellin, Jean Fagan. *Women and Sisters: The Antislavery Feminists in American Culture.* New Haven, Conn.: Yale Univ. Press, 1989.

ARTICLES AND BOOK CHAPTERS

Alexander, Adele Logan. "How I Discovered My Grandmother . . . ." *Ms.* 12 (Nov. 1983): 29–37.

Baker, Paula. "The Domestication of Politics: Women and American Political Society, 1780–1920." *American Historical Review* 89 (June 1984): 620–47.

Billington, Rosamund. "Ideology and Feminism: Why the Suffragettes Were 'Wild Women.'" *Women's Studies* 5 (1982): 663–73.

Blair, Karen. "Pageantry for Women's Rights: The Career of Hazel MacKaye 1913–1923." *Theatre Survey* 31 (1990): 25–45.

Bland, Sidney. "'Never Quite as Committed as We'd Like': The Suffrage Militancy of Lucy Burns." *Journal of Long Island History* (Summer/Fall 1981): 4–23.

Blocker, Jack. "Separate Paths: Suffragists and the Women's Temperance Crusade." *Signs* 10 (1985): 460–76.

Bosmajian, Haig. "The Abrogation of the Suffragists' First Amendment Rights." *Western Speech* 38 (1974): 218–32.

Campbell, Karlyn Kohrs. "Femininity and Feminism: To Be or Not to Be a Woman." *Communication Quarterly* 31 (Spring 1983): 101–8.

Cheney, Lynne. "How Alice Paul Became the Most Militant Feminist of Them All." *Smithsonian* 3 (1972): 94–100.

Cole, Terry. "The Right to Speak: The Free Speech Fights of the Industrial Workers of the World." *Free Speech Yearbook* (1978): 113–19.

Daniels, Doris. "Building a Winning Coalition: The Suffrage Fight in New York State." *New York History* 60 (1979): 59–80.

DuBois, Ellen Carol. "The Radicalism of the Woman Suffrage Movement: Notes Toward the Reconstruction of Nineteenth Century Feminism." *Feminist Studies* 3 (Fall 1975): 63–71.

———. "Working Women, Class Relations, and Suffrage Militance: Harriot Stanton Blatch and the New York Woman Suffrage Movement, 1894–1909." *Journal of American History* 74 (1987): 34–58.

Eaton, Clement. "Mob Violence in the Old South." *Mississippi Valley Historical Review* 29 (1942): 351–70.

Fortas, Abe. "Concerning Dissent and Civil Disobedience." In *Dissent, Symbolic Behavior and Rhetorical Strategies,* ed. Haig Bosmajian. Westport, Conn.: Greenwood Press, 1980.

Freedman, Estelle. "Separatism as Strategy: Female Institution Building and American Feminism, 1870–1930." *Feminist Studies* 5 (Fall 1979): 512–49.

Fry, Amelia. "Along the Suffrage Trail." *American West* 6 (Jan. 1969): 16–25.

Gallagher, Robert. "I Was Arrested, Of Course." *American Heritage,* Feb. 1974, 17–24, 92–94.

Hall, Jacquelyn. "Disorderly Women: Gender and Labor Militancy in the Appalachian South." *Journal of American History* 73 (Sept. 1986): 354–82.

Jensen, Billie Barnes. "Colorado Woman Suffrage Campaigns of the 1870s." *Journal of the West* 12 (Apr. 1973): 254–71.

Kiely, Kathy. "A Capital Commotion—75 Years Late." *Working Woman* (Aug. 1995): 11.

Krout, Maurice. "Symbolism." In *The Rhetoric of Nonverbal Communication,* ed. Haig Bosmajian. Glenview, Ill.: Scott, Foresman, 1971.

Lakey, George. "Techniques and Ethos in Nonviolent Action: The Woman Suffrage Case." In *Dissent, Symbolic Behavior and Rhetorical Strategies,* ed. Haig Bosmajian. Westport, Conn.: Greenwood Press, 1980.

Landsman, Gail. "The 'Other' as Political Symbol: Images of Indians in the Woman Suffrage Movement." *Ethnohistory* 39 (Summer 1992): 247–84.

Louis, James. "Sue White and the Woman Suffrage Movement in Tennessee." *Tennessee Historical Quarterly* 22 (1963): 170–90.

Marshall, Susan. "Ladies Against Women: Mobilization Dilemmas of Antifeminist Movements." *Social Problems* 32 (Apr. 1985): 348–61.

McGerr, Michael. "Popular Style and Women's Power, 1830–1930." *Journal of American History* 77 (Dec. 1990): 864–85.

McGovern, James. "The American Woman's Pre–World War I Freedom in Manners and Morals." *Journal of American History* 55 (Sept. 1968): 315–33.

Mitchell, Catherine. "Historiography on the Woman's Rights Press." In *Outsiders in 19th-Century Press History: Multicultural Perspectives,* ed. Frankie Hutton and Barbara Straus Reed. Bowling Green, Ohio: Bowling Green Univ. Popular Press, 1995. 159–68.

Morse, Minna. "The Object at Hand." *Smithsonian* 23 (Mar. 1993): 28–32.

Schaffer, Ronald. "The New York City Woman Suffrage Party, 1909–1919." *New York History* 43 (1962): 269–87.

Sloan, Kay. "Sexual Warfare in the Silent Cinema: Comedies and Melodramas of Woman Suffragism." *American Quarterly* 33 (Fall 1981): 412–36.

Smith-Rosenberg, Carroll. "The Female World of Love and Ritual: Relations Between Women in Nineteenth-Century America." In *Disorderly Conduct: Visions of Gender in Victorian America.* New York: Alfred A. Knopf, 1985. 53–76.

Smith-Rosenberg, Carroll, and Charles Rosenberg. "The Female Animal: Medical and Biological Views of Woman and Her Role in 19th-Century America." *Journal of American History* 60 (173–74): 332–56.

Steiner, Linda. "Finding Community in Nineteenth Century Suffrage Periodicals." *American Journalism* 1 (1983): 1–15.

Strom, Sharon Hartman. "Leadership and Tactics in the American Woman Suffrage Movement: A New Perspective from Massachusetts." *Journal of American History* 62 (1975): 269–315.

Thurner, Manuela. "Better Citizens Without the Ballot": American AntiSuffrage Women and Their Rationale during the Progressive Era." *Journal of Women's History* 5 (Spring 1993): 33–60.

Trecker, Janice Law. "The Suffrage Prisoners." *American Scholar* 21 (Summer 1972): 409–23.

Welter, Barbara. "The Cult of True Womanhood." In *Dimity Convictions: The American Woman in the Nineteenth Century.* Athens: Ohio Univ. Press, 1976, 21–41.

"When Sara Comes, It's Always a Holiday!" *Bancroftiana* (Oct. 1980): 1–3.

Wood, Gordon. "A Note on Mobs in the American Revolution." *William and Mary Quarterly,* 3rd ser., 23 (1966): 635–42.

Dissertations

Bland, Sidney. "Techniques of Persuasion: The National Woman's Party and Woman Suffrage, 1913–1919." Ph.D. diss., George Washington Univ., 1972.

Nelson, Marjory. "Ladies in the Street: A Sociological Analysis of the National Woman's Party, 1910–1930." Ph.D. diss., State Univ. of New York at Buffalo, 1976.

Terborg-Penn, Rosalyn. "Afro-Americans in the Struggle for Woman Suffrage." Ph.D. diss., Howard Univ., 1977.

Zimmerman, Loretta. "Alice Paul and the National Woman's Party 1912–1920." Ph.D. diss., Tulane Univ., 1964.

INDEX

Blackwell, Antoinette Brown, 77
Blackwell, Henry, xxviii
Blatch, Harriot Stanton, 27, 164, 196n;
and class, 45, 154, 220n; in England,
26; and Equal Rights Amendment,
157; and Equality League of Self-
Supporting Women, 27, 75, 162, 220n;
and League of Nations, 157; on
NAWSA, 27; and open-air meetings,
28–29, 37, 45, 144, 168; and pageants,
99; and parades, 75, 76, 77, 80, 81, 83–
84; and picketing, 118; on suffrage
assemblies, 17–18; and war work, 126;
and Women's Political Union, 77, 99,
163, 230n
Blount, Anna, 31
Boston Equal Suffrage Association for
Good Government, 19, 46, 164
Boston Tea Party, allusions to, xxix, xxxi,
123, 124, 136, 147, 150, 173
Brady, James, 92
Brannan, Eleanor, 171
Brannan, Eunice, 123
Breckinridge, Madeline, 32, 76
Brisbane, Arthur, 127
British influence, 25–27, 149, 151–52; on
open-air campaigns, 41, 45; on
parades, 74–75, 125–26, 195n, 224n; on
picketing, 118; on plays and pageants,
225n
Brown, Olympia, 126
Bugbee, Emma, 61
Burns, Lucy, 157, 164; arrests of at
White House, 121, 133, 172; and CU,
161, 170; force-feeding of, 134; and
NAWSA Congressional Committee,
169; and NWP, 171; and picketing of
White House, 125, 126, 133; and
prison, 122, 129, 130
Byrne, Edith, 236n

Carey, Mary Ann Shadd, 5, 17, 184n
Cartoons, suffrage, 43–44
Catt, Carrie Chapman, 164; chairs
Committee on the Cause and Cure of

War, 157; and class, 154; criticizes
White House pickets, 139; and Empire
State Campaign Committee, 161; in
England, 26–27; on feminism, 43; and
International Woman Suffrage
Association, 162; as NAWSA president,
15, 16, 127, 132, 139, 162, 234n; and New
York City Woman Suffrage Party, 162,
169; and 1917 New York referendum,
67–68; and open-air meetings, 24; and
pageants, 110; on parades, 75, 81, 146,
213n; on petitions, 52, 58, 63, 211n; and
racism, 16, 154; on suffrage movement,
196n; her "winning plan," 12, 190n; and
woman's temperance movement, xxxi
Censorious suffragists, 50–51, 127, 155
Chaplin, Charlie, 225n
Chapman, Maria Weston, 182n
Children and suffrage movement, 18, 19,
43, 47, 87, 93, 159; see also Motherhood and suffrage
Civil disobedience, 121–22; and British
suffragettes, 142–43; and civil rights
movement, 142–43, 158; and Mahatma
Gandhi, 142–43; nineteenth-century
suffragists' use of, xxviii, xxx; Alice
Paul's use of, 152; and woman
temperance movement, xxxi; and
White House pickets, 117, 123, 126, 140
Civil rights movement, 142–43, 158–59
Clark, Septima, 158
Class in suffrage movement, 15, 35, 149,
153–54; and open-air campaigns, 32,
37, 44–46, 50, 146; and parades, 88;
and plays and pageants, 107; and
picketing of White House, 116, 129,
141; and prison, 128
Clay, Laura, 13, 14, 32, 58, 76, 208n
Clayton Anti-Trust Act, 115, 228n
Colby, Bainbridge, 173
College women, 40, 44, 91, 146, 153
College Women's Equal Suffrage League,
161, 164, 165, 194n
Colored Woman's Progressive Franchise
Association, 17

demonstrates, these assemblies helped change the nation's concept of democracy and helped women move from the private, domestic sphere into the public, political sphere. An exciting exploration of a turning point in American history, *Rampant Women* is a unique chronicle of how freedom of expression effected peaceful social change.

The Author: Linda J. Lumsden is assistant professor of journalism at Western Kentucky University. She is the author of *Adirondack Craftspeople*.